Without Warning:

Threat Assessment, Intelligence, and Global Struggle

Without Warning:

Threat Assessment, Intelligence, and Global Struggle

Mikhail A. Alexseev

St. Martin's Press
New York

ISBN 0-312-17538-8

Library of Congress Cataloging-in-Publication Data

Alexseev, Mikhail A., 1963—
    Without warning : threat assessment, intelligence, and global
struggle / by Mikhail A. Alexseev.
        p. cm.
    Includes bibliographical references and index.
    ISBN 0-312-17538-8
    1. World politics. 2. International relations. I. Title.
D32.A54 1997
327—dc21   97-28936
                                                            CIP

Design by Milton Heiberg Studios

Printed in the United States of America by
Haddon Craftsmen
Bloomsburg, PA

First edition: November, 1997
10 9 8 7 6 5 4 3 2 1

For Jan, Leach, Ludmila, and Anatohy

Contents

Acknowledgements

I am indebted to many people for helping me with this project and with the life-changing transition from Soviet journalism to American academe. Professor George Modelski, who chaired my dissertation committee, inspired me with the changes he had wrought by his lifetime work in political science. Changes that included: broadening the confines of the international relations field through promoting and developing the concept of world politics; the assessment of communism as a competing world system; focusing on the dimension of time in world politics; and, applying evolutionary theory in a discipline consistently being accused of ignoring change. George also encouraged me to include the case of the Mongol Empire, a historical case hitherto ignored by the students of international relations in North America, and one in which, in retrospect, was the most exciting case to investigate and write about. (Unlike Soviet kids, most American kids have not grown up reading blockbuster historical thrillers about the Mongol conquests of China, Central Asia, and Russia.)

Professor Stephen Hanson, who shared my confusion—and many a good chat—in redefining what used to be the field of Soviet studies, creatively challenged the book's arguments. In many ways, this book would not have happened had Steve and I not been satisfied that the arguments could be sustained in other cases of global struggle—such as Napoleon's invasion of Russia, World War I, Hitler's initiation of World War II, or Stalin's designs for expanding communist influence worldwide after the Cold War. A true comparativist, Steve also helped me work out in detail how this project relates to the work of others in international relations and comparative politics, especially to those working on deterrence, democratic peace, rational choice, decision psychology, and game theory. I omitted a very detailed discussion of my arguments' theoretical implications, deciding that experts in their respective theoretical niches would be best suited to glean useful insights for their theories without much prompting from me—something which less theory-minded readers will surely appreciate.

Professor W. Lance Bennett, who guided me in the American Politics field, was the first to introduce me to the discipline of political science as practiced in the United States when he agreed to collaborate on a comparative study of press-state relationship in the United States, Britain, and Russia, for which I got the NATO fellowship. Work on this project gave me hands-on experience with academic writing for publication—and many pages of this book were rewritten using Lance's editing methods. Lance also reminded me to keep making it clear why each particular piece of evidence matters.

Raymond Garthoff, of the Brookings Institution, read several chapters and gave me a very detailed feedback that only an insider and a lifetime expert, such as he, could give, regarding U.S.-Soviet interactions during the Cold War and the workings of the estimative process in the CIA. Professor Christopher Jones deserves many thanks for clarifying many practical issues in CIA-KGB confrontation—to say nothing of reading this work before it was substantially revised to be published as a book. My research on the CIA chapters was supported by a grant from the Kennan Institute for Advanced Russian Studies at the Woodrow Wilson International Center for Scholars, in Washington, D.C. I very much appreciate the help of the National Archives staff in locating the recently declassified CIA National Intelligence Estimates on the Soviet Union, and also the help of the staff at the National Security Archives in locating a broader range of U.S. government documents, dealing with my case. I also appreciate comments on my ideas—some very brief, some extensive—by Daniel Abele, James Caporaso, Ron Diebert, John Lewis Gaddis, John Keeler, William Lee, Nodarii Simoniia, David Singer, Viktor Sumsky, and Vladislav Zubok. A series of workshops at Seattle's Battelle Center on evolutionary paradigms in social sciences—organized by George Modelski and Kaz Poznanski—allowed me to run my ideas by Robert Gilpin, Jacek Kugler, Ken Osterkamp, and William Thompson. Jere Bacharach and Tom Rekdal helped me get a post-doctoral niche at the University of Washington during the critical stages of manuscript revision. My appreciation is also extended to the anonymous reviewers of the book's chapters.

This book would have been impossible without my St. Martin's Press editor, Karen Wolny, who is responsible for one of the most memorable phone calls in my life when she initially got interested and enthusiastic about the project. (Although I'm still mystified as to how many cups of coffee she needed to get her through the manuscript). But with or without caffeine, Karen's editorial guidance was impeccable, and her ability to have the manuscript reviewed in a matter of two month evokes my admiration. Karen's editorial assistant, Elizabeth Paukstis helped me find my way through the necessary publication and marketing paperwork. Production editor Ruth Mannes painstakingly explained the copyediting process and helped me to avoid hours (if not days) of extra work. The copy editor Wendy Jacobs deserves much praise for cleaning up my writing (especially those long sentences) and for having me appreciate the amount of detail required for completing bibliographical references. The publisher's job was made easier by June Rugh who edited and proofread my manuscript in Seattle before it hit St. Martin's. She straightened out my use of articles (after all, English is only my "father tongue") and much of the stylistic clumsiness that creeps into books from dissertations. Chris Davis of Horsepower Design in Seattle deserves great credit for his patience listening to my explanations of political geography in the Mongol era and for nicely designed maps that will help the readers navigate through the book.

Above all, a huge thanks goes to my wife, JaneAnne Wilder, who gave me all her love and support over the years, tolerated my long hours by the computer, inspired me to persevere when I got discouraged, and—as a marketing expert—helped write the prospectus that attracted publishers and suggested "Without Warning" as this book's title. (Jan's friends, Katie Lindberg and Jan Monti also helped me to brainstorm title ideas.) My parents, Anatoly and Lyudmila, on their frequent visits from the former Soviet Union to Seattle kept bringing recently published Russian books—some of which I used extensively. My brain might not have sustained the stress of book writing as well as it did, were it not for periodic infusions of my mother's blinis and true Ukrainian borscht (sumptuous multivegetable bonanza). My daughter, Leah Alexseev, three years old at this writing, had me remembering that my love for her matters more to me than global struggle.

Preface

This book is about global change without warning—such as the one most of us went through in the past decade when the Soviet Union collapsed and the Cold War ended. This book also marks a tectonic shift in my own life—one from a Soviet journalist to an American scholar and writer. My transition began in earnest in December 1989. At that time, I covered the Congress of People's Deputies in the Kremlin for an English-language weekly published by the Ukrainian government for Ukrainians worldwide. At every step, at every quick glance at the computers delivering news updates, at every briefing in the crowded press room, and in every huddle with top political players in the Kremlin corridors, I felt I could see and touch history as it was made. The Berlin Wall just went tumbling down, the Velvet Revolution swept the Soviet-style government away in Czechoslovakia, Romania's communist dictator, Nicholae Ceausescu, was dead, and in the Soviet Union, the Lithuanian communists stunned Gorbachev by seceding from the Communist Party of the Soviet Union. All these events resonated in thousands of ways in the Kremlin—more journalists flocking to opposition deputies during the breaks in parliamentary proceedings, a broader and more confident smile on Yeltsin's face when he turned up in the corridors, a shade of redness coloring Gorbachev's face more often, and more "red squares"—blocks of empty seats—appearing in the deputies' stalls as whole delegations from Lithuania, Latvia, Estonia, and Georgia walked out in protest against Moscow's rule.

Though elated by the changes, I was saddened, seeing how little time I had, as a journalist, to probe into the complex causes of these momentous developments. Also, as a Soviet citizen I soon realized, observing my Western colleagues, that my access to information was still extremely limited, and that my training in Marxist research methodology—the only one available under the Soviet system—was woefully inadequate. Hence came the decision to go global and move into the academe. On my way, I wrote a weekly column in *The Seattle Times,* held the Reuters Fellowship at the University of Oxford in Britain, and a NATO's Democratic Institutions' Fellowship (both were open to Soviet participants for the first time). Eventually, I earned my Ph.D. in political science at the University of Washington. This book is based on my doctoral dissertation.

Having crossed the East-West divide as the Cold War faded away and the Information Age dawned, I found myself greatly stimulated by the role of information in global struggle. I took a "big picture" view both of world politics and international relations theory: international outcomes do, indeed, hinge a great deal on the distribution of military and economic power, on domestic politics and institutions, and on patterns of decision making by groups and individuals. However, I also found that incumbent world powers and their challengers have had systematically different priorities for assessing threats and opportunities—especially when it comes to life and death or war and peace. In this sense, global events stem from asymmetric decisions—these asymmetries go beyond the cost of or access to information and are qualitative in nature. To give a mundane example, the idea of having pickled tomatoes, mashed potatoes, and a beefsteak for breakfast is unlikely to appeal—or even occur—to an American. But as somebody coming from Russia, I have often craved such a matinal menu. And, as someone who worked for the Cold War to end in a draw, I experience different feelings than most Americans, when the United States is declared a winner, and Russia a loser in that struggle.

With this in mind, I turned to intelligence as a "critical element in creation and reproduction of political reality" and found that remarkably little work had been done to integrate the literatures of international relations and intelligence studies. This book will thus be the first to analyze, by the method of structured, focused comparison, how and why the leaders and challengers in the past millennium started or averted global wars by acting on systematically divergent strategic intelligence "feeds." I look at the rise of the Mongol Empire and decline of Sung China (1206-1221); British-French rivalry leading into the Revolutionary and Napoleonic Wars (1784-1805); and the "New Cold War" followed by the collapse of the Soviet Union (1975-1991). Viewing threat assessment in the long perspective helps discern divergent patterns: the leading powers see security primarily in military and economic terms, and the challengers focus primarily on political vulnerabilities. In pursuing quick gain strategies, the challengers lose in the long run, and the incumbents ultimately prevail. But the price of this struggle is paid in traumas, turmoil, and massive loss of human life. The hope for preventing this dynamic from recurring on a global scale thus lies with global institutions where diverse political grievances can be expressed and through which collective preventive action against determined aggressors can be taken.

The book is organized into an introductory chapter and two parts. The introductory chapter explains why the leading powers and challengers develop predictably divergent preferences for intelligence collection and analysis. Part I looks into the causes of asymmetric threat assessment, things that are at the heart of the struggle for global leadership: sea versus land power; pluralism versus centralization; and high versus low degree of involvement in the global economy's lead sectors. In Part II, I look at key strategic decisions stemming from these divergent threat assessments, such as why the Mongols attacked the Chin and Khwarazm, and France attacked Britain, against all odds; why Sung China and Britain considered themselves secure in the face of the rising challengers; and why Moscow and Washington came to realize they were no longer enemies, by each following a very different logic. The book's first two cases are based on library research, and the third on recently declassified National Intelligence Estimates (NIEs) of the Central Intelligence Agency, and on texts of KGB instructions for global operations, including Operation RYAN (about 1983, when the Soviet leadership anticipated a nuclear attack against the USSR to be launched by NATO).

Relying on my foreign language fluency, I used many sources in Russian and French that have been rarely (or never) analyzed in the North American political science literature. They range from various chronicles relevant to the Mongol World Empire case to the recent memoirs of top Soviet intelligence officials that remain unpublished in the West. The latter include books by Vadim Bakatin, the last KGB chairman, Leonid Shebarshin, former head of the First Chief Directorate (foreign intelligence), and Nikolai Leonov, head of the KGB analysis directorate that provided estimates to the Politburo.

List of Maps

List of Tables

Chapter 1

"Limits of the Known World" and the End of Deterrence: Asymmetric War Threat Assessment

Assessment of threats and opportunities is a primary concern of every government. Moreover, few leaders pass into their nations' history in a more ignominious light than those who fail to anticipate security threats to their state. Thus, despite enormous popularity in the West for his vision of an interdependent, peaceful world and for engineering the collapse of Soviet communism and the end of the Cold War, Mikhail Gorbachev is profoundly despised by most Russians in the 1990s. Incapable of winning even 1 percent of the vote in the first post-Soviet presidential election in 1996, while on the campaign trail Gorbachev was spat at and punched by the same people who ten years before would have idolized him as Russia's savior. If the Cold War had ended with the Soviet Union intact and the United States no longer on the map, Ronald Reagan would most likely have been reviled in America—yet be a hero in Russia.

INFORMATION SELECTION AND POLITICAL THEORY

This asymmetric packaging of former statesmen into heroes and villains, though it underscores the importance of threat assessment in world politics, illuminates a major problem concerning both the conduct of international actors and the ability to explain and predict the outcomes of their conduct—what I call the *information selection problem* in international relations theory and the practice of world politics.

One intelligence studies expert, Philippe Baumard, has put the problem in perspective, noting that "we never act, strategize, or decide outside the limits of the known world."[1] Therefore, any act, strategy, or decision in world politics is a function of the "limits of the known world" as perceived by major actors—be they states, corporations, government institutions, or individuals. All face the problem of selecting the essential from among countless bits of information or indicators, especially regarding threats and opportunities. As this book's case studies will show, the indicators that individual policymakers deem critical may be extremely diverse: some would favor the size of a nation's gold reserve, whereas others would consider the number of lights left on in government buildings after working hours; some would put more emphasis on battleships and others, on the revolutionary potential of an adversary's populace. The type, number, weighting, and combination of indicators selected for any given issue sets the limits of the known world. Hence, any decision in world politics, as an outcome of all the methods of information collection and analysis, is informed by the initial choice of indicators. These indicators in turn shape strategy even *before* calculations of power balances, rationality, cognitive or psychological constraints, or bureaucratic politics begin to play their part.

As an analogy to the information selection problem, one may think of the sky on a clear night, filled with myriad stars, large and small, and various observers admiring diverse stellar combinations. In world politics, the stars would represent innumerable bits of information or indicators. The skywatchers would represent decision makers, each capable of perceiving only a limited and very distinct combination of stars at any given time. Neither the night sky in its entirety nor any uniform pattern of constellations assumed as a given will be consistent with the limits of the sky known to these hypothetical skywatchers-policymakers. The actual images will differ according to which stars are included, their physical properties, and the linkages that transform groups of stars into meaningful patterns.

Thus described, the information selection problem affects international relations theory in three distinct ways. First, the choice of indicators regarding the capabilities and motivations of international actors, such as nuclear warheads, GNP, birthrates, or popular support of government, is critical in shaping strategies, policies, and decisions. Second, among different actors, the choice of indicators is usually asymmetric, meaning that indicators are unlikely to overlap or carry equal weight among policymakers. Third, the analysis of systematic patterns of information selection needs to be factored into assumptions about information selection preferences, to refine existing theories of world politics.

The information selection problem calls for recasting key issues in international relations theory—balances of power, deterrence, threat assessment, interdependence, rationality, worst case scenarios, global leadership—in terms of the question, based on what indicators? Would a despotic totalitarian regime and the most benign of democracies attach equal or different relative value to indicators of national power? Would a decision maker bent on aggressive territorial expansion be more likely to be deterred by air strikes or by an oil embargo if the predominant religion of that decision makers' state is Orthodox Christianity or Islam? Would a tit-for-tat escalation of military preparedness in a crisis be more or less likely to trigger war if the escalation involves combat helicopters on one side and tanks on the other, as opposed to, say, Stealth bombers and medium-range missiles against chemical weapons? Which state will have higher per capita income a decade hence—those emphasizing innovation in biotechnology or an expansion of space defense programs?

These questions are far from being hypothetical. The example that follows demonstrates that asymmetry in the threat indicators selected has a real impact on world affairs and may have been critical in hastening the end of the Cold War—arguably the major global event of this century. In closing an international conference on Pacific Rim affairs, held more than half a year after the fall of the Berlin Wall, a member of the U.S. National Security Council staff surprised the participants by stating that the Soviet Union was still considered a major security threat to the United States in the Asia Pacific region. This judgment, he explained, was shaped by the U.S. government's explicit preoccupation with still-sizable Soviet nuclear capabilities rather than the improved political climate between East and West. In contrast, Moscow officials were preoccupied with entirely different indicators. Among the Soviet participants at that conference was Vladimir Lukin, who later became Russia's ambassador to the United States, Yeltsin's adviser on Asian politics, and eventually, chairman of the Foreign Relations Committee of the Russian lower chamber of parliament, the

State Duma. According to Lukin, the rational calculation of nuclear capabilities played a negligible role in the Kremlin's major decisions, such as agreeing to German reunification under NATO. Critical to the Soviet moves, Lukin argued, were symbolic events such as Chancellor Kohl's visit to Gorbachev's native village in the steppes of southern Russia; Soviet foreign minister, Eduard Shevardnadze fishing in Wyoming with his U.S. counterpart, James Baker; long, heartfelt conversations with Western leaders lasting after midnight; and exchanges of pens used to sign arms control treaties. The American statesmen overseeing the winding down of the Cold War failed to emphasize precisely these factors in their memoirs, making Lukin wonder if James Baker and George Shultz really understood anything about the Soviet motivation for concluding four decades of global confrontation.[2]

This stark asymmetry between the U.S. and Soviet choices of threat indicators, practical versus symbolic, suggests a major paradox: that the clash between "Western rationality" and "Eastern irrationality"—considered by none other than Winston Churchill as a major source of enduring hostility between Russia and the West—turned out to be instrumental in breaking down the Iron Curtain. The clash of interpretations to end all such confrontations became possible through an asymmetric information selection that traded off heartfelt chats after midnight with military presence in vital geographical locations—a development that is largely beyond the scope of conventional international relations theories. This example also shows that the entire debate about Western rationality versus Oriental irrationality misses an important point: to speak of rationality or irrationality makes sense "only relative to a possessed body of information . . . in terms of which the merits of the available course of action can be evaluated."[3] Thus, the decisive impact of asymmetric information selection on world events may be a major yet unacknowledged lesson of the Cold War.

INFORMATION SELECTION AFTER THE COLD WAR

The end of the Cold War meant the end of competition for leadership in world politics between the United States and the Soviet Union. For the only remaining superpower, the United States, the end of this competition has exacerbated the information selection problem as it relates to major security threats. In particular, the post–Cold War security environment makes it much harder to derive the intentions of potential aggressors from their capabilities or to assess security threats on the basis of capabilities. Thus, the principal Cold War era analytical practices in threat assessment by the intelligence, decision making, and scholarly communities in the United States are increasingly called into question. The conceptual focus on a single existential threat to the United States and its allies must be replaced with multiple concepts as decision makers debate over which problems to target and how to weigh the relevant evidence from numerous and far-flung sources.

Several key factors explain why it is increasingly difficult to derive political intentions from capabilities in the post–Cold War world. First, the decision to use destructive capabilities has become much more complex. The Kremlin is no longer the only or the major source of aggressive strategies; instead the sources of potential danger are dispersed globally. This source dispersion has been driven by several processes, such as the proliferation of weapons of mass destruction (including their geographical spread, potential access to them by groups and individuals rather than states, and technological weapons innovation); the rise of terrorism and organized crime, with multiple operational centers worldwide; the proliferation of aggressive challenges from states taking on the role of "regional bullies" (such as China, Iraq, Iran, Libya); and the rise in internal wars spilling over state boundaries (as in Bosnia, sub-Saharan Africa, or Afghanistan).

Second, threat analysis must encompass multiple doctrines, since communism and world socialist revolution are no longer the primary conceptual source of challenges to the Western alliance's leading position in world politics. Ideational influences on the strategic intentions of potential aggressors represent a diverse mix of religious doctrines, ethnocultural traditions, regional histories, and regional political thought. National security advisers in Azerbaijan or China, for example, may not have internalized Western political science approaches to world politics.

Third, the relatively greater importance of the economic dimensions of security and the decline of the bloc mentality (which assumed the primacy of East-West military confrontation) engender competing interpretations for the motives behind the spread of conventional weapons and so-called dual use technologies which may be employed to manufacture nuclear weapons. The old assumption—that the acquisition of military capabilities is a function of superpower competition—no longer holds, thus undermining the implicit negative conceptualization of massive military capabilities as the tools of Armageddon. The debate about the merits of "opaque deterrence" in an age of "opaque proliferation" indicates the difficulties inherent in efforts to define what constitutes a "clear and present danger" in a post–Cold War world.[4]

Fourth, the price of failure in threat assessment now appears to be lower, as analysts primarily focus on smaller threats to the diverse interests of the United States worldwide, rather than on the probability of intercontinental attack and global war. This shift—from a concern with survival to the monitoring of a kaleidoscope of interests—makes it harder to assess intentions of aggressors and design weighting schemes for indicators of aggression, which are diffused among many interest domains.

Other factors amplifying the information selection problem in post–Cold War threat assessment include the geographical dispersion of challengers (mainly from Europe to everywhere in the world), as well as a shift in military threats from predominantly high-tech, massive forces to a mix of high-, medium-, and low-tech forces. Moreover, a small nuclear bomb, hidden in the back of a dilapidated truck and driven to the Potomac with the express threat to wipe out the U.S. capital on behalf of some elusive conglomeration of terrorist groups and rogue states, would make a mockery of the deterrence value of the most high-tech missile defense, while underscoring the futility of the billions of dollars invested over the years in every type of defense system. Extrapolating the intentions of potential aggressors from known capabilities under such a scenario is next to impossible, unless it happens by luck.

The quantum increase in observable threat indicators after the Cold War makes threat assessment strikingly similar to the problem of deterring the Invisible Man in the famous story by H. G. Wells, who dreams of holding the world in constant terror. My argument goes further than simply saying that deterrence after the Cold War has to focus on smaller, regional challenges. The argument implies that deterrence, as the stronger powers' strategy to prevent aggression, will become less relevant in the decades to come. The end of the Cold War signals not the end of history or ideology, but the end of deterrence. The continuing ability of deterrence as an international relations theory to explain the failures of deterrence as strategy will therefore be of little solace to failing statesmen.

INTERNATIONAL RELATIONS THEORY AFTER THE COLD WAR

This problem of extrapolating intentions from material capabilities, implicit in the major global shifts that have taken place since the Cold War, also confounds the mainstream international relations paradigms—realism, decision making, and domestic sources of foreign policy—that government analysts, academics, and the media rely on to discern patterns in the conduct of actors on the world stage. Most of these theoretical models have a diminishing explanatory and predictive capacity for assessing precisely those threats of aggression that are more likely to dominate security concerns in the post–Cold War world. A critical reassessment of these models, particularly in relation to deterrence theory—which, some have argued, has been at the heart of America's government thinking on security since the Monroe Doctrine and especially after World War II—is needed to help scholars and policy makers cope with the growing problem of information selection. Below I analyze these paradigms' capacity to interpret threat indicators—especially those that go beyond material capabilities.

The Realist Tradition

It is hard to argue with the key assertion of the realist theory: national power matters in world politics, often decisively. The central role of power in the realist worldview—particularly among structural or neorealists—rests on the largely untested assumption that the ordering principle of the international system is anarchy, resembling a Hobbesian state of nature, in which major actors (states) are permanently insecure. At the systemic level, this implies that structure, or the distribution of power, "defines the arrangement, or the ordering, of the parts of a system."[5] The strategic priorities of major units in the system (states) are to expand their military capabilities, and prevent others from expanding and using theirs.[6] Consequently, neorealists argue that states "base their strategic behavior on the capabilities, not intentions, of other states."[7] The information selection problem as defined in this book, is, thus, irrelevant from the realist perspective, since power is measured in terms of capabilities supposed to exist "independently of the actors' knowing or will."[8]

Yet the information selection problem has bedeviled scholars who have sought to explain what realism presents as the central issue of world politics: the causes of war and the conditions of peace. At the heart of the problem is the lack of reliable method for predicting which configurations and indices of power among states would lead to war, even though some of the most brilliant practitioners in the field have addressed the problem. One review of the literature spanning almost half a century searched for the key indicators of national power and concluded that either designing a universal scale to measure each nation-state's power relative to that of all other nation-states or selecting "the best index of power" amounted to a political scientist's pipe dream.[9]

Despite all the sophistication and ingenuity of principal researchers, statistical tests of *probabilities* that one or another type of indicator scale would be a better predictor of international outcomes have also failed to resolve the information selection problem. Perhaps the best example of research efforts along these lines is the Correlates of War (COW) project.[10] According to this approach, national capabilities consist of demographic, industrial, and military characteristics, measured in percentages. These characteristics include total national population; the number of cities with populations of 20,000 or more; the coal ton equivalent of energy consumption; iron or steel production; military expenditures; and armed forces size, excluding reserves. Consistent with the reductionist approach of neorealism, the COW study argued that "separate indicators of social organization, national unity and motivation, and technical skills" could be excluded, since each "was adequately reflected in one or more of the six specific indices."[11] In short, material capabilities automatically subsume other, less concrete forms of power.

Although analyses of past patterns of state conduct that relied on the COW project data sets often generated findings with high levels of statistical reliability, one would use the COW indicators for political prediction only at great peril. By confining the substantive content of strategic information to a restricted set of capability indicators, studies derived from the COW project, as with other realist models focusing on global power distributions, failed to explain such massive structural transformations in world politics as the outbreak of global wars, the collapse of the communist bloc,[12] and the post–Cold War outbreak of ethnopolitical conflict in the former Soviet area.

Noting that the indexes of relative capabilities for the years 1915, 1940, and 1945 became distorted, the COW Project investigators replaced data for those years with the data for 1913, 1938, and 1946 to ensure a close fit with the theory, tacitly acknowledging measurement problems because of war.[13] Composite power capability ranks, constructed on the basis of the COW data set for 1980, showed the Soviet Union in first place and overtaking the United States. In the real world, however, the late 1970s and early 1980s demonstrated the conclusive incapacity of the Soviet political and economic system to generate innovation, growth, and vitality in critical civilian and military industrial sectors, such as electronics and computer applications. Moreover, when adjusted for disparities among major powers, the COW index of power indicators made the Soviet Union appear almost twice as powerful as the United States—in a sharp contradiction to the reality of Soviet decline, especially in comparative global terms.[14] An inability to discern shifts in leading economic sectors was one of several reasons for the strong bias against change in the world system implicit in structural realism. A prediction implicit in Kenneth Waltz's work, and also made in the early 1980s—that the Soviet Union would outlast Ford, IBM, or Shell—is a perfect illustration of the general failure of realism to anticipate the Soviet collapse.[15]

Although the number of internal wars, especially those originating in ethnopolitical conflict, has risen steadily since the 1960s, models employing power indicators associated with the realist paradigm estimated that between the mid-1980s and the year 2000, collective protest within states would decline steadily and that most internal wars would occur in India, China, Indonesia, Nigeria, and Pakistan, rather than in Somalia, Rwanda, or Yugoslavia. Only a marginal increase in the incidence of internal war was predicted for the former Soviet Union.[16] The lack of political intention indicators disassociated from capabilities, such as the impact of Tito's death on the Yugoslav polity, goes a long way toward explaining why some of the most sophisticated regression and factor analysis models failed to predict the severity of the ethnic conflict that ripped apart the former Yugoslavia.[17]

Classical Deterrence Theory

In other words, realist models, by default, fail to capture political intentions of actors that influence events independently of capability distributions or that play critical roles in determining which power indicators should be emphasized in decision making. The logic of the classical (realist) deterrence theory illustrates this point.

The basic formula of deterrence—peace through strength—implies that potential aggressors would abstain from resorting to military action if the party supporting the status quo convinces them that the cost of using force would outweigh the benefits.[18] A statement by President Kennedy conveyed the essence of deterrence as strategy: "Only when arms are sufficient beyond doubt can we be certain without doubt that they will never be employed."[19] Sufficient capabilities and the credibility of threats to use them are therefore at the heart of deterrence. But how is credibility transmitted in real life? Paul Huth's *Extended Deterrence and the Prevention of War* offers a classic illustration of how credibility estimates are subsumed by indicators of material capabilities and how the independent impact of political intentions is neglected in deterrence theory. As such, credibility was exclusively linked by Huth to material capabilities—demonstrated military actions with which a defender could counter a potential aggressor, a history of past military action, and in the case of extended deterrence, the strength of military and economic ties between a defender and its protégés.

Thus, credibility is measured by such indicators as naval visits to ports, naval exercises or war games close to areas of potential aggression, reinforcement of ground forces along borders, buildup of ground and naval forces, general or partial mobilization, outcome of past military engagements (defeat, victory, or capitulation), presence of formal military alliances often involving military presence of the defender on the protégés' territory, arms transfers, and trade in strategic materials, such as coal and iron ore prior to World War I and petroleum, copper, chromium, titanium and cobalt after World War II.[20]

In practice, however, the independent impact of political intentions is a critical ingredient that is often neglected. Khrushchev's decision to deploy Soviet missiles in Cuba in 1962, boldly challenging a massive U.S. predominance in military capabilities in the region and worldwide, stemmed, to a large extent, from a peculiar Kremlin mix of power politics and Marxism—concepts that remained impenetrable to the Washington's Kremlin watchers. In addition, at the June 1961 Vienna summit, Khrushchev concluded that Kennedy was a wishy-washy "boy" who would be vulnerable to pressure—a poor match to Khrushchev's own hardened worldliness amplified by cunning wit. In another example, Kennedy's predecessor, Dwight Eisenhower, did not realize when sending the U-2 spy planes deep into the Soviet territory in April and May 1960—following talks with Khrushchev at Camp David—that these acts made Khrushchev politically vulnerable to the Kremlin opponents of détente with the United States (especially in the face of worsening Sino-Soviet relations). Consequently, Eisenhower sought no intelligence assessments of political ramifications of his policies within the Kremlin.[21]

Political intentions may also be critical in identifying the relative value of all the measurements of capabilities and credibility in deterrence models. A note in Paul Huth's book both acknowledges and explains the essential nature of the information selection problem in deterrence theory: "A critical source of measurement error could be caused by the use of objective [i.e. quantifiable] indicators, rather than the potential attacker's perception of strength or presence, for the measurement of the independent variables. If subjective estimates do, however, diverge from objective indicators, then the model should have poor predictive value."[22]

Without specifying national capabilities on which the political intentions of actors are more likely to focus, research relying on realism and classical deterrence theory has generated findings that contradict the initial assumptions of the realist paradigm. If various realist claims are given equal weight, one would conclude that neither the balance of power nor an asymmetric distribution of power are good predictors of either deterrence stability or war and peace. Why, then, would estimates of relative power among nations have significant predictive value in world politics?[23]

According to one view, if equality of power among nations minimized the likelihood of war, then World War I, the Franco-Prussian War, the Russo-Japanese War, World War II, the Seven Weeks War, the Crimean War, and the wars of Italian reunification—to name but a few in the past 200 years—should never have been fought. Other findings indicate, however, that states with a window of opportunity because of a favorable capability distribution do not automatically attack states facing a window of vulnerability. A major empirical paradox in this regard is the absence of a superpower war during the periods of American nuclear superiority and the striking absence of Soviet aggression against China.[24] Even harder to explain would be developments such as the Soviet Union returning Manchuria to China when the former had nuclear weapons and the latter did not. Conversely, even with a negligible nuclear capability relative to the Soviet Union, China initiated military attacks on Russian border posts in the late 1960s to gain possession of several Amur River islands.

These last examples suggest that asymmetries in strategy are inconsistent with asymmetries in power distribution and are explicable only given differentiated information selection among key actors. That political intentions matter in strategy decisions at least as much as ultimately destructive capabilities is underscored by systematic empirical evidence showing that in 14 major postwar disputes, nuclear weapons capability failed to deter conflicts or influence decisively the outcomes of extreme crises.[25] A statistical analysis of deterrence cases spanning the period from 1900 to 1980 showed that "the long-term balance of forces and the defender's possession of nuclear weapons makes little difference" for deterrence success or failure.[26] And without accounting for the asymmetric selection of power indicators, realist and deterrence theories provide only an asymmetric, one-sided picture of motivations underlying conflict and war. As Richard Betts has observed, "both the balance of interests and the balance of power theories prove useful for explaining either the threat or the response, but neither appears adequate to account for *both sides' behavior at the same time*" [emphasis added].[27]

Decision Theories
Decision theories in international relations introduce information processing as a variable in world politics. Global conflicts and wars, for example, are

not automatically attributed to tectonic shifts in national capabilities and alliance configurations. For example, decision theorists see in deterrence the interplay of preferences, choices, and outcomes. Key studies within this paradigm, however, suggest that preferences are assumed to be constant, exogenous, and retroactively defined. Choices follow preferences, and outcomes follow choices. The assumption of rationality, either in a classic economic sense or modified by psychological and cognitive constraints in a uniform fashion, means that the fabric of world politics is woven from interactions among rational unitary actors in search of maximum security and economic benefit.[28] Information processing methods within the prevailing decision-making paradigms do not, however, resolve the information selection problem.

Theories of rational choice emphasizing the theoretical rigor of formal models dominate the decision-making paradigm within international relations (and, perhaps, the entire discipline of political science). Yet just as realist theorists are confounded from the outset by the problem of defining power, decision theorists are confounded by the definitions of rationality and utility. In short, rationality means that decision-makers have some kind of unified and universal scale for ranking preferences, have unrestricted (except by cost) access to all available information, and can always tell the best from the worst and choose the best. But even in economics, where rational choice models originated and where preferences can be pegged to one universal parameter—money—problems of information choice are legion, particularly in predicting the performance of command economies (in no small part because the role of political intentions is infinitely higher there than in market economies). Absent a universal indicator of power, such as money, in economics, political outcomes are immeasurably more sensitive to a greater variety of initial conditions. The metaphor of a butterfly flapping its wings in Beijing and causing a storm in New York, borrowed from chaos theory, may be readily evoked to describe the impact of information selection on supposedly "rational" choices.

In attempting to resolve this problem, rational choice theories define the interests of nation-states and the structure of international alliances as a function of the states' relative power to one another. In one of the best applications of rational choice (expected utility) theory in international relations, Bruce Bueno de Mesquita argues that the strategies of states depend on calculations of the expected probability of success and the expected utility or risk with respect to gains. His measure of the expected probability of success in war for any State A against State B is, essentially, a ratio of State A's index of gross national capabilities (based on the Corre-lates of War indicators) over the same index of national capabilities of State B. Expected utility includes a noncapability indicator—presence of trea-ties, pacts, or *ententes* among the key states—but is contingent on the num-ber of great powers lined up against any given actor, thus requiring a calculation of capabilities. Capability estimates, therefore, typically play a dominant role in strategic assessments, and the independent impact of political intentions is discounted.[29] As the onset of World War II showed, however, both global capability balances and instruments of diplomacy, such as treaties, are poor indicators of political intentions.

The information selection problem within theories of decision making thus parallels the problem within the realist paradigm. Translated into the language of decision theories, a realist's problem in explaining restraint by dominant powers and the initiation of war by weaker powers becomes one of explaining irrational outcomes (such as war) in rational situations (such as the balance of power) and rational outcomes (peace) in irrational situa-tions (as in tense and politically charged phases of the Cold War). Most decision models of deterrence, for example, attempt to bypass the problem of defining rationality by assuming the underlying logic of the game of chicken. The operational metaphor for this game is two teenagers racing their cars at each other in a test of wills, each with the option to collide head-on or "chicken out." Applied to world politics, the structure of the game presupposes that war is the worst possible outcome; therefore, it can only be chosen irrationally. Since a rational leader under a balance of power would never purposefully initiate war, decision-theoretic models presup-pose that "only irrational and accidental wars are possible"[30]—a proposi-tion easily falsified by examining Mein Kampf or the pronouncements of European leaders prior to World War I that emphasize the "cult of the offensive."[31]

Also, game theoretic models assume a symmetrical payoff structure (that is, if A gets four points when defecting against B, whereas B gets two, B would get four points when defecting against A, whereas A would get two, according to the payoff structured into the game). Decisions in the real world more often originate in highly asymmetrical assumptions about pay-offs. Therefore, decision models are likely to duplicate the problem ex-posed in the empirical testing of realist theories—either threats or the responses to these threats (moves or countermoves) can be accounted for, but not both. Thus, for example, in playing chicken, an opponent trying to avoid one disaster (head-on collision) must face another (turning away and again risking collision with the other player, who may decide to turn away at the same time). Once the U.S.-Soviet rivalry during the Cold War was conceptualized in these terms, expecting either side to play for reconciliation (that is, for canceling the test of wills altogether) became theoretically impossible. It is small wonder, then, that international relations theorists, influenced by the classical deterrence school, failed to register shifts in the Soviet global outlook in the early and mid-1980s and were then surprised by the seeming abruptness with which the Cold War ended.

Psychological models of political decision making, represented in the work of such authors as John Steinbruner, Robert Jervis, and Richard Ned Lebow, have concentrated on patterns of selective perception and misperception, emphasizing the reluctance of decision makers to acknowledge information that is inconsistent with their preconceptions or bolsters fears of political divisiveness. Their studies emphasize the role of persistent images, values, and expectations acting independently of material capabilities calculated on the basis of formal models. Robert Jervis, for example, using the concept of the state's "basic intention," has argued that "a major determinant of the effect of threats is the intention of the other side."[32] He presents the perception problem as a source of strategic conflicts in and of itself, making the general conclusion that "states are willing to pay a higher price to protect what they have than to increase their values."[33] Therefore, intentions are defined largely as a function of perceived costs of action and, therefore, are subject to the same asymmetric indicator selection problem as realist and rational choice theories.

Although perception theories introduced an important new dimension to analyses of strategic conduct, the theories lack the rigor of formal models and concentrate on the *process* of information assessment rather than on substantive information preferences of key policymakers. Thus, psychological models have been of very limited value in explaining policy changes leading to systemic transformations, such as the end of the Cold War. The psychological dynamics of spiraling threat perceptions, developed by Jervis, broke down in a brief span of three years (1986-1989), when the key decision makers of the Soviet Union and the United States redefined the ways of assimilating information to pre-existing beliefs—if not the beliefs themselves—and overcame "excessive and premature cognitive closure."[34]

Theories of Domestic Politics and War
Many studies have examined linkages between the character of domestic political systems and the decision to go to war. Though acknowledging

that states' foreign policies are constrained by their military and economic capabilities, this type of research emphasizes the impact of a leader's "willingness and political ability to respond to systemic imperatives."[35] Research in this tradition has generated what comes closest to a law in political science: clear-cut, robust, and multidimensional empirical evidence demonstrates that democracies have a very low proclivity to fight one another because of shared democratic culture and democratic institutional constraints.[36]

Other studies of domestic politics and war have focused on what is described as "power intangibles," or factors that have an independent impact on political intentions in world politics—such as state ideology, government's capacity to mobilize resources and manpower and to exploit people's willingness to suffer, the maintenance of ruling coalitions, a fear of domestic revolutions or opposition movements, or the rise of hardline "war parties."[37] Whereas systemic theories such as neorealism stress continuities in world politics, theories of domestic politics often focus on change, arguing, for example, that domestic revolutions or power transitions have a decisive impact on structural transformations in world politics, such as war and shifts in the global power balance.[38] Nonetheless, scholarly reassessments of domestic politics theories have highlighted lack of systematic explanations for the war propensities of democracies toward non-democracies and of authoritarian governments in general. Critics have called for "placing democratic peace into a broader configuration of political systems."[39]

Casting theories of domestic politics and war in the light of the information selection problem helps to deconstruct the meaning of democratic peace and place it within this broader configuration of political systems. In the same way that realism is confounded by weaker actors attacking stronger ones and decision theories fail to explain irrational outcomes among rational actors, theories of domestic politics and war have to contend with several paradoxes that characterize interactions between democracies and autocracies. While it has been known at least since Kant's *Perpetual Peace* that democratic governments are less belligerent and almost never go to war with one another, the record of behavior of democracies in relation to autocracies is mixed. Despite favoring peace, democracies are often poor and dubious peacekeepers. Theories of domestic politics and war can rarely predict which of these two aspects of democracy is more likely to prevail at any given time. If democracies can successfully contain autocracies, such as the United States with regard to the Soviet Union during the Cold War, why do they fail so disastrously at other times, as in the events leading up to World Wars I and II? Why are democracies sometimes resolute and ready to risk major embarrassments internationally and domestically to contain their autocratic adversaries, as was the United States over Vietnam? At other times, however, they act without will and resolve, missing opportunities to deter aggressive challenges with low risks, as Britain did in late eighteenth century at the onset of the French Revolutionary Wars, or Britain, United States, and France did when initially attempting to appease Hitler. The record for autocratic, despotic governments is also mixed: some despotisms are clearly more benign than others; some states with long autocratic traditions are averse to initiating war. The Soviet Union under Stalin—probably the most totalitarian state in history—nevertheless consistently criticized Western democratic governments in the 1930s for their appeasement policies, took steps to forge an anti-Hitler coalition, and fought World War II on the side of democracies. As Joshua Goldstein has concluded, "If there are principles to explain why some societies at some times are more peaceful than others and why they change under different conditions, political scientists have not identified them."[40]

From the perspective of this book, the asymmetric behavior of democracies and autocracies may be explained in terms of asymmetric information selection. Democracies and autocracies usually have divergent, often institutionalized, preferences about which information matters to them. This divergence therefore explains asymmetric choices of strategy both within and between autocracies and democracies. Thus, the question to be posed after examining theories of domestic politics and war through the prism of information selection problem is, "democratic peace" and "autocratic war"—based on what indicators?

To sum up, the information selection problem poses a serious challenge to mainstream international relations theories. In particular, these theories are most deficient in anticipating two classes of international political phenomena: (1) the independent impact of changes in political intentions on changes in strategy, including the proclivity for war (with respect to aggressive strategies, this implies that most international relations theories will do much better in a world where aggressive political intentions play no role—a counterintuitive and dangerous assumption), and consequently (2) changes or major transformations at the global level, arising from changes in political intentions (with the two world wars, the end of the Cold War, and the collapse of the Soviet Union presenting the biggest puzzles in this respect).

This conceptual oversight is precisely why much international relations research fails to explain the interplay between short- and long-term causes of upheavals in world politics. It is also why we can predict we can predict 70-80 percent of the instances of war initiation—no mean achievement in social science terms—but not global wars, of which five account for an estimated 80 percent of all the war casualties in the past 500 years.[41] The question of why global wars are initiated by powers with a weaker global reach, both economically and militarily, continues to confound the dominant theories.[42] Thus, the problem identified as central to the theory of international relations as far back as the 1960s—the "discovery of the links between gross characteristics of nations, such as measures of national power, and the specific behavior of individuals acting for nations"—remains unresolved.[43]

Given this state of the art in international relations theory, we may be hardly better prepared today to anticipate the rise of war-prone challengers determined to change the world than were decision makers in the past who failed to anticipate the outbreak of devastating world wars. Since international relations theories permeate the educational system and implicitly frame debates and discourses on international affairs, in coming decades the public and decision makers may be desensitized to critical global security issues precisely when greater attention to these issues may be crucial to averting massive armed conflicts. With security giving precedence to economics in the minds of Western policymakers after the Cold War, the aggressive political intentions of potential challengers may be more easily misread.

WHAT ARE THE ALTERNATIVES?

In considering the magnitude of the information selection problem, this book suggests that political scientists could profitably reexamine the research and address the asymmetric targeting of threat indicators among major actors in world politics. The tools and building blocks for a theory of information selection are available; the question is how to use the tools and how to assemble the building blocks.

If information selection should be treated as a dependent variable and is the principal phenomenon under investigation, the logical place to begin is with intelligence, especially strategic intelligence involving estimates of threats and the opportunities of actors in world politics.[44] The historical record of what is often termed "the second oldest profession" is the record of a gradually unfolding process of the "creation and reproduction of international political reality."[45] In this respect, "intelligence assessments, broadly conceived, provide a unique insight into both the prevailing spoken and unspoken assumptions of government agencies tasked with the making of foreign policy and military decisions."[46]

For example, consider the meaning of intelligence as used to describe government institutions responsible for collecting and analyzing strategic information: In Japanese, *joho* implies knowing both facts and purpose; in Russian, *razvedka* connotes knowledge mingled with surmise, divination, trust, and exercise of authority. In the West, however, information signifies objective fact valued as much as a commodity as for its intrinsic worth.[47] Changes in the meaning of intelligence over time similarly reflect shifts in institutional patterns of information collection and analysis by governments. In standard English usage of the fifteenth century, when the church played a key role in political intelligence, intelligence primarily referred to "the basic eternal quality of divine Mind" or the angels guiding the earth along the celestial crystal spheres. But by the turn of the twentieth century, intelligence came to signify government departments dealing with information on potential adversaries or allies.[48]

Since the information selection problem has a particularly strong negative effect on the ability of international relations theory to deal with changes at the global level (also defined as structural changes or transformations in world politics), this book focuses on intelligence assessments among major powers that were competing for global leadership—the Mongol Empire and Sung China in the thirteenth century, Britain and France in the late eighteenth century, and the United States and the Soviet Union during the Cold War. I address several principal questions: How are asymmetries in relative power and domestic political institutions factored into intelligence assessments of threat and opportunity by global powers? Do major powers have systematically different intelligence collection priorities? If so, how do these differences affect crucial decisions and key strategies, particularly prior to conflict? Moreover, in what way may information selection priorities—or priorities for intelligence collection and intelligence set by governments—differ systematically among major global powers (if they differ at all)?

First, it is intuitively plausible that differences in intelligence assessment, representing the information selection process as practiced by governments, would reflect differences in the relative military and economic capabilities of states, their political systems, and socioeconomic organization, and a broad range of cultural traditions permeating state institutions. Since in the real world these characteristics are highly diverse, intelligence assessment priorities are likely to differ as well, and in some generally predictable fashion. Thus, conventional recipes for intelligence collection and analysis within divergent national institutional settings are likely to differ accordingly, and over time these differences will become deeply rooted. As Philippe Baumard has observed, "Organizations have memory, not only within their archival department, with their old newspapers, and dusty boxes of internal mail, but a real history, carried from mouth to ear, as warnings for newcomers, in advice from the experienced 'old boys,' in evolving tacit rules for interpersonal communication and *in developing the intelligence process*" [emphasis added].[49]

Second, in analyses of global leadership competition, also known as "the rise and fall of great powers," intelligence assessments of the two principal actors—the leaders (or status quo powers) and the challengers—are likely to exhibit the most consistent patterns of systematic differentiation or asymmetry. This is also highly plausible intuitively, since the contrasts between global powers that rise and those that fall are both pronounced and persistent.

It is therefore quite likely that asymmetric threat assessment is a function of the rise and fall process among global powers and that the causes of the rise and fall will also shape intelligence collection and analysis preferences. In this book, I suggest that an evolutionary theory of world politics, one that identifies the conditions consistently resulting in the rise and fall of major powers over the long term, is critical in explaining intelligence preferences among contenders for global leadership. The application of evolutionary theory will also help to address the implicit information selection problem in two ways. First, most international relations analyses, including longitudinal studies based on such data sets as the Correlates of War, focus on static relationships. For example, studies of the impact of power distribution on war initiation since 1815 would produce the same probability scores regardless of whether this relationship was stronger in the 1830s or 1950s or whether the frequency of war in the 1830s had an impact on the frequency of war in the 1950s. In contrast, an evolutionary approach in international relations—the theory of long cycles of world politics—examines the impact of one class of events or indicators on another after specified periods of time. This research established, for example, that states succeeding in coalition-building 30-40 years prior to global wars usually win those wars. A higher rate of economic performance, especially innovation, in the leading sectors of the global economy was shown to be a better predictor of a state's rise in world politics over 30, 60, or 90 years than were the GNP growth rates of the entire economy.[50] In other words, the problem of selection is endogenous to evolutionary theory; the thrust of the research is to identify which indicators of state power or national economy are more successful in the long run and therefore more likely to induce changes at the global level.

THE EVOLUTIONARY MODEL

Like any other theory in international relations, the evolutionary model has underlying assumptions about the nature of world politics or the international system. I assume that world politics is a self-organizing process combining elements of both anarchy and structure, randomness and regularity, change and continuity, insecurity and confidence, all in varying degrees at different times. The evolution of the world politics implies the continuous emergence of various actors and strategies with different capacities to adapt to the external environment, a process resulting in the retention of more successful (adaptive) strategies and actors. Among the major global powers, this process of responsive and interactive adaptation takes the form of *competition* for global leadership, or the proverbial "rise and fall." Although highly random initially, tryouts or combinations of strategies are gradually structured into recognizable and enduring patterns, as the less adaptable approaches (usually at the extreme ends of the choice spectrum) are winnowed out over time. Computer simulations have suggested, for example, that middle-range cooperative strategies outcompete both consistent defectors and unconditional cooperators even in one-shot games because of the implications of projecting one's intentions onto prospective partners. Evolutionary sequences result in still greater advances for these moderately cooperative strategies.[51]

The evolutionary process is also assumed to be nonlinear, meaning that the continual selection and reproduction of more adaptable strategies and actors in world politics does not necessarily culminate in any kind of finite and unalterable state of the system. Multiple feedbacks between the world system and domestic political and economic imperatives (including random phenomena) may periodically result in punctuated equilibria in power balances, domestic regime stability, or war proneness. From this perspective, no theoretical claim can be made that cruel and violent means of resolving international disputes, such as wars, may ever become obsolete (nor would the world ever likely to lapse into total pandemonium, or a war of all against all). The application of genetic algorithms to Axelrod's evolution of cooperation model has demonstrated, for example, that even stable, benign clusters of tit-for-tat strategies break down in the long run (when the number of game iterations is extended to 700 and above) under massive and sudden attacks by "defective genes" challenging the status quo.[52]

From this perspective, global wars are more than mechanisms to "redraft the rules by which relations among nations work" and establish "who will govern the international system and whose interests will be primarily served by the new international order."[53] They are viewed as macrodecision points in the process of global leadership competition and selection linked *longitudinally* to the setting of political agendas, coalition-building, and the emergence of new institutional structures for global system management. In the context of world time, or what Fernand Braudel described as the "superstructure of world history,"[54] these processes can be seen as distinct phases in the evolution of world politics. According to George Modelski, these phases

> make it explicit that problem resolution requires, in the first place, information, and an exploration of alternative courses of action. That is followed by the coalescence of coalitions around prominent leaders, and certain prominent alternatives, some of which are bound to offend vested interests. The coalitions are then likely to square off in sustained conflict but one of them will prevail through a collective choice process. Claimants to global leadership all participate in this process but with special intensity in the phase of macrodecision. They activate and lead the coalitions that via a global trial of strength (in past cases, a global war) validate the set of policies that will be carried to fruition . . .[55]

Strategies in global leadership competition, including global wars, are conditioned by this evolutionary process, which drives the selection of global leaders and the "deselection" of challengers. Studies in long cycles of world politics have identified three major conditions that in combination have ensured a nation's rise to global leadership in the past 500 years: a superior politico-military organization for global reach (naval, airspace, and information power); an open democratic polity anchored in a system of popular representation, institutional checks and balances, and the rule of law;[56] and a lead economy sufficiently large to support global operations yet deriving growth and vitality from innovation rather than extension.[57]

This global selection process also results in the rise of challengers seeking to modify existing configurations of power in world politics in their favor; however, no longer accepting the rules of the game set by the incumbent world power and its coalition, challengers strive to develop alternative forms of military, political, and economic organization. Historically, challengers have emphasized rapid regional concentrations of military force (usually large land armies); highly centralized and less open political systems; and economies favoring direct and centralized government intervention.[58]

Since about 1500, four powers have risen to the position of global leadership according to these criteria: Portugal in the sixteenth century, the Netherlands in the eighteenth, England (Great Britain) in the eighteenth and nineteenth centuries, and the United States in the twentieth century. And states that clashed with the incumbents in wars contesting global leadership—Spain and France (both twice), Germany, and the Soviet Union—clearly fit the challenger profile. Before 1500, initial conditions of global leadership were observed in Sung China and Venice, with the Mongols (from Genghis Khan to Kubilai Khan) exhibiting the traits of global challengers.

Table 1.1 illustrates the differentiation of major global powers into leaders and challengers after 1500 on the basis of their capacity to control the transoceanic network of political, military and economic interactions within the world system. This capacity shows the decisive role of ocean navies and, in modern times, nuclear missile and air force capabilities.

Over the centuries, differentiation among global powers, particularly among leaders and challengers, has necessitated the differentiation of strategic priorities and, hence, priorities in intelligence collection and analysis. Leaders and governments are never supplied with complete information about the world by their intelligence services. Rather, intelligence efforts are directed where their high-placed consumers request, thus perpetuating established patterns. In this manner, asymmetric differentiation in strategic priorities between incumbent world powers and challengers is further reinforced by the "limits of the known world" or by decision paths resulting from policymakers' adapting their domestic requirements to global conditions. Metaphorically speaking, incumbent world powers (global leaders) and their challengers use parallel and separate information highways to reach strategic decisions.

The examples of national variations in the meaning of intelligence[59] mentioned earlier suggest that a systematic distinction is possible between

Table 1.1
Concentration of Global Reach
Capabilities and World Powers

World Power	Periods of Global Reach Capability Concentration Exceeding 50% of Total	Competing Global Powers
1. Portugal	1502-44	England, Spain, France, Netherlands
2. Netherlands	1608-42	England, Spain, France
3. Britain	1714-38	France, Netherlands, Russia, Spain
4. Britain	1809-34	France, Russia, USA, Germany, Japan
5. United States	1944-	Soviet Union, (China)

Source: William R. Thompson, On Global War: Historical-Structural Approaches to World Politics (Columbia: University of South Carolina Press, 1988), 46, 76-77.

intelligence assessments about facts and purpose, or capabilities and intentions, in the language of intelligence experts. In fact, the assessment of capabilities and the intentions of other actors in world politics has been the main traditional concern of intelligence institutions.[60] In intelligence studies, threat assessment has traditionally comprised both capabilities and intentions linked to a broad range of factors. In analyzing how the intelligence product reaches decision makers, Sherman Kent has emphasized personalities, geography, military capabilities, the economy, political alignments, social attributes, moral "doctrines of life," and scientific-technological development (including the social sciences). In broader terms, he distinguishes between nonmilitary instrumentalities and war potential constituting the overall strategic stature of a given actor.[61] Thus, asymmetries in the assessment of intelligence among governments will be based on diverse weights assigned to intentions and capabilities, as well as on different methods of interpreting intentions.

Studies in intelligence suggest that incumbent world powers structure intelligence collection and analysis, emphasizing precise and quantifiable information on the global reach capabilities of all major powers, the centrality of analysis, verifiable open source collection, the higher salience of global issues, and access by public representatives to intelligence data. These elements comprise what is known as the American view of intelligence.[62] Sherman Kent, one of the pioneers and major proponents of the American view, also argued that capabilities are the minimum and the critical predictor in assessing strategic threats, particularly in wartime.[63]

At the same time, intelligence studies indicate strongly that totalitarian, expansionist challengers are more likely to give priority in their intelligence process to direct assessment of the political intentions of adversaries, to the ability of opponents' alliances to ensure regional concentrations of military force, and to strong personal leadership, coercion, mobilization, war tolerance, and morale. Within the challenger paradigm, intelligence collection and analysis is more concerned with strategic deception and surprise, whereas autocratic governments usually impose blanket restrictions on public access to intelligence data. The challenger mode of information collection and analysis, therefore, conforms to what is known as the traditional view of intelligence.[64]

Intelligence studies and the evolutionary theory of long cycles in world politics each in their own right make no explicit and systematic connection either between global leadership characteristics and the American view of intelligence, or between challenger characteristics and the traditional view. This connection, however, is logically very plausible and is tentatively supported by a substantial body of literature.

To restate the hypothesis in terms of international relations theory, the conditions of global leadership are likely to engender strategies based on the systematic analysis of globally available tangible military and economic capabilities. Estimates of material capabilities typically center on the size and technical characteristics of navies, airpower, nuclear missiles, land armies, cavalry (for various historical periods); population size; economic indicators, such as steel output; natural resources; and similar data. Conditions exhibited by challengers are more likely to favor strategies derived from the direct assessment of political intentions and motivations, particularly intentions affecting regional concentrations of land power. These asymmetric priorities for strategy should translate into distinct national institutional patterns of intelligence collection and analysis. With respect to strategic intelligence, in policymaking jargon incumbent world powers may then be called "bean counters," and their challengers, "palm readers." In this way, the evolutionary dynamics of world politics, including global leadership competition and global wars, account for the phenomenon of asymmetric threat assessment among major actors. Intelligence assessment asymmetries between leaders and challengers in turn should help explain the presence or absence of global war between the contenders for world leadership.

It can be argued that both leaders and challengers will pay attention to intentions, and they do, but the divergent emphases are critical. By analogy with the American view of intelligence, global leaders are more likely to extrapolate political intentions of challengers from estimated material capabilities. I shall term this method as *capability-based intention assessment*. Intention is measured by calculating which threats are feasible, given the estimated capabilities. From this perspective, an army concentrated on a border would signal an intention to initiate war and would trigger countermeasures. For example, the U. S. government received signals of Japan's hostile intentions regarding Pearl Harbor, especially through intercepted diplomatic cables but failed to react because the Japanese strike force was not detected.[65]

Challengers, on the other hand, are more likely to accentuate *direct intention assessment.* Here the stress is on the independent impact of political intentions on capability deployment and use. When conducting direct intention assessments, an intelligence consumer focuses on how political plans, designs, and intentions may animate the adversary's capabilities. In a sense, estimates of the adversary's usable capabilities are extrapolated from political intentions that are assessed independently. From the perspective of direct intention assessment, a concentration of troops on the border signals war only if there is direct, additional evidence of hostile intention. Recently declassified Soviet intelligence files of the prewar period show that reports on German troop concentration near Soviet borders in spring 1941 presented overwhelming evidence of Hitler's aggressive plans.[66] Stalin, however, failed to counteract the threat, believing that Hitler had no *political intention* to attack—a belief that was only strengthened by Britain's disclosure of Plan Barbarossa to Moscow in 1941. Stalin could not impute aggressive political intentions to Hitler even when faced with "Ultra" intelligence from decrypted German communications supplied by Winston Churchill—his belief in a British global conspiracy against Russia was too strong.[67] Thus, the distinction between intentions extrapolated from capabilities and direct intentions matters critically in decisions affecting the course of history.

"Bean Counters" and "Palm Readers"

Why does global leadership competition, the process of the rise and fall of global powers, result in the systematic differentiation of information preferences between incumbent world powers and challengers? The causal mechanism reflects the asymmetry between leaders and challengers as to global reach capabilities, the lead sectors of the world economy, and domestic political and economic organization. Furthermore, the bean-counter and palm-reader patterns are mutually reinforced when leader and challenger interact in global leadership competition. At the high point of threat assessment asymmetry, leader and challenger may be likened to two invisible men playing catch with one another.

The Global Level

Within their limits of the known world, the incumbent world powers (see Table 1.1) must constantly concentrate on the security and maintenance of their global reach capabilities—whether it be the caravels dispatched by the Portuguese to the Calicut, or the hardware of British gunboat diplomacy, or U.S. naval bases in the Philippines. With the possession of more than 50 percent of ships of the line in 1655-1859 or pre- and postdreadnought battleships in 1860-1945, or attack aircraft carriers and nuclear attack submarines after World War II, the governments of incumbent world powers may be expected to deploy more institutional resources than would challengers. Government agencies of the world powers will be occupied with processing information about the movements of these forces, the quality and quantity of military hardware, and the emerging balance of military and economic capabilities in diverse locations worldwide. Throughout the nineteenth century and early in the twentieth century, Britain exemplified this tendency with such institutional methods of strategic estimates as the "two-power standard" and the "one-power standard plus 60 percent." The United States, as Defense Secretary William Perry stated in 1996, based the size and composition of its military forces "on the need to deter and, if necessary, fight and win, in concert with regional allies, two major regional conflicts nearly simultaneously."[68] The buildup of regional armies by potential challengers or outbreaks of internal political violence are therefore unlikely to play a decisive role in threat assessments, unless the challenger's military expansion threatens the nerve centers of the world system or some "domino effect" was anticipated. The rapid mobilization of the U. S.-led coalition against Iraq, in contrast to the stalemate over NATO involvement in Bosnia in the early 1990s, provides a recent example of this threat assessment pattern.

Occupying a dominant position in lead sectors of the world economy and thus possessing a global competitive advantage in cutting-edge industries gives the incumbent world powers an additional incentive to favor a global focus and capability-based estimates in government information management. A global focus on tangible economic indicators such as gold reserves, exchange and inflation rates, productivity, or money supply has been essential for incumbent world powers to maintain leadership in the world economy.[69]

With inferior global reach capabilities, challengers are driven to seek shortcuts that compensate for their inferior position. According to Michael Handel, an intelligence studies expert, countries that are only too cognizant of their relative vulnerability when preparing to challenge a stronger incumbent have a powerful incentive to design strategies based on strategic surprise as well as deception. Thus, when seeking opportunities to challenge the incumbent, the actor with inferior capabilities will seek *adaptation* to an unfavorable global position by taking the initiative and "concentrating superior forces at the time and place of its choosing, thereby vastly improving the likelihood of achieving decisive victory."[70]

Patterns of global power distribution increase the value that challengers place on strategic deception of a world power and its coalition. Fostering disagreement within the world power's coalition regarding the challenger's strategy is also perceived as critical. Germany's conduct during its buildup to both world wars, Japan prior to the attack on Pearl Harbor, or Soviet attempts to disrupt political cohesion of NATO illustrate this tendency. Challengers may be expected to stress noncapability power multipliers based on political decisions, which regulate the timing and place of attack (or defender's response), troop movements, or the use of new weapons. Other power multipliers used by challengers include the frequent appearance of new doctrines and innovative tactics, surprise methods for using existing military technology, and the choice of political-military goals for war.[71]

Outperformed in the lead sectors of the global economy, challengers have an incentive to set up intelligence collection to elucidate the strategy, aims, plans, and intentions of the world power and its coalition "so well that one can devise means of circumventing and defeating it at the lowest possible cost."[72]

The Domestic Level

The differentiation of domestic political structures is part of another evolutionary process in world politics. All global powers that have attained superior military capabilities of global reach represent "what in retrospect might be called the democratic lineage."[73] In his analysis of democratic polities, Robert Dahl identified about twenty countries where "the institutions of polyarchy evolved more or less steadily, took root, and endured."[74] A good measure of belonging to this group is membership in the Organization for Economic Cooperation and Development (OECD), which embraces twenty-four industrialized, stable democracies.[75] The political systems of these states are distinguished by their institutions: free and fair elections; inclusive suffrage; the right to run for office; freedom of expression; alternative sources of information; and, the autonomy of political associations from central government control.[76] Despite inevitable gaps between theory and practice, democratic polities are based on institutional arrangements whose underlying purpose is, in the words of Justice Brandeis, "to preclude the exercise of arbitrary power."[77]

Studies in American politics indicate that the systematic use of quantitative indicators, such as patterns of federal expenditure, highway deaths, disease rates, or costs of entitlement programs, is one of the bedrocks of public policy in a democratic setting.[78] David McLellan's examination of the conceptual evolution of ideology since the late 1700s explained why hard data and scientific analysis have achieved a high priority in democratic polities (if not becoming dominant ideologies in themselves):

> The increase in information available and the fact that it issued from highly divergent sources meant that its interpretation became problematic and competing frameworks, reflecting different interests, emerged to make sense of all the new material. But these frameworks, or ideologies, in spite of their inevitably partial origin had to have a universal appeal. For with the increased participation of the masses in politics, persuasion rather than mere command was the order of the day. In the age of liberty, fraternity and equality, the only approaches that could even aspire to universal acceptance were those based on the apparently universal ideas of reason and science.[79]

Pressure to quantify arises from other factors as well. Perhaps the most salient feature of democracy, identified as a high degree of "executive constraint" by Eckstein and Gurr, requires executive branch officials to abide by clear and distinct institutionalized rules in making policy decisions.[80] How does this mechanism work? We can expect that the separation of powers, especially entrusting the power of the purse to legislatures, will increase the pressure on governments to account for expenditures and therefore put a price tag on policies. Putting a price tag on policies favors the use of quantifiable indicators and statistics. At some point, this practice may become vexing to government officials. In a speech at the University of Washington in Seattle in 1996 (attended by the author), the former U.S. ambassador to Moscow, Jack Matlock, complained, the U.S. government was obsessed with "quantifying the unquantifiable."

The due process of law and free market practices also reinforce preferences for capability-based estimates. Thus, hard data and physical evidence is more likely to sway jurors from diverse social backgrounds. And when a government cannot run every shoe factory, software company, or commodity distribution system by decree, government policies must target supposedly objective quantitative indicators to ensure a smoothly running economy and to avoid economic crises.

As Dahl has observed, "in most countries, polyarchy has not developed," despite considerable expansion during the second half of the twentieth century.[81] Outside the circle of twenty or so stable and prosperous democracies are quasi-democracies and the autocracies, which are based on a hierarchical political order and have very weak institutional constraints on the executive branch. Polities of this type have been common among the world power challengers. In such polities, authoritarian pressures come to bear on information collection and analysis, including intelligence institutions, and encourage the quickest and most direct methods of access to top-level decision makers of the leading world powers. From an authoritarian ruler's perspective, an overwhelming sense of confusion accompanying the political processes in a democracy signifies a state-sponsored effort to conceal the true strategic intentions. The domestic system of the challenger confirms the perception that these supposedly hidden intentions could be accessed directly and cheaply by planting the right "mole" in the right place at the right time. Other persistent measures directed at more open societies by challengers include manipulation of the domestic media— an opportunity denied to democracies in countries where the entire media is constantly censored by the state.

At the same time, authoritarian governments try to protect their hold on power by denying outsiders any information considered potentially threatening to the official political image of the state. The scope of classified information is higher than in democracies, and the public exchange of ideas is tightly controlled. The lack of popular legitimacy and predictability in power succession predicates an excessive emphasis on conspiracy. With a politics of suspicion underlying these governments' survival and hold on power, disproportionately large intelligence collection and analysis efforts are channeled inward, targeting the entire domestic population in an attempt to enforce ideological uniformity. Former CIA director Allen Dulles found that "the size and power of an internal security service, is generally in direct ratio to the extent of the suspicion and fear of the ruling clique."[82] The correlation between authoritarianism and the domestic uses of intelligence, especially for political surveillance, is among the findings of intelligence studies that come closest to social theory.[83] Even in democratic polities, authoritarian tendencies within certain subsets of institutional policy making may lead to an escalation of covert domestic surveillance.[84] Relative to nondemocracies, however, these practices have

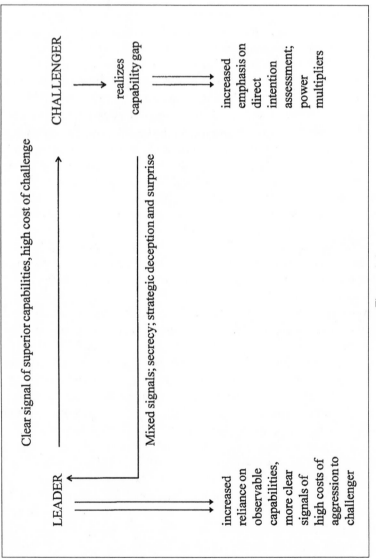

Figure 1.1

been narrower in scope, and most have subsequently been outlawed through intervention on the part of representative institutions, such as the U.S. Congress or the British Parliament, and the media.[85]

Interactive Effects

The asymmetry between the bean-counting and palm-reading methods of threat assessment is also likely to be magnified in the interactions between world powers and challengers.

At the global level, this interactive reinforcement will follow the process, illustrated in Figure 1.1. With superior global reach capabilities, a leader assumes that sending clear signals of superior capabilities to a challenger will deter attempts to transgress on the leader's position. This mode of thinking permeates modern deterrence theory in the United States. Since the United States is the incumbent world power, we may say that deterrence theory provisions are evidence that incumbent global leaders believe in the deterrence value of clear signals about superior capabilities. The problem is that a determined challenger, upon realizing the true extent of the capability gap, will only step up its efforts to develop noncapability power multipliers, as was discussed earlier. Secrecy will be increased, an emphasis on strategic deception and surprise will be greater, and schemes to disrupt domestic economies or the political stability of world powers will be more devious. Confronted with this type of information strategy, the global leader is likely in turn to redouble its attempts to convince the challenger that aggression would be too costly and to send even clearer signals of superior capabilities. Depending on the issues and the timing, such spirals of asymmetry may be of varying length and intensity, and even the most intensive ones will not necessarily lead to war. Yet this dynamic of interactive reinforcement of bean-counting and palm-reading assessments is a necessary condition of the irrational initiation of global wars by challengers. From an evolutionary perspective, spirals of asymmetry need not be a permanent fixture, but they are likely to persist as long as the rise and fall of global powers is the central process in world politics (a separate problem in international relations theory). These asymmetry spirals may be latent while the challenger takes time to design and develop alternative strategies and to enhance noncapability power multipliers while temporarily accepting the global leader's superiority, responding well to threats or "bribes" and abstaining from aggressive military challenges.

At the domestic level, similar interactive reinforcement of asymmetric preferences may be observed. Take, for example, the differences in access-to-information costs among democracies and autocratic polities. Democracies assign a higher value to an individual human life than do authoritarian regimes. In contrast, autocracies impose high costs (such as imprisonment, forced labor, torture, and death) on human agents seeking information, the exposure of which is considered damaging to the state or beneficial to the adversary. Thus, the standard punitive practices of autocracies make intelligence collection by human agents (HUMINT) a much less attractive intelligence collection method for democratic states. In adapting to a lack of access to routine domestic indicators, world powers have the incentive to develop improved analytical techniques as well as technical means of remote intelligence collection that transcend the domestic control of other actors. For example, when denied information on Soviet military and industrial capabilities, the United States developed the U-2 and SR-71 aircraft, sophisticated photo equipment, photogrammetric analysis, and policy research institutions, such as the Rand Corporation.[86]

This logic of differentiated information preferences makes challengers in global leadership competition more likely to attack even when their capabilities relative to the incumbent are weak, to seek political gains even at the cost of military defeat, to gamble that a surprise attack will have decisive force-multiplier effect, and to stress not so much the capabilities per se as the political intentions to use them. Systematic emphasis on these factors by challengers because of a convergence of domestic and global conditions make the calculation of global capability balances irrelevant, and aggressive strategies increasingly undeterrable.

ASYMMETRIC THREAT ASSESSMENT: THREE CASE STUDIES

This book employs the method of structured, focused, and controlled comparison by examining strategic information collection and analysis by the status quo world powers and their challengers in instances of conflict over global leadership.[87] Some formal theorists have criticized this method for lacking rigorous, "scientific" standards of theory construction and verification.[88] Nevertheless, it has an advantage over formal models when it comes to developing differentiated typological theories that comprise conditional generalizations rather than frequency distribution. This comparative method is well suited for the study of strategies concerning global conflicts and wars which, due to their relatively low incidence in world history, pose the problem of small n. An investigator employing the method of structured focused comparison "seeks to identify *the conditions under which each dis-*

tinctive type of causal pattern occurs rather than attempting to address the question of *how often* each outcome and/or causal pattern does occur."[89] Other advantages of the method are historical depth and empirical verifiability.[90]

I examines the intelligence assessment preferences in three historical cases of global leadership competition: the Mongol world empire strategy (1206-1220), British and French strategies leading to the French Revolutionary and Napoleonic wars (1783-1800), and the U.S. and Soviet strategic threat assessment in the final phases of the Cold War (1975-1990). My choice of cases extending over eight centuries serves two purposes. First, theories that hold across highly diverse settings are considered from a methodological perspective to be "more impressive than confirmation under similar conditions."[91] Second, rather than being random samples, the cases represent distinct stages in the evolution of world politics: the emerging preconditions for the global system (from about 930 A.D.), the formation of the Eurocentric world system (from about 1430), and the transition to global organization (from about 1850).[92] This design makes it possible to draw inferences about the impact of changes in the systemic conditions and domestic organization of global powers in terms strategic intelligence content. Current debates about the possible role of global intelligence institutions (such as the UKUSA Agreement or the UN's Early Warning systems) and the benefits of global governance may also be placed in historical context.

Set in different periods and geographical regions, the cases share essential characteristics while displaying sufficient variations that allow for a controlled comparison.

First, they represent examples of competition among global powers. The Mongol case qualifies, because the scale of the territorial conquest was among the greatest in world history and affected the most politically and economically active regions in the emerging global system. The Mongols built the largest land empire in history, creating the preconditions for the rise of Europe as a nucleus of world politics after 1500. The other cases involve powers whose military global reach capabilities ranked first and second, respectively, at the time.

Second, in each instance, the central issue is systemic (or global) leadership, implying control over major political, military, and economic operations at the world system (or principal subsystem/Eurasian) level.

Third, all the cases feature one active challenger (the Mongols, France, the USSR) seeking to improve its inferior military and economic position and to change the global and domestic environment in its favor. The cases also include the incumbent world power (Great Britain, the United States), as well as the most likely world power candidate (Sung China) in the Mongol case.[93]

Fourth, the cases emphasize periods of high global war threat for both the leading world powers and their challengers. These high-threat periods were associated with large-scale wars in two cases (the Mongol Empire, the French Revolutionary Wars) and in a sustained political and military competition on a global scale (the Cold War). The U.S.-Soviet case is, in many ways, a critical test, focusing on whether asymmetric threat assessment may also lead to peace and resolve conflicts over global leadership competition.

Fifth, in each instance attention is concentrated on strategic intelligence collection and analysis (i.e., information inputs and sources) as regards threat assessments by each participant in global competition. The focus on intelligence preferences, with regard to the method of estimating intentions and capabilities by key policymakers, helps in comparison of cases widely dispersed in time and space. The focus on assessment types also enables comparison across diverse institutions and methods of intelligence collection and analysis.

Finally, the cases examine time periods of approximately equal duration sufficient to represent major developments pertaining to each instance of systemic competition (the Mongol campaigns against the Chin and Khwarazm; the French Revolutionary Wars; and the late-1970s escalation of the Cold War and its subsequent demise).

A standard set of questions applies to each case:

- What share of global reach military capabilities and regional forces did the principal actors in the global leadership conflicts possess? What were the participants' share of the leading sectors of the world economy?
- What were the formal coalitions and alliances of the leading world power and the challenger at the time of increasing global war threat? How were global and regional capability balances affected?
- What was the state of four indicators pertaining to the domestic political organization of the leading world power and/or the challenger (i.e., institutional power structure, political participation, due process, civil rights)?
- What was the state of three indicators pertaining to the domestic economic organization of the leading world power and/or the challenger

(i.e., forms of economic ownership/production, goods distribution, and economic growth)?

- What were the most prominent types of strategic intelligence with respect to threat assessment requested and/or used by policy makers in major global conflict decisions? In other words, how were threats defined, and which threat indicators received greater consideration? Which intelligence inputs were given priority?

- Which changes in indicators used in intelligence analysis were closely associated with changes in threat assessment? What kinds of information increased or decreased threat-related estimates of war success probability for both the leading world powers and their challengers in periods of anticipated global conflict initiation? To what extent was the estimated probability of success in war a function of the known composite capability assessments or direct intention assessments?

- What conditions account for intelligence content preferences in a given case, and how do these conditions reflect on the salience of the causal variables?

The case studies are based on multiple tests of the hypothesis, including content analysis of primary sources, such as Mongol, Persian, and Chinese chronicles; government documents of eighteenth-century Britain and France, including declarations of war; diplomatic and intelligence correspondence; and lists of locations of intelligence sources. The U.S.-Soviet case is based on recently declassified National Intelligence Estimates (NIEs) of the Central Intelligence Agency and on texts of KGB instructions for global operations, including Operation RYAN in late 1983, when the KGB made an estimate that the United States and NATO might launch a nuclear strike against the Soviet Union.

Part I describes differentiations among global leaders and challengers in the past 800 years by examining global reach capabilities, political systems, and patterns of economic development, and how divergent settings shape intelligence collection and the analysis priorities of governments. Part II looks at whether divergent rise and fall conditions correspond to asymmetric patterns of threat assessment and whether these asymmetries account for the decision to initiate wars challenging global leadership (by the Mongols and France), the failure to contain aggressive challenges in a timely fashion by the incumbents (Sung China and Britain), and the peaceful resolution of global military confrontation in the time period after a world war. In the Conclusion, I discuss global intelligence organizations after

World War II and prospects for reducing the negative impact of asymmetric threat assessment in the face of increased globalization of security threats, including interstate aggression, internal wars, ethnic conflict, and weapons proliferation.

Part I

Causes of Asymmetric Threat Assessment: Divergent Lineages in World Politics

Chapter 2

Global Reach Capabilities: Sea Power and Land Power Lineages

THE MONGOLS AND SUNG CHINA: THE HOUNDS OF THE STEPPE, THE MASTERS OF SOUTHERN SEAS

Few locations in thirteenth-century Eurasia were more inhospitable and farther from the most advanced centers of human civilization than the barren, desolate stretches of rocks, desert, and steppe at the source of the Onon River. The Grand Assembly *(khuriltai)* of the nomadic tribes and groupings who congregated there in 1206 to pledge their allegiance to Genghis Khan (universal ruler) and endorse his ambition to expand the Mongol domain to all corners of the known world, was at best a marginal event in Eurasian politics. Despite a respectable size of 380 million acres,[1] the nascent Mongol Empire in 1206 was set deeply inland and was isolated from the main lines of communication to the south, east and west by the more populous, economically advanced, and better armed empires, kingdoms, and sultanates of northern China and Central Asia.

The Mongols could not project their power globally in 1206, even if they had known of the existence of continents separated from Eurasia by oceans. Nor do we have any records indicating that the grand strategy of Genghis Khan emphasized the centrality of a strong naval force for maximizing power, wealth, or mobility on the Eurasian continent and beyond. In the first two major campaigns, the movements of the Mongol forces (both advances and retreats) were almost entirely inland, as if guided by some invisible hand away from oceanic coastlines. After conquering the Chin capital of Zhongdu (Beijing) in 1215, the Mongols plundered and pillaged the city, raping and massacring thousands of inhabitants. They then set the city ablaze, causing massive destruction of property. (A few years later, according to a medieval chronicler, the leader of a mission from Khwarazm to China, upon entering Zhongdu, saw a white hill made up of the bones of the people massacred). Though they invested great effort in plundering the city, the Mongols failed to recognize the potential of Zhongdu as an avenue to the sea or to start work on a seaport for their emerging empire. Instead of establishing a major military presence by the ocean, the main armies of Genghis Khan either turned inland or returned to Mongolia, as they did after conquering all the other coastal Chin cities.[2]

In the annals of the Mongol Empire no evidence is found that the Genghis Khan's elite understood that a world-class cavalry was perhaps less important than a world-class navy, if the khan's vision of the "universal empire" were ever to be attained. The importance of the sea routes linking the east coast of Africa from Madagascar to the Red Sea with India, Malaysia, and China escaped Mongol strategists in 1206. This network had evolved slowly over the preceding five centuries and constituted perhaps the largest and most-developed segment of what would become the future global system of communications and trade, yet Genghis Khan was thoroughly isolated from it.[3] In designing his campaigns, the future world conqueror had no substantial capability that he could immediately project to South China, East Asia, India, or East Africa. His strategic focus was the Eurasian heartland, and the main objects of his conquests were predominantly inland empires.

Given the gaps in historical evidence, the full extent of Mongol strategic military capabilities for every given year in that period is hard to estimate. Nevertheless, what we do know from surviving primary sources is often sufficient to draw a picture of the power balances in Eurasia. The Mongol Empire emerged as a military state after tribal armies were consolidated under Genghis Khan's rule in 1206. The army subsequently became the Mongols' greatest strategic asset. It was not, however, size or physical power alone that put the Mongol army in a class of its own, but rather the institutionalized cult of the army, permeating both politics and society, especially after the advent of Genghis Khan.

The size of the Mongol army proper from the 1211 campaign against the Chin (the rulers of North China and Manchuria) to 1227, at the death of Genghis Khan, fluctuated between 110,000 and 150,000 men, according to the chronicles—many fewer than the Chin or Khwarazm could send to battle at the time. These estimates are confirmed when the size of the Mongol army is calculated on the basis of population (approximately 1 million) and mobilization rates, this computation yields about 138,000 troops. Even after the Mongol Empire expanded from China to the Black Sea, the largest Mongol field force that could be documented—the army assembled under general Bayan in 1275 for the conquest of the Southern Sung—numbered less than 200,000.[4]

Moreover, despite formidable skill in archery and horsemanship that dazzled European witnesses, a warrior in the service of Genghis Khan would not necessarily be an overpowering phenomenon if pitted against a cavalryman of most Central Asian armies. Consisting entirely of cavalry, the Mongol army no doubt would be a surprise in the Roman Empire or the Middle East. It was a common sight, however, in the steppes north of the Black Sea, as well as in Central and North Asia. According to H. Desmond Martin, a foremost specialist on the Mongol army, "Within the Asia of Genghis Khan's day the fighting material opposed to him was never surpassed." That fighting material consisted of Turkish horse archers, who replaced the Arab troops and peasant levies throughout Islamic Asia—first as mercenaries and then as conquerors of the lands from the Aral Sea to the Indian Ocean, and from the Bay of Bengal to the Mediterranean. "Inured to war, and able to ride and use the bow as the people of the steppe alone knew how, the Turkish horse archer was the most formidable soldier that the world of Islam had ever seen."[5]

But their skill in coordination and collective performance, reinforced by draconian discipline—all virtually nonexistent in other contemporary societies—gave Genghis Khan's troops a decisive edge over the armies of the most formidable kingdoms of Central Asia and China. The army cult affected every Mongol almost from birth and shaped political and social institutions. The Mongol toddlers routinely were tied by their mothers onto the back of a horse and taught to ride. At four or five, a child received his first bow and arrows and was encouraged to spend as much time as possible hunting on horseback. This Mongol practice was customary among many other peoples of the Asian steppe—babies of the Hsiung-nu nomads in the third century B.C. reportedly were taught to ride on sheep and shoot birds and rats with miniature bows and arrows.⁶ While strengthening his political grip on Mongol society, Genghis Khan molded the ancient nomadic traditions and practices into the building blocks for a powerful army. In turn, army appointments became the ultimate measure of political power and social status, as traditional ways of life were militarized in a highly centralized fashion. In the military reorganization under Genghis Khan, men were forbidden, under threat of death and punishment of their superiors, to leave the army units they had been assigned to. Their entire families were subordinated to the unit's military commander.⁷ To the muscles and sinews of iron that traditionally characterized the armies of the north Asian nomads, Genghis Khan added nerves of steel. Mirroring this newly forged synergy of military muscle and nerve, the Mongol war machine was perfectly crafted for the massive blitzkrieg campaigns that swept across the Eurasian continent.

Capable of enduring the bitterest cold and the most oppressive heat, accustomed to sleeping mounted, well adapted to cover hundreds of miles on scant rations (usually ten pounds of dried milk curds, two liters of fermented mare's milk, and a small quantity of cured meat), and always ready in dire necessity to drink the blood of his horse by opening a vein in the animal's neck or to eat the flesh of a fellow warrior slaughtered for food, the Mongol soldier also possessed extraordinary sense of direction, without the benefit of compass or maps. Taking these qualities to the limit of what was possible for individuals as well as for thousands of troops en masse was a key ingredient in Genghis Khan's preparations for transcontinental campaigns. The iron authority of the Great Khan was absolutely critical to suppress any outbreak of discontent commonly aroused by such extreme deprivations.

Mongol horses, and the especially the training they received, epitomized a similarly strong emphasis on endurance and coordination. Measuring only thirteen to fourteen hands in size, these Mongol ponies had unusual stamina. They needed water only once a day and fed mostly on grass, relieving the army of the logistical burden of transporting large quantities of grain fodder. According to some records, these horses were known to travel 600 miles in nine days and to sustain 60-70 mile-per-day marches, even across some of the roughest mountainous terrain in the world.⁸ Genghis Khan commanded that his warriors acquire and perfect uniform skills in horse handling, which made the Mongol cavalry extremely adaptable to adverse conditions, resilient in the face of the stubbornest opposition, and well suited for surprise attacks. Thus, not only were Mongol horses unique in their exceptional obedience to voice (freeing the rider's hands), but they were also trained to allow the archer to shoot both while in the saddle and while dismounted, standing or kneeling behind the horse. The saddles, designed by the Mongols for conquest, were made of wood and rubbed with sheep's fat to prevent them from swelling in the rain or parching in the heat. Elevated both in back and in front, the saddles firmly anchored riders to the seat, giving secure balance that allowed shooting in any direction.[9] Marco Polo, who spent many years observing life in the Orient, was astonished by how well the Mongols trained their horses to "double hither and thither, just like a dog."[10]

Even more astonishing was the ability of thousands of Genghis Khan's warriors to use their remarkable horsemanship in good coordination with one another in inhospitable environments and dire circumstances, whether in battle or on a march. These capabilities—the foundation of Genghis Khan's bid for universal empire—allowed the Mongol cavalry to ride for hours, if not days, while directing massive salvos of arrows at the enemy. Their superb horsemanship also gave the Mongols more tactical versatility, trust in which was so unshakable in Genghis Khan's camp that it was elevated to strategic decision making. As Marco Polo later noted, "They fight to as good purpose in running away as if they stood and faced the enemy, because of the vast volleys of arrows that they shoot in this way, turning round upon their pursuers, who are fancying that they won the battle." No less astounding than this capacity to deliver synchronized "Parthian shots" en masse, were the lightning yet orderly river crossings— thousands of horses swimming with the warriors holding onto their animals' bodies and their equipment floating behind in leather bags attached to the horses' tails.[11]

Lacking other contemporary, "hi-tech" war tools, such as the crossbow and the flame-throwing machines of China and the metal craftsmanship of Central Asia, Mongol military equipment prior to the start of massive campaigns against the Chin, was the emblematic of Genghis Khan's strategic emphasis on speed, economy, maneuverability, and organization. (If Genghis Khan was an ingenious strategist, it was due to his astute measurement of these power intangibles and correct assessment of their imperceptible yet decisive impact in battles with more technologically advanced opponents.) The Mongols' answer to the Chinese crossbow, invented sometime in the Han period (200 B.C. to A.D. 200), was a large but light compound bow with a killing range of 200 to 300 yards—impressive even by comparison with modern automatic weapons. Most troopers carried 60 arrows, 30 light sharp-pointed ones for long-range shooting, and 30 heavy ones with large, broad heads for close volleys. It is possible that some Mongol archers, like the Khitans before them, carried up to 400 arrows. A Chinese general and contemporary of Genghis Khan, Meng Hung reported (as did in later years a papal envoy to the Mongol court, Plano Carpini) that the Mongols commonly used arrows that "cut two ways like a sword" and could pierce armor.[12]

Other equipment strongly emphasized speed and economy as well. Mongol "armor" was mostly made of hide, and was mercilessly tight-fitting. Large (but also lightweight) shields, made of skin or willow wood, were probably issued exclusively for sentry duty. In battle formations only the front-rank warriors carried shields, which were much smaller. The Mongols' light, sharp sabres were copied from the Muslim Turks, as were their lances. But the lances the Mongols used were lighter and often equipped with hooks for pulling enemy horsemen out of the saddle.[13]

The institution that perhaps best epitomized the Mongol army cult, with its particular emphasis on military skills, strict discipline, and coordination, was the annual winter hunt, in which all males eligible for military service were obliged to participate. During Genghis Khan's reign the hunt embodied the empire's political and military system, taking the form of a military campaign against the animals of the forest and steppe under the personal command of the khan, who opened the chase. Others were allowed to use weapons only after the khan had killed his choice of game. At the conclusion, Genghis Khan analyzed and discussed with his generals the execution of the hunt, much as one would critique military operations. The massive scale of these regular operations and the personal involvement of the khan strengthened the ruler's trust in the superior skills, resolve, and savvy of his Mongol warriors.

The institutions of command and control were designed to train skilled archers and cavalrymen who could quickly communicate with one another and change direction as an integrated unit, while moving at maximum speed along river bends, through forests, or under the cover of a mountain crest. Clearly, these military and political institutions were oriented toward land power. The great captains of Genghis Khan navigated the steppes, not the ocean. The military and political leaders occupying the four top positions in the Mongol Empire were known as the "Four Steeds" and the "Four Hounds"[14] (not the "Four Seawolves" or "Four Sharks").

The Sung Empire, lying mostly to the south of the Yangtze River, occupied a leading position in East Asia by the early thirteenth century with respect to sea power. The idea of training and supporting a large land army was discussed at the Sung court from time to time but was never a priority policy. There is little doubt, however, that the high Sung officials who argued at the emperor's court in favor of buying off aggressive northerners with tribute as a cheaper alternative to raising a powerful horse army would have been summarily executed had they expressed such opinions at the court of Genghis Khan. In contrast to the virile, aggressive cult of the army and the total militarization of society for continental conquests, the Sung promoted a measured, serene, and well-calculated pride in naval power and overseas commerce.

By the early thirteenth century, the Sung's naval leadership, not only in East Asia, but also on a global scale, was demonstrated most amply by the invention and use of the compass, which became a decisive innovation, allowing to navigate with confidence in the open ocean. Another striking manifestation of Sung maritime capabilities were the junks, some of which were large, four-deck ocean-going vessels with four or more masts and twelve big sails that could carry up to several hundred persons and deploy firearms. In 1132, responding to the Chin invasion in the north, the Sung expanded their naval forces by founding a High Sea Fleet for coastal defenses that was separate from river squadrons and equipped with larger ships. The Sung further strengthened their naval posture by destroying the Chin fleet off the coast of Shantung (1161), suppressing piracy and maintaining the security of maritime activities.[15]

China's global leadership in sea power during that period was well documented by Joseph Needham, who studied the transmission of all key technologies and inventions between China and the West. Regarding sea power, all such transmissions were in one direction only—from China to the West. Thus, the nautical construction principles employed by the thirteenth-century Sung were developed ten centuries ahead of the West; the stern-post rudder, four centuries earlier; and the magnetic compass used for navigation, two centuries earlier.[16]

Although they were not used for trade, exploration, and the acquisition of colonies on the same scale as in the West after about 1500, these innovations and capabilities gave Sung fleets a competitive advantage in ocean travel, communications, and commerce. By the end of the twelfth century, the Sung were supplanting the Muslims in the east and in Southeast Asian waters. By late 1200, Chinese merchants were well established in the ports of Southeast Asia and on the Indian subcontinent. The formidable Sung junks provided regular and safer communication than the overland silk roads from India to China. The extent of this maritime competitive advantage gained by the Sung was especially evident when China, still reeling from the turmoil of Mongol conquests and occupation, organized seven ocean expeditions in 1405-1433 under the command of admiral Cheng Ho. With 62 ships (or about three times as many ocean-going ships than Portugal, England, France, and Spain combined had in 1500) and 28,000 men, Cheng Ho sailed to Java, Ceylon, the Calicut, the east coast of Africa, the Persian Gulf and the Red Sea. Covering more than 10,000 miles on their way from China, these expeditions dwarfed similar European efforts of the time. The Portuguese had gone only as far as Cape Verde on the west coast of Africa by 1455, a reach of less than 3,000 miles. In Paul Kennedy's view, with ships 400 feet long and displacing more than 1,500 tons, the Cheng Ho expeditions may well have been able "to sail around Africa and 'discover' Portugal several decades before Henry the Navigator's expeditions began earnestly to push south of Ceuta."[17]

According to Jung-pang Lo, an expert on the history of the Chinese sea power, by the time Mongol power was on the rise in the north (in the early 1200s), the Sung navy was at its zenith. Sung naval forces numbered 3,000 men and 11 squadrons in 1130; 21,000 men and 15 squadrons in 1174; and 52,000 men and 20 squadrons in 1237. The Mongol naval fleets, called "wings," first appeared only as late as 1257, chiefly as a continuation of the Chinese naval tradition. By comparison, the British navy reached 50,000 personnel for the first time only in 1756—more than six centuries after the Sung. The Byzantine navy at its peak (ca. 600-1,000 A.D.) numbered an estimated 40,000 sailors. This emphasis on naval capabilities offset Sung weaknesses on land and accounted for the survival of the Sung dynasty in southern China for 150 years after the fall of the Northern Sung. The maritime orientation of the Sung, in contrast to continental orientation of the Mongols, was also reinforced by the migration of the mass of China's population from the north to the south and coastal southeast during the period from late T'ang (618-906) to the Northern Sung (960-1127), which markedly exceeded similar population movements in the past in territorial sweep, numbers, and socioeconomic consequences. Prior to 742 A.D., about 43 percent of the empire's population lived in the south. By 1078, the balance had reversed, with 65 percent of the population in the south and 35 percent in the north.[18] These mass migrations reflected a persistent and mutually reinforcing asymmetry between the rise of continental powers in the northern Eurasia and the increase in Sung maritime activities. The migrants were fleeing from the northern plains, which were more vulnerable to nomadic cavalry attacks, to the fertile lands separated from the invaders by the Huang (Yellow) and Yangtze Rivers and to the coastal areas behind the mountainous ridges of Wuyi Shan.

In this overall portrait of the distribution of military capabilities in the east and in northeastern Asia, the Sung emerge as the prototype of later global maritime powers—Portugal, the Netherlands, Britain, and the United States. The Mongols, by contrast, developed their war machine in line with numerous other (ultimately failed) attempts (which later included Napoleon and Hitler) to organize the world on a continental basis. Placing this contrast between the Mongols and the Sung in the long perspective, Modelski and Thompson concluded: "In evaluating the Sung, we find for the first time, on a scale that moves toward global significance, evidence of the basic strategic tension of modern world politics: that between land and modern sea power, or better still between continental and oceanic power. This makes the relationship between the Sung and . . . the Mongols proto-typical in at least some respects to later strategic contests between world powers and their challengers."[19]

BRITAIN AND FRANCE IN THE 1700s:
THE WHALE AND THE ELEPHANT OF THE EUROCENTRIC WORLD

In the centuries following the rise of the Mongol Empire, the voyages of Columbus, Cabot, Vespucci, Magellan, and other daring seamen set the stage for the increasing importance of navies and merchant fleets on a global scale. In an eloquent account of South American voyages, published in 1600 as *The Discovery of the Large, Rich, and Beautiful Empire of Guiana,* Sir Walter Raleigh voiced the emerging understanding of the fundamental advantages of sea power in world politics: "Whoever commands the sea commands the trade; whoever commands the trade commands the riches of the world, and consequently the world itself."[20]

With these developments, power struggles were becoming increasingly global and Eurocentric. The Chinese navy's defeat in the mid-fifteenth century cleared the way for Venetian, Portuguese, Spanish, Dutch, and then British fleets to dominate oceanic communications and establish strongholds for European power in Asia, Africa, Australia, and Latin America. Portuguese ships appearing off China's coast in the sixteenth century signified a profound global shift in the distribution of sea power in

Europe's favor after 1500. Among Europe's various political entities, too, the differences in global reach were increasingly played out on a global scale. First Portugal, then Spain, the Netherlands, and Britain emerged as the leading sea powers from the sixteenth to the late eighteenth century. Britain's progressively naval orientation weathered the 1649 and 1688 revolutions, and British naval superiority was definitive throughout the eighteenth century. From 1714 to the late 1770s, Britain possessed about half of the entire world's fleet of gun-carrying ships of the line—the mainstay of naval power at the time. On average, Britain enjoyed an approximately twofold advantage against France and a threefold advantage against Spain.[21] In the mid-eighteenth century, senior policy makers in London viewed Britain's preponderance in sea power as a viable counterbalance to the superior armies of continental Europe. The Duke of Newcastle, secretary of state for the Northern Department, wrote to the Earl of Hardwicke, Lord Chancellor, in September 1749 that without this sea power advantage "all alliances, all subsidies, will signify nothing: but a known, established, avowed, superiority at sea, will give weight to an inferior alliance upon the Continent; and, perhaps, upon the whole, put us near upon equality; at least, so near as that no attempt will be made upon us."[22]

Such attempts were made repeatedly, with most challenges to British global dominance in the eighteenth century coming from France. These challenges reflected France's attempts to acquire a higher share of maritime and colonial trade and dominate west-central Europe—ultimately by force of arms, which generated a series of wars in 1689-1697, 1702-1714, 1756-1763, and 1776-1783. Between 1689 and 1793, England and France were consistently at war for 48 years, or 46 percent of the time. Opposing France were various alliances of maritime and continental neighbors cemented politically and financially from across La Manche. As George Modelski observed, after defeat during the decisive naval battle for the control of the Channel at La Hogue in 1692, "the basic pattern of Anglo-French warfare for the next 123 years was established. With some exceptions France concentrated on its land campaigns within Europe and commerce raiding at sea. England or Great Britain concentrated on mounting blockades, protecting commercial convoys, engaging in naval skirmishes in more distant waters (Caribbean, Mediterranean, and Indian Ocean) with only occasional fleet encounters . . . and supplementing its ground efforts with subsidized allies."[23]

This basic pattern of Anglo-French warfare can be traced to the asymmetric evolution of military capabilities, with Britain favoring sea power and France favoring land power. Britain had more ocean warships and France had a larger continental army throughout the entire eighteenth century. In the decade preceding the French Revolutionary Wars, Britain had a stable and nearly twofold advantage in warships, whereas France had a three- to fivefold advantage in army size. This asymmetry endured well into the French Revolutionary and Napoleonic Wars (1792-1815), with France persistently lagging in global reach (naval) capabilities, at about 35 percent of major power share, yet maintaining numerical superiority on land, at about 54 percent of major power share. This asymmetric global contest between Britain and France is succinctly summed up in Paul Kennedy's metaphor as the struggle between the whale and the elephant.[24]

Even a successful French campaign against Britain during the American War of Independence failed to overturn this long-established asymmetry in military capabilities. The success of the French cause in this war served, on the one hand, to sustain the global aspirations and the challenger impulse of France. As a result of the 1783 Treaty of Paris, France gained Tobago and some former ports in Senegal, won greater access to Newfoundland fishing resources, regained Louisiana, and had restrictions on the fortification of Dunkirk removed. On the other hand, France failed to prevail over Britain at sea by losing battles at the Saintes (Dominica Channel) and off Trincomalee in 1782, where, in both cases, the French fleets enjoyed numerical superiority. Although the combined fleets of France and Spain outnumbered the Royal Navy at the close of the American War of Independence—and the French spirit was high—the French *global* challenge was exhausted. France's economy lacked dynamism, and finances were overstrained. France no longer had enough momentum to take over British positions in the West Indies or at Gibraltar. Most of France's conquests, gained at a tremendous cost to the domestic economy, were restored. Thus, France had made a great effort in the American war but gained comparatively little in the subsequent peace settlement. According to E. H. Jenkins, a historian of the French navy, "The result of the war [for France] was a disappointment. One of her two objects of making it, revenge on England, had been obtained by freeing the American colonies and partially destroying the Mediterranean base; the other object, recovery from her own losses by the Peace of Paris [1763], had not been achieved, nor had she fulfilled her promise to her ally of recovering Gibraltar."[25]

In the end, despite helping to deny Britain sovereignty over the thirteen North American colonies, France's sea power capacity proved inadequate to sustain a commanding global presence. Having failed to become a global "whale" in addition to being a European "elephant," France was also unsuccessful in pulling the British "whale" closer to shore. Britain maintained control over the key nerve centers of global maritime communication. In a memorandum for a parliamentary inquiry into the state of naval affairs in December 1781, while Britain was still fighting a losing battle with France, Holland, and America, the First Lord of the Admiralty, Lord Sandwich, pointed out that despite its losses, Britain had not been "brought into disgrace." Britannia still ruled the waves in key strategic locations such as the Baltic; the West Indies; the East Indies; the Dutch fisheries area; St. Eustatius, Demerera, and Essequibo; the Bay of Saldanha; Gibraltar; the English Channel; parts of the Mediterranean; New South Wales, New Zealand, the Leeward Islands, the Cape of Good Hope, and the Isle of St. Helena; the Newfoundland fisheries, Nova Scotia, and Vancouver; and several positions on the West African coast and in East and Southeast Asia.[26] The ensuing Peace of Versailles of 1783 confirmed Lord Sandwich's view. As one British historian put it, "Our retention of Canada, Gibraltar and nearly all our East and West Indies, showed that the victors had not dictated terms."[27]

The contrast between Britain and France in terms of sea power versus land power orientation was not as stark as the one between the Mongols and the Sung. The scale of the France's global challenge rested on substantial naval capabilities. France, as Paul Kennedy aptly observed, was a "hybrid power"—one with strong continental and maritime capacity but clearly leaning toward land power and limiting its strategic focus to regional affairs. Frustrated in its attempts to dominate Britain in the Channel, the West Indies, Lower Canada, and the Indian Ocean, France intensified efforts to bolster its position in northwest Europe and northern Italy. Eighteenth-century France, in Kennedy's view, "remained, by its size and population and wealth, always the greatest of the European states; but it was not big enough or efficiently organized enough to be a 'superpower,' and, restricted on land and diverted by sea, it could not prevail against the coalition which its ambitions inevitably aroused."[28]

The overthrow of the ancien régime in 1789 added an important ideological dimension to the relations among the powers of Europe, pitting republicans and monarchists against each other. Revolutionary fervor took on a life of its own and resulted in many policy decisions and outcomes that would otherwise not have occurred, yet these decisions and outcomes did not overrule the long-term pattern of British-French rivalry. The domestic political motives of the French Revolution were linked explicitly with the idea of challenging Britain's political and economic preeminence on a global scale. By late 1792 Jacobin leaders consistently urged the people of France "to dictate peace on the ruins of the Tower of London" and to cut off "the sources of England's corrupting wealth" (i.e., naval power, global commerce, and colonies). The events of 1789 only added fuel to France's long-standing efforts to roll back Britain's global empire, perceived as seriously shaken by the loss of the American colonies in 1783. The same logic underlay the French challenge with the declaration of war on Britain on February 1, 1793, a war that led to nearly 700 battles over 23 years and was driven by "far-flung schemes which embroiled the world in a conflict *reverting more and more to the traditional Anglo-French type*" [emphasis added].[29]

Moreover, the French Revolution magnified the whale-versus-elephant asymmetry between these two powers. Britain's margin of superiority over France in ships of the line with more than sixty guns—one of the key indicators of naval capabilities at that time—increased from 34 to 40 percent between 1783 and 1793. At the start of the war in 1793, British ships of the line carried 8,718 guns, and French ships, 6,002 guns (giving Britain a 36 percent advantage). Despite heavier French guns, Britain still had an advantage of one-sixth of the aggregate weight of broadside.[30]

Underlying this asymmetry were the different national responses in Britain and France to the mounting European crisis in the early 1790s. By 1793 both countries had a system of setting aside furniture and stores, as well as stocking the magazines at several dockyards with imperishable stores for each sea-going ship. In the crisis years after the French Revolution—despite poor pay, desertions, mutinies, and manpower shortages on both sides—Great Britain bettered the stockpiling system, while France displayed growing neglect of naval supplies. Thus, when orders to arm against the French challenge were received in 1793, Britain raised the number of ships of the line in commission from 26 to 54 and the total size of its naval force from 136 ships to more than 200.[31]

In contrast, after 1789, a fine French navy with more than 70 ships of the line, 64 frigates, and about 80 smaller craft was reduced to chaos. Although British and French seamen on board faced similar challenges of hard, continuous service with low pay "under conditions of monotony and isolation generally unfavorable to health," the incidence of illness was much lower among British sailors. For example, after a ten-week pursuit of the French fleet to the West Indies in 1805, Lord Nelson reported that among his nearly 7,000 subordinates, "neither officer nor man" was lost by sickness.

The French and the Spaniards, according to Nelson's dispatches, lost a thousand to sickness at Martinique.[32]

In 1793 France faced stiff opposition both at sea and on land. France maintained on average a more than threefold advantage in army size over Britain, but it could not match the combined army strength of states such as Prussia, Austria, and the Netherlands, all of which later joined Britain in the First Coalition against France from 1793 to 1795. Even considering only the size of the armies involved in the opening round of hostilities against France in 1792 (those of Austria, Prussia, and the Netherlands), the First Coalition (which Spain and Russia also pledged to join) could field an army 67 percent larger than that of France. In 1792, prior to the outbreak of war, Britain, the Netherlands, Prussia, and Austria still held more than a two-to-one advantage in army size over France. Adding Spain and Russia, this advantage increased to three to one.[33] With an estimated population of around 29 million by the end of the eighteenth century, France had a larger mobilization potential than any of its major adversaries taken separately, Russia excepted. And Russia was much removed from the scene of immediate hostilities. The combined population of First Coalition members numbered approximately 99 million, or 3.4 times higher than that of France, and this should have weighed heavily in France's decision making, at least according to most of the contemporary international relations theories. Even without Russia and Spain, the First Coalition had a population of 51 million, almost double that of France, to back up its military power.[34]

Faced with Britain's stiff opposition at sea, confronted with First Coalition powers on land, and urged to action by an entire nation aroused to its depths, the leaders of revolutionary France invested mostly, if short-sightedly, in France's continental lineage at the expense of its maritime capability. Thus, the newly liberated energies and passions of the French nation, when channeled into the military buildup, spawned massive and magnificent land armies but simultaneously caused "the utter weakness of the sister service [navy], not only amid the disorders of the Republic, but also under the powerful organization of the Empire." In the fiery parliamentary debates that called upon the French people to rise in arms against the old monarchies of Europe, France's military power was measured against that of Sparta and the Mongol Empire (under Genghis Khan and Tamerlane), representing the "continental power lineage" in world politics, rather than against Athens, Portugal, or Britain, representing the "oceanic lineage."[35]

This rhetoric, fanning a sense of empire envy among the people yearning for a new identity amid political, economic, and social upheaval, propelled the famous national mobilizations, *the levées en masse,* which swelled the ranks of the French army to 650,000 by late summer 1793. Naval stores were depleted, however; able captains were driven into exile, imprisoned, hanged, or subordinated to revolutionary committees ignorant of special naval requirements; personnel training was neglected; and skilled seamen were equated with the aristocracy and all its political vices. "The seamen and navy of France," noted Mahan, "were swept away by the same current of thoughts and feelings which was carrying before it the whole nation; and the government, tossed to and fro by every wave of popular emotion, was at once too weak and too ignorant of the needs of the service to repress principles and to amend defects which were fatal to its healthy life."[36]

THE UNITED STATES AND THE SOVIET UNION: MISSILES OF THE OCEAN AND MISSILES OF THE FOREST

Technological advances in the second half of the twentieth century, especially the advent of nuclear power as well as the aerospace and computer industries, have considerably changed the nature of global reach capabilities. In the post-1945 world, projecting military power worldwide required heavy or attack aircraft carriers, nuclear attack submarines, ballistic missiles, long-range bombers, supersonic fighter aircraft, reconnaissance and communication satellites, and electronic and computer technology, in addition to intensive research and development. Robust, innovative, and globally competitive economies increasingly became part of efforts to sustain the global military reach.[37]

By the mid-1970s, the Soviet Union reached approximate parity with the United States in intercontinental ballistic missiles (1,899 Soviet missiles against 2,154 for the United States). At the time, world politics was readily perceived as, above all, the arena of global competition between the two nuclear giants. The "superpower" label, when applied to both the United States and the Soviet Union, misleadingly presented them as equals in terms of global reach. In reality, the structure of Soviet and U.S. strategic nuclear forces remained very much as asymmetric in the distribution of land- versus sea-based forces as were the military capabilities of the Mongols and the Sung, and of Britain and France. Of the two superpowers, the United States was the nuclear whale, and the Soviet Union, a nuclear elephant. From the darker days of the Cold War, around the time of the Cuban Missile Crisis through the nuclear arms reductions of the late 1980s and early 1990s, the United States retained its advantage in sea-launched nuclear missiles and air-launched bombs and missiles, or the globally mobile components of the strategic nuclear triad. By contrast, the Soviet challenge to U.S. global military supremacy relied on persistent increases in the number of intercontinental ballistic missiles (ICBMs), representing the land-based component of the nuclear triad. The U.S. combined share of submarine-launched ballistic missiles and air-launched bombs and missiles in the U.S.-Soviet strategic balance was 72 percent in 1962, and it was still 70 percent in 1988, with few and insignificant fluctuations in between. The Soviet share of the intercontinental ballistic missiles in the same balance, however, though only 21 percent in 1962, grew to 73 percent in 1988.[38]

Further underscoring the persistent U.S. naval superiority and Soviet reliance on continental forces is the asymmetry in nuclear delivery vehicle (bombs and missiles) deployment on long- and medium-range bombers. By 1975, the United States deployed 437 delivery vehicles on long-range bombers, as opposed to 140 by the Soviet Union. Soviet medium-range bombers carried an estimated 800 bombs and missiles in contrast to America's 66 on this type of aircraft.[39] Among the major underlying factors of America's relative superiority at sea was the failure of the Soviet Union (or any other global power) during that time to develop anything that could match the strike power of the U.S. Navy's fifteen carrier task forces.[40]

The approximately twofold advantage enjoyed by the United States in naval and air power in 1960-1990 was paralleled by the Soviet Union's more than twofold advantage in army size (with the exception of the Vietnam War mobilization around 1970). The U.S. army was about half the size of the Soviet army in 1965; 66 percent the size of the Soviet army in 1970; 43 percent in 1975; 42 percent in 1980; 32.5 percent in 1985; and 41 percent in 1990.[41]

To aggregate these indicators for 1970-1990, the United States had about three quarters of the sea- and air-launched nuclear delivery vehicles (missiles of the ocean) in the strategic forces balance with the Soviet Union. In contrast, the Soviet Union had on average a 60-percent cumulative share of the land-based intercontinental missiles (missiles of the forest) and an army size in the same balance. Thus, the American sea- and air-power predominance was matched by the Soviet land predominance. In this manner, the competition between the United States and the Soviet Union during the Cold War continued to resemble the struggle between a whale and an elephant, as in the past cases of asymmetric competition between the Mongols and Sung China, and between Britain and France.

The impact of Cold War alliances on the balance between U.S. and Soviet strategic forces may be discounted if one considers only crude macro indicators of global reach capabilities, such as megatonnage or number of military hardware pieces. For example, in terms of aircraft carriers, nuclear attack submarines and submarine-launched nuclear warheads, the contribution of non-U.S. NATO forces to the American global power share added up to 7.8 percent in 1960, 7.3 in 1975, 3.1 in 1980, and 3.9 in 1985. The Soviet Union owned all of the Warsaw Pact's nuclear warheads.

But U.S. military-political alliances, such as NATO, ANZUS, CENTO, and SEATO, were dispersed globally, whereas Soviet and Warsaw Pact military power was predominantly concentrated in northern Eurasia. This was a further illustration of the global orientation of U.S. power, in contrast to the regional, mostly continental, concentration of Soviet military capabilities. Contributing to these patterns of power distribution was the structure of the naval forces balance between NATO and the Warsaw Pact, the two principal coalitions in the Soviet-U.S. strategic competition. The United States accounted for about 90 percent of NATO's naval aircraft and 88 percent of NATO's nuclear submarines, while relying on its Western European allies for 96 percent of diesel submarines and 60 percent of noncarrier surface warships in the European theater of operations. As did Britain in the eighteenth and nineteenth centuries, the United States concentrated on naval capabilities suited for global operations, while delegating to an allied coalition the task of supplying regional naval forces. In contrast, the contribution of the Eastern European allies to Soviet naval capabilities was marginal, compelling Moscow to devote greater resources to regional forces. In addition to possessing all Warsaw Pact nuclear submarines, the Soviet Union accounted for 97 percent of diesel submarines and 98 percent of noncarrier surface warships. Given this asymmetric capability distribution, the alliance with NATO gave the United States twice as many major surface warships and three times as many naval aircraft as the Soviet bloc had. This NATO edge also undercut Soviet superiority in diesel submarines, against a background of nuclear submarine parity.[42]

The global reach of Soviet and Warsaw Pact military capabilities was further undermined by several other factors: the Warsaw Pact had a higher proportion of submarines and large surface ships more than 20 years old by the mid-1980s; Soviet submarine detection technologies remained more limited than NATO's; conscripts as opposed to long-service professionals

constituted 75 percent of the Soviet navy's personnel; the newer and larger
Soviet warships entering service in the 1980s still had little surplus force
to disrupt NATO's maritime lines of communication; only a few major
overseas bases were operated by the Soviet Union (in Vietnam, Ethiopia,
South Yemen, Syria, and Cuba); and supply lines were vulnerable to Western wartime pressures. As with eighteenth-century France, weaknesses in
maritime capabilities made the USSR an "incomplete superpower," one
capable of challenging but not denying the United States a global "command of the sea."[43]

Interestingly enough, in 1975 the KGB's Analysis and Assessments
Directorate prepared a report on the prospects for Soviet global strategy.
The report suggested that the Soviet Union should emulate the strategy of
the great sea powers of the past, such as Great Britain. Apparently, the chief
of the Analysis and Assessments Directorate, General Nikolai Leonov, noted
in the report that Britain attained global leadership by dominating the
major ocean route from Europe to India, a strategy that required control of
a relatively small number of "points on the map, such as Gibraltar, Malta,
Suez, Aden and Singapore." Therefore, the KGB report proposed that the
Soviet Union should concentrate its limited economic resources in a few,
strategically chosen states, such as South Yemen, while granting other allies
only political and moral support. The proposal, however, clearly failed to
fit into the limits of the world known to the Politburo. It follows from
Leonov's account that the Soviet leadership was unenthusiastic about mod-
eling its strategy on the great sea powers of the past. Yuri Andropov, the
KGB chairman and a member of the ruling Politburo, considered the report for a few days, then returned the document with a recommendation
to shorten it. The shortened version was also returned, this time with
Andropov's order to "remove the proposals and leave the facts only." In the
end, Leonov wrote, KGB analysts concluded that "the proposal was discussed [by Andropov] in person with the Politburo members, but won no
support and died, without even being presented as an official KGB report
addressed to the Soviet Communist Party Central Committee."[44]

Another complication for the Kremlin was a clearly perceived ideological imperative to encourage the arrival in power of communist governments worldwide while maintaining "fortress socialism in one country."
With these benchmarks for the vitality and future prospects of the entire
Soviet regime firmly institutionalized, the rulers in Moscow unwittingly
set themselves up to be vulnerable to ideological challenges, especially from
the group of states classified as socialist and developing countries. Thus the

Soviet fear of rising Chinese power was greatly compounded by ideological tensions in the wake of Khrushchev's denunciation of Stalin in 1956 and ongoing disputes over the leadership in the world communist and anticolonial movements—all major factors in the Sino-Soviet split of the early 1960s. In less than a decade, with the ideological bonds severed, China came to pose a major military threat to the Soviet Union along the world's longest (8,000 miles) border, further enhancing the continental pattern of Soviet military power distribution.

Adding to Soviet strategic concerns in the late 1970s and early 1980s were the economic recovery of Japan, the increasing self-assertiveness of India, a U.S.-oriented Pakistan, the spread of Muslim fundamentalism along the Caucasian and Central Asian borders of the USSR, and after 1979, a protracted military involvement in Afghanistan. In other words, regional competition in northern Eurasia helped the United State's containment strategy and its world power-status by diverting Soviet resources from global competition and global issues toward its own continental borders.[45] The Soviet equivalent to American military bases spread all the way across the globe from Osnabrück, Germany, to Okinawa, Japan, were the hundreds of thousands of troops stationed along the perimeter of the Soviet border (especially the border with China) and in the adjacent territories of Poland, Czechoslovakia, Hungary, and East Germany.

Although it launched the world's first space satellite, Sputnik, in 1957 and was the first to send a man into space, in 1961, the Soviet Union was consistently outperformed by the United States in the air and in space. From the start to the end of the Cold War, the United States possessed more powerful and sophisticated aerial and space equipment, including global surveillance capabilities, than did the Soviet Union. American preponderance in air- and space power, in addition to the fleet of aircraft carriers that made U.S. airpower highly adaptable to diverse geographic conditions, was also demonstrated by the advent of high-technology air- and spacecraft, such as the U-2, the SR-71 Blackbird, geostationary satellites, and the Stealth bomber. In space technology, U.S. leadership was convincingly demonstrated by moon landings and the development of space-shuttle aircraft. The SR-71 Blackbird is a good example of the early American lead in highly sophisticated airpower, which also gave Washington a global information edge over Moscow. Developed in 1959, with its "sooty, heat-resistant titanium skin, which glows cherry-red as it flashed across the heavens at Mach 3.32 [2,100 mph]," the SR-71 could fly around the world nonstop, with aerial refueling. Cameras mounted on board could photograph 100,000 square miles of the earth's surface in less than an hour from a height of more than 80,000 feet.[46]

In satellite power, America's global leadership was also decisive. The Soviet Union lacked truly global satellite networks, such as INTELSAT, which the United States started in 1965 and which, by 1980, was supported from 263 earth stations in 134 countries. Though it achieved a spectacular propaganda victory over the United States by first launching three dogs into space in the late 1950s, the Soviet Union only put its first signals intelligence (SIGINT) satellite into orbit in 1967—five years after the United States. By the end of the Cold War, Moscow was still unable to match highly sophisticated U.S. geostationary SIGINT satellites, such as Rhyolite/Aqaucade and Chalet/Vortex. The U.S. lead in space-based global early warning systems was highlighted in 1968 with the launch of the first in the series of Byeman generation of space satellites, designated DSP Code 949 (Big Bird). This piece of space gear, looking like a large oil drum with a noselike infrared telescope, could orbit at the same speed as the earth. "Perched over Singapore," according to an expert on U.S. intelligence, James Bamford, "the long-nosed bird could 'see' almost half the earth." This advantage was further enhanced with the development of KH-11 Keyhole massive low-altitude surveillance platforms with a longevity of about two years and the capability to send back to earth high-quality telephoto signals from a 300-mile-high orbit.[47]

At about the same time, the Soviet Union was still relying on first-generation (nongeostationary) SIGINT satellites with circular orbits and altitudes of only about 205 miles that had to be launched in constellations of four to provide reliable coverage. The Soviet Union was still launching those satellites in 1982. The second generation of Soviet SIGINT satellites, with an altitude increased to 372 miles, appeared only in 1977. These Soviet space "birds" were still launched in groups of six and had a life expectancy limited to 180 days—four times less than the American KH-11. In short, during the Cold War the United States developed more enduring and more global space surveillance capabilities, whereas the Soviet Union threw larger numbers of smaller and short-lived satellites into space, particularly during international crises, such as those in the Middle East (1973) or the Falklands (1982). In the words of one satellite expert, when compared to the United States, the Soviet Union pursued "Genghis Khan-style satellite launching"—implicitly making the exercise of power in space akin to the lightning cavalry attacks of the medieval nomads.[48]

The asymmetric distribution of military capabilities among incumbents and challengers has been an enduring feature at the global level since the Mongols launched their bid for universal empire in the early thirteenth century. These enduring asymmetries can be viewed as lineages in capability distribution in world politics. In the three cases analyzed, Sung China, Britain, and the United States all had a preponderance of global reach capabilities, from the Sung junks sailing out of the Yangtze estuary to Indonesia, to Britain's superior handling of ships of the line, to the U.S. aircraft carriers, Stealth bombers, and KH-11 satellites. In contrast, the Mongol Empire, France, and the Soviet Union had superior land forces, ranging from tightly coordinated Mongol archer-horsemen to French armies drawing on revolutionary mobilizations, to the Soviet buildup in intercontinental ballistic missiles.

From a long-term, global perspective, this differentiation gives incumbent world powers and their challengers systematically divergent vantage points or observation platforms from which to exercise military power. The bulk of the Mongol, French, and Soviet military capabilities were regionally concentrated, mainly confined within distinct segments of the Eurasian landmass. The main components of Sung, British, and U.S. military power, with some variations and a few provisos, transcended regional continental boundaries, were globally distributed, and perhaps even more importantly, were much more globally mobile. In a symbolic passing of the oceanic lineage through time, the same naval outposts that the Sung maintained in South and Southeast Asia were later integrated wholesale into the global naval network of Britain and the United States.

Chapter 3

Political Systems and Information Control: Force of Reason and Reason of Force

The Mongol Empire emerged in the early thirteenth century as an antithesis to the very idea of political pluralism and separation of powers. When Temuchin, a warrior-chieftain who won the war of Mongol unification, declared himself supreme ruler of the Mongol tribes under the title of Genghis Khan, he inherited a society deeply divided along social as well as ethnic and territorial lines. The victorious Temuchin knew only too well that Mongol unification was achieved at a high cost: the 1206 peace came after a violent and protracted struggle among many local tribal units led by military chiefs *(noyons)* "for better grassland, cattle, and influence over the neighboring tribes."[1] Temuchin (meaning "Man of Iron")[2] zealously implemented his vision of monolithic political unity among these feuding aristocrats of the steppe. While forging his empire out of the crucible of multiple civil wars—and wiping out political discord in the process—Temuchin developed institutions of government and information control explicitly aimed to suppress social impulses toward political pluralism.

UNIVERSAL RULERS AND RULES OF SILENCE

Temuchin's wars of Mongol unification (1203-1206) culminated in the struggle against his best friend, military ally, and sworn brother *(anda)*

Jamuka. In the view of Barthold and several other experts on the Mongols, Jamuka represented a political movement among the nomadic elites who advocated political unity, allowing commoners' greater access to decision making, or greater political pluralism. Genghis Khan, on the other hand, stood for a conservative faction of rich tribal nobles who advocated unification based on strict, top-down subordination. According the *Secret History,* the contemporary Mongol chronicle that survived in the original, the split between Temuchin and Jamuka occurred when they were moving their main encampment *(nutuj-ece).* Jamuka suggested that the new location be close to the mountains, "where horse and cattle herders can pitch their yurts," and also to a river, "where sheep herders will find food ready to be shoved into their throats." That is, Jamuka suggested a location that could accommodate the economic interests of the two major social groups among the Mongols. According to Barthold, "Those who grazed horses were the aristocracy of the steppe; those tending to the sheep and lambs and thinking only about food for their throats were commoners." Temuchin was confused by Jamuka's suggestion that the choice of camp should take into account some kind of social pluralism. As Temuchin began to suspect, this suggestion could imply a shift in Jamuka's sympathies toward the sheep herders, or the commoners. Perceiving Jamuka's position as a source of potential threat to Mongol unity—which was especially alarming when articulated by his closest political and military ally—Temuchin broke with Jamuka and made the painful decision to eliminate this potential threat. This meant war with his sworn brother and closest friend.[3]

For Temuchin, breaking with and then defeating Jamuka's alliance was tantamount to conquering the last frontier on the path to Mongol unification. With the powerful proponents of the embryonic "democracy of the steppe" as well as other sources of elite opposition out of the way, Temuchin could mold Mongol political institutions and the social fabric to his liking. He adopted the self-styled title of "Genghis Khan," meaning the strong, superior, greater, global, "oceanic" ruler—wording deliberately setting him apart from the more traditional nomadic title of *gurkhan* ("universal ruler").[4] Temuchin's bid for a world empire was combined with an insistence on absolute power. At his enthronement in 1206, he declared, "There cannot be two suns in the sky, two swords in one sheath, two eyes in one eyepit, nor two kings in one empire."[5] The new title reflected Genghis Khan's ambition to create a government stronger than any previous among the Mongols or elsewhere in Asia.

To legalize his accession to power according to Mongol tradition, in 1206 Genghis Khan convened a *khuriltai,* an assembly of diverse tribal leaders and the only known prototype of anything resembling a representative institution in the Mongol Empire.[6] With the advent of Genghis Khan, the *khuriltais* became distinctly less of a forum for any kind of policy and strategy debate, and distinctly more of a rubber-stamp body. According to Vladimirtsov, these general assemblies "did nothing else but sanction what a small group of aristocrats had already decided upon several years in advance."[7] The *khuriltai* of 1206 was a particularly good case of popular assembly to end government by popular assembly. The main issue was addressed immediately: a white standard with nine flags was raised and Temuchin was proclaimed emperor, with the title of Genghis Khan. The rest of the Khuriltai consisted of a long list of orders and speeches made by Genghis Khan, responses by other members of the Mongol elite pledging to serve him, and the singing of an anthem glorifying the army.[8]

The *khuriltai* was not a representative institution like the contemporary baronial council in England, whose members signed the Magna Carta (1215) and laid down the beginnings of the institutional separation of powers.[9] Genghis Khan's *khuriltais* served primarily as a show of pan-tribal support symbolizing legitimization of an autocratic ruler's power. Absent in the primary sources are not only records of debates on the laws or organization of government but also any mention of voting—by show of hands, by voice, or by any other means. Regarding the program of world conquest, the assemblies passed but never challenged military campaign plans after 1206. Conspicuously absent from such forums was any discussion of the costs and benefits to Mongol society and the economy of strategies advanced by Genghis Khan. Instead, the post-1206 *khuriltais,* by their very lack of opposition to the khan, were designed to symbolize political unity among the Mongol tribes.[10]

In contrast, the grand assembly held in 1203, prior to Genghis Khan's enthronement, was an exception to this rubber-stamp pattern. A heated policy debate took place over Temuchin's plans to start a military campaign against the people of Ongut, who inhabited the lands to the southeast of the Mongols. At this *khuriltai,* a group of Mongol chieftains argued that the campaign had to be postponed, because the Mongols' horses were too thin and weak. Temuchin and his supporters responded that attacking with weaker capabilities, but without delay, would give the Mongols the advantage of surprise. Temuchin insisted that the surprise factor would be decisive, coming at a time of internecine political conflict among the Onguts.[11]

In this example, the expression of alternative views in the Mongol tribal assembly raised the issue of capability analysis in adopting a campaign strategy. Temuchin's opposition linked the probability of success with cost calculations (i.e., the condition of their horses). The lesson drawn by Temuchin was that such open policy debates jeopardized his personal preference for basing strategy on political factors (i.e., discord among the Onguts). Since Genghis Khan had to address intensive political debates before attacking even a small tribal group close to home, what would it take to have the plans for conquering far-flung powerful empires and sultanates endorsed by an independent assembly of tribal leaders preoccupied with material costs? Could Genghis Khan, illiterate and without experience in political debates, prevail and have the chance to test his plans on the battlefield? Political pluralism would only undermine Temuchin's grand design for a Mongol universal empire. It is little surprise, then, that on assuming power, Genghis Khan suppressed opposition at the *khuriltais* and rigorously centralized Mongol political institutions. Fearing manifestations of dissent such as that at the 1203 grand assembly, Genghis Khan organized his government as an aristocratic clan on a grand scale. Genghis Khan's lineage was officially proclaimed the Clan of Gold *(altan uruq),* designed to rule eternally over all the Mongols ("all the offspring living in the felt tents") and, in the final count, over all of the known world.[12]

Fearing voices of reason such as those opposed to his war plans at the 1203 assembly, Genghis Khan responded with reasoning by force. Upon his ascension to power, he expanded the Khan's Guard from about 1,550 to 13,000. With this nearly tenfold increase, Genghis Khan could use the guard more effectively as an instrument of political domination and administrative control. This control was especially important for keeping in check the Mongol military aristocracy, the chiefs commanding the units of Ten, One Hundred, and One Thousand, into which Genghis Khan subdivided the Mongol army and all of Mongol society. The guard was also designed as an intelligence source for identifying and eliminating political dissent in the court of the Great Khan. The guard was thus Genghis Khan's tool for imposing and sustaining a monolithic political structure.[13] Subject to the strictest discipline in the empire, those serving in the guard made up a pool of cadres uniquely trusted by Genghis Khan to govern what he saw as a nascent world empire. The majority of his generals came from this guard and "thus, thanks to this institution, the leadership of his military forces throughout the whole extent of the empire was in the hands of men who had been personally tested by the Khan."[14] In this sense, the supreme ruler's monopoly on information selection, institutionalized in the functions of the guard, was extended to the growing empire. Positioning himself as primary information gatekeeper, Genghis Khan closed the channels through which commoners could convey to his court their concerns about the burden of military campaigns. Simultaneously, Genghis Khan intensified propaganda that promised his warriors limitless riches and sexual conquests that could only be attained in a sweeping global campaign.

Very early in his rule Genghis Khan also eliminated the sources of conflict between secular and religious authority by establishing the supremacy of imperial power over the shamanic priests. Immediately after Genghis Khan's accession, a major internal challenge to his power came from the high priest, Kokochu, who was the son of Monglik, a servant to the father of Genghis Khan. Credited with uncovering an assassination plot against Temuchin during the wars of unification, Kokochu carved out a uniquely influential position for himself and the entire Monglik family in Genghis Khan's entourage. Becoming the chief shaman with the title of Teb-tengri (The Most Heavenly), Kokochu harbored the ambition to achieve supreme authority among the Mongols. This claim had much weight, since among deeply superstitious Mongols the shamans evoked an association with magical, divine powers. As a result, the shamans were no less influential among the nomads than among the tribal chiefs.

Uniting around himself those dissatisfied with Genghis Khan's reforms, Teb-tengri began to spread slander couched as divine prophecies about Genghis Khan's younger brother, Kasar (Khazar). Kasar was accused of contemplating high treason. By humiliating Kasar, Teb-tengri sought both to undermine Genghis Khan's trust in his own Clan of Gold and dampen the reputation and prestige of the ruler. The shaman succeeded in this, but perhaps too quickly. As "the peoples of the nine tongues" (the major Mongol tribes) began a mass migration to the lands owned by Teb-tengri, Genghis Khan became suspicious of the shaman. Recognizing the immense potential of Teb-tengri to disrupt the political unity of his empire, Genghis Khan dealt with the chief shaman swiftly and ruthlessly. Upon the authority of his brother the khan, Temuge-otchigin hid three strong men around the ruler's tent and invited the shaman for a talk. At the appropriate moment, the men seized Teb-tengri, broke his spine, threw his corpse in the dirt by the horse carts, and announced that the shaman was unwell.[15]

In place of Teb-tengri, Genghis Khan appointed Usun of the Ba'arin, known for his absolute devotion to the khan, as the new arch-shaman. By Genghis Khan's decree, the chief shaman was confined largely to ceremonial duties: to ride a white horse, wear a white robe in public, take a seat of honor during public functions, and bestow divine grace on the months and years selected by Genghis Khan for his undertakings.[16]

From the Great Khan down to his soldier-nomads, the Mongol system of government resembled a set of nesting dolls. Each conquered political entity was equated to adopted kin. Thus, the foreign rulers who chose submission over resistance in battle were granted the official status of "the fifth son of Genghis Khan" (who had four sons of his own).[17] In this way, Genghis Khan strove to buttress his expanding realm by creating a veritable fifth column of political adoptees. The most revered political institution, the Khan's Guard, was also designed as a structure of nested personal loyalties from the top down. The pivotal positions in this structure were occupied by the sons of regimental commanders of the original (1203) formation. These commanders had to bring with them one kinsman and ten companions.[18]

Reasoning by force triumphed over enforcement by reason in the local government of the Mongol Empire. There the emphasis was on political loyalties rather than capability assessments. From Karakorum, the Mongol capital, irrational and draconian forms of taxation, economic regulations, and codes of social conduct were imposed on the conquered territories. These rules, regulations and codes were enforced by the local governors *(darugachi* and *basqaq)* who reported directly to the Great Khan. Any kind of insubordination in these territories (whether to the rules set by the khan or to the many whims of his satraps) could immediately be interpreted as a breach of political loyalty and trigger off brutal, sudden, and massive retribution.[19]

The elites from among the nobility in territories under Mongol rule were allowed no political debates among themselves. Instead, feuding local nobles would be escorted to Karakorum, often from hundreds of miles away, and the Great Khan or his closest confidants would mediate the dispute.[20] This practice reveals the importance that Genghis Khan attached to exploiting local political rivalries among his enemies and eradicating such rivalries in his realm. This strategy was used to enhance the khan's central authority, and Genghis Khan did this with great skill, bonding local chieftains to himself by personally confirming or withholding their privileges. The Mongol khans also sought to enforce strict hierarchical subordination of local administrators by issuing state seals and tablets of authority *(paitze)* to trusted officials. The *darugachi* and *basqaq* were monitored and received orders through the system of official messengers *(elchi)* that, under Ogodei, evolved into a sophisticated and highly efficient postal service with a wide network of postal stations *(yams)*. According to Paul Ratchnevsky, an eminent historian of the Mongol Empire, the *elchi* "rode hither and thither through the occupied territories," regularly abusing their vast powers. They represented a physical embodiment of the khan's personal authority, as well as the khan's political intelligence network, leaving local residents no choice but to tolerate constant mistreatment.[21] Given that the Mongol nobles, including Genghis Khan, were illiterate, the official functions at the very top of the bureaucratic hierarchy were trusted to a handful of clerks and officers whose loyalty had been tested rigorously and who were experienced in clerical and administrative tasks. Characteristically, out of the many cultured peoples who initially clashed with the Mongols, the Uighurs were predominantly entrusted with key administrative positions, chiefly because their leader was the first among the non-Mongol tribes to accept Genghis Khan's suzerainty voluntarily.[22]

Communications and the movement of all members of the Mongol *ulus* were subject to strong central control. Once the population of any given area was assigned to the units Thousands, Hundreds, and Tens under the appropriate commanders, no one was free to change units. According to Juvaini, any soldier guilty of transferring without permission from one commander to another was to be executed in front of the whole army. The commander who agreed to receive such a soldier under his jurisdiction was also subject to strict punishment (usually by whipping and demotion). From a fear of treachery and conspiracies, Genghis Khan forbid Army commanders to associate with one another. The expression of independent views was discouraged. Genghis Khan instructed his subjects to measure whatever they wanted to say in public, or heard others say, against the official position: "Compare your own word and the words of others with those of the sages; if they match, it may be uttered, otherwise it should not be pronounced." Commanders were told to reprimand subordinates who dared speak first and to send such unfortunates to "hammer cold iron."[23]

The Great Khan was also the sole source of law. Even ancient Mongol traditions that existed independently of the universal ruler mattered only in terms of how they were interpreted by the khan.[24] Research on the Mongol legal system suggests strongly that Genghis Khan's new law code, the *Yasa*, adapted the old tribal laws to strengthen central authority and secure forever the rule of the Genghisides.[25] According to al-'Umari: "Everything in the Yasa which is ascribed to him [Genghis Khan] arose solely from his reasoning, his empathy and his ability to give of his best."[26] This code of law was an iron and merciless one. According to Juzjani, a thirteenth-century chronicler and historian: "Genghis Khan bound the people of all tribes by oaths and vows to obey him in all things. If he ordered a son to kill a father, the son would have to obey."[27]

Decisions on what constituted a crime were made personally by Genghis Khan (in cases regarding members of his guard) or by his closest aide, Shigi-khutukhu. Mongol laws exempted Genghis Khan's direct relatives from many of the legal code's provisions. For example, they were allowed to commit nine crimes without retribution. Moreover, access to the very texts of the *Yasa* as well as the monopoly on interpretation of the laws were granted exclusively to members of the Clan of Gold.[28] Anyone who wished to become emperor "on his own authority" was to be put to death immediately, and no peace was to be made with any state unless it submitted to the Mongols. Thus, the legal system emphasized the centrality of monitoring political intentions in Mongol society at large. In this manner the whole world was to be brought into submission.

If anything was legally binding to the Mongol rulers, it was above all the will of Genghis Khan, deified and codified in the *Yasa*—an embodiment of the supreme calling to expand the empire or face the threat of extinction. One royal edict *(bilik)* stated: "If in the future, even after 500, 1,000, or 10,000 years, the great men, the *bahadurs* [brave warriors] and the emirs at the service of the many children of the rulers who will see the light of day in the future, should not adhere strictly to the law, the power of the state will be shattered and interrupted; then they will be searching for Genghis Khan with great passion, but they shall not find him."[29]

Confident in the formidable information machine ensuring the political loyalty of his subjects, Genghis Khan could assess the political landscape in foreign lands from a position of greater military power and wealth, looking for signs of discord among the local aristocracy, weaknesses of character among leaders, acrimony between secular and religious leaders, and court intrigues eroding the capacity of these opponents to resist the blitzkriegs for which the entire Mongol population was trained from birth.

THE SUNG CONTRAST:
NASCENT PLURALISM, ENDURING RATIONALISM

Forms of political and socioeconomic organization distinctly divergent from those of the Mongols emerged in the tenth through the twelfth centuries in Sung China. The Sung remained an empire under an autocratic monarch, and its internal administration was patterned on the centralized government of the T'ang period. Even such a persistent and opinionated reformer as Wang An-Shih, chief minister in 1068-1076, never questioned the accepted form of government or entertained ideas about class equality and the rights of man.[30] Yet even though autocracy was unchallenged in principle, a gradual shift toward what may be described as "enlightened monarchy" started during the T'ang-Sung transition (especially after 960 A.D.). This shift was associated with the introduction of many, albeit prototypical, elements of political pluralism, the rise of a national market economy, and in particular, the rationalization of government functions.

The Sung polity emerged as a distinct alternative to the ephemeral military dictatorships that controlled the North China provinces between 907 and 960 A.D. (the period of the "Five Dynasties"). The Sung "founding fathers" based their political system civilian control over the military. The final and chaotic phase after the demise of the T'ang dynasty gave impetus to the Sung's enduring and unique adherence to the "testament of distrust for military solutions." The transition was launched by the first Northern Sung emperor, general Chao Kuang-yin. Chao came to power as a result of a mutiny initiated by the military leaders—a solution he opposed and desired not to be repeated. Determined to end the vicious cycle of coups d'état associated with the T'ang decline, Chao convinced the same generals who had enthroned him to resign voluntarily, under the pretence of supposed maladies. In a famous address to these military leaders, Chao said: "The life of man is short. Happiness is to have the wealth and means to enjoy life, and then to be able to leave the same prosperity for one's descendants. If you, my officers, will renounce your military authority, retire to the provinces, and choose there the best lands and most delightful dwelling-places, there to pass the rest of your lives in pleasure and peace until you die of old age, would this not be better than to live a life of peril and uncertainty?"[31]

In stark contrast to Genghis Khan's life philosophy and militarization of government and society, this conversion of swords into plowshares among the Sung encouraged rule-based civilian government and civilian control over the military. Unlike Genghis Khan, who aligned the political institutions of the Mongols with his personal vision of global conquest, Sung leaders were convinced that whereas one could *win* empires on horseback, one could not *rule* empires from horseback. This decided preference toward civilian government was buttressed by a unique and very strong Confucian tradition: China's civil service had been recruited on the basis of competitive examinations (instituted 2,000 years earlier than in the West). Within such an institutional framework, the influence of scholar-officials—chosen through performance-based written examinations—increased at the expense of tribal aristocratic military leaders. (Among the Mongols, civilian administration was subordinated to the requirements of the military.) Promoting rule-based civic norms by such methods, the Sung government was designed to embrace commoners with diverse talents and qualifications. Even though only about 2 percent of candidates passed the first round of exams held in the district and prefectural cities (and even fewer passed the subsequent prefectural exams qualifying them for minor government posts), the regularity and predictability of the exams fit well with the idea that rulers should adhere to rational, impersonal procedures.[32]

An intricate and well-defined system of rules was elaborated for finding appropriate positions in the political and social hierarchy. According to Yuan Ts'ai, a county magistrate in Wen-chou, Chekiang province, in the middle of the Southern Sung era, the best thing was to become a Confucian scholar: "Those of them who are endowed with outstanding talents and able to pursue the calling of a scholar fitting himself for appointment of office will, if of first quality, gain riches and honors through success in the examinations, and if of the second quality, give instruction to disciples and receive the offering due to a master." Those scoring lower on government exams but still passing, could "fulfill the tasks of writing letters and drawing up documents for others, and . . . give primary instruction in the arts of punctuating and reading." Those incapable of being Confucian scholars "may make their living without disgracing their ancestors by working as spirit-mediums, doctors, Buddhists, Taoists, farmers, merchants or experts of some sort."[33] In promoting the social status of scholar-officials, "the Sung stripped the civil service recruitment system of its least rational accretions in order to tap human resources of the whole society for the duty of governance."[34]

Furthermore, a prototype of pluralistic party politics emerged within the ranks of the scholar-officials (even though in the absence of popular franchise, the political game was still centered on the emperor). The two main parties were the innovators and the conservatives (or the "new" and the "old" parties). The innovators emphasized pacifism and economic reform, and they strove to ensure sustained prosperity for most Sung subjects. Apparently, Jeremy Bentham's maxim, "the greatest happiness for the greatest number," had antecedents in the Sung China. The conservatives, on the other hand, emphasized the goal of reconquering the territories between the Yangtze and the Huang Rivers, lost to the northern nomads (the Jurchen). The "old" party also resisted the commercialization of the economy, seeing in it a threat to the traditional government practices. Moreover, the party divide had religious overtones, with the innovators, in contrast to the conservatives, supporting greater tolerance of Taoism and Buddhism. These religions were influential among commoners. By serving as intragovernmental outlets for divergent interests and viewpoints, these two parties promoted a system in which politicians "carried on their warfare with pens rather than death sentences."[35] The political ascendance—and very existence—of the "new" party in Sung China was in direct contrast with the Mongol Empire, where political opponents daring to expound their views openly were quickly made corpses by Genghis Khan (as evidenced, for example, by the extermination of the Jamuka party). The distinctive feature of the Sung politics, however, starting with the accession of Chao, was that deposed ministers were not put to death.[36]

If Genghis Khan was the ultimate source of all laws, the Sung rulers were constrained by Confucianism, a dominant, official creed urging the government to adhere to the rules of propriety. Though fundamentally conservative, Confucianism required individual rulers to abide by external norms: successful governance was rationalized as issuing from the five virtues of a gentleman—integrity, righteousness, loyalty, altruism, and love, or "humanheartedness." Confucian norms were also steeped in rationalism and demanded that the government be concerned mostly with financial management (taxes) and the security of its subjects, and that government should be derived from knowledge of hard facts. "Recognize," Confucius instructed rulers, "that you know what you know, and that you are ignorant of what you do not know." This rationalism is also manifested in a popular saying among China's Confucian bureaucrats: "Governing a country is like cooking small fish: neither should be overdone."[37]

In addition to moderation, the Confucian conception of government service emphasized meritocracy. According to one of the most prominent Confucian scholars of the thirteenth century, Liu Yin, every person, "whether old or young, tall or short, shallow or deep, slow or quick" can reach their full potential through study. Having achieved "completeness," a ruler's minister or general was expected to be able to transform the ruler into a *Yao* or *Shun,* the legendary sage-kings who brought about great harmony and peace.[38] As an ultimate goal of government and of government philosophy, this is a striking contrast to Genghis Khan's plan to conquer the world by sword. In 1208, about the same time that Genghis Khan assumed his title meaning "universal ruler," the Sung emperor, Ning-tsung, adopted the title of *Chia-ting,* meaning "in praise of stability." And at the same time as Genghis Khan passed edicts suppressing policy debates among his vassals, the Sung ruler issued a broad call *(ch'iu-yen)* to all officials for criticism and discussion—in the words of one American historian, "a Sung version of 'Let a hundred flowers bloom'."[39] The sublime "intoxication" with rationalism, moderation, and "civilianism" among Sung officials contrasted sharply with Genghis Khan's goals and the world conqueror's philosophy that "a man's fulfillment was to be found in the intoxication of battle."[40]

BRITAIN AND FRANCE:
MEN OF NUMBERS AND MEN OF SPIRIT

In the last quarter of the eighteenth century, Britain was ruled by stable political institutions characterized by a gradually evolving system of multiple constitutional checks on royal powers. France, however, after the fall of the Bastille in 1789, found itself in a revolutionary vortex, with a political system in a catastrophically rapid transition.[41] Grounded in major institutional differences throughout this period of momentous political change, this asymmetry between continuity and change also mirrored Britain's greater reliance on the force of reason in policy making and France's impulsive slippage into governing by reason of force.

Like France under the ancien régime, Britain was a monarchy with strong executive powers. Like national assemblies in revolutionary France, the British parliament played an important part in political life. Yet both before and after the French Revolution, British monarchs and the Parliament faced greater institutional and legal constraints on their power than did the French monarchs, parliaments, or revolutionary committees. Whereas in England it was said that the "king's government was the king's,"[42] in France the king's government *was* the king. Derived from Louis XIV's famous principle—*L'état, c'est moi*—the constitution of the ancien régime granted French kings absolute authority to pass laws, appoint state officials, maintain supreme judicial power, and levy taxes. Though he enjoyed the incomparably greater merit of a genteel upbringing, Louis XV explicitly abided by the same political philosophy as Genghis Khan. "Sovereign power resides in my person alone," Louis XV proclaimed in 1766. "To me alone belongs all legislative power with neither any responsibility to others nor any division of that power. Public order in all its entirety emanates from me, and the rights and interests of the nation are necessarily bound up with my own and rest only in my hands."[43]

Given these norms and institutional structure, political considerations took precedence over cost constraints, as demonstrated by France's involvement in the War of American Independence. Lacking institutional mechanisms that would balance executive action against rigorous estimates of economic and financial capacity, the rulers of France launched a daring global crusade to inflict massive political damage on the traditional rival, England—a crusade that proved successful in the short term but disastrous a decade later. The French polity operated as if guided by some devious hand to reject policies that made financial sense. In the 1780s, France had virtually no system of national accounting and no annual tallies of revenue and expenses. As Paul Kennedy concluded, as long as the French monarchy could "raise funds for the immediate military needs and the court, the steady escalation of the national debt was of little import." Attempts to register government loans by the controller-generals Turgot and Necker were continually frustrated by the increasingly close alliance of the *noblesse de robe* (civilian aristocracy that dominated unrepresentative *parlements*) and *noblesse d'épée* (military aristocracy), which derived its very livelihood and prosperity from fiscally irresponsible conduct.[44]

Within this system, checks on the executive by a representative legislature, with all the "bean-counting" methods accompanying them, were evoked only as a last resort. In theory, France did have a quasi-representative supreme legislative body, the Estates General, but this legislature had not assembled for 175 years. When finally convened in 1789, out of desperation to resolve an acute government debt crisis over massive spending in the War of American Independence, this parliamentary assembly proved to be too little, too late. Thus, in Jenkins' analysis, "Instead of peaceably reorganizing chaotic finances and adjusting social inequalities, France had incurred war expenditure that had brought her into bankruptcy, and the Bourbon despot who had betrayed his caste by aiding the establishment of a republic was to find his sin recoil upon his own head, not a little because of the example that the Americans had set to his own subjects."[45]

After the revolution, attempts to institute some political checks and balances in France were discernable in the constitutional documents adopted in 1789-1795, especially in the Declaration of the Rights of Man and Citizen (1789) and the Constitution of 1791. The focus of both documents, however, was on the powers of the nation as a whole as exercised by its representatives and the king; the role of the judiciary and the rule of law was left out. In Godechot's view, "Political contingencies forced the Assembly to resolve first of all the question of the royal powers, then the organization of the Legislative Assembly, and only in the end work out the laws."[46] In this tumultuous transition, general principles triumphed. Institutions that could hold the revolutionary governments accountable had no time to evolve. Thus, the Declaration mentions many general principles, including the separation of powers, but not a single specific political institution. The majority of its articles list only general definitions of the rights of the individual (Articles 2, 4, 7-11, 17) and the rights of the nation (3, 6, 12, 13-16). Godechot called the Declaration "a dogma of universal value, which anyone could make their own." Thus, the declaration proclaimed the right to universal suffrage regardless of sex or race, whereas in actuality its authors had "a firm intention to institute a very narrow franchise." Having spoken for the abolition of slavery in principle, nowhere did the Declaration specify that human rights had to be observed, not only in France but also in the French colonies, where such rights were the most blatantly violated.[47]

Ironically, while idolizing the people, the French constitutional documents implicitly favored governance by political zealots who could mobilize national passions and offered few checks on their power other than revolutionary consciousness. The Declaration defined law as "the expression of the general will." By using popular revolutionary rhetoric to defend the members of the Constituent Assembly and the social groups it represented from the despotism of absolute monarchy, the creators of the Declaration failed to "protect other classes of the nation, especially the poor, from the eventual tyranny of those who later rose to power."[48]

In 1789, the convening of the Estates General and the National Assembly, followed by the storming of the Bastille, triggered institutional chaos in France. The executive apparatus was weakened; the national legislature was disbanded and reconvened three times; institutions of the judiciary, by sweeping association with the royal tyranny of the ancien régime, were abolished or neglected. In the process, the legislature subsumed both executive and judiciary powers, ruling through such agencies as the Committee of Public Safety and the revolutionary tribunals. Major executive and judiciary powers were thus sustained, while independent institutions capable of checking the power of the Convention and revolutionary committees were weakened. Bernard Silberman, in examining the changes in the French government bureaucracy during the revolutionary transitions, concluded that "the members of the assemblies that brought an end to the monarchy as it had traditionally existed had acted as *self-selected revolution-*

aries. . . . More important, no specific constraint (no notion of constituency or contract) which could inhibit members of these assemblies from constantly redefining collective action emerged from this transformation" [emphasis added]. The rules by which leadership and decision making were systematically organized remained both ambivalent and disconnected from the elective structures of leadership in the French governments, despite the advent of *liberté.*[49]

Without proper institutional guidelines in the face of a widely perceived threat of foreign military intervention, the passionate debates (especially between the Montagnards and the Girondins) degenerated into publicly waged propaganda wars inciting the people to save the revolution from the rich. Emergency statutes and new unrestrained executive agencies with equivocal jurisdictions multiplied amidst the legislative turmoil. The Constitution of Year I (June 24, 1793), for example, concentrated power in the legislature, which in turn gave unlimited executive authority over domestic and foreign affairs to the exclusive and secretive 24-member Committee of Public Safety.[50] Nor did the public right to a referendum granted by the 1793 Constitution, as a gesture to popular revolutionary sentiment, constitute an effective institutional check on the unicameral National Convention. A referendum could be called only if 10 percent of the primary assemblies in more than half of the more than 90 departments of France objected to a proposed law within 40 days—an unlikely occurrence, given the political chaos.

As a result, France in that period was governed increasingly by highly politicized and arbitrary revolutionary committees with extraordinary powers that derived an added sense of legitimacy from the absence of referenda. The political power centralized in these committees superseded that of the old government structures still in existence. The Committee of Public Safety and the Committee of General Security, which rose to prominence at the onset of the revolutionary wars, prepared measures prior to their being discussed and voted on in the Convention. All financial measures were decided by the Finance Committee and kept secret from any outside review. The Military Committee restricted any public debate on the organization of the war effort from late 1792 on. Implementation of these decrees was entrusted to *représentants en mission* and their commissaires, the watch committees, and the public prosecutors *(procureur-syndics)*—all part of a new executive machine and Revolutionary meritocracy, as practiced by the various assemblies and committees, made decision making and appointments contingent primarily on personal and revolutionary loyalties.[51]

In England, by contrast, the Bill of Rights (1689), together with subsequent acts and court cases, codified a system of checks and balances among the executive, the legislature and the judiciary, and established multiple mechanisms for unpersonal fact-checking and evidence-testing procedures in government. Key to this system, as advanced in the Bill of Rights, were thirteen specific measures by which the people of England could assert their rights and liberties. Thus, without the consent of Parliament, the king could not pass laws, levy and disburse public money, or elect the Court of Commissioners for ecclesiastical causes. The king was prohibited from raising or keeping a standing army without parliamentary approval. All subjects had the right to petition the king and jurors in trials for high treason had to be freeholders. The English constitutional acts "removed a vast mass of evil without shocking a vast mass of prejudice."[52]

In this political balancing act, the English crown controlled the administration, key appointments and the design of policy, but parliament took an increasingly assertive role in commanding the nation's finances and making statutes. Parliaments were convened regularly (with little deviation from the average of once every six years in 1754-1790). The legislative power of the purse was deeply imbedded in institutional practices.[53] This political balancing game resembled a tug-of-war in which neither side ever let go of the opponent. John Louis de Lolme, a Swiss barrister who lived in England in the 1770s and 1780s, and studied British law and government for many years, highlighted the workings of institutional checks and balances, which France did not have at the time:

> The king of England . . . has the prerogative of commanding the armies and equipping the fleets; but without the concurrence of his parliament he cannot maintain them. He can bestow places and employments; but without his parliaments he cannot pay for the salaries attending on them. He can declare war; but without his parliament it is impossible for him to carry it on. In a word, the royal prerogative, destitute as it is of the power of imposing taxes, is like a vast body, which cannot of itself accomplish its motions; or, if you please, it is like a ship completely equipped, but from which the parliament can at pleasure draw off water, and leave it aground,— and also set it afloat again, by granting subsidies.[54]

Thus, in England the most successful statesmen of the eighteenth century—Walpole, Pitt the Elder, and Pitt the Younger—were known as men of the crown, men of Parliament and also as "men of numbers." These qualities best matched the institutional configurations described by de Lolme and embodied in the position of prime minister. The balance of power between crown and Parliament was expressed in the official titles bestowed upon the prime minister—Minister of the King in the House of Commons and Minister of the Commons in the King's Closet. In France, no minister owed political debts to representative institutions, and no minister would need to say what Walpole once told the House of Commons: "I have lived long enough in the world, Sir, to know that the safety of a minister lies in his having the approbation of this House."[55]

The political mastery of English prime ministers, who had to balance political imperatives and the constraints of the state purse, became necessarily associated with the mastery of finance. This symbiotic fusion between political and fiscal mastery is clearly seen in the careers of Walpole, Pelham, and the two Pitts, and was a critical factor in their rise and fall. Adept in hardnosed management of his own estate, Walpole became Britain's first prime minister after a distinguished record as treasurer of the Navy, First Lord of the Treasury, and paymaster general. In 1717, Walpole introduced England's first Sinking Fund, a major tool for fiscal accountability by government and a hedge against state bankruptcy in forthcoming centuries. Appointed First Lord of the Treasury in 1721, Walpole evolved into a de facto prime minister. Henry Pelham, prime minister during 1744-1754, was first appointed to government by Walpole as Paymaster of the Forces and, like Walpole, served as First Lord of the Treasury (1743-1754), combining this position with that of prime minister. The elder Pitt also served as paymaster general prior to becoming secretary of state and rose to prominence after successfully implementing a well-designed maritime strategy against France in 1756. But Pitt's neglect of England's war weariness (closely associated with the financial strain), resulted in his becoming isolated in the Cabinet and led to his subsequent resignation, despite Britain's military victories and the growth of the British Empire. The remarkable accession of Pitt the younger as Prime Minister was particularly indicative of this trend. Having become the youngest British prime minister at the age of 24, Pitt remained head of government for nearly a quarter century, largely because his power base was uniquely well balanced between the king and the Parliament, with major political factions recognizing his sound financial management skills. Like Walpole, Pitt distinguished himself by reforming the Sinking Fund and reducing the national debt.[56]

Financial checks on executive authority in Britain helped London stave off many a financial disaster such as befell France from overextending its

resources during the American War of Independence. Parliamentary opposition to George III succeeded in terminating the American military
campaigns, and a series of corrective measures were adopted. These measures exemplified the tight institutional linkages between separation of
powers and the political importance of quantitative indicators in government: the increasing influence of financial probity and Pitt's restructuring
of the Sinking Fund was accompanied by Place Acts, legislation banning
from the House of Commons those members who held offices for profit
under the crown (and had been relied on by the king to sustain government's
parliamentary majority). Characteristically, a major legislation package aiming to abolish sinecures and reduce administrative waste was called "economic" reform.[57] Whereas the French system pushed the government to
borrow without accountability, the British system put a premium on government accountability in borrowing. After the collapse of the South Sea
Bubble in 1720, for the rest of the century the English system of public
finance "remained more honest, as well as more efficient, than that of any
other in Europe."[58]

Few other issues demonstrate the propensity of British political institutions (particularly in contrast with France) to favor evidence testing than
the issue of the death penalty. When Voltaire and Montesquieu visited
England, they praised the judicial safeguards for the individual that they
did not have at home: habeas corpus and trial by jury, the great law schools
at the Inns of Court, freedom from arrest without a legal warrant, and
precise laws. The judiciary's greater institutional independence promoted
the rule of law. The conviction of an individual on criminal charges had to
be based on specific evidence related to a concrete offense on the statute
books, as defined by juries appointed from outside the government and
selected through procedures designed to enhance the courts' impartiality.[59]

Lacking these institutional evidence-testing mechanisms, France was
shaken by the wholesale execution of enemies of the state and the restoration of punishment for imaginary crimes during the Reign of Terror (1793-
1795). This reign started after the monarchy was overthrown, with the
"First Terror" of August-September 1792, culminating in the heyday of
the Committee of Public Safety in the spring and summer of 1793, the
period known as the "Great Terror." At that time alone, institutionalized
revolutionary arbitrariness claimed approximately 35,000-40,000 deaths,
with the victims denied the benefits of due process. Instead, French revolutionary jurisdiction favored swift, punitive measures, as symbolized by

the guillotines that executed suspected subversives and political dissent-ers—many of them innocent.[60]

In contrast, British law required that convictions be based on specific rules, procedures, and the interpretation of admissible evidence by court-impanelled jurors, despite the rise of public sentiment against foreigners at the time of the French Revolutionary Wars, despite the passage of legisla-tion suspending habeas corpus, and despite the crown being endowed with greater powers to arrest individuals on charges of treason. Thus, even in wartime, mechanisms of due process were critical in the acquittal of many prominent members of English radical societies, those supporters of French revolutionary ideals who probably would have ended up under the guillo-tine had they dared to challenge publicly the Committee of Public Safety in the same way they challenged the British government. Even in the face of France's invasion of Ireland in 1798, the Irish Court of King's Bench dismissed the death sentence passed by court-martial on Theobald Wolfe Tone, an Irish rebel. Following procedural canon, the court ruled that since Tone was not a British soldier, he could not be tried under military law. His life was thus spared. A. V. Dicey, an expert on the history of the British legal system, concluded: "When it is remembered that Wolfe Tone's sub-stantial guilt was admitted, that the court was made up of judges who detested the rebels, and that in 1798 Ireland was in the midst of a revolu-tionary crisis, it will be admitted that no more splendid assertion of the supremacy of law can be found than the protection of Wolfe Tone by the Irish Bench."[61]

The British and French political systems were also divided by differ-ences in the government's ability to censor the press and suppress popular expression. In England, direct institutional control of the press was abol-ished in the Revolution Settlement of 1688. After 1695, Parliament was denied authority to censorship, which, in Macaulay's view, did "more for liberty and for civilization than the Great Charter or the Bill of Rights."[62] Even though libel law was very strong,[63] Parliament eventually yielded to the arguments of the opposition and passed the Libel Act of 1792, which denied the courts or judges the prerogative of bypassing a jury and finding the defendant guilty solely on the proof of publication. On the whole, juries were far less likely to yield to executive pressure than judges; thus the Libel Act introduced important safeguards for freedom of expression in Britain amid the rising panic of the French Revolution and the Great War.[64]

Freedom of the press was characterized by permission to publish the most unfavorable representations of the head of state. Gillray's satirical caricatures publicly attacked George III's slovenly manners, ungraceful and undignified deportment, and predilection for naïve and pointless questions bordering on callous stupidity. These attacks lasted throughout the entire revolutionary period, and the king sometimes examined Gillray's sketches before publication. Royally displeased by many of these uncomplimentary cartoons, George was still unwilling to challenge institutional safeguards on press freedoms, and he let the presses run.[65] Records of House of Commons debates appeared regularly in the British newspapers. (Among the anonymous parliamentary reporters supplying these records was Dr. Johnson, early in his career.) Another famous politician and writer, John Wilkes—at one time cleared of treason charges over the antiroyalist writings in issue number 45 of *North Briton* (1762)—became lord mayor of London in 1774. In this capacity, Wilkes two years later prevented the sergeant-at-arms of the Commons from arresting a printer who published parliamentary proceedings. After Lord North allowed the charges against Wilkes to be quietly dismissed, Parliament informally acquiesced to the public's right to know what its representatives said at Westminster. From 1771 on, journalists were admitted into the gallery more often; after 1783, they were allowed to take notes. By the early 1800s newswriters were routinely recognized by the Speaker at the start of the proceedings, as part of the House audience.[66]

Even the restrictions on freedom of expression, imposed amid the rising international crisis of the early 1790s, had a built-in system of constraints: suspension of the Habeas Corpus Act in 1794 had to be renewed annually and eventually expired in 1801; the Treasonable and Seditious Practices Act of 1795 was to last only for three years and "until the end of the next session of parliament," with charges under the same act limited to high misdemeanor; and the Seditious Meetings Act of 1795 did not extend to universities or to "institutions of youth."[67]

The prevalence of economical reforms' advocates in the British Parliament in the early 1780s also reflected the mounting socioeconomic distress caused by the America's War of Independence. Greater popular participation in government was demanded. A grassroots parliamentary reform movement emerged, pressing for greater involvement of popular press in politics, county meetings, resolutions, petitions to Parliament, instructions to members of Parliament, and remonstrances to the king. In 1780 this reform movement established a central association "to coordinate the efforts of the nation and perhaps take action should parliament remain unresponsive."[68] The increasing openness of the British political system to growing popular activism is illustrated by the number of political petitions to Parliament at the turn of the nineteenth century, increasing from 880 in 1784-1789 to nearly 4,500 in 1810-1815. In eighteenth-century England, petitioning filled Parliament's institutional role as "grand inquest of the nation," and "adopting a petition to parliament remained the standard justification for holding a public political meeting."[69]

Overall, the structure of British political institutions, as well as the norms and standards that evolved through these institutions, strongly favored rule-based evidence-testing in decision making. Competitive information channels were developed. Conversely, French institutions encouraged elaborate mechanisms for centralized, top-heavy information controls and emphasized the primacy of political and personal loyalties over impersonal procedures. Voltaire's sojourns in the Bastille were vivid testimony to the ability of the French government to exercise direct control over the public circulation of critical ideas. Under the ancien régime, ministers in the king's administration widely used the so-called *lettres de cachet* to prod government into action by evading the rules; the *lettres* also proved a powerful means for controlling freedom of expression. Because of one such letter, the poet Desforges was incarcerated for six years in an iron cage for denouncing the government's expulsion of the Young Pretender from France; another commanded the poet Charles Favart to add his wife to the list of concubines for Maurice de Saxe, in order to show the government's gratitude for the latter's victories in war. As Will and Ariel Durant have pointed out, "Any offense to a noble by a commoner, any major criticism of the government, might bring a *lettre de cachet* and imprisonment without trial or stated cause."[70]

Protests in the Paris municipal government in 1787 and 1788 against the use of *lettres de cachet* to silence political opposition eventually compelled the king to issue an edict inviting opinions on the convening of the Estates General and establishing de facto freedom of the press. What these examples show is that repairing the damage to national finances and social welfare after decades of rampant royal profligacy was tightly linked to the reinstatement of the legislature and the lifting of government monopoly on political expression. A massive wave of political pamphleteering followed in the wake of the abolition of *lettres de cachet*. In 1789-1791 newspapers were allowed to print parliamentary proceedings verbatim; Protestants were granted the right to hold public office; and freedom for theatrical performance was proclaimed along with the "Declaration of the Rights of Genius." This period was very short-lived, however. Beginning in 1791, the revolutionary government restored the government's information monopoly: collective petitioning was made illegal; pro-royalist newspapers were closed down; the death penalty was introduced for statements in support of the monarchy, land reform, and the dissolution of the Convention; theater censorship was tightened; popular societies and clubs were closed; the Girondin press was suppressed; and by 1795 newspaper vendors were allowed to shout out only the titles of newspapers.

Of the 44 major revolutionary and counterrevolutionary newspapers in France during that period, 41 (93 percent) were started after 1788, and 31 (70 percent) were shut down after 1795. Only five newspapers survived after 1800, including the three that had existed before 1788. The remaining two owed their survival to strict adherence to the publication of documents of whatever government was in power.[72] Throughout most of the revolutionary period, France closely resembled the Soviet Union. Both can be regarded as a "counterintelligence state . . . characterized by the presence of a large, elite force acting as the watchdog of a security defined so broadly and arbitrarily that the state must maintain an enormous vigilance and enforcement apparatus far out of proportion to the needs of a real democracy."[73]

Operating as part of this political system, French intelligence remained distinctly unaccountable, with few reliable clues in the archives of the period as to the sources of financing and government authorization of operations. Most likely, the French government had but a vague notion of the cost effectiveness of its secret service. With a solid tradition of executive information monopoly, the French polity was inhospitable to the concept and the practice of intelligence cost-accounting. In sharp contrast, intelligence collection and analysis in Britain was subject to stringent and well-defined procedural accountability. Cost-accounting procedures with respect to foreign intelligence were made possible by a 1782 act dealing with the Civil List (which by order of the British Parliament fixed the personal expenses of the sovereign). Passed in the spirit of economical reforms, this act illustrates the impact of checks and balances, due process, and competitive representation on the design of intelligence institutions. The precise wording of the relevant clause, especially when contrasted with French procedural ambiguity regarding intelligence, is striking:

> That when it shall be deemed expedient by the Commissioners of
> his Majesty's Treasury, or the High Treasurer, for the time being, to
> issue, or in any Manner to direct the Payment of any Sum or Sums

of Money from the Civil List Revenues, for [the] foreign Secret Service, the same shall be issued and paid to one of his Majesty's Principal Secretaries of States, or to the first Commissioner of the Admiralty: and the said Secretary or Secretaries of State, or first Commissioner of the Admiralty, shall, for his Discharge at the Exchequer, within three Years from the issuing the said Money, produce the receipt of his Majesty's Minister, Commissioner or Consul in Foreign Parts, or of any Commander in Chief or other Commander of his Majesty's navy or Land Forces, to whom the said Money shall have been sent or given, that the same hath been received for the Purpose for which the same hath been issued.[74]

As a result, the records of British secret service spending have been carefully maintained and preserved down to the present. We know the amounts spent on intelligence, to the penny, for any given year, whereas French intelligence expenses of the period are still shrouded in secrecy.

SUPERPOWERS AND SUPERASYMMETRIES

Introduced by Lenin after the 1917 victory of the Bolshevik "Great October" Revolution, the Soviet political system was explicitly designed as an antipode to Western democracies, with Lenin claiming that communist rule would be a more humane and viable form of government than had ever existed. Central to this argument was the concept that Western political institutions were completely under the control of big business and therefore incapable of representing working people. The political power of "capitalist fat cats," insisted the Russian communists, should be replaced by political institutions operating as "true representatives of the working class interests." Unwavering and supposedly incorruptible oversight was to be provided by what Lenin called "the brain, the honor and the consciousness of our epoch" that is, the Soviet Communist Party.

Thus, what may be termed a *superasymmetry* of political systems was a key feature in the international competition between the United States and the Soviet Union. The American tradition of government prided itself on checks and balances, limited government, open and competitive elections, due process of law, freedom of the press, and safeguards for individual privacy. In contrast, the Soviet political tradition emphasized that the Communist Party was "the leading and guiding force of Soviet society." The state, as a collective, symbolic entity, was designed to benefit individuals in equal measure: the legitimacy of the centralized party state rested with the provision of universal employment, universal (and inexpensive) public housing, and universal (and free) health care, as well as universal public education, with all college and university students exempt from paying tuition and most receiving monthly stipends. This superasymmetry in political systems reflected the vastly divergent constitutional foundations of the two superpowers. The U.S. Constitution focuses on specific institutional and procedural mechanisms designed to safeguard the system of checks and balances and individual freedoms. The Soviet constitution, while providing a general description of government institutions and the rights of citizens, failed to specify institutional mechanisms that would prevent members of the ruling communist party elite from abusing their monopoly on power.[75] In American political science literature, these asymmetries in Soviet and American government have been quantified.[76] The Polity II research database, widely accepted by international relations specialists, provides an index of democracy and autocracy measures applied to states for every year since 1815. According to this index, the United States scored ten points to the Soviet Union's one point on democracy in the 1970s and the 1980s. On autocracy, the scores were reversed.[77]

These "supercontrasts" between the forms of government in the Soviet Union and the United States extended to the relationship between political institutions and intelligence services. The resulting asymmetric political pressures favored the bean counting of military and economic capabilities in the U.S. intelligence community and the palm reading of political intentions in Soviet intelligence agencies. A congressional investigation in the mid-1970s into suspected unconstitutional activities in the intelligence services are emblematic of these asymmetric political pressures and the resulting differences in intelligence collection and analysis priorities, particularly when contrasted with the Soviet system, which granted the KGB much greater powers over the legislature than the legislature had over the KGB. The work of Congress' oversight committees deserves a closer look here, precisely because the Soviet Union never had this type of monitoring mechanism. The story of these committees not only shows how the U.S. intelligence community interacts with political institutions but also highlights the absence of checks by publicly accountable institutions in Soviet intelligence agencies.

In the early 1970s, the resignation of President Richard Nixon in the aftermath of the Watergate scandal unleashed congressional investigators on the U.S. intelligence community with unprecedented zeal. For all the political drama surrounding Nixon's resignation, the president's departure came as a result of Congress showing its intention to activate impeachment procedures established in the Constitution. In contrast, none of the Soviet leaders, from Lenin to Gorbachev, was removed from office—nor could they have feasibly been removed—in a constitutional or rule-based manner.[78] (Of the seven Soviet leaders, only two were still alive when they left office: Khrushchev was ousted in a Politburo coup, and Gorbachev was forced to resign by the collapse of the state of which he was president.) The competitive and open system of representation in American politics made public opinion central to the initiation of the "grand inquest" into the workings of the CIA by Congress. Two intelligence oversight committees were formed. In the Senate, Frank Church made no secret about his ambition to run for president in 1976 or 1980 and saw the congressional investigations as a major campaign springboard. In the House, liberal democrat Otis Pike also sought a public opinion dividend from the Watergate fallout.

Both politicians had good reasons to expect substantial public relations benefits from their investigations. The early 1970s marked a watershed in American public opinion: after the debacle of Vietnam and the Nixon-Kissinger rapprochement with Moscow and Beijing, anticommunism was increasingly viewed by many Americans as a cover-up justifying flawed (if not illegal) executive practices, rather than as a doctrine vital to national security. For example, a compilation of data from major U.S. polling organizations by Richard Niemi shows that in 1973 more Americans—47 to 44 percent—said they liked, rather than disliked, Russia. In contrast, in 1966—and consistent with the more than decade-long pattern—only 17 percent of American respondents liked Russia (to 74 percent who disliked Russia). According to polls, in the early 1970s, in contrast to the 1950s and 1960s, the majority of Americans no longer objected to communists singing on the radio, making public speeches in their communities, teaching in a college, or advertising soap. At the same time, Americans were much more wary of intelligence agencies abusing their constitutional freedoms. Whereas in 1969 the American public was evenly split (46 to 46 percent) on the admissibility of government wiretapping of private communications, five years later 80 percent of respondents opposed wiretapping.[79] According to a Harris poll, between 77 and 81 percent of Americans in August 1974 objected to the government tapping phone conversations, opening private mail, or spying by any kind of electronic surveillance.[80] Public opinion was also galvanized by sensational information published in the mainstream press, such as the Pentagon Papers, which were run in the *New York Times* and the Watergate story, carried in the *Washington Post*. Thus, changes in public opinion trends and in the exposure of illegal government acts by the media made any appearance of stonewalling politically suicidal—a pressure that was passed on from elected officials to political appointees and civil servants. Even J. Edgar Hoover, whose superb political instincts enabled him to survive for decades as head of the FBI despite his alleged involvement in shady deals, changed his lassez-faire attitudes of the 1950s and 1960s with respect to domestic surveillance: "For years and years and years," he said, "I have approved opening mail and other similar operations, but no. It is becoming more and more dangerous and we are apt to get caught."[81] In the Soviet Union, the KGB chiefs in any city or region had unrestrained powers to wiretap or, in KGB jargon, "push a button on" anyone's telephone conversations. Only a handful of local political leaders were exempt: the local communist party's first and second secretaries, heads of local soviets (councils), Komsomol and trade union chiefs, and the People's Deputies. But even with respect to these elites, wiretapping warrants could be issued arbitrarily by the Central Committee of the Communist Party, and not subject to anything like due process or legal recourse.[82]

Although this acute and widespread fear of getting caught may have been unique to the post-Watergate political climate in the United States, the pressures to reform government oversight of the intelligence community illustrate the typical institutional pressures on government agencies that arise from the system of checks and balances: Congress demanded that the intelligence agencies become more publicly accountable, cost-conscious (including publication of the total size of the intelligence budget), and specific in defining the nature of intelligence operations. But despite the clear ideological advantage of going after the CIA in public, focusing on evidence and numbers proved more effective than instigating wholesale political witch hunts.[83]

The pressure for greater accountability took the form of a growing number of congressional committees demanding that top CIA officials testify in public. In his memoir on the agency, William Colby, Director of Central Intelligence during the Church and Pike investigations, described the "clutches of Congress" at work: "As it became ever more obvious that the nation's attention and the media's limelight were now to be focused mercilessly on the agency, a number of other Congressional committees discovered that they too had some jurisdiction in the intelligence area and moved quickly to get their share of the headlines. CIA's former Congressional protectors helplessly asked me to go ahead and testify before those committees and not claim my exclusive responsibility to the old watchdogs. In this fashion I ended up adding such audiences as the House Post Office Committee to the groups I had to tell about CIA's past activities."[84]

That a CIA chief could openly publish his reminiscences, or indeed anything, with a major press—and only a few years after leaving government—would be unthinkable in the Soviet context. While the Soviet Union existed, not a single memoir by the heads of Soviet intelligence was published. Even at the peak of Gorbachev's glasnost in 1989, a KGB general who ventured to demand greater parliamentary oversight of Soviet intelligence, Oleg Kalugin, was unceremoniously retired, and his story became an instant blockbuster political scandal. It is little surprise, then, the prospects for any KGB chairman giving public testimony on any wrongdoing were impossible in the Soviet context. If anything, the Soviet legislature met only twice a year for a few days to rubber-stamp laws worked out in the executive departments and in the party's Central Committee. (It met more often than the *khuriltais* convened by Genghis Khan, but the Mongol and the Soviet assemblies were not too much different in substance.) Moreover, the deputies to the Supreme Soviet were legislative dilettantes: they spent most of their time in the jobs which they had held before being elected, and they lacked the staff or the facilities to conduct independent investigations of executive agencies. What was even more important, Soviet legislators owed their allegiance not to their constituents but to the party, which nominated them for Supreme Soviet seats. As for polling agencies, there were simply none from the early 1930s on, when Stalin had pollsters executed, imprisoned, or exiled, until 1988, when Gorbachev authorized the establishment of the All-Union Center for the Study of Public Opinion. In a system that had only one candidate nominated for each (supposedly freely elected) position and a guaranteed 99.9 percent turnout to vote these candidates into office, Communist Party control of the legislature was secure, and the party's monopoly on executive information was insulated from any independent legislative inquiry. An American president would sooner be investigated by Donald Duck than Soviet intelligence chiefs (such as Beria or Andropov) would testify before the Supreme Soviet. (Donald Duck's investigation would arguably be more effective, too.)

The Church Committee questioned three directors of Central Intelligence: John McCone, Richard Helms, and William Colby. Richard Helms's testimony before the committee strongly indicated that the system of checks and balances made the information monopoly even over dubious covert operations—such as the killing of foreign leaders—hard to sustain: "It is almost impossible in a democracy to keep anything like that secret. . . . Somebody would go to his Congressman, his Senator, he might go to a newspaperman, whatever the case may be, but it [killing foreign leaders] is just not a practical alternative, it seems to me, in our society."[85]

Congressional demands for greater political accountability were accompanied by pressures to release more information on the operational costs of intelligence, pressures that clearly stemmed from constitutionally granted powers of the purse. Having concluded that the American people deserved to know more about the workings of intelligence institutions, the Church Committee immediately suggested that the Congress and the public must "determine whether the amount spent on intelligence, or by the intelligence agencies individually, is appropriate, given the priorities."[86] In applying pressure for greater fiscal transparency, the Church Committee explicitly relied on concrete constitutional provisions: "No Money shall be spent drawn from the Treasury but in Consequence of Appropriations made by Law; and a regular Statement and Account shall be published from time to time."[87] The Church Committee recommended that the direct costs to the United States for its national intelligence programs be made public, revealing that for 1976 these costs represented about 3 percent of the total federal budget and about 8 percent of controllable federal spending. This congressional push for greater fiscal responsibility also included institutional mechanisms to facilitate cost accountability within the intelligence community; staff members of the General Accounting Office (GAO) were to conduct "full audits, both for compliance and for management of the intelligence community." Demonstrating how pressures for political accountability are translated into pressures for cost-accountability, the Church Committee recommended that the GAO obtain the necessary clearances and "have full access to all necessary intelligence community files and records."[88]

Complementing the push for fiscal and political accountability, congressional investigators also called for more specific language to be used in authorizing intelligence operations. Thus, the Church Committee challenged the doctrine of "plausible denial," designed to conceal knowledge of U.S. involvement in covert operations from foreign countries by obfuscating the definitions of such operations. The push for evidence on behalf of congressional investigators led the committee to conclude that the plau-

sible denial doctrine placed "elected officials on the periphery of the decision-making process" and thus amounted to nothing less but "an invita-
tion to error," an abdication of responsibility, and a "perversion of democratic
government" that constituted an "antithesis to accountability." Consequently, the Church Committee moved to excize circumlocution and euphemism from government documents: "Subordinate officials should
describe their proposals in clear, precise, and brutally frank language; superiors are entitled to, and should demand, no less. . . . Failing to call dirty
business by its rightful name may have increased the risk of dirty business
being done." The committee also made the recommendation to ban "specific acts to be taken on the basis of general approvals of broad strategies
(e.g., keep Allende from assuming office, get rid of the Castro regime)"—
again, to enhance responsibility and accountability. Similarly, the Church
committee recommended abandoning the assumption of "floating authorization" (such as when Richard Helms justified not informing Director of
Central Intelligence John McCone about plans to assassinate Castro because such authorization had been granted earlier by Allen Dulles, McCone's
predecessor). The committee instead recommended a system of floating
accountability, through which newly appointed officials would automatically review all existing programs. The committee also objected to creating
new covert operation capabilities—again, on typically procedural, congressional grounds—to avoid the danger that "authorization for the mere creation of a capability may be misunderstood as permitting its use without
further authorization."[89]

The conduct of the Church investigation also demonstrates how the
principles of due process of law embedded in the American political system put pressure on all sides to quantify the unquantifiable. CIA Director
William Colby, drawing on his experience as a private lawyer with the law
firm of Donovan and Leisure, viewed the Church Committee investigation as if it were a major antitrust action, and he prepared to deal with the
inquiry accordingly. An intimate knowledge of the institutional wheels of
justice was instrumental in Colby's strategy of handling the investigation.
Colby's legalist approach proved viable. "In those [antitrust] cases," rea-
soned Colby, "an enormous number of documents are demanded by the
prosecution, meticulously examined and then three or four specific papers
are extracted to prove the case. The only real defense in such actions, I
pointed out, was not to fight over the investigators' right to obtain the
documents, as the courts would almost invariably rule against you, but
to come forward with the documents selected by the investigators and

explain that they had another significance than guilt." As John Ranelagh, a CIA historian, has observed, Colby's was "a quantitative rather than a qualitative approach," stressing the volume of documentation rather than theorizing about the place of intelligence in American society.[90]

The proliferation of quantify-the-unquantifiable procedures in CIA analyses is illustrated by the complex methodologies used to estimate the size of the Soviet economy and Soviet military expenditures. The utility of such an exercise is immediately questionable when one considers that in the Soviet Union's command economy prices were set, and all costs were determined by executive decision making monopolies, such as the Soviet state planning agency, Gosplan. Economic decision making in these monopolies was politically micromanaged by the Communist Party and was distinctly designed to ignore market logic. The ruble was not convertible, and more than a hundred widely divergent exchange rates for foreign currencies were used in different Soviet departments. And yet, year after year, the CIA was obligated to go through the looking glass into the upside down, topsy-turvy world of the Soviet state-run economy and return with supposedly accurate and trend-predictive estimates of Soviet economic performance. What amounted to one of the most bizarre practices at the CIA was also one of the agency's major analytical functions in the Cold War. Publications such as *Estimated Soviet Defense Spending: Trends and Prospects* and *USSR: Toward a Reconciliation of Marxist and Western Measures of National Income* were considered among the most important products of the CIA's Foreign Assessment Center. At the heart of these estimates was the so-called direct costing method. Under this accounting procedure, the CIA counted individual Soviet weapons systems and classified them according to a standard nomenclature. Then the weapons systems were valued in dollars, based on estimated ruble prices and ruble-dollar ratios. By multiplying these prices by the number of weapons systems, the CIA arrived at estimates of Soviet military spending. This building block method had major methodological flaws: for example, in 1970-1982 a CIA price sample listed only about a dozen actual ruble prices for Soviet equipment. The price sample collected over three decades was still too small: only 135 prices, often out of date, were available, covering mostly component parts rather than major-end items such as tanks, guns, ships, aircraft, and missiles.[91] What was even more important, this bean-counting approach misrepresented the very essence of the Soviet economy and product development. The Soviet economic system depended critically on political management. Economic development was driven primarily by party-inspired campaigns such as the collectivization of agriculture and the Stakhanovite shock worker movement under Stalin; the movement to create communist labor cities and the plowing of Kazakhstan's virgin lands under Khrushchev; the expansion of the nuclear power industry and construction of the Baikal-Amur railway under Brezhnev; the production discipline drive under Andropov; and productivity acceleration strategy *(strategiya uskoreniya)* under Gorbachev. Engineered by Communist Party elites, these campaigns were designed in explicit defiance of rational cost estimates.

Despite being "at times a delusion, at times a snare," and resembling an exercise in economic circumlocution, the CIA's dollar estimates of the Soviet economy were not only spared congressional scrutiny but on the contrary were deemed to represent the finest products of the intelligence community, along with assessments of Soviet military capabilities. Even proponents of terminating the CIA's National Intelligence Estimates wanted to keep the assessments of Soviet capabilities on the payroll. Robert Gates, while head of the Office of Soviet Analysis in 1982-1989, had intimate knowledge of the flaws in the direct costing method, and decided to abolish the dollar estimates of the Soviet economy, but the system of checks and balances quickly forced him to restore the practice. According to Gates, after his decision to discontinue the dollar estimates was announced, key officials in the Pentagon and on Capitol Hill immediately registered complaints. The Department of Defense and Congress insisted that without quantitative data, however flawed, on the Soviet economy and military spending, the United States would have tremendous difficulties in passing its own budget. The Defense Department needed to measure procurement requirements against some quantifiable benchmarks to draft defense budget proposals. Lawmakers needed dollar estimates of the Soviet economy and military spending to assess the validity of the Pentagon's requests.[92]

The story of the CIA's dollar estimates is especially revealing about the political superasymmetries between the United States and the Soviet Union, since in Moscow the KGB was explicitly responsible for the blanket protection of "state secrets"—a concept that had no specific legal definition. Protection of state secrets thus spread to concealment of basic economic data from both foreign governments and domestic users outside the inner circle of top party and government officials. In the early 1980s, for example, one of the KGB's special information management tasks was to protect data on Soviet grain harvests, which the party arbitrarily declared a state secret. Such information was confined to Information Bulletins, classified documents published by the party's Central Committee. Nikolai Leonov, who as head of the KGB analytical service from 1973 to 1984 regularly read these bulletins, was annoyed that "information on the real state of affairs in the country at large and in the [communist] party was invariably stamped 'Secret.'"[93] Whereas in the United States, the CIA could at least periodically be scrutinized by congressional investigators, in the Soviet Union all major political institutions were under surveillance by the KGB. From its headquarters in Lubyanka, near the Red Square, the KGB reigned over Soviet society and the government. It had several mechanisms for ensuring the information monopoly of the Communist Party: personal files were kept on all Soviet citizens who, unlike their U.S. counterparts, had no constitutional right to access their records; all appointments, promotions, or demotions in the party, the government, in industry or in agriculture were subject to KGB screening; every university, factory, research institute, farm, or editorial office had either a "First Department" or a special agent reporting regularly to the KGB on the political reliability of each institution; all government buildings and top officials were protected (and thus kept under constant surveillance) by the KGB's Ninth Directorate; every Soviet citizen traveling abroad had to be interviewed and debriefed by a KGB officer; ministries of defense and internal affairs were subject to constant oversight by the KGB's Third Directorate (military counterintelligence); the State Procuracy and the courts were obliged to follow KGB instructions; the Inter-Regional Bar Association allowed KGB lawyers to intervene in the judicial process anywhere in the country; a 240,000-man standing army was maintained by the KGB, as well as a network of prisons; all government communications were run by the KGB; the investigative branch of the KGB had a permanent license to issue warrants and conduct seizures without restraint; and the bunkers to protect the Soviet leadership in case of a nuclear attack were maintained from the Lubyanka.[94]

Deriving political power from this information monopoly, Soviet leaders were extremely sensitive to the public circulation of any potentially damaging information. In this context, reading the political tea-leaves and correctly gauging the political intentions of key party leaders who controlled government information was more prudent than making decisions on the basis of evidence-testing. The memoirs of high-level KGB officials published after the collapse of the Soviet Union reveal the decisive impact of ideological loyalties on shaping the institutions responsible for keeping the leaders informed. According to Leonid Shebarshin, a career KGB officer and Soviet intelligence chief in 1989-1991, the KGB modeled its operating procedures on the (communist) party: "No alternative existed. These procedures were uniformly adopted in the whole [Soviet] system." At the KGB Analysis and Assessments Directorate, General Leonov lamented that a "gerontocratic" Soviet Politburo was bombarded daily with 300-400 pages of reports on foreign affairs. Despite Brezhnev's order to retype all the reports in capital letters, Soviet decision makers could not physically process the amount of information they received. Ailing Politburo members increasingly relied on oral summaries conveyed to them by their aides over the phone. Conscious of their jobs and promotions, these aides painstakingly filtered out information that was either negative or did not square with the orthodox Marxist-Leninist interpretation of events. "Exactly the same way as the *boyars* and nobles of the old times [in Russia] jockeyed for position closest to the ear of the Czar-Patriarch," Leonov noted, "the ministers in charge of various departments refused point-blank to change the existing procedure of informing the government. In line with this 'procedure,' all the countless telegrams and reports were addressed exclusively to one person who was the head of the party and the government. Everyone [among these ministers] jealously guarded the 'untouchableness' of their right of access to the General Secretary's ear."[95]

Whereas in the United States, as stated earlier, Congress put pressure on the executive agencies to produce quantifiable data and explain their validity, in the Soviet Union hard data on the military were excluded from the budget and from political decision processes, by the very design of the Soviet political system. Policy makers were deliberately isolated from information on tangible military capabilities. In spring 1975, Lieutenant General Daniel O. Graham debriefed an official of Gosplan—the administrative leviathan charged with drafting the five-year plans for the entire Soviet economy. This Gosplan official played a special role in the Soviet state planning process by integrating the defense budget into the five year plan: "This was a tough job, since the Soviet Ministry of Defense refused to provide copies of their highly classified budget figures to civilian Gosplan. Instead they allowed one Gosplan representative to come to the Ministry and *read* the budget, but not take notes."[96] Moreover, no legislative or any other kind of institutional oversight was at hand to encourage a comprehensive assessment of the economic, political, and social costs of military programs, especially in the long term.

To a large extent this was conditioned by the highly centralized nature of the Soviet system of government and the strong role of the military, which zealously guarded their avenues of access to key figures in the Polit-buro. Gosplan was not the only Soviet government agency that required specific quantitative information on Soviet military yet was explicitly de-nied such information. Surprising their American counterparts, Soviet military negotiators at the Strategic Arms Limitation Talks (SALT I and SALT II) were "always anxious that their civilian colleagues should not hear American statements and assessments of Soviet military capabilities; they showed more concern for their own domestic political considerations than for the accuracy of U.S. intelligence."[97]

Officially, the Soviet defense budget in the late 1970s and early 1980s amounted to 17 billion rubles (about $26 billion at the Soviet consumer exchange rate). When I learned this number for first time, while a Soviet high school student, doubt immediately set in—how could the Soviet Union compete with the U. S. military machine, given such a paltry budget? Our teachers' official explanation was that patriotism and the devotion to com-munist ideas on the part of Soviet workforce gave a quantum boost to Soviet industrial productivity just as in World War II. Unspecified and unsubstantiated, this claim appeared shaky even to Soviet high school stu-dents. Budget numbers thus represented the political intentions of the party elite in a very crude manner and for all intents and purposes, were utopian, unless interpreted within the conceptual framework of Soviet ideology. For this reason, posting a very small amount for defense spending made good political and ideological sense by showing that the Soviet Union was "in the vanguard of global forces of peace and progress" (a key propaganda theme under Brezhnev). By manipulating the numbers this way, Soviet leaders also implied that a socialist economy based on collective values could provide security for the state at a much lower cost than a capitalist economy driven by individual profit and greed. In the case of the KGB, the budget was cloaked in complete secrecy. This absence of cost account-ability of the Soviet intelligence community is clearly attributable to the absence of institutional checks and balances, similar to those in the United States. Thus, the Soviet political system had no oversight committees re-porting to representative institutions and no audit staffs holding the intel-ligence community financially accountable. There was no Soviet equivalent of minutely detailed congressional budget justification books, which the oversight committees in the United States could routinely use to review intelligence budgets line by line.[98] The highly centralized political system was run by the all-powerful Politburo, dominated by aging party apparatchiks, government ministers charged with political affairs, the military, and token representatives of the non-Russian republics. In linking the KGB to the overarching Soviet predicament, General Leonov noted, "Those who spent the money ran the Politburo; those who made the money were not represented."

In the absence of legislative and judicial restraints outside the one-party system, the Soviet intelligence community evolved, together with the Soviet Union as a whole, into a veritable counterintelligence state. A Russian parliamentary commission on intelligence, the oversight body established after the failure of the 1991 Moscow coup against Gorbachev to conduct a postmortem on the KGB, concluded: "In functioning for a long time in the absence of practically any kind of legal basis to regulate its activities, the KGB became, in essence, a supercentralized structure, exercising control over all aspects of [Soviet] society and amassed—under the pretext of protecting state security—an immense political and military power. . . . The Committee of State Security [KGB] thus turned into a . . . supragovernmental institution, placed above the organs of supreme power and administrative agencies of the Soviet Union and Union republics."[99]

The asymmetric evolution of the domestic political systems of the incumbent world powers and their challengers was traced from the thirteenth-century Mongol Empire and Sung China. At the heart of this asymmetric evolution is the divergence between the more open, pluralistic polities of the leading world powers and the more closed, autocratic polities of their challengers. Global leadership has been consistently achieved by actors with strong institutions for checks and balances, civilian control over the military, competitiveness and openness of representation, and due process of law. Under such systems, multiple sources of political information outside of direct government control emerge and become the political norm, and they are embedded in standard operating procedures and upheld by the rule of law. Elements of political pluralism—more common among the leading global powers—set the stage for the framing of political debates in terms of material costs and benefits. In this way, pluralistic institutions encourage the politics of reason. In Sung China, the rationalization of political decision making was associated with the system of competitive examinations for government service and institutionalized party pluralism. In Great Britain, ruled by men of numbers balancing the demands of the crown and of Parliament, procedural and financial norms for accountability were extended to the secret intelligence services. In the United States, public opinion pressures and congressional oversight forced the intelligence community to abandon some of its most secret surveillance programs (including eavesdropping on Politburo phone conversations during the Cold War), while dollar estimates of the size of the Soviet economy, which the CIA knew to be fundamentally flawed, nevertheless persisted to the last days of the Soviet Union, to accommodate a budget process embedded in the world's perhaps most fully realized system of checks and balances.

In contrast, challengers are more prone to centralization of power in the executive, militarization of political institutions, government monopoly of political information, and strong regimentation of private activity, as well as executive monopoly of law and the legal process. In these political systems, information on material costs and benefits associated with government strategies is not only closely guarded by a few select gatekeepers but is also often unknown to the very people charged with making and adopting these strategies. Having silenced political debates among the aristocracy of the steppe and restricted access to law texts to direct-line family, Genghis Khan launched dazzling military campaigns in his quest for a universal (but short-lived) empire, all the while censoring information that could have threatened his grand strategic design. France, whether under the government of the king, the National Assembly, the Constituent Assembly, the Legislative Assembly, the Convention, or the Committee of Public Safety, lacked the critical institutional mechanisms to weigh the costs of massive global military engagements when taking up arms against the whole of Europe. In the Soviet context, the defense ministry denied its data to key political institutions such as the agency responsible for drafting five-year economic development plans for the entire Soviet Union, and the KGB was as much in charge of information collection and analysis as of maintaining the Soviet Union as a counterintelligence superstate.

Chapter 4

The Economic Imperative: Global Lead Sectors, Innovation, and Government Control

The thirteenth-century Eurasian economy revolved around large agrarian societies, especially in India and China, with sedentary patterns of food production and the beginnings of industry in the processing of agricultural raw materials; city-state ports such as Venice, Aden, Palembang, and Malacca, that linked international and local trade networks; strategic locations that served as pathways between flanking trading partners, such as India, Champagne, Samarkand, the Levant, and ports along the Persian Gulf; trade in valuable raw materials limited to specific areas, such as fine wool from England, camphor from Sumatra, frankincense and myrrh from the Arabian Peninsula, spices from India, jewels from Ceylon, ivory and ostrich feathers from Africa, as well as military slaves supplied from Eastern Europe; and active, export-oriented zones with manufacturing industries. Critical to these economic activities were the development of national markets, printing, the production of paper and paper money, rice production, iron and coal industries, maritime trade, champagne fairs, galley fleets, and the pepper and spice traffic.[1]

THE MONGOL EMPIRE AND THE
ECONOMICS OF TOTALITARIAN EXPANSION

In 1206 the Mongol Empire lay outside these zones of globally significant economic and industrial innovation. The land of Genghis Khan offered no "strategic crossroads location, unique industrial productive capacity, nor transport functions."[2] Reliable statistical information on the aggregate performance of the Mongol economy is unavailable. Yet it is safe to say that the Mongol Empire failed to develop any of the lead sectors in the Eurasian subsystem of the emerging global economy in the 1200s. Even the military equipment that Mongols used, although of solid craftsmanship, would hardly be competitive in Eurasian markets, having been designed to suit the military system and mission unique to the Mongols. If anything, the transfer of military technology at the initial stages of the Mongol expansion, especially the wall-breaking machines and incendiary charges, was from the conquered to the conquerors. Contemporary eyewitness accounts attest to the low level of the Mongols' economic capacity even when compared to minor actors in Asia, such as the Uighurs or the kingdom of Xi-Xia. Contemporary records of the Mongols' daily activities portray a rather primitive economy based on large-scale animal herding. Manufacturing played an auxiliary role to herd tending and military campaigns, or served the very basic household needs. More than three decades after Genghis Khan's arrival, the Mongol economy appears still to have been primitive, as described in the account by a European traveler, William of Rubruck: "The men make bows and arrows, manufacture stirrups and bits and make saddles; they build the houses and carts, they look after horses and milk the mares, churn the cosmos, that is, mare's milk, and make the skins in which it is kept, and they also look after the camels and load them. Both sexes look after the sheep and goats, and sometimes the men, sometimes the women, milk them. They dress skins with the sour milk of ewes, thickened and salted."[3] Another reputable observer, John of Plano Carpini, a papal envoy to the Mongol court in the early 1240s, confirms this impression: "Their women make everything, leather garments, tunics, shoes, leggings and everything made of leather; they also drive the carts and repair them, they load the camels, and in all their tasks they are very swift and energetic."[4]

These travelers left no record of bustling industrial development at the hub of the then-vast Mongol Empire. Thus, a confusing puzzle for realist and rationalist theorists is that the Mongols set out to establish a universal empire from a position of economic weakness and backwardness. Even cattle herding, the main sector of the Mongol economy, declined substantially by 1206. The wars of Mongol unification and climatic changes reportedly decimated the Mongol flocks.[5]

Genghis Khan and his generals were illiterate, which is hardly surprising, since the Mongols had no written language until a modified version of the Uighur script was adopted during the early stages of the empire. Artisans, merchants, and clerics in the service of the empire were overwhelmingly and, in the early years, exclusively outsiders, from China or the Muslim regions. In 1206 the budding empire had no capital city. The capital later established by Ogodei at Karakorum was hardly a match to Rome, Samarkand, or Huangchow. Even though it had a palace where clarified mare's milk, fermented honey drink and rice mead[6] flowed, cascading, from a large silver tree, four silver lions and a gilded serpent, Karakorum resembled more of an army camp amid the steppes than an administrative and trade center. For most of the year it was a lonely storage area that housed the emperor's provisions and treasures in "many buildings as long as barns." The emperor stayed at the palace only twice a year, for what William of Rubruck described as "drinking festivals;" these took place "once about Easter, when he passes there, and once in summer when he goes back [westward]."[7] The chronicles have no record of permanently operating markets, artisan's quarters, merchant guilds, manufacturing centers, or places of mass entertainment (such as the Roman coliseums). The city itself was remarkably small for the capital of the largest empire on earth, and the benefits of craftsmanship and trade were mostly confined to the khan's palace.[8]

Evidence of the economic backwardness and dependence of the early Mongol Empire on more economically advanced regions can also be found in the Chinese chronicles. In the *Meng Ta Pei-lu,* general Meng Hung analyzed why the Mongols were better equipped at the time of their war with the Chin than were any previous invaders of China. Their advantage attributed to the collapse of the pre-Chin embargo on supplies of iron to the Mongols. Exported north in considerable quantities, the iron came in the shape of coins that earlier had been circulated by the Sung in the province of Ho-Tung (Shan-hsi). Upon the conquest of the latter, the Chin abolished the money and sold it to the T'a-T'a (Tatars).[9]

By most accounts, the Mongols lacked any basic socioeconomic organization. Even after their sweeping victories against the Chin in 1211-1212, they had to relinquish the majority of the territories conquered due to a lack of personnel accustomed to garrison and administrative work. Genghis Khan seemed to have had neither the experience nor the desire to govern the agricultural and urban areas of the Chin; he appeared content to withdraw behind Feng Chou and hold on to the lands of the Ongut, the small towns on the steppes and strategic points controlling access to the south. Sections of the Mongol army were reported to have crossed the Gobi Desert on their way back to Mongolia. The Mongols found it easier to traverse 500 miles of desert than to manage the highly civilized areas of China.[10]

Thus, the economic dimension of the Mongols' national capabilities calculated as a share of the output of domestic lead industries among the major powers in the region approximated zero percent, with the possible exception of leather processing and arrow making.[11] The Mongols' world empire strategy therefore had to allow for a substantial lack of economic capacity.

The *Ulus* System: The Core of Economic Totalitarianism

In formal diplomatic correspondence and in the text of state seals after 1212, the Mongol rulers referred to themselves as "khans of the Great Ulus."[12] The term *ulus* can be defined as a state *(ulus irgen)* that is also "personal property of the whole family [or the clan] of a person who established that state and became a khan."[13] Prior to Genghis Khan, this type of social organization was a source of internal squabbles among diverse families or tribes. Determined to build an empire that would last forever, Genghis Khan transformed the social structure of the Mongols radically. Using the old *ulus* blueprint, he organized the empire as if it were his personal property by diminishing the power of tribal chieftains and creating political and military institutions absolutely loyal and obedient to the khan.

Vital to Genghis Khan's version of the *ulus* was a decimal system of social subordination. The state structure paralleled the organization of the Mongol army. Under Mongol rule, land was divided into territories corresponding to the army's two major segments, the left and the right wings. Within the wing territories were segments assigned to units of Ten Thousand *(tumen)*, of One Thousand (regiments), of Hundreds (squadrons) and of Tens (troops). Those denominations included both the warriors in a unit of the Mongol army and the socioeconomic formations capable of supporting military units of corresponding size. Everyday life in the Mongol *ulus* revolved around the *kurens* (circles), consisting of carts in which the Mongols transported their possessions. (Hence, the cossack circles or *kurens,* units blending military service and socioeconomic activity that have continued to this day in Russia.) To ensure complete control over the life of his subjects, Genghis Khan overhauled the old patriarchal *kurens.* New chiefs *(nukers)* were appointed directly by the khan, who now claimed supreme authority over the *kurens,* while families were moved between *kurens* to break up traditional patriarchal loyalties.[14] According to Fedorov-Davydov, an expert on the economics of the Mongol Empire: "In the epoch of the *ulus* system during the reign of Genghis Khan and his successors, the *uluses* as landed estates fitted almost entirely into the military subdivisions. Thus the whole population was subdivided into military units corresponding to a particular status of a given *ulus.* Unlike in the past, however, the *ulus* was not merely a tribe or a clan. . . . It was a conglomerate of variegated groups and fragments of the old groups. The replacement of the old patriarchal and tribal organization required a [strict] discipline and subordination to Genghis Khan."[15]

Throughout its dramatic territorial expansion, the Mongol army and corresponding socioeconomic structure continued to be based on the same 95 Thousands established by Genghis Khan at the 1206 *khuriltai.* Mongol conquests were thus designed to expand a totalitarian economy. In fact, as part and parcel of the *ulus* system, the Mongol economy paralleled the highly centralized political system and a society patterned after the army. This economy rested on militarized food procurement (when all able Mongols took part in the annual royal hunt), rent from conquered cities and kingdoms, a universal welfare system (the centralized distribution of looted goods and resources, aid to poor herdsmen), a state monopoly of trade and communication (the *yam* system), and bureaucratic micromanagement. Conspicuous by their absence among the Mongols were the free market elements found in contemporary economies of Europe and Asia: business immunities, private property and rules of law, autonomous business associations (such as guilds or peasant assemblies), money markets, private investment, laws of contract and compensation, urban growth, trade and usury capital, and limitations on the government's power of taxation.[16]

Illustrative of the Mongol command economy, prestigious economic functions were assigned to the political and military units entrusted with the empire's most important security tasks. Thus, the distribution of goods obtained through rent and looting—the major source of "revenue" during the Mongol expansion—was assigned by Genghis Khan to members of his night guard *(kebteuls),* the most privileged military unit. They were in charge of distributing bows, armor, lances, fabrics, and clothes; servicing the work horses; and loading and unloading trade cargos.[17]

The history of economic management in the Mongol Empire is also the history of unregulated taxation and bureaucratic tyranny exercised by the *basqaqs, darugachi,* and *elchi.* Oppression and despotism accompanied the collection of numerous taxes levied at will. Among the heaviest taxes were the corvée and the property tax *(alban kubchiri),* the land tax *(chang),* and the trading tax *(tamgha).* Extortion by the *elchi,* who extracted rent from the conquered lands to maintain their numerous escorts (sometimes as many as 500 to 1,000 men), became widespread as the empire expanded. A Russian folk song dating to the times of the Mongol conquest in the late 1230s ran: "If a man had no money, they took his child. If he had no child, they took his wife. If he had no wife, he himself was taken."[18]

Though initially serving Genghis Khan's policy of centralization well, this type of economic organization led to widespread abuse of office, excessive bureaucracy, the suppression of grassroots economic initiative, and in later years, devastating poverty among the bulk of the population. Above all, this was disproportionately a system of economic mobilization for swift and sweeping military campaigns. Decision making was fashioned accordingly: this system encouraged the Mongol rulers to favor strategies for immediate gratification without consideration of long-range economic consequences. These strategies proved disastrous to the Mongols some fifty years after the advent of Genghis Khan. A major Chinese chronicle of the Mongol conquest, *Yuan-shi,* speaks of devastating cattle plagues; frequent outbreaks of famine affecting the army up to the regimental commanders; rampant corruption and contraband trade in gold, silver, slaves, bows, arrows, and horses; the sale of land, property, and even wives and children by impoverished Mongol soldiers and border guards; mass resettlements of starving populations; and consistent bureaucratic denials of these dire conditions.[19] Spreading west into Russia and Europe with the Mongol expansion, these problems gave rise to many of the conditions that triggered the Great Plague of 1348.

THE SUNG CONTRAST:
RISING MARKETS AND RATIONALIZATION OF GOVERNMENT

Sung governments made decisive moves away from the more traditional patterns of centralized socioeconomic organization. Sung China is widely credited with such breakthroughs to modernity as urbanization, commercial revolution, formation of a national market with fiscal and administrative frameworks, and expansion of maritime trade.[20] Cities with population exceeding 1 million, internal waterways linking a growing number of small- and medium-sized marketplaces, an amazing diversity of traded commodities, ranging from rhinoceros horn and pearls to lumber, copper, lacquer, oil, and silk, were evidence of an emerging market economy replacing the old ward system and "official market" system.

Sung China also stands as the prime example of innovation and intensive manufacturing at the time, taking the lead in the production of cotton, iron goods, porcelain, silks, linens, chemicals, sugar, and books.[21] The introduction of paper production and movable-block printing by the Sung around 930-990 marked a turning point, comparable in significance to the invention of writing 4,000 years earlier.[22] As suggested by Joseph Needham, Chinese wood-block printing techniques were employed by Johannes Gutenberg in Europe about four centuries later.[23] Contributing to the dynamism of the leading sectors of the thirteenth-century Eurasian economy was the growing use of money and credit (including paper money in Sung China), the emergence of capital-raising practices, and an increase in merchant wealth. With respect to commerce, Sung China was at the forefront of two major innovations: the replacement of tribute with trade, and the expansion of maritime trade at the expense of land-based and agrarian-centered transactions—strongly associated with the emergence of thriving overseas Chinese communities in Southeast Asia and the declining significance of the northern silk road traffic to Central Asia.[24]

The development of gunpowder and firearms in the Sung era also stand out as major economic and military innovations that had a profound impact on the world system. The first use of gunpowder to ignite flamethrowers was traced to 919; a model for a "fire arrow" designed around 969 was developed by the early eleventh century. By the middle of the twelfth century, the range of available firearms included smoke-producing incendiary grenades, land- and sea-based catapults for launching incendiary bombs, explosive grenades, and fire lances (primitive flamethrowers).[25]

Although the Sung were leaders in the most important sectors of the world economy, innovation in these sectors proceeded amid tension with some elements of Confucian doctrine. Many mandarins disliked traders just as much as they disliked warriors, and in some periods, government officials confiscated merchants' property or banned businesses. Yet by virtue of Chinese institutions, even the officials who most detested trade wanted the market economy to prosper. And despite the mandarins' suspicions, foreign trade kept expanding, because it was less controlled by government than was domestic trade. John W. Haeger, a Sung historian has described the linkages between the market system evolution in Sung China and the increasing rationalization of government decision making:

The T'ang-Sung transition not only created the obvious necessity of feeding the capital from a significant distance, but also stimulated recognition for the basic idea of specialized economic function. When this was translated into the organization of the national market, it had a dramatic impact on regional trade. Self-sufficiency in given townships or cities not only disappeared in fact but was also eradicated in theory. As increasingly specialized commercial and craft guilds appeared in all the major cities of the south, they had no difficulty gaining official recognition, and as they proliferated, the national use of labor was increasingly rationalized. The circulation of money and the consequent determination of a money value for goods and services alike gave great impetus to the rationalization of the entire social order. By the middle of the dynasty, compulsory labor and administrative services had been almost entirely transformed into simple taxation, eliminating cumbersome status gradations between households, permitting labor to be weighed against profit in the determination of value, and allowing the government to find and buy exactly the goods and services it required, instead of having to make do whatever was available in a given year in a given locality. . . . Commercially generated wealth became a means of access to education, and education, in effect, the only significant means of access to official position. The mobility which this engendered served to reinforce the linkage between government and society and between society and its civilized heritage.[26]

As I will show later, this rationalization of the social and political spheres is critical to understanding Sung preferences in threat assessment and strategy selection at the time of the Mongol expansion into China in 1211-1214.

BRITAIN AND FRANCE

Lead Sectors and Global Market Competition

Cotton textiles and the iron industry, undergirded by the increasing industrial use of coal and the internal combustion engine, were key technologies driving the eighteenth-century Industrial Revolution. These industries are widely considered as representing the lead sectors of the late-eighteenth century global economy.[27] For this reason, scholars have measured world economic leadership during the 1780-1790s in terms of raw cotton consumption and pig iron output. Data for these industrial sectors are considered "proxies for complexes which far transcend their narrow, literal scope." Thus, performance in these two sectors can serve as an indicator of the relative economic power and prospects of the major global actors.[28]

When measured in three critical indicators—share of the iron and cotton industries, per capita levels of industrialization, and percentage of world manufacturing output—the British and French economies show distinctly asymmetric growth patterns in the second half of the eighteenth century, particularly after 1750.[29] In mid-century, Britain and France had approximate economic parity in levels of industrialization per capita (at about 10 percent of the U.K. industrialization level in 1900) and in per capita world manufacturing output share. And as late as 1780, France had a slightly higher share (31 percent) of the world's textiles and iron industry than England (29 percent).[30]

But between 1780 and 1800 the British economy expanded rapidly in globally significant industrial sectors, whereas the French economy was at a standstill or declined. Thus, in 1790, Britain accounted for about 46 percent of the world's cotton textiles and iron production, with the British share increasing 17 percent in a decade. In contrast, France's global share of the same industries was only 16.3 percent in 1790, registering a 15 percent or almost twofold decrease from a decade earlier. In the 1790s this asymmetry continued to widen. By 1800, Britain was responsible for more than 53 percent of the world's leading sectors (again posting a relative gain of nearly 9 percent), whereas France was still in the same position, with its share sliding a further 0.3 percent.[31] Between 1750 and 1800, Britain's share of world manufacturing output rose 2.3 times (1.9 to 4.3 percent), whereas the French share barely increased at all (4.0 to 4.2 percent). The levels of industrialization per capita followed the same asymmetric pattern: France posted no change at all between 1750 and 1800, whereas Britain surged ahead (from 10 to 16 percent of its 1900 level). As a result, by 1800, Britain's level of industrialization was almost twice that of France. With the Industrial Revolution picking up steam, France's superior population size was no longer decisive in determining its share in world manufacturing output. Data from 1830 ex post facto confirm this trend in the relative economic positions of Britain and France. The British world output share increased another 2.2 times from 1800, and levels of industrialization rose again by 1.6 times, whereas France's world output share and industrialization levels showed little gain.[32]

At the end of the eighteenth century, the structure of international commerce further favored Great Britain's position in the world economy, against a backdrop of British preponderance in the leading sectors on the one hand and a strong French position in terms of trading volumes on the other. France's superiority over Britain in terms of the manufacturing output in the mid-1700s and its subsequent decline are mirrored by the shifts in the import-export structure of France in the second half of the eighteenth century. In 1754 France had a positive balance of trade, with exports exceeding imports by over 65 million *livres tournois*. In the same year, France exported 20 percent more goods to Britain than Britain exported to France. By 1787, however, France's balance of trade was negative, with a deficit of more than a 62 million *livres tournois,* reflecting a 41 percent drop in the export-import ratio from 1754. Also in 1787, France's exports to Britain were only about 60 percent of Britain's exports to France.[33]

The Franco-British Treaty on Navigation and Commerce of 1786, which became effective in May 1787, also revealed Britain's increasing superiority over France in lead industrial sectors. Following decades of trade and tariff wars, the treaty allowed for the admission of British iron and cotton goods into France, while French batiste and lawn (fine linen of Laon) were to be admitted into Britain. What first appeared to be an equitable trade agreement soon led to asymmetric consequences by disproportionately favoring the British economy. Solid quality at lower prices made British exports more competitive, causing insurmountable difficulties for French manufacturing industries and widening export-import ratios in favor of Britain.[34]

Paralleling these developments was the import of raw cotton into Britain, which rose from 4 million pounds in 1761 to 56 million in 1800. This trend continued into the nineteenth century, with the figure reaching 100 million pounds in 1805, the year the battle at Waterloo was fought. The iron industry experienced a similar boom: pig iron production kept rising, from 17,000 tons in 1740 to 125,000 in 1796, and to 256,000 in 1806. The tonnage of ships clearing British ports increased 7.4 times from 1709 to 1800. High lead industrial sector capacity that emerged after the 1750s was demonstrated by the construction of 30 acres of iron docks in London at the height of the Napoleonic Wars, thus turning the British capital into the world's greatest port and increasing its sea-power potential. Exports of British products also increased, from 21.7 million pounds in 1794-1796 to 37.5 million a decade later, due largely to trade with Asia, Africa, the West Indies, Latin America, and the Near East, and despite the loss of the North American colonies.[35]

Domestic Economies, Finances, and Government Strategies
During the second half of the eighteenth century, the asymmetries between Britain and France in the global economy's lead sectors were mirrored by domestic economic asymmetries. In Britain, the protection of private property rights, the stability of major government institutions, the rise of contract law grounded in due process, and the decentralization of

economic decision making created a socioeconomic environment that encouraged interaction among scientists, engineers, businessmen, and landed and commercial interests. These interactions were variegated and flexible, fostering business' adaptability to changing conditions and more rapid commercialization of innovations in British industry and agriculture. Between 1760 and 1800, increases in productivity accounted for 70 percent of the total per capita economic growth in Britain but for less than 50 percent in France.[36]

In this period Britain held an absolute advantage in what economists call *macroinventions,* or inventions that give rise to new industries or revolutionize existing industries. In Britain, the principal macroinventions—such as the spinning jenny, the coke furnace, and the steam engine—greatly boosted performance in the world economy's lead industrial sectors (pig iron and cotton thread production). In addition, Britain maintained a comparative advantage over France in microinventions, or incremental improvements in adapting technology to specific markets. Britain's market structure was, in turn, more receptive to innovation, in great contrast to France (both under the ancien régime and during the revolutionary period). In Britain, economic development relied on market forces, as opposed to direct government management, much more than in France. This is evident in Britain's higher nonsalaried-to-salaried income ratio; its higher share of private investment in scientific research, education, and public projects (such as construction of national transportation networks); greater security of private investment; stronger private patent and contract laws; wider proliferation of nongovernmental business associations, associations for scientific and technical knowledge, and private universities; and greater delegation of economic management to the provinces.[37]

It would be too simplistic to state that Britain at the time had an entirely laissez-faire economy. For example, the British government collected a higher percentage of income in taxes than the French government; Britain's Poor Laws (providing welfare for compulsory labor) were a unique feature in Europe; and many ancient statutes restricting innovation beyond prescribed types of equipment and know-how were still on the books. In practice, however, the British system proved much less top-heavy than the French, especially regarding the government's ability to impose sudden and arbitrary regulations and taxes or to impose coercive measures on individual producers to bolster production of state-designated products. Thus, France's military expenditure in peacetime was about 75 percent higher than in Britain around 1790. French governments, particularly during the revolutionary period, had the power to change at a moment's notice the nation's currency or to declare nationwide economic wars, such as the "flour war" of 1775—measures that would be deemed unthinkable and quixotic in Britain. Moreover, French governments under the ancien régime and the National Assembly, the Constituent Assembly, the Legislative Assembly, the Convention, and the Committee of Public Safety maintained a system of internal travel permits and internal tolls restricting freedom of domestic travel and commerce, a system of permanent employment registration *(cahiers)* restricting change of occupation, and a system of government quality control in manufacturing industries. French executive authorities had arbitrary powers for granting tax exemptions as well. Finally, French governments zealously maintained stringent control over science, research, and the development and commercialization of technology.[38] Whereas in Britain any enterprising individual with some private capital could acquire the necessary technical knowledge for starting a business in provincial society, in France one had to take a much more cumbersome road that led through the *grandes écoles* in Paris. Out of a sample of 498 applied scientists and engineers in Britain born between 1700 and 1850, only 50 were educated at the elite universities of Oxford and Cambridge, whereas about two-thirds (329) had no university education, in contrast to France, where government training was required for all engineers.[39]

It should be noted, however, that in the decade prior to 1789, and especially between the storming of the Bastille and the rise of the Great Terror, the governments of France attempted measures to increase economic productivity by bolstering private enterprise. Some of them lasted, like the abolition of serfdom. But many of the socioeconomic adjustments proved more difficult an accomplishment than the overthrow of governments. For example, the tolls and many other obstacles to internal trade were abolished in autumn 1790, only to be de facto reinforced with the introduction of a rigid system of economic management in the provinces through directly appointed représentants en mission. The decree of December 5-19, 1790, abolished the existing rights of registration of financial institutions but at the same time introduced a new, "universal system" of registration that favored citizens with political credentials "regenerated by the revolution." This system led to administrative abuses amounting to a "retreat to feudalism."[40]

Critical differences in the British and French systems of public finance illustrate the association between domestic economic systems and government decision-making patterns. In Britain, the higher degree of economic decentralization spurred the evolution of institutions for raising and re-paying long-term loans in an efficient fashion. The institutionally autono-mous Bank of England (created in 1694); the regularization of the national debt with sinking funds, consolidated revenue funds, and improved public accounts; and the growth of "country banks" in eighteenth-century Britain were critical factors in increasing the amount of money available to both government and businesses. Explicitly linking this synergy between gov-ernment and private businesses with the entire nation's well-being, Britain instituted a system of public finance that encouraged prime ministers to adopt verifiable, economically proportionate policies and strategies. After the financial scandal that followed the collapse of the South Sea Bubble in 1720, British prime ministers, from Walpole to the younger Pitt, "worked hard to convince their bankers in particular and the public in general that they, too, were actuated by the principles of financial rectitude and 'eco-nomical' government."[41]

In contrast, the French system of taxation and public finance, more centralized and more direct, spawned multitudes of tax farmers, parish collectors, district receivers, regional receivers general, and during the revo-lutionary upheavals, *représentants en mission*. These agents of government buttressed the crown's and then the revolutionary committees' central con-trol over the economy and thus were highly interested in taking the largest possible cut before passing the collected revenues on to Paris. In this con-text, individuals with surplus capital often found it much more attractive to buy an office or an annuity instead of investing in a business. Under such arrangements, and in a virtual absence of the system of public ac-counts, French governments were easily sustained in the belief that raising any amount of revenue was possible with sufficient enforcement—it was all a matter of political will. At the same time, no proper and viable system of public finance or financial accountability was feasible, since no mea-surement system was in place to assess the true cost of politically driven centralized fundraising on the French economy. Given these conditions, it is little wonder that plans to rationalize government decision making in France encountered powerful and insurmountable resistance by those with high stakes in the status quo. And the revolutionary governments, even when they preached total freedom, put an even higher premium on centralized control over the economy, fearing the collapse of the entire state from internal and external pressure. As Paul Kennedy has noted, "The French government's financial policy was therefore always a hand-to-mouth affair."[42]

THE UNITED STATES AND THE SOVIET UNION

The Global Economy and the Leading Sectors

America's leadership in the post-1945 world economy has been well established and its origins documented by economic historians. In the classical sequence of leading economic sectors from the eighteenth century on,[43] the United States held a convincing lead over the Soviet Union by the beginning of the Cold War. According to data marshaled by Walt Rostow on the beginning dates for national leading sectors, the United States was 50 years ahead in cotton textiles and pig iron, 60 years ahead in the development of railroads, 40 in motor vehicle production, and 20-30 years in steel and electricity.[44]

This U.S. lead persisted into the Cold War. In addition to the continuing importance of steel, electricity, and motor vehicle production, studies of the long cycles of world politics link global leadership after 1960 to the production of chemicals (nitrogen fertilizers, plastics, and resins), semiconductors, and civilian jet airframes.

America's share in these leading sectors was 3.4 times that of the Soviet Union by 1980, despite an overall decline from 64 to 49 percent. The decline in the U.S. share of such sectors as steel or electricity production was not necessarily testimony to America's loss of global economic leadership. From the early 1970s on, the increasing role in the lead industries has been played by information-intensive sectors, such as computers, telecommunications, biogenetics, robotics, lasers, and financial services. In these new, critical industrial sectors, Soviet performance was considerably weaker, and the U.S. lead (as well as the potential for increasing it) was more pronounced.[45]

The United States and its major Cold War allies (Britain, France, West Germany, and Japan) convincingly controlled the world economy. Throughout the Cold War, the United States and its European and Asian allies also maintained a comfortable advantage in the overall size of the economy. Thus, in 1950 the U.S. gross national product (GNP) was three times the size of the estimated (or, more accurately, guesstimated) Soviet GNP. Even though the gap somewhat narrowed during the relatively successful Soviet economic expansion of 1950-1965, the United States still had a twofold advantage in 1980. The Soviet bloc as a whole, including the Warsaw Pact states along with Cuba, Mongolia, Vietnam, Cambodia, and Laos, had an estimated GNP of $1.78 trillion in 1980. At that time, the U.S. coalition, which included European and Pacific allies (the NATO states, Japan, Australia, New Zealand, Taiwan, and South Korea), generated a GNP of $6.15 trillion.[46]

The strategic advantage of global incumbency is also illustrated by the total GNP for the United States and the coalition of its European and Pacific allies, which exceeded the Soviet bloc GNP by a relatively constant margin (by 3.7 times in 1950 and 3.5 in 1980). Thus, relative to the United States and its allies, the Soviet bloc economies gained only about 5 percent in thirty years. At that rate, it would have taken the Soviet bloc about 600 years to catch up with the U. S. coalition. Data on the gross world product corroborate this relative position of the U. S. and Soviet coalitions. The combined share of the United States, the European Community, and Japan in 1960 was estimated at 56.4 percent in 1960, at 55.4 percent in 1970, and at 53.0 percent in 1980; the combined Soviet bloc share was, respectively, 19.3, 18.6, and 17.5 percent.[47]

Domestic Socioeconomic Organization

The asymmetry between the United States' free market economy and the Soviet Union's centrally planned economy was also conspicuous.[48] Freedom House's annual cross-country survey of political-economic systems ranked the United States and the Soviet Union at opposite ends of the capitalism-socialism continuum, noting that during the Cold War years, "the Leninist-socialist style of political organization was exported along with the socialist concept of economic organization, just as constitutional democracy had been exported along with capitalist economic concepts." Both systems were also ranked as "inclusive," meaning that most economic activity was organized in accordance with the dominant system.[49] Moreover, the Soviet economy was explicitly designed as a historical alternative to capitalism, capable of outperforming it in the long-term "competition between the two global politico-social systems."[50] The existence of a challenger with this type of economic organization for most of the twentieth century made the distinctions between the two systems clear-cut: private versus state ownership, and the marketplace versus central planning.[51] The strength of the institutional and cultural legacy of the state monopoly on property ownership and central planning in the Soviet period was vividly demonstrated in the early 1990s by the difficulties of Westernizing and marketizing post-communist economies.[52] An economic freedom ranking for 1995 published by the Heritage Foundation emphasizes such factors as the size of the state sector and the degree of legal protection for private property: the United States occupies a position near the top, among the 65 economies considered to be free-market, whereas Russia is ranked one hundredth and on a par with Moldova, Bulgaria, and Nepal, out of the 142 countries surveyed.[53]

In the development of the global economy, innovation rather than the sheer size of the economy have been critical to global leadership. Here the difference between U.S. and Soviet economic growth patterns is striking. By the mid-1970s, the structural shift in the world economy, from smokestack industries to "post-industrial" sectors such as computer electronics, biogenetics, and services, emphasized better management and information exchange. At this stage, the Soviet experience with a centrally planned economy was one of short term, success and long-term failure. In the short term, the industrialization of the 1930s gave the Soviet Union its steel manufacturing and machine-building industries, which proved crucial in defeating the Nazi invasion in 1941-1945, served as a basis for the postwar economic recovery and expansion, and allowed the Soviet Union to stockpile ICBMs matching those of the United States. The merger of the Communist Party and secret police control over the Soviet atomic bomb program under Lavrentii Beria made possible a unique Soviet synergy—that between the worldwide hunt for industrial secrets and the mobilization of war-torn domestic industries—enabling Stalin to surprise the world with a nuclear test in 1949. In other words, this typical Soviet fusion of ideological and coercive institutions for control over industry paved the way to Soviet "superpower" status.[54]

The same experiences of combining a politically repressive form of government with a centrally planned economy, however, substantially undermined long-term Soviet performance in developing globally based strategic nuclear forces and in the newly emerging leading industrial sectors. Rigid party control over the economy and research and development programs set the Soviet Union back several decades by the late 1970s in the three critical sectors: aerospace, biotechnology, and computer electronics. In the aerospace industries, the Great Terror of the 1930s led to the cancellation of a jet engine program despite some successful flight tests, from fear that the program would boost the political standing of Marshal Tukhachevsky. As a result of high party intrigue and disinformation, Tukhachevsky was executed, both he and his project were branded enemies of the people, and the Soviet Union missed the chance to face Nazi Germany with jet aircraft in the coming war. Similarly, the officially endorsed monopoly of Lysenko and his theories stifled research in biogenetics while innovative scientists were being executed or sent to labor camps. Soviet computer science and engineering missed the crucial turning point associated with von Neumann's work in cybernetics. As part of a campaign against "cosmopolitanism" in the late 1940s and early 1950s, cybernetics was declared a "pseudo-science."[55]

The Soviet system of implementing technological innovation *(vnedreniye)* had been crippled by central control—instead of innovation, the Kremlin emphasized meeting five-year production targets. By 1980s, the *vnedreniye* system, which was supposed to keep the Soviet Union globally competitive, was an embarrassment even to the Soviet leaders. Nikolai Ryzhkov, the Soviet prime minister in 1985-1990 and, prior to that, a director of the giant Uralmash turbine conglomerate in Sverdlovsk, expressed his frustrations over the lack of technological progress in the Soviet Union:

> That delightful term, *vnedreniye,* was linked in my mind with forcing needless things upon people. But anyway, since we live in a country of bent mirrors, it is quite logical that scientific research which industrial managers in the West court, cherish and revere, was treated in our country as a kind of "sleeping beauty": it appeared that we had it, but it was better not to wake it up, for otherwise it would get you way too much trouble. . . . At Uralmash we developed a method of continuous steel casting with a 10-percent metal economy. What a great impact, if applied across the whole industry! Yet by 1984 only 13 percent of steel was cast by that method in the USSR, compared to 79 percent in Japan to which we sold the manufacturing license. Is any further comment necessary?[56]

The combined effect of low incentive to produce cost-effective goods, a hierarchical multilevel institutional structure bogged down with detailed instructions, and a priority given to meet state plan production targets rather than encourage innovation, led to the wasting of resources on a vast scale. For example, Soviet goods used two to two and a half times more energy and raw materials than analogous Western products. Early attempts by Gorbachev in 1985-1988 to reform this system through decentralization and increased production efficiency ran up against deeply entrenched institutional structures: despite pledges that central planning would cover only 25 percent of production at individual industrial enterprises by 1989, the state in 1990 still directly controlled an estimated 90 percent of Soviet industrial output.[57]

The United States also had economic problems, but they were much less severe than the ones facing the Kremlin. Labor productivity in the

United States was at least 2.5 times higher than in the Soviet Union. In addition, the U. S. economy was much more flexible and adaptable to shifts in the lead industrial sectors, due in many ways to "the very unstructured, laissez-faire nature of American society." Thus, the adjustment problems therefore were less severe than "a rigid and *dirigiste* power would have."[58]

The increasing U.S. lead in the development of new sector technologies (despite the decline of both powers in terms of gross product share) is evidenced by a comparison of their military applications. By the early 1980s the significant lag times in a large number of technological processes were increasing, and the Soviet military saw their weaponry consistently outclassed in regional conflicts. This widening technological gap was particularly evident in the increasing military applications of superior American avionics, radar equipment, miniaturized guidance systems, and Stealth technology, as a growing number of mirror-image U.S. weapons systems began emerging on the Soviet side after a lag of several years. A systematic evaluation of the U.S.-Soviet balance in high-technology development by the Canadian Institute of Strategic Studies shows that by the late 1980s, the Soviet Union could claim a lead in none of the primary, cutting-edge technologies. With respect to air and space technology, the United States was ahead in research and development areas critical to lead-sector growth and global reach capacity—aero- and fluid dynamics, computers and software, electro-optical sensors, guidance and navigation systems, life sciences, material sciences, the development of microelectronic matrices, aviation propulsion systems, radar sensors, robotics and machine intelligence, signal processing, signature reduction, submarine detection, and telecommunications. The Soviet Union at best reached parity with the United States in nuclear and conventional warhead technology, directed energy (e.g., laser systems) research, optics, and power sources.[59]

Despite its impressive size, the Soviet economy was much harder to sustain, and its continuing growth required nationwide mobilization campaigns in the name of a bright communist future. By the mid-1970s, people were getting much more cynical toward and weary of sacrifice on behalf of the Soviet economic experiment, for they realized that the quantum leap to the communist consumer paradise promised by the Communist Party would not materialize in their (or their children's) lifetime. By the early 1980s, the last of the huge state-run industry-building campaigns, the Baikal-Amur Railway, fizzled out, an the increasing number of convicts filled in for absent Komsomol volunteers. As Soviet economic growth ground to a halt, the loss of vitality and enthusiasm combined with the mellowing of the brutally coercive system forged by Stalin was deadly to the Soviet Union. When Bill Gates was starting Microsoft, which in less than two decades would become the world's leading provider of operating systems for personal computers, Soviet scientists were still forbidden free access to copying machines. Upon entering the Soviet Union, each machine had to be registered with the KGB. In every institution, photocopying was supervised by specially assigned interior ministry (MVD) officers. These officers were to ensure that no unauthorized copies were made, for the potential to disseminate anti-Soviet views by means of the machines was well recognized. The officers regularly took readings from copy meters and checked the compulsory ledgers listing all copied documents. When photocopies were made of any document, a special form had to be filled out and signed by top-level officials in a given institution.[60] The failure to loosen police control and censorship in Soviet society had an increasingly negative impact on the dissemination of word processing, computers, electronic mail, fax machines, and communication networks that could enhance the exchange of ideas and innovation.[61] In the early 1980s, there were only 50,000 personal computers in the Soviet Union, as compared to 30 million in the United States (600 times as many); moreover, most of the large mainframe computers used by the Soviet government were a generation behind Western machines.[62] Innovation and growth in computer-related industries was further stifled by the exigencies of the state-planned economy—more sophisticated equipment required longer building times and more complex and diversified maintenance schedules.[63] At the close of the 1980s, Paul Kennedy argued: "Its own [Soviet] autocratic and bureaucratic habits, the privileges which cushion the party elites, the restrictions upon the free interchange of knowledge, and the lack of a personal-incentive system make it horribly ill-equipped to handle the explosive but subtle high-tech future which is already emerging in Japan and California. Above all, while its party leaders frequently insist that the USSR will never again accept a position of military inferiority, and even more frequently urge the nation to increase production, it has clearly found it difficult to reconcile those two aims."[64]

Thus, the U.S. and Soviet governments found themselves in highly asymmetric decision-making contexts. Living in the United States, one soon grasps the immense role of bean-counting institutions, from the Federal Reserve to the General Accounting Office, to the Office of Management and Budget, to the New York stock market and the Dow Jones' Industrial Average, to government agencies furnishing monthly figures on unemployment, housing construction starts, and consumer prices. One also discovers how much the political and economic debates revolve around numbers—from budget balancing to taxes to welfare to Medicare. In the Soviet Union in the early 1980s, one was accustomed to a different information flow—constant reports about efforts to overfulfill five-year production targets or about yet another phase in the nationwide "battle for the harvest," or about shortfalls in the state-incited supposedly volunteer scrap-metal recycling programs. The asymmetry between these two decision-making environments was obvious when U.S. and Soviet government officials met their counterparts. When Mikhail Gorbachev visited Canada (whose free market economy is essentially the same as that of the United States) as a new member of the Politburo charged with agriculture, he was surprised to hear from prosperous cattle ranchers in Alberta that agriculture was not cost-effective without government subsidies and credits. Conditioned by his Soviet background, Gorbachev saw cost effectiveness in terms of farms' meeting five-year plan targets set by the Soviet government for grain, milk, eggs, poultry, or machine-to-manual labor rates. Interpreting cost effectiveness in depoliticized, purely monetary terms was beyond the limits of the known world of the future Soviet leader. Gorbachev was also stunned to learn during his visit that Canadian farmers did not take month-long vacations, such as those ones the Soviet government guaranteed farmers back home.[65]

In turn, a group of U.S. Federal Reserve experts who visited the Soviet Union in 1989 was appalled at the management of Soviet public finances. "They could not figure it out, even in their imagination," reported General Leonov, chief of the KGB's analytical service, "how the [Soviet] economic system could run as a coherent unit with a currency, the ruble, having a hundred different values assigned to it [by various government agencies]. They said, this would be the same as building a house, with each worker using a measuring stick of different length, yet all believing the stick was one meter long."[66] Proposals to rationalize Soviet government decision making consistently led nowhere. According to Gavriil Popov, a Soviet management analyst and later one of the key members of Boris Yeltsin's reform team, "In the socialist countries, the application of electronic data processing technology for economic management was outside the governments' field of vision. It was a sideline, something peripheral." Having worked at the United Nations and traveled abroad extensively, Popov submitted numerous analytical papers to the Central Committee, the Council of Ministers, and the KGB recommending that priority be given to cost accounting and technological innovation, while economic management and decision making should be decentralized. "These proposals were politely approved, a few recommendations would be adopted here and there, but the economic system as whole continued to decline unchanged. . . . The growing decrepitude of the political leaders and the expanding power of government bureaucrats [over the economy], were killing my last hopes for change."[67]

The very concept of time management was fundamentally different in the Soviet Union by comparison with the capitalist market economies, of which the United States was the best exponent. The quintessence of capitalist management—"time is money"—was rendered meaningless by the very design of Soviet institutions. Stanislav Strumilin, one of the founding fathers of Gosplan, which had responsibility for the entire Soviet economy, considered that total government control of work and leisure time would enable the Soviet Union to surpass capitalist production levels, and possibly control time itself. Central to economic performance in this system, which lasted to the collapse of the Soviet Union, was not cost accounting, or convertible currency, or rational evaluation of the existing levels of production but the ability of the government apparatus to find the right planning formula for the entire state.[68] Then, according to Strumilin, socialism would beat capitalism into the ground: "We are bound by no laws. There are no fortresses the Bolsheviks cannot storm."[69] Little wonder that when Russia embarked on market reforms in the early 1990s to change this "fortress storming" pattern, one of the biggest challenges was summed up by the popular Russian magazine, *Ogonyok,* as "learning to count."[70]

In the same way as the Soviet economy relied primarily on mass mobilization to storm fortresses, as opposed to intensive innovation and commercialization of new technology, the KGB relied on mass mobilization for intelligence collection as opposed to intensive, rigorous analysis. General Leonov regretted that in the KGB's foreign intelligence service, the ratio of information collectors (spies) to information analysts was ten to one, compared to about one to one (in Leonov's estimate) at the CIA.[71]

By the early 1980s, the Analysis and Assessments Directorate was increasingly operating in this fortress storming mode, trusted by ailing Politburo members to provide politically correct assessments even on issues that KGB analysts had no prior experience with. In Leonov's words, the KGB intelligence service was used as "a plug for every hole." Thus, the directorate was ordered to forecast gold price fluctuations on the world market, just as the Soviet Union was preparing a large sale. A minor error could cost hundreds of millions of dollars. The assignment was highly classified, with tight restrictions on the number of analysts that could take part—and none of them were professional market analysts. When presented with the task, the analysts balked, wondering why they were given this assignment instead of experts at the State Bank and the Ministry of Foreign Trade. This was also a puzzle to Leonov, but he considered that KGB analysts "were trusted more than these [financial] experts, since the latter's reputation may have been compromised by their links with foreign states." Flattered nevertheless that they were trusted by the Soviet government in this delicate task, KGB analysts started to brainstorm the gold fortress. They were given one week by the government to come up with the estimate.

Working on the estimate, according to Leonov, was "improvisation from start to finish." The first group of analysts compiled data for a diagram reflecting changes in the gold price over the preceding three years; the second group researched the capacity of global gold deposits; the third group looked into the state of gold mining technology and the impact of technological innovation on the cost of gold extraction; the fourth group documented the incidence of strikes at gold mines; the fifth group studied industrial and commercial gold consumption. KGB analysts polled many specialists dealing with gold production and sales without revealing the object of their investigation. Finally, Leonov convened all of these and other groups working on the estimate for a final brainstorming session that lasted several hours. Afterward, the KGB issued an assessment predicting that gold prices in the world market would rise steadily over the next three to four weeks. An informal working paper was submitted to the head of the KGB. As for Leonov and his team, during these four weeks they "monitored the ups and downs of the blasted gold prices around the world in a state of indescribable nervous tension"; the analysts were well aware that their forecasts were at best a good try. According to General Leonov, "We had no competence to conduct this kind of assignment and based our analysis on village knowledge combined with some superficial research. Luckily, Lord had mercy on us. The gold prices, indeed, continued to climb during that time period. We were as happy as a bunch of kids for coming up with the right guess. Yet, deep in our hearts, we were also concerned for the country that assigned tasks such as this one to us."[72]

This chapter described the distinct asymmetry between the leader-type powers, Sung China, Britain, and the United States, and the challenger-type powers—the Mongol Empire, revolutionary France, and the Soviet Union. Among the first group, economies evolved with public intervention married to private incentives. Among the second group, governments attempted to revolutionize economies and societies by maximizing control over individual economic activity and substituting political mobilization for private incentive. This distinct asymmetry is evidenced by the development among the leading world powers of such characteristics as private property, business immunities, contract and patent laws, business associations, money markets, urban growth, usury capital, statutory limitations on the executive capacity to tax, private investment in public projects, research, and development, and private technology commercialization. In contrast, challenger powers excel in militarization of the economy, bureaucratic micromanagement of the daily running of businesses, wholesale government monopoly on foreign and domestic trade, total government control over currency rates, unlimited taxation powers vested in the executive, and government control over the media (and in the USSR, even over copying machines). The leader-type characteristics of economic systems show a clear long-term advantage, especially with the increasing globalization of the economy from the thirteenth century to the late twentieth century. Thus, Sung China had global leadership in key economic sectors such as printing, paper money, iron production, and coal mining. Britain led in pig iron and cotton thread production, as well as in global maritime trade. The United States took the lead in motor vehicle production, aviation, and electricity, and is well positioned in the lead sectors of the information age. The challengers' economic systems proved best fit to "storm the fortresses" and mobilize vast resources in the hands of a highly centralized government at breakneck speed, often with the promise of fabulous gains to the population at the cost of massive immediate sacrifices.

These asymmetries also set the institutional context for divergent decision-making patterns or cultures, what may be termed the cost-accounting decision-making culture among global leaders, in contrast to the mass-mobilization decision-making culture among challengers. For example, one feature of government decision making among the leading powers, spanning eight centuries, has been that the providers of revenue to the state had a strong autonomous role and political leaders had to contend with them. Conversely, among the challenger powers, rulers were unconstrained by the revenue providers and were thus compelled to gear their decision-making apparatus for the political mobilization of economic resources. In all cases, the evidence strongly suggests, these divergent decision-making patterns shaped the limits of the known world of the institutions trusted with intelligence collection and analysis in war threat assessment.

Part II

Outcomes of Asymmetric Threat Assessment: Global Wars and Confrontation

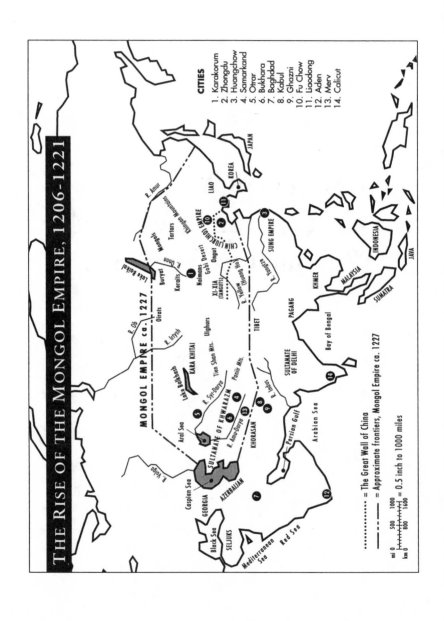

THE RISE OF THE MONGOL EMPIRE, 1206-1221

CITIES
1. Karakorum
2. Zhongdu
3. Huangchow
4. Samarkand
5. Otrar
6. Bukhara
7. Baghdad
8. Kabul
9. Ghazni
10. Fu Chow
11. Liaodong
12. Aden
13. Merv
14. Calicut

MONGOL EMPIRE ca. 1227

········ = The Great Wall of China
—·—·— = Approximate frontiers, Mongol Empire ca. 1227
——— = 0.5 inch to 1000 miles

mi 0   500   1000
km 0   800   1600

Chapter 5

The Mongol Bid for "Universal Empire," 1206–1221

In 1206 an obscure leader of nomadic hunters and herdsmen united a number of Turkic-Mongolian tribes of Central Asia, adopted the title of Genghis Khan (universal ruler) and went on to subjugate militarily more powerful and economically more advanced Asian states, such as the Empire of Chin and the Sultanate of Khwarazm. Twenty years later the empire of Genghis Khan stretched from the Sea of Japan in the east to the Black Sea in the west, and from the Indus River in the south to the Ural Mountains in the north. By the late thirteenth century the Mongol Empire extended to eastern Europe, Syria, and the South China Sea, encompassing approximately 40 percent of the world population—a degree of global domination greater than any other empire or state ever attained before or since.[1]

Political scientists in the United States have largely ignored this momentous development in world politics. Yet the Peloponnesian wars fought between two Greek city-states in the fifth century B.C. have been the subject of a disproportionately large number of studies with the aim of validating the fundamental assumptions of political realism about power and rationality.[2] Perhaps not coincidentally, the case of the Mongol Empire challenges many of these assumptions. If Genghis Khan were a rational power seeker, how could he have designed a long-term strategy that called for a small, poor, backward nation of animal breeders scattered around Mongolian steppes to defeat vastly more powerful and civilized Asian states? Why did the Mongols, unlike the Sung, for example, repeatedly ignore the economic costs of war? Why did the strategy envision the elimination and suppression of more advanced civilizations rather than a peaceful imitation of their patterns of wealth and power accumulation through learning, competition, or cooperation? If, on the other hand, Genghis Khan was a political madman or adventurist, how could he have succeeded so brilliantly in maximizing his power? Traditional explanations of this paradox sought in a military context have proven inadequate: Genghis Khan was defeated in battle about as many times as he was victorious; his celebrated feigned retreats and flanking maneuvers were nothing new to many of his major adversaries; the Mongol armies were vastly inferior in numbers and equipment to those of the Chin emperors; and several of the astounding Mongol victories in Persia were not decided by cavalry.[3] Moreover, when Genghis Khan laid down his grand design for the Mongol universal empire, he predicted that it could collapse within two decades and its rulers be put to death.[4] Why would Genghis Khan and his successors so devoutly espouse a strategy explicitly envisioning self-destruction?

On the basis of what body of information, if any, did the Mongol leaders after 1206 adopt and pursue their aggressive universal empire strategy? What factors were critical in threat and opportunity assessments? Why would a leader attach so much weight to such intangibles as organization, discipline, coordination, loyalty, deception and strategic surprise in making long-term strategy—at the expense of military and economic capabilities?

THE RISE OF GENGHIS KHAN:
"WE COUNT AS NOTHING THE NUMBER OF OUR ENEMIES"

When Genghis Khan embarked on a course of global conquest in 1206, the new Mongol Empire faced momentous obstacles, from the Gobi Desert and the Himalayas to the powerful armies of Chinese and Central Asian states. Genghis Khan's two most powerful immediate adversaries, blocking his expansion throughout the Eurasian continent, were the Empire of Chin to the east and the Sultanate of Khwarazm to the west. The exact balance of military power in the early thirteenth century between the Mongols and these two adversaries is impossible to quantify on a year-by-year basis. Yet the picture that emerges from analyzing major sources is unambiguous: Genghis Khan's numbers were greatly inferior to that of his two main prospective opponents. In 1211, shortly before Genghis Khan's invasion, the Chin army was estimated at 120,000 mounted archers, whose equipment surpassed that of the Mongols, as well as almost 500,000 infantry. The total size of the Chin army was thus estimated at over 600,000. The Mongol army at that time had 110,000 horsemen at the most. The Chin Empire also had a vastly superior population: of 48,490,000 people officially registered in 1195, the army was drawn from 6,158,636. Even though the Mongols instituted universal conscription, the entire population of the Mongol Empire when Genghis Khan completed unification (inclusive of the peripheral lands of Buryat Mongolia and North Chakhar) was approximately 1 million. This Mongol-Chin population ratio matches the Mongol-Chin army size ratio. Moreover, in 1206—the year Genghis Khan came to power—the Chin army demonstrated its fighting power by marching 145,000 troops into the Sung Empire and forcing the latter to sue for peace in 1207.[5]

A well-ramified system of defense installations added greatly to Chin military capabilities. As H. Desmond Martin notes, the empire was extremely difficult to penetrate. It was protected by the Xi-Xia kingdom and the Huang Ho River in the west, by deserts to the north, by forests to the northeast, and by the sea to the east. The imperial cavalry's main recruiting grounds, located right behind the line of Khinghan, would have indicated to any potential invader that much hard fighting and little loot were to be expected in the vicinity. The heavily fortified cities of Hsi Ching (the western capital, now the city of Ta-T'ung), Te-hsing Chou, and Hsuan-Te Chou were located south of the Mongolian plateau, in the valleys of the Sang-Kan Ho and Yang Ho rivers. The nearly impregnable forts of Chu-yung Kuan and Tzu-ching Kuan protected the capital Zhongdu (Chung Tu, modern Beijing), to the northwest and southeast.[6]

The Great Wall system had fallen into disrepair by the time Genghis Khan rose to power, but two walls were added at some distance beyond the Great Wall proper in the last years of the twelfth century. The old Khitan frontier was repaired in 1181 with the construction of a wall along the Khingan escarpment. The second wall (known to the Chinese as the *Wai pao* and to the local nomads as the *Ongu*) ran from the Khingan to the frontiers of Xi-Xia along the outer fringe of the southern Mongolian grasslands. Although, as Desmond Martin noted, "neither can have been intended to withstand more than raiding expeditions," the imperial cavalry's recruiting grounds buttressed the Khingan wall. This left the *Wai pao* as the only plausible entry point and, consequently, the perfect location for the Chin to concentrate forces to crush any prospective invaders, whose troops would also be physically exhausted after a long march across the desert. In addition, the southern rim of the Ongut prairies, lying between China and South Manchuria on one side and Outer Mongolia on the other, was turned by the Chin into a social, economic, and political cordon sanitaire against invasions from the north. A flourishing "small town belt" in that area, including Huan Chou, Chu'ang Chou, Fu Chou, Ching Chou, Feng Chou, and Yun-nei, served as a support network for military operations against invaders.[7]

Genghis Khan was aware of the superior military capabilities and economic resources of the Chin Empire. (The chronicles provide no clue, however, as to whether the Mongol ruler knew the exact number of Chin troops.) According to one chronicler, Rashid ad-Din, the Mongols believed that Altan-khan [Golden Khan, the Chin emperor] was a mighty and great sovereign, whose army was numerous beyond any limit, whose lands were vast beyond any limit, and whose fortifications were impregnable beyond any limit." As late as September 1208, Genghis paid an annual tribute tax to the Chin emperor.[8]

At the time of unification under Genghis Khan, the Sultanate of Khwarazm, to the west and southwest of the Mongols, was at its zenith. Beginning in the 1150s the Khwarazm rulers subjugated Kara-Khitai, conquered the western part of Khorassan, destroyed the Seljuk dynasty in Persia, and obtained the investiture of their states from the Caliph of Baghdad. With the arrival of Alai ud din Muhammed (Sultan Muhammad II, the Khwarazm shah) in 1200, only six years before Genghis Khan's enthronement, Khwarazm expanded further by completing the subjection of Khorassan; reducing to submission Mazanderan, Kirman, and Transoxania; annexing Ghur; and subduing Gazni. In March 1206, Shihab ad-Din, the last of the Muslim rulers capable of competing with the Shah of Khwarazm, was mysteriously assassinated. The capital was moved in the early 1200s to Samarkand, "a trade oasis city of Central Asia *par excellence*" with a population of over 500,000, three circles of walls surrounding an impressive *shahristan* (the walled citadel of the ruler's palace), and a garden in almost every household.[9] The Khwarazmian dominion at the invasion of the Mongols stretched from the Aral Sea to the Persian Gulf, and from the Indus River to Iraq and Azerbaijan.[10]

At the time, the Sultanate of Khwarazm could mobilize an estimated 300,000 troops, according to Desmond Martin, and 400,000, according to Henry Howorth.[11] At Samarkand alone, the size of the garrison was put by Juvaini at 110,000 elite troops, creating the impression among the Khwarazmian rulers that their capital would be able to withstand any attack for years.[12] According to an-Nasawi's biography of Jalal ad-Din, Muhammad's son, when the Khwarazm-shah learned about the Mongol victory over the Chin, he ordered a 78-80 kilometer wall to be built around Samarkand and started gathering troops for military operations against the Mongols.[13] The same source indicates that in his offer of peace to the sultan in 1218, Genghis Khan couched his claim of suzerainty over Khwarazm in a diplomatic turn of phrase by referring to Muhammad as "the best loved of my sons," instead of issuing a traditionally direct demand to submit. Overtures such as that notwithstanding, Muhammad was reportedly outraged by the Mongol offers of peace and expressed confidence in being the strongest military power in Asia.[14] To the cities of the Maverannakhr region, another 100,000 troops were dispatched by the shah as an advance barrier against the Mongols.[15]

The major primary and secondary sources for that period lack information on the composition of the Khwarazmian army; it is therefore impossible to determine the exact balance between cavalry and infantry in the army of Sultan Muhammad. This is a serious deficiency, given that military historians have often attributed the Mongol successes to their overwhelming reliance on cavalry, and some have even claimed it was a unique development in the history of war.[16] Reliable circumstantial evidence gleaned from Chinese records, however, suggests that "from the rise of the Hsiung-nu in the third century B.C. to the fall of the Dzungar in the eighteenth century A.D., the armies of the steppes closely resembled each other in organization, strategy and tactics." Although armies composed entirely of cavalry were an almost unknown phenomenon in the Roman Empire and the Near East, "among the pastoral peoples dwelling north of the Black Sea and in Central and Northern Asia mounted forces had long been used." The majority of the troops in service of the Khwarazm were formidable Turkish horse archers.[17]

Barriers to the Mongol Tide: Intermediate Powers and Geography
In 1206 the Mongol Empire was separated from the Sultanate of Khwarazm and the Empire of Chin by a layer of kingdoms and tribal groupings including the Black Irtysh, Kirgiz, Oirat, Karluk, Naiman, Merkit, Tumat, Kara-Khitai, Uighur, Tangut (Xi-Xia), Buryat, and Jurchen.[18] Major sources indicate, however, that even though some tactical advantages could have been and were derived by Genghis Khan from interactions with these peoples, he could count on the military capabilities of but a handful of

these smaller powers and formed no overarching military alliance with them. At best, the khan was seeking to free his existing forces from the necessity to protect the flanks rather than to increase his army's size.

Genghis Khan's relations with these intermediate powers were highly volatile. For every people such as the Uighurs or the Karluk who pledged allegiance to Genghis Khan without a fight, there were others, such as the Kara-Khitans, who switched allegiances back and forth. The Tangut people, from Xi-Xia, valiantly resisted the Mongols. When conquered, the Tangut refused to provide auxiliary troops to the world conqueror for his critical first attacks on the Chin and Khwarazm. The kingdom of Xi-Xia, possessing the largest military force among these intermediate powers, sought to carve out an independent niche for themselves and kept threatening the Mongols with periodic uprisings while also staging sting operations against the Mongol's major rivals, the Chin.[19] The reliability of agreements between the Mongols and the intermediate powers was extremely low, thus complicating a rational estimate of "a nation's war-related utility for another nation."[20]

The majority of these smaller powers were ruled by groups defeated by Genghis Khan in the wars for the Mongol unification (1203-1206) and therefore presented a significant danger. On the whole, for every case of submission there were two cases of opposition, resistance, and insubordination. The groups that pledged allegiance and loyalty to Genghis Khan—the Uighur, Oirat, Kirgiz, Karluk, and Kara-Khitai—could contribute approximately 50,000-60,000 troops. Conversely, the size of the armies engaged in prolonged and bitter opposition to Genghis Khan's advancement toward the Chin and Khwarazm empires are estimated conservatively at 270,000.[21] Even areas subjugated by force could not be counted on: Xi-Xia rulers refused to provide auxiliary troops to Genghis Khan during his decisive campaigns against the Chin and Khwarazm, and the Naimans and Keraits posed a constant threat, forcing Genghis Khan to leave a contingent of 2,000-3,000 scouts and more than 20,000 troops in his rear guard before advancing on China in 1211.[22] This shows that Genghis Khan invested no trust in the conquered peoples that dared stage armed resistance, yet trust in their political loyalty was what he sought most. Another poignantly telling example was Genghis Khan's campaign against the Merkit tribes, led by Kodu, the brother of Genghis Khan's longstanding enemy, Tokto'a-beki. Genghis Khan ordered that the Merkits be massacred "to the last man." That last man turned out to be Kodu's youngest son, well known to Genghis Khan's generals for his unparalleled skills in archery. None other than Jochi, one of the celebrated "Four Hounds" leading the Mongol army, requested pardon for Kodu's son. But to Genghis Khan the prospect of political disloyalty to the Mongol Empire, however remote, outweighed the prospect of augmenting the capability of the Mongol archers. The Great Khan's reply to Jochi was, "It is for you that I have conquered so many empires and armies. Why do we require him?"[23] Successful campaigns and the suppression of numerous intermediate powers lying between the Mongols, the Chin Empire, and the Sultanate of Khwarazm, while strengthening the Mongol army's morale, discipline and coordination, did little to increase the number of warriors fighting under Genghis Khan's banners.

Geography also posed formidable challenges to any rational decision maker planning to conquer Asia from a base in the Mongolian steppes.[24] The expansion of the Mongol Empire toward China and Central Asia was very sporadic, defying geostrategic common sense. Instead of setting up convenient bases for the first mass offensive against the Chin Empire in the territories conquered between 1206 and 1211, for example, Mongol troops returned all the way to inner Mongolia. In particular, the Tangut territories of Xi-Xia kingdom subjugated in 1209 provided a strategic bridgehead from which the Mongols could attack the Chin, thus obviating the Great Wall, but were not used as such. Instead, after 1209, Mongol forces recrossed 500 miles of the Gobi Desert and had to traverse the same desert in 1211. To reach the points where the Chin forces could be seriously engaged in battle, the Mongol armies had to cover approximately 600 miles. It was possible for the Mongol army to cover this distance in a single march in six to nine days—and then it faced the Great Wall.[25] In addition to transporting 110,000 soldiers across the Gobi Desert, the Mongols also needed to provide food on the march for approximately 330,000 horses (with at least two extra mounts per soldier). Moreover, the entire army would be advancing through barren, arid lands at altitudes of 2,000-5,000 feet—an extraordinary logistic enterprise that would confound any rational decision maker. In Desmond Martin's assessment, provisioning 110,000 men on such a march "would constitute a major commissariat problem" even in the mid-twentieth century.[26]

Geographical obstacles to the Mongol advance on the Sultanate of Khwarazm were even more formidable. From their winter encampment at the foot of the Altai Mountains and the upper Irtysh area, Genghis Khan's army had to cover 900 miles just to reach the outer limits of the sultanate (requiring at least 8-12 days on the march). The Mongols faced approximately

250 miles of the Sary-Ishikotrau desert, 150 miles of the Muyun-Kum desert, and at least 200 miles of rugged terrain in the northern Tien Shan, with mountain ridges 1,000-10,000 feet high.[27]

The Mongol economy—weak, small, and backward by comparison with the economies of the Chin and Khwarazm—hardly improved the odds of overcoming these geographical obstacles and then defeating the larger armies of the key Mongol adversaries. Yet even if one leaves aside the economic dimension of the power balance between the Mongols and their main rivals—if anything, for lack of reliable economic data—a realist, rational actor in Genghis Khan's place should never have pursued a universal empire strategy that relied on capability estimates. Statistically speaking, if the Mongol army and population size were to be weighed against the army and population size of other major powers in Central Asia and China, and the adverse effects of geography considered, the expected probability of a Mongol victory against Xi-Xia in 1209 would stand at about 39 percent, against the Chin Empire in 1211 at about 16 percent, and against the Sultanate of Khwarazm at slightly over 27 percent.[28] Given these considerations, a rational political analyst would conclude that Genghis Khan's aspiration to become a universal ruler was but a megalomaniac's daydream. And yet this "daydream strategy" was adopted and carried out, bringing 40 percent of the world's population under Mongol rule.

The theory I have developed this far suggests that Genghis Khan attached greater weight to such parameters of political power as unity, discipline, obedience, morale, divine support, propensity for surprise, and other factors of direct intention assessment. In this sense, the khan was still a shrewd, power-seeking ruler, but he relied on other types of operands than those presumed by theories grounded in political realism's assumptions about power.

The Sung Factor

At the time of Genghis Khan's ascendance as the supreme ruler of the Mongols, the Sung were far removed from areas in which the Mongol bid for universal empire began to unfold; moreover, naval power was irrelevant to those initial stages of conflict. The Sung did possess a large army with an estimated 504,000 troops in 1206 and did wage war on the Chin in 1206-1208. At the time of the Mongol invasion of North China in 1211, however, the Sung and the Chin had been faithfully pursuing peaceful relations. These well-regulated relations were maintained after the Sung were defeated in 1208, as witnessed by diplomatic exchanges and payments of tribute. Twice a year the Sung and the Chin exchanged envoys bringing salutations for the new year and for royal birthdays. Envoys were also dispatched on some other special occasions, such as a monarch's accession or death, as well as for the collection of the Sung's annual tribute. The perceived interdependence of the Sung and the Chin was evident in the proverbial diplomatic language with which the last Chin emperor appealed for an alliance against the first wave of the Mongol invasions: "We are to you as the lips to the teeth; when the lips are gone the teeth will feel the cold."[29] Nevertheless, I found no evidence of formal military alliances between the Sung and the Chin in the face a Mongol invasion.

For their part, the Mongols had no understanding with the Sung on mutual assistance or noninterference prior to Genghis Khan's first attacks on the Chin in 1211. More than that, official Mongol-Sung contacts before 1233 had been rare, if any, and had been characterized by mistrust on the Sung side. No exchange of envoys took place until 1221-1223, a whole decade after the initial Mongol attack on China. In the view of Charles Peterson, "Early Mongol initiatives to establish relations had been rebuffed by a court which remembered all too well that, almost exactly a century earlier, an alliance with a new barbarian power (the Jurchen) against a common enemy (the Khitan) had resulted in that court's permanent exile to Hang-chou." As late as the 1220s, the Sung refused to allow the Mongol army free passage from the west against the Chin.[30]

In contrast, the Sung still maintained amicable relations with the Chin well *after* the Mongols' first massive invasion of the Chin Empire in 1211. The Sung continued sending regular diplomatic and tribute missions north well into 1214. In 1213, for example, the Sung dispatched all three of their regular diplomatic missions to the Chin: the first conveyed birthday salutations in the sixth month; the second delivered formal congratulation upon accession of the new Chin monarch in the tenth month; and the third delivered new year greetings the same month. The three missions failed to reach the Chin court for logistical reasons. Nevertheless, attempts to transfer tribute (silver and silk) to the Chin continued into 1214, when, at one point in that year, Sung officials were given no formal receipt *(kuo-shu)* after depositing the funds. Thus, compliance with treaty obligations to the Chin remained the focus of the Sung's northern policy.[31] That is, the Sung economy continued to support the Mongol rivals for three years after war was initiated. Thus, in rational-choice terms, the Sung should have had more use for the Chin, with whom they had trade and diplomatic relations, than for the Mongols, with whom Sung had no treaties or meaningful relations in 1211-1214. The Mongols, for their part, could hardly expect the Sung to weigh in on their side during the North China campaign.

The Northern China Campaign

While taking account of the highly unfavorable balance of military, economic, and demographic capabilities, Genghis Khan conducted thorough direct intention assessments in preparation for his campaigns. These assessments predominantly concerned political unity in the Mongol heartland, domestic political tensions and the state of military command, opportunities for deception and surprise, and the political intentions of intermediary powers, Xi-Xia in particular.

Domestic political priorities subordinated to the universal empire strategy were a powerful factor in Genghis Khan's decision to attack the Chin. The khan was aware that quick military victories and rich spoils were critical to maintaining the support of Mongol tribal leaders, as well as political unity. It was imperative for Genghis Khan to demonstrate that under his leadership, the Mongols could overcome deeply embedded nomadic rivalries that had weakened them in previous decades and put the Mongols effectively under Chin suzerainty. This vassalage over the Mongols extended into the early years of Genghis Khan's rule. A successful campaign against the Chin would therefore avenge past humiliations, enhance national unity, and solidify support for Genghis Khan's political centralization of the Mongol Empire. The Great Khan also needed frequent campaigns to integrate the soldiers from various tribal backgrounds into the "melting pot" of the newly forged Great *ulus,* thus reducing the potential for internal strife.[32]

Evidence suggests that Genghis Khan was first advised to attack the Chin even before he assumed power. The information available to Genghis Khan by and large conveyed an image of the Chin Empire as less organized, disciplined, and cohesive than the Mongol Empire. At the same time, to Genghis Khan the Chin appeared more likely to allow internal political dissent to undermine the government. One early recommendation to make war on the Chin came from a Khitan defector, Ila Ahai (Yeh-lu A-hai, in Chinese transcription), in 1206. Prior to entering the khan's service, Ila Ahai had been the Chin envoy to Wang-khan of the Keraits, one of Genghis Khan's major rivals in the wars of unification. Transferred to the court of Genghis Khan, Ila Ahai was impressed by the Mongol ruler at their first meeting and immediately offered his services to the khan as an adviser (hence, de facto, as double agent). To ensure Ila Ahai's loyalty, his brother Tuke was enlisted into the Mongol guard as a hostage. Ila Ahai's intelligence services were valued highly, and he was posthumously granted an honorary title, that of "Loyal Military Duke," by Khubilai Khan.[33] From a military viewpoint, the 1206-1207 period also presented a good window of opportunity to strike at the Chin; at the time, north Chinese leaders had sent 145,000 of their troops against their large southern neighbor, the Sung.

But Genghis Khan preferred to bypass that window of opportunity, at least temporarily: the Chin Empire was still under the rulership of Zhaozong (Madagu), whose military prowess had impressed and intimidated Genghis Khan when he served as a centurion under the Chin against a recalcitrant group of Tatars in 1196. The overall performance of the Chin army gave an unambiguous impression of strength—as was confirmed by the Chin successes of 1207 against the Sung.[34]

Genghis Khan's perception of the Chin power was changing, however. Though he paid his annual tribute tax to the Golden Khan of Chin China in 1208, the Mongol emperor staged no customary ceremony of deference. In that year Genghis Khan also received direct evidence that the Chin ruler was reluctant to use military force against the Mongols. Moreover, four senior Chin officials—Li Zhao, Wu Fengchen, Bai Lun, and Tian Guangming—defected to the Mongols. The defectors had urged the Chin emperor to suppress the expanding Mongol Empire by force; in response, the emperor had sentenced them to one hundred strokes. Appearing at Genghis Khan's court—their very defection being a potent symbol of political discord at the highest levels of the Chin government—these officials advised the Mongol ruler to attack their former master.[35]

Around 1206, important information about potential social unrest among some large tribal units subordinate to the Chin emperor reached Genghis Khan. According to the official history of the Yuan China, *Yuanshi,* a delegation from Liaodong (in southern Manchuria) "informed Genghis Khan of the despotism and cruelty of the Chin ruler." Hearing this petition, Genghis Khan decided "to bring the emperor to justice" in due course.[36]

The Mongols also received reliable information about political discord and rivalry between the Chin emperor and the rulers of his provinces.[37] Of particular strategic importance were the political intentions of the Ongut. This people had settled just to the south of the Gobi Desert and controlled the *Wai pao,* the addition to the Great Wall that the Chin had erected along the edge of southern Mongolian grasslands late in the twelfth century. The nomads referred to it as *Ongu.* The name *Ongut* therefore referred to those in charge of the new part of the Great Wall, or Ongu.

Between 1204 and 1211 the Ongut had conflicting loyalties. On the one hand, they were in a special treaty of tribal intermarriage with the Naimans, who consistently opposed Genghis Khan's drive for Mongol unification. On the other hand, the Ongut had also achieved peace with Genghis Khan. Above all, the Ongut were under the suzerainty of Chin China. After 1207, Ongut allegiances shifted decisively in the Mongols' favor. In that year, the Juyin peoples—who included the majority of and, possibly, all of the Onguts—staged an uprising that distanced the local rulers from the Chin and made the Mongols' political influence paramount in the Sino-Mongolian border zone. By 1211, the Ongut emirs were leaning toward the party of Alakush-Tagin, who regarded Genghis Khan as a political and military genius. With Alakush-Tagin in charge of the Ongut, the Mongols had a reliable friend at the most vulnerable area along the Great Wall. Alakush-Tagin later allowed Mongol troops through the wall and placed a corps of auxiliaries under Genghis Khan's command.[38] Genghis Khan regularly received intelligence about these propitious shifts in Ongut political leadership from special merchant-envoys, such as Chingai (Cinqai) and Hasan. Chingai's role in supplying this kind of political intelligence to Genghis Khan was noted in the *Meng-ta pei-lu,* the major Chinese chronicle, of 1221: "Now there was an Uighur by surname T'ien [in some Chinese sources this surname is prefixed to Chingai's name]. He was very rich and made enormous profits from trade. He travelled back and forth in Shantung and Ho-pei, and provided detailed information (to the Tatars [Ta' ta as Mongols were known in China]) about the people and things (of the area). Together with the Juyin (people) he persuaded the Tatars to raise an army and enter the frontiers to raid. Temujin was angered by the (Chin) oppression and thus violated the frontiers. The (Chin) prefectures along the border were all destroyed."[39]

Chinese sources suggest that Genghis Khan could also count on support from the country of the Upper Liao Ho, which had a history of unsuccessful rebellions against the Chin. Genghis Khan correctly estimated the political intentions of anti-Chin leaders in Liaodong as well, from which he received a delegation in 1206. Later in the campaign Genghis Khan obtained valuable help from this province, where a member of the former Khitan royal family, Ila Liuge (Yeh-lu Liu-ke), put together an anti-Chin rebel force of 100,000, joined forces with the invading Mongols, and struck successfully against the Chin in spring 1212.[40]

Loyalty assurances from the two major intermediary powers to the south and east of the Mongols—the kingdom of Xi-Xia and the Uighurs—were another major factor in the timing of Genghis Khan's campaign against the Chin. Alliances with those two powers had at best a marginal impact on the balance of military capabilities between the Mongols and the Chin. The Tangut from (Xi-Xia) refused to provide auxiliary troops to Genghis Khan and instead supplied camels with herders, woolen and silk goods, and falcons trained for the hunt. The Tangut ruler explained his decision diplomatically: "The Tangut people are ready to serve as your right hand and share with you our forces. But what can we give you? We do not migrate far from our dwellings [i.e., we are a sedentary society] . . . we will not be able to catch up with you on fast marches or stand up to an enemy in a heated battle."[41] The implied message was that the vengeance with which the Tangut fought the Mongol invasion of 1209 would fail to work in promoting Genghis Khan's conquests. Yet the statement of loyalty, backed up by rich tribute and by the gift of one of the Tangut leader's daughters as a wife to Genghis Khan, proved a sufficient token of the Xi-Xia intention to submit. The khan thus could discount the danger of a Xi-Xia attack on his army's flanks or rear and, more importantly, the disastrous prospects for Mongol political unity should such a treachery be attempted. In 1209-1211 Genghis Khan also accepted an offer of suzerainty over the Uighurs—the first people outside the Mongol nation who voluntarily acknowledged Genghis Khan's rule. To test the firmness of the political intentions of the Uighur leader, the *idikut,* Genghis Khan insisted that he must come personally before him, "bringing gold and silver, small and large pearls, brocade, damask and silks." For his part, Genghis Khan gave his daughter, Altun, in marriage to the Uighur ruler.[42]

In addition to receiving reports of questionable loyalties to the Chin emperor on the part of several strategically crucial borderline provinces and to his perception of the Chin emperor as incapable of governing, Genghis Khan received intelligence on serious deficiencies in the cohesiveness of the Chin army. The defection of several top-ranking Chin officials to the Mongols in 1208 enhanced the khan's perception that political loyalty, coordination, organization, and subordination were causing major problems in the top echelons of the Chin government and the armed forces. Information about the firmness of political control over the adversary's army was especially highly valued and acted upon by Genghis Khan. For this reason, Genghis Khan's order for an advance on the Chin troops at Huan-erh-Tsui early in the Chin campaign came immediately after he received a report claiming that the enemy appeared disorganized and incapable of coordinated military action. The report had come from Chakhan, one of Genghis Khan's key agents with the Chin. As noted earlier, Genghis Khan was aware of and impressed by the superior size and equipment of the Chin army. Therefore, Chakhan's information on the lack of organization among the Chin outweighed information on their numerical strength. The General Chinese History *(Gan'-mu)*, in explaining Genghis Khan's subsequent rout of the superior Chin armies, provides insight into the kind of reports Genghis Khan received on the state of command and control in the Chin army: "The [Chin] Sovereign deviated from the correct principles of command. . . . The rules of military science required selection of an old and experienced leader. But to field a four hundred thousand strong army without unified control and to entrust this army to people who are weak in spirits—would not that pave the way to defeat? What else could be the cause for an utter thrashing of 400,000 cavalry and infantry?"[43]

In planning for world conquest, Genghis Khan also counted on the effective use of surprise and deception. Information about an impending attack was supplied to known Mongol sympathizers among the Jurchen, such as Ila Nieers, who had assembled forces to take revenge upon Chin rulers and upon the sinicized upper classes in the provinces. Later, Genghis Khan appointed Ila Nieers general of his home area of Jizhou. The Mongols routinely spread rumors vastly overstating their numbers in order to sow panic and disunity among the enemy, including the Chin. A specific example occurred some years later, prior to the invasion of the Sung in 1258, when Mongke Khan claimed that his 40,000 force was 100,000 strong. The pattern for this type of disinformation tactic was well established in the early Mongol campaigns. Other standard deception techniques factored into the Mongol strategic calculus included extending the main body of the army in a single line; using shock troops for ambushes; whipping up clouds of dust to enshroud the army's flanks and secretly envelop enemy formations; using "storms of arrows" tactics; putting stuffed dummies on spare horses; lighting five fires per soldier at night; leaving the fires burning when changing location at night; and various types of feigned retreats.[44] Firmly in control of and constantly practicing this repertoire of techniques, Genghis Khan received implicit validation of the Mongol's superiority in coordinated military operations over the more numerous and advanced armies of his opponents.

Mongol strategists led by Genghis Khan also saw an opportunity to start a campaign against the Chin after the death of Emperor Zhaozong (Madagu) in 1210. According to *Yuan-shi*, the new emperor, Yunji, a former prince of Wei, sent an ambassador to Genghis Khan with news of his accession to the throne, demanding that the old Chin suzerainty over the Mongols be confirmed and that the khan formally kowtow to the ambassador. After receiving this message, *Gan'-mu* tells us: "Genghis Khan asked the ambassador who the new Sovereign was. 'Prince Yunji,' responded the ambassador. Genghis Khan immediately turned his face south, spat and said: 'I thought that some kind of an extraordinary person ascended to the throne of Zhung-Yuan; how could that imbecile be a ruler? He does not deserve obedience.'" Having spoken, Genghis Khan mounted his horse and rode off.[45] This was a direct challenge to Chin political authority in the region.

Belief in divine support for the 1211 campaign against the Chin also figured strongly in Genghis Khan's decision. The Great Khan's appeal to the heavenly powers was linked to avenging the blood of his relatives and also eliminating the Chin as a source of internecine rivalries among the Mongols. Rashid ad-Din reports that orders to advance were given after Genghis Khan withdrew to the top of a hill, untied his belt, put it over his neck, untied the ribbons on his vest *(kaba),* went down on his knees, and said: "Oh, Eternal Heaven, you know and understand that Altan-Khan[46] was the wind which [fanned] the tumult, that it was he who began the quarrel. He executed, without cause, Okin-barkak and Khambakai-khan who had been captured and delivered to him by the Tartar tribes. And these were the elder relatives of my father and grandfather and I seek to repay for their blood, but only as a revenge [for them]."[47]

Juzjani provides important circumstantial evidence on the role of spiritual considerations in Mongol strategy. According to Juzjani, Genghis Khan communed with the Eternal Heaven in a felt tent for three days. He issued orders to Mongol families to spend three days and three nights bareheaded and fasting.[48] The spiritual factor overshadowed material considerations, such as feeding the Mongol army. For example, the three days of fasting were ordered just before the army had to cross 500 miles of the Gobi Desert. This crossing took more than a week of strenuous riding, with the army subsisting on extremely meager rations and no supplies awaiting them after the crossing.

The divine factor had also an important symbolic value, since most Mongols linked the selection of Genghis Khan as their leader at the 1206 assembly with the idea of heavenly predestination. In this sense, religious ideas were tied to the core principles of Mongol unity, autocratic rule, and universal empire.[49]

In 1211 Genghis Khan was facing a monumental dilemma. On the one hand, the political situation in and around the Chin Empire was extremely advantageous—a society increasingly dissatisfied with its rulers' oppression; the empire's ethnic and tribal patchwork quilt was coming apart at the seams; an army command increasingly incapacitated by political discord and bad appointments; a new emperor considered an imbecile; elites that still harbored a perception of insecurity about the southern frontier, where campaigns against the Sung had been waged in 1206-1208; rebellions rising in the provinces; and the Tangut plundering the northwestern frontier zone. On the other hand, the Chin army was numerically superior and better supplied, Chin army reserves were virtually inexhaustible, and economic resources were essentially limitless in comparison to the Mongols. Facing Genghis Khan's main force of about 90,000 and Ongut auxiliaries numbering about 10,000 was the Chin army, which had a nominal strength of 600,000, including 120,000 imperial cavalry—warriors equal to the Mongol mounted archers.[50]

This situation was a perfect case of asymmetric threat (or opportunity) assessment. The decision to invade the Chin thus depended on Genghis Khan weighing favorable but unquantifiable political factors on which he had detailed and trusted intelligence against unfavorable but quantifiable military capabilities on which specific intelligence was most probably lacking. A decision to go to war in this situation would be a gamble. In the end, the assessment of political intentions carried greater weight with the Mongol leader, who saw the unstoppable expansion of the Mongol realm as critical to his very survival in power. Estimating that the tide of political allegiances in the Sino-Mongolian frontier zone—and much deeper in the Chin Empire—was in his favor, Genghis Khan seized the opportunity, took the gamble, and won. Rather than waiting until the balance of military power shifted in his favor, Genghis Khan forced momentous geopolitical shifts in Eurasia by striking first against militarily superior but politically vulnerable opponents. According to Rashid ad-Din, Genghis Khan's resounding victories over the Golden Khan of Chin China were primarily due to "adherence to the right cause and correct intentions."[51]

The Central Asia Campaign

Mongol strategy leading to the attack on the Sultanate of Khwarazm in 1219-1221 followed much the same decision blueprint as Mongol strategy against the Chin Empire. Once again, the Mongols faced a superior army drawn from a much larger population in a much more economically potent region. Although the army of the Khwarazm-shah was somewhat less numerous and most likely not as well organized as that of the Chin Empire, the new target of the Mongol conquests was almost 1,000 miles away from Genghis Khan's last home base. Once again, Mongol strategic assessments of threat and opportunity focused predominantly on political unity in the heartland of the Mongol Empire; on the political tensions, the state of military command, and the tensions between secular and religious leaders affecting the Sultanate of Khwarazm; on the political intentions of smaller, intermediary powers; and on opportunities for deception and surprise. In the end, as in the case of the Chin invasion, Genghis Khan took the gamble, counting on political advantages to outweigh inferior military capabilities and the formidable geologistics of the Central Asian invasion.

Attention to sources of discord among the Khwarazmian elite was highest on the list of intelligence collection targets of Genghis Khan's Central Asian sources. This intelligence collection was conducted through an increasing number of Muslim merchants and craftsmen who found permanent employment under the tribal nobility of the Mongols. These merchant-spies were assigned intelligence targets before setting out on trade missions and then were personally debriefed by Genghis Khan upon their return. According to the Russian historians Grekov and Yakubovsky, Genghis Khan obtained "a considerable amount of spy reports from the Muslim merchants about the states and principalities of the Central Asia and Near East, as well as valuable assistance in the struggles he waged outside Mongolia against various enemies." Merchants reporting to Genghis Khan had diverse connections in high places, covering both the court of the Khwarazmian ruler, the shah, and his emirs, feudal lords, and the clergy. High-level political defectors from the shah's court, such as Badr ad-Din al-'Amid, also contributed to Genghis Khan's detailed knowledge of the sultanate's politics. Particular attention was paid by the Mongols to "the disposition [loyalty] of the troops, the morale of the population and the party factions at court."[52]

Those sources informed Genghis Khan of several major fault lines in the politics of the sultanate that would give rise to tensions and open feuds. In February and March 1218 a bitter rivalry erupted between Muhammad and his mother, Turkan-khatun, over royal succession and the administration of territories. The system of dual power had considerably weakened the sultan's capacity to govern. Turkan-khatun had her own court, her own executives, and controlled the governments of provinces, appendages, and fiefs—a bifurcation of authority that Genghis Khan knew from his own experience would undermine the sultanate. Turkan-khatun hated Muhammad's wife, Ai Chichen, and his eldest son, Prince Jalal ad-Din Mangubirti. Turkhan-khatun insisted that the sultan must appoint his youngest son, Qutb ad-Din Uzlagh-shah, as heir to the throne, instead of Jalal ad-Din. This succession crisis was exacerbated in 1218, when Turkan-khatun challenged Muhammad's appointment of Nizam al-Mulk as *wazir* (chief minister) to the royal successor. Given the chief minister's functions, the political rivalry in Khwarazm now centered on political control over the provinces. According to Persian chronicler Nasawi, the two royal administrations—Muhammad's court and Turkan-khatun's court—began to issue contradictory orders on a regular basis. In the ensuing governing crisis, only the most recently dated instructions were obeyed, as the local elite clearly preferred wait-and-see tactics.[53]

The gravity of this feud was revealed in retrospect when the Mongols conquered Khwarazm and Turkan-khatun was captured. Refusing to contemplate escape from Mongol captivity, Turkan-khatun cited her strong hatred of Jalal ad-Din's mother, Ai Chichen: "Even imprisonment by Genghis Khan and my present humiliation and shame are better than that [sharing the royal quarters with Ai Chichen]."[54]

This split at the very top of the power hierarchy had wide scale repercussions. By the late 1210s, Muhammad had the worst of both worlds. While political dissent was on rise, the Khwarazm-shah's capacity to enforce his authority was declining rapidly. Thus, Muhammad had 22 feudal lords in prison at Urgench for obstructing his policies of centralization, but the shah could not bring himself to execute the dissenters, as Genghis Khan doubtless would have done. Furthermore, the Khwarazm-shah never mustered enough courage to depose two of the strongest dissenting vassals, the *atabeks* (provincial rulers) of Fars and Luristan. Even civil servants in regional bureaucracies and the armed corps of Turkish nomadic tribes, who had always strongly supported power centralization, split into two opposing camps.[55]

Muhammad further weakened the administration of the provinces by transferring the duties of the imperial *wazir* (chief minister) to a college of six *wakils* (high officials) of the court. This new arrangement meant that any decision required the unanimous support of the *wakils*. Consequently, a longstanding bureaucratic tradition that supported centralized government in the sultanate was challenged, pitting many powerful bureaucrats against the shah, whom they blamed for this reform. The switch to "collective government" also raised discontent among the general population. The commoners, too, regretted the loss of government by a single *wazir*, seeing the new arrangement as both less efficient and more open to corruption. However arbitrary and unjust the *wazir* might have been considered in the past, many concluded that "to satisfy one is in any case easier than to satisfy six."[56]

Another fault line of discord ran between the shah and the merchants (including merchants seeking trade with the Mongols), who wanted less government regulation. These disputes alienated critical sectors of the urban population from the Khwarazm-shah, such as common craftsmen and powerful feudal lords who had a stake in commerce. These internal political tensions began to directly affect relations between the Mongols and the sultanate. After the news of the fall of the Chin capital, Zhongdu, to the Mongols in 1215 reached Central Asia, three merchants from Bukhara set out with a caravan to Genghis Khan. The Mongol ruler paid high prices for the merchants' goods and in turn sent a trading caravan to the Khwarazm-shah with an offer of a treaty on mutual trade protection. Genghis Khan offered Shah Muhammad to "ensure the security of the caravan routes from deadly incidents in order that merchants, on whose continual visitations the welfare of the world depends, may move hither and thither with peace at heart."[57] When the caravan arrived in the Central Asian city of Otrar (Utrar), however, the local governor, a cousin of the sultan's mother, Turkan-khatun, informed the shah that the merchant-envoys were on a spy mission and were trying to stir panic among the population. With the permission or, at the very least, tacit approval of the sultan, the merchants were murdered. This development, in addition to provoking Genghis Khan, further alienated many merchants and craftsmen from the Khwarazm-shah. These social groups later helped the invading Mongol army to seize many cities in the sultanate.[58]

Genghis Khan, by contrast, settled the issue of imperial succession by playing the role of a wise, strong monarch and forging a consensus among his sons and chief advisers in favor of Ogodei. The succession was publicly endorsed by the *khuriltai* summoned in 1218. Notably, this general assembly was convened both to approve the choice of Genghis Khan's successor and to announce the campaign against Khwarazm. In addition, Genghis Khan reaffirmed his role as supreme ruler in the expanding Mongol Empire by confirming in person the appointment of commanders of the largest military units—the Ten Thousands (*tumen*), the Thousands, and the Hundreds. After that, Genghis Khan once again "proclaimed among them his own guiding rules [*ain*], the law [*yasa*] and the ancient custom [*yusun*] and then set on a march against the country of Khwarazm-shah."[59]

In further contrast to the Khwarazm-shah's deteriorating capacity to assemble and prepare an army for battle, Genghis Khan personally made sure that the Mongol army sharpened its critical coordination skills and draconian discipline. In summer 1219, Genghis Khan assembled his army on the Black Irtysh, in southwestern Siberia, and carried out a royal hunt to surpass all royal hunts—a series of large-scale *battues,* staged to exercise the army and gather provisions for the western campaign.[60] Successful campaigns in China by that time boosted Genghis Khan's trust in the superior physical condition of his troops and especially their capacity for lightning-fast marches over long distances.

Discord among the ruling elite in Khwarazm, coupled with bureaucratic ambivalence, prevented the shah from exercising effective control over defense—vulnerabilities of which Genghis Khan was keenly aware. Upon learning of the Mongol conquest of Zhongdu, Muhammad started preparing for war with the Mongols. In 1217, the sultan collected the nationwide mobilization levy *(rusum)* for 1219 (two years in advance) and ordered payment of the land tax *(kharaj)* ahead of schedule to finance the construction of an 80-kilometer wall around Samarkand. Neither the wall nor mass mobilization could be completed in time for the Mongol invasion—the former, through bureaucratic inefficiency, and the latter, due to Muhammad's fear for his political future. Upon hearing the news of Genghis Khan's advance, the sultan dispersed what the chronicles called "an incredibly multitudinous army" among the military garrisons in Maverannakhr.[61] According to Grekov and Yakubovsky, "Muhammad the Khwarazm-shah could not muster courage to allow for a large concentration of troops in one place, fearing the military chiefs. He had good grounds to believe that the latter could turn their arms against him. That is why he never fielded a large army that would engage the main forces of Genghis Khan in a decisive battle. The khan therefore had the opportunity to demolish the enemy forces piecemeal, concentrating the troops where he saw it as more advantageous. . . . Bukhara, Samarkand, Merv, Urgench, and other cities of Central Asia were taken one by one due to poor coordination of defense."[62]

Genghis Khan was most likely informed by his last envoy to Khwarazm that Muhammad had rejected the earlier advice of Imam Shihab ad-Din Khiwaqi to confront the khan in a major battle on the bank of the Syr-Darya River—before the Mongols could recover from their extended march across the mountains. The imam recommended that the sultan should seize the advantage of pitting a numerically superior, well-equipped, and fresh force against the Mongols.[63] The Khwarazm-shah feared, however, that a victory against Genghis Khan would strengthen the hand of the military aristocracy dominated by members of the Turkic tribe of Kankalis. This was precisely the tribe to which Muhammad's mother (and key political rival), Turkan-khatun, belonged. Muhammad was therefore rightly afraid that the concentration of forces would eventually strengthen the hand of his dynasty's principal political rivals.[64] As Barthold has aptly observed, the sultan "could only have assembled his forces in one place if they had been as docile an instrument in his hands as was the Mongol army in those of Genghis Khan."[65] But the Khwarazm-shah had no such power. Exacerbating these problems were the personal character weaknesses of Shah Muhammad, of which Genghis Khan was well informed.

Genghis Khan also restated his claim to divine authority for running the empire and directing the Mongol campaigns of conquest at the 1219 *khuriltai*. Great attention was paid to averting discord on religious grounds in the diverse regions of the Mongols' expanding dominion. Freedom of religious worship was granted to local inhabitants as long as they pledged not to challenge the supreme authority of the universal ruler. The relative absence of religious feuds achieved as a result of this policy contrasted sharply with the deep-seated and violent religious conflicts that were tearing apart the Khwarazmian sultanate. These disputes were made worse by an act of political violence. In 1216 the Khwarazm-shah, in a fit of anger he later regretted, ordered the execution of the popular sheikh Majd ad-Din Baghdadi. This act greatly offended Turkan-khatun, the Sufi Muslim priesthood, and the population at large. Testifying to the political significance of the Sufi saints in Khwarazm is the fact that some of them, such as Hakimata and Ahmad Yasawi, were revered by common people in parts of Central Asia up to the twentieth century. Muhammad's discontent with the sheikh can be partly explained by the warning he got from some Khwarazmian officials that the priests were winning greater influence over the general public.[66]

It is not established whether Genghis Khan knew about this event, but given the quality of the available sources in Central Asia, the regularity of reports, and the widespread popularity of Majd ad-Din, Genghis Khan was unlikely to be entirely unaware of the story. The khan certainly knew about the hostile relationship between the Khwarazm-shah and the caliph an-Nasir of Baghdad. After dazzling military successes earlier in the century, the sultan claimed the prerogative to act as supreme spiritual leader of all Muslims, relegating the caliph to a more ceremonial role, and administering a new position of Imam-caliph above that of an-Nasir. This news reached Genghis Khan because the caliph (most likely in 1217) dispatched envoys to the Naimans and the Mongols, seeking military support against Muhammad. More importantly, Genghis Khan's Islamic advisers duly informed the khan of the political consequences of this feud: Muhammad could no longer proclaim a holy war that would have united his vast and diverse provinces against an invasion by infidels.[67]

The intentions of intermediate powers, from Xi-Xia (Tangut) to the Kara-Khitai, were factored into Genghis Khan's strategic estimates predominantly in terms of their impact on the internal cohesion of the Mongol Empire. The 1218 campaign against the *Gurkhan* ("universal ruler") of the Kara-Khitans, Kuchlug, was undertaken to eradicate the last rallying point for the Naiman rebels who had threatened Genghis Khan's hold on power from the very beginning of the Mongol Empire. At that time, the khan was not concerned with using the area as a springboard for his war on Khwarazm. But by defeating Kuchlug—a "Buddhist neophyte," in the words of Ratchnevsky—Genghis Khan came to be regarded as a liberator of the local Muslims against religious encroachment and high taxes.[68]

Auxiliary contingents from Han and Khitan subjects in China, the *idikut* of the Uighurs, Arslan-khan in the Kayalag, and King Suktak-beki of Almalik did not significantly augment the numbers of the Mongol expeditionary force in Central Asia. The size of this force is assessed by military historians to have been around 140,000 at the maximum and most probably under 100,000 for any major battle.[69] Based on Juzjani's account, it is unlikely that any of these auxiliary contingents exceeded 6,000.[70] At the same time, Genghis Khan could not employ the 60,000-strong forces of the left wing kept in China under Mukali to suppress the Jurchen resistance.[71] As in the case of the campaign against the Chin in 1211, the state of Xi-Xia, which could draft 125,000 men (see chapter 2), refused the Mongol request for additional troops. The message from the ruler of Xi-Xia to Genghis Khan was: "If you do not have enough troops, you have no business being a Khan!"[72]

Genghis Khan skillfully exploited rivalries, suspicions, and animosities within the Khwarazmian polity by spreading false information, further weakening the sultanate's capacity to resist the Mongol invasion. Perhaps the most significant use of deception was the attempt to capitalize on the feud between the sultan and his mother. Chamberlain Danishmand was dispatched by Genghis Khan to Turkan-khatun with an offer of defection. The message read: "You know how dishonorably your son has dealt with your rights. I am now, with the consent of several of his emirs, taking field against him, but I shall not attack your possessions. If you accept this offer, send someone to me who will reassure you [that you can rely upon my word] and we will then cede to you Khwarazm, Khorassan and the parts of [territories] which lie on this side of Amu-Darya."[73] This dispatch was preceded by a message informing the Khwarazm-shah of the planned campaign, which did not fail to raise tensions among the sultan's and the Queen Mother's factions.

After the fall of Samarkand in March 1220, Genghis Khan exploited the shah's mistrust of his generals who were ethnically related to the Queen Mother (who was of the Turkish Kankalis tribe), by arranging the delivery of forged letters to the shah. This was done on the advice of the defector Badr ad-Din al-'Amid, whose father, uncle, and a number of cousins had been murdered for religious dissent, and who was thus acutely aware of the full scope of discord at the top echelons of government in Khwarazm. Ostensibly written by Turkan-khatun's emirs to offer their services to Genghis Khan, the letters were presented to Muhammad by a member of Genghis Khan's entourage who pretended to be a defector. He succeeded in convincing the shah that a considerable part of his army was plotting a coup. As a result, Muhammad abandoned resistance to the Mongols in the east, where the Amu-Darya River would have greatly helped him impede the Mongol advance, and moved west to raise a new army in Persian Iraq. In this way, he passed up a chance to concentrate his forces and stall Genghis Khan's invasion.[74]

Genghis Khan also directed skillful propaganda campaigns against the peoples of Central Asia, promising mercy in return for quick submission and portraying himself as a champion of religious tolerance, lower taxes, and trans-Asian commerce. Most cities that submitted without resistance were spared destruction and pillage, and received a copy of Genghis Khan's proclamation and a special seal (*al-tamgha*).[75] The diverse deception and surprise tactics of the Chin campaign were also employed.

In the end, as was the case with the Chin Empire, the threat and opportunity assessment for the massive military attack on the Sultanate of Khwarazm presented Genghis Khan with a dilemma: were internal political tensions in the sultanate strong enough to compensate for the Mongols' inferior military and economic capacity? Ultimately, threat assessment was derived not from the balance of military strength nor from the balance of political vulnerabilities, taken separately. Rather, these assessments were derived from the "balance of balances": Genghis Khan struck after calculating that the political vulnerabilities of Khwarazm were more serious than the military vulnerabilities of the Mongols.

Threat Assessment Preferences: Inside Mongol Decision Making

Mongol leaders were aware that the distribution of military and economic capabilities in Eurasia did not favor them. As the supreme ruler of the empire, Genghis Khan made efforts to procure information about the material capabilities of his potential adversaries. After the decision to attack an adversary was made, "None [of the intelligence reports] were of greater importance [to the Mongols] than those concerning roads, passes, river folds, fortified places, towns and cities, and the military forces to be encountered." It was established, for example, that prior to the invasion of the Chin Empire, detachments of Mongol scouts explored the topography of the Gobi Desert to locate water sources and areas that could be used for grazing. The Mongol army advanced in two groups; both penetrated the Chin territories in places where good grazing was plentiful and the terrain "admirably adapted to Mongol tactics," reflecting the effective work of the scouts. Regarding Khwarazm, it is possible that Genghis Khan's decision to invade was influenced by reports that the sultan had authorized the construction of a new wall around Samarkand.[76]

General Meng Hung, a Chinese contemporary of Genghis Khan, noted that information of this type was discussed and evaluated by top Mongol commanders around the time of major *khuriltais*.[77] Genghis Khan and his generals drew up campaign plans and determined the number of men to be drafted, the number of horses (ranging from two to seven spare mounts to each man), and the amount of supplies needed, which included an estimate of the required number of livestock driven on hoof.[78] After the army of invasion was assembled, Genghis Khan and his top commanders held an inspection to make sure that all the requirements had been met. Troops were counted and horses and equipment checked.[79]

The evidence strongly suggests, however, that Genghis Khan collected the bulk of intelligence on enemy capabilities only after major decisions had been made on the basis of other information. The procurement of intelligence on water sources and grazing in the Gobi Desert is a case in point. The Mongols had to traverse 500-530 miles of dry and barren land, providing water and food for at least 110,000 men and 330,000 horses. Water could be found along the route followed by the Mongols in wells and waterholes, but that supply was inadequate; in their reports to Genghis Khan, the scouts had to estimate the amount of water that could be produced from melted snow found in clay troughs and hollows. This suggests that the scouts were dispatched after the principal decision to cross the desert had been made and that knowing Genghis Khan's disposition, they preferred to provide optimistic estimates. By any account, this type of water supply was risky and unpredictable, and impossible to calculate precisely. Grazing was also found to be poor in those areas at the time of the invasion of the Chin, and no advance supply depots were set for that campaign.[80]

Major Arabic and Chinese sources confirm that the Mongols were so highly motivated in their quest for universal empire that decision makers discounted inferior material capabilities (for example, the number of troops) and serious geographic or meteorological impediments. While preparing to attack the last Chin stronghold in Shan-Tung (Shandong province) during the 1211-1215 campaign, Mukali's son Po-lu (Boru) of Wu-mu-hu was at one point confronted by officers who argued that the mission should be postponed because of the summer heat. Boru summoned the dissenting officers and instructed them, "I have never heard that in the west Genghis Khan deferred an expedition on account of the hot weather; how then can we his subjects remain inactive!" The attack was carried out triumphantly.[81]

This discounting of capability estimates at times had dire consequences and is illustrated vividly by Genghis Khan's neglect in provisioning the Mongol army and providing sanitation. At the spring 1214 siege of Zhongdu, for instance, Genghis Khan had to authorize the killing of some of his own soldiers for food. During the same siege, unsanitary conditions in the Mongol camp caused an outbreak of plague among men and livestock. The Mongols were forced to accept a truce and restore many possessions won during the previous three years. Several other emergencies in which the Mongol army survived by eating human flesh have been recorded. Whatever information the khan had on the Mongols' economic potential also proved cursory and unreliable.[82]

Yet despite these glaring inadequacies in threat assessment, the Mongols carried out their conquest of Eurasia. The Mongol command's faith in their superior resolve to endure physical hardship, as compared to the sedentary civilizations of China and Central Asia, is also recorded in the chronicles. Combined with trust in their own superior system of military command and control, this was often a pivotal factor in strategic considerations. Chinese sources convey an episode in which Mukali, though impressed with the numbers of the Chin army, nevertheless recommended an attack on Chin troops at the decisive battle of Huan-erh-Tsui in 1211. To

Genghis Khan, he said, "The soldiers of the Chin are far more numerous than our own and unless we fight to the utmost we shall be beaten."[83]

In another well-documented case, a Georgian officer serving the Mongols warned his superiors that the Seljuk army they were planning to attack at Kuzadagh in Armenia, in a battle that took place on June 26, 1243, was much larger than their own. The apprehension of the Georgian adviser was confidently brushed aside by the commander Baiju, who remained calm and determined to execute the mission: "You know not the valor of our Mongol people; God has given us the victory, and *we count as nothing the numbers of our enemies;* the more they are the more glorious it is to win and the more plunder we shall secure."[84]

THE FALL OF SUNG CHINA: RATIONAL THREAT ASSESSMENT FAILS

The assessment of the Mongol threat by decision makers in Sung China differed substantially from the Mongols' assessment of opportunities for expansion. Ultimately, the Sung's failure to correctly assess the political intentions of the Mongol rulers resulted in denial and appeasement that left Sung China surprised, ill prepared, and lacking allies in the face of the massive invasion.

As noted in chapter 3, the rationalization of political and economic decision making became a distinct feature of the Sung government and was reinforced in the second half of the twelfth century with fiscal and market management techniques that were increasingly viable in the expanding maritime trade. The replacement of the tribute system with markets and monetization of the economy was conducive to the emergence of a system of policy preferences based on cost-and-benefit analysis. As a result, military spending became increasingly linked to economic resources. In the 1060s, an official estimate revealed that supporting more than 1 million troops in peacetime required 80 percent of the government's entire income. By the 1140s, Sung armed forces were reduced to about 215,000 troops, or more than fivefold by comparison with 1068. According to John W. Haeger, "In the end the Sung became so immersed in the rationalization of affairs and so enamored of the universal convertibility of goods, services and intangible benefits that they even became willing to set a price on war and peace. When they negotiated treaties with the Liao and Chin, whose terms called for subsidies to guarantee freedom from attack, however pragmatic their approach to the problems at hand, the Sung in effect committed the ultimate rationalization: prosperity in the towns and the countryside was used to buy the peace their armies could not win."[85]

The decision to pay tribute to Liao (whose role was later taken by the Chin) exemplifies the rationalization and quantification of threat assessment on the part of the Sung. Sung policy makers estimated that paying tribute would be a much more cost-effective alternative to war. According to their estimates, the amount of tribute required to buy peace from northern tribes accounted for only about 2 percent of Sung revenues and less than 1 percent of the projected costs of military operations.[86]

It is easy to see why, having followed this pattern of buying off the barbarian "Northerners" for more than two hundred years, Sung leaders discounted the magnitude of the threat associated with the rise of Genghis Khan. In a detailed study of Sung reactions to early Mongol invasions of North China, Charles Peterson analyzed practically all references to Mongolian tribes in Chinese sources up to the early thirteenth century. These sources showed "how sparse available information on the Mongols and related tribes was to the native dynasty in the south." Contacts between the Sung court and the Mongols broke down at the beginning of the Northern Sung period (ca. 1030). As Peterson concluded, "Since its establishment [ca. 1160] Southern Sung had virtually no intelligence on that part of the world [Mongolia]," except some general knowledge that an assemblage of peoples existed "out there." Although primary Chinese sources indicate that news of the Mongol campaign against Xi-Xia (1209-1210) reached the Sung court at Huang-chou, as well as that in 1210 an alert against a rumored Mongol invasion was ordered at the Chin capital, specific and accurate information on the Mongols was lacking.[87] In other words, it may be considered well established that Sung decision makers failed to collect and analyze intelligence on the Mongols' intentions and capabilities.

In the absence of specific information, the prevalent patterns of threat assessment by the Sung can be examined by studying an address to the imperial throne by Chen Te-hsiu, a secretary in the Royal Library apparently charged with preparing a report in connection with the invasion of the Chin by the Mongols in 1211. Although the report reveals at best weak factual knowledge of the strategic situation in the north, the rise of the Mongols and the decline of the Chin are defined as part of "the cycle of barbarian fortunes." Indiscriminate references to the Chin and the Mongols as "the slaves" (*lu*) or "the northern slaves" (*pei-lu*) show that the Sung neither considered northern political units as equal opponents nor distinguished between Mongol or Chin strategic proclivities. This analytical framework supports the traditional rationalization by the Sung court of the nature of the northern threat as one that could be easily neutralized with tributes and payoffs. The strategy resulting from this rationalization of threat—proposed by Chen and adopted, for the most part, by the emperor—was to have a military force large enough to deter a rational challenger and to assemble a stock of goods for tribute to buy off such a challenger. The emphasis was on the smooth running of the bureaucratic apparatus and the "proper use of resources." This assessment of the Mongol threat explains why Sung leaders neglected appeals for an alliance on the part of the last Chin emperor and chose instead a traditional strategy of buying off northern aggressors.[88] Genghis Khan's design for universal empire in the *yasa,* as well as the Mongols' distinct political and socioeconomic organization, which helped propel implementation of this grand design, were not factored into the Sung strategic calculus. This lack of understanding of the Mongols' political intentions turned out to be a fatal mistake for the Sung. By the time Sung decision makers grasped the seriousness of the Mongols' political intentions, it was too late to repel the mounted archers charging from the northern steppes. In 1237 this miscalculation was brought home with the massive Mongol invasion and, in a few decades, the Sung Empire ceased to exist.

A decision maker guided by contemporary North American concepts of realism and rationality would be loathe to pursue the strategy of universal expansion of Genghis Khan. The balance of military capabilities and populations, as well as the long stretches of hostile geography the Mongol army had to traverse, suggest that Genghis Khan had less than one chance in six to defeat the Chin Empire and about one chance in four to prevail over the Sultanate of Khwarazm.

Explicitly defying these dire estimates, the Mongols attached a higher value to the assessment of political intentions. Mongol intelligence reports that preceded major strategic decisions focused on such factors as the political loyalty of key members of the enemy elite to the leader; war resolve and the tolerance of the population at large; the state of military discipline and coordination; and relations between secular and religious elites. In the context of strategic deployment in China, commander Baiju's insistence that the Mongols "count as nothing the number of our enemies" underscores Genghis Khan's intelligence priorities. For example, an evaluation of the Chin leader as "an imbecile" who could not run his rich and powerful empire, coupled with the information on Khwarazm-shah's feuds with his powerful mother and the Caliph of Baghdad, made Genghis Khan estimate his own system of political control as vastly superior. Although the

Mongols did not ignore the size of the armies arrayed against them in
China and Central Asia, the direct assessment of political intentions played
a decisive role in strategy selection. These estimates signaled to Genghis
Khan when, where, and how the idea of world conquest could be implemented with the best results. The specific combination of political intention estimates that made the advance against Khwarazm feasible in 1219
was not present in 1206 or 1211; the confluence of political conditions
that opened a window of opportunity for devastating the Chin in 1211
was absent in 1206 or 1208. Each time, Genghis Khan seized the moment,
illustrating the great usefulness of direct intention assessment in strategies
for quick gains. Both the Chin Empire and the Sultanate of Khwarazm
had ample opportunity to crush Genghis Khan's forces in decisive battles,
if only their much more numerous and better-equipped armies had been
concentrated under a unified command and turned against the Mongols.
The Mongol attacks, however, took both adversaries by surprise, and both
failed to assemble their armies against Genghis Khan in the right place and
at the right time. Major primary and secondary sources indicate that Genghis
Khan was aware in both cases that his adversaries lacked the necessary
political authority and administrative nimbleness to assemble forces for a
decisive battle against him. In contrast, the entire Mongol army, as well as
the entire Mongol population, were at the beck and call of the Great Khan
in his pursuit of a universal empire. Strategies to implement this vision
thus emerged from the felt tents of the Mongol commanders and were
forcefully deployed in the battlefields of East and Central Asia.

In contrast to the Sung, the Mongols had no institutions and no system for estimating the costs and benefits of their strategy in a rigorous,
quantitative fashion. Sung rulers knew exactly what percentage of the national income would be required to support an army of whatever size.
They also believed that they knew exactly what percentage of the national
income could buy off potential northern invaders. One may consider, however, what would have happened if the Mongols and the Sung had exchanged methods of threat assessment. In that case, Mongol rulers would
likely have seen that in the long run the universal empire strategy was self-
defeating. These rulers would also have been more likely to anticipate the
famines, destruction, massacres, plagues, and mass impoverishment that
the Mongol conquest brought to many parts of the world and, with painful irony, to the Mongol Empire itself. Sung leaders, in turn, most probably would have had much a greater appreciation for the Mongols'
single-minded determination to implement Genghis Khan's world empire strategy.

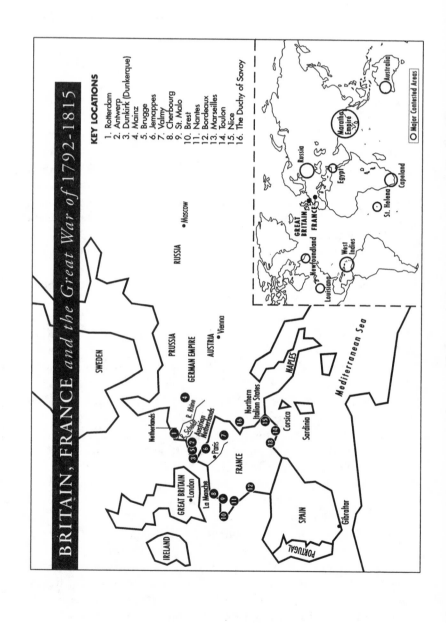

BRITAIN, FRANCE *and the Great War of 1792-1815*

KEY LOCATIONS

1. Rotterdam
2. Antwerp
3. Dunkirk (Dunkerque)
4. Mainz
5. Brugge
6. Jemappes
7. Valmy
8. Cherbourg
9. St. Malo
10. Brest
11. Nantes
12. Bordeaux
13. Marseilles
14. Toulon
15. Nice
16. The Duchy of Savoy

○ Major Contested Areas

Chapter 6

Britain, France, and "The Great War" of 1792–1815

The Great War of 1792–1815, classified by international relations scholars for its magnitude as "general," "hegemonic," "systemic," or "global" war, took Europe by surprise.[1] In the decade leading up to the outbreak of hostilities, occasional conflicts involving the great powers of Europe, such as Britain, France, Prussia, Austria, Spain, and Russia, were seen as isolated quarrels. Among these quarrels were the division of Poland; the rolling back of the Ottoman Empire; the intervention of Britain, France, and Prussia in the "Patriot" party crisis in the Netherlands; and the Anglo-Spanish contest over Nootka Sound off Vancouver. In the aftermath of the 1789 revolution, France's challenge of other major European powers, especially Britain, escalated into twenty years of warfare. These global hostilities spread from Gibraltar to Moscow, and from the Caribbean to the Cape of Good Hope. Time and again, Britain emerged as the main opponent of the French challenge, on the Continent and at sea.[2]

Declarations of war on Austria, Prussia, Britain, and Holland in 1792–1793 at the onset of the Great War made France play against odds that, in Paul Kennedy's estimate, "were more uneven than in *any* preceding war." Yet much like the Mongols under Genghis Khan, France took the gamble. France defied the balance of military and economic power consistently throughout the war—a pattern culminating with Napoleon's militarily disastrous campaign in Russia and with an economically self-defeating continental blockade.[3]

For their part, Great Britain and its anti-French coalitions failed to capitalize in a timely fashion on their military and economic superiority. This was especially apparent in 1793, when troops and resources of the formidable anti-French alliance were not committed to "a direct thrust at the heart of France" weakened by almost four years of political, economic, and social turmoil. As the hostilities increased and France consolidated its power on the Continent, the two powers persisted in their own ways in warfare that led to more than two decades of intensive global conflict— once again resembling what Paul Kennedy alluded to as a struggle between a whale and an elephant, "each by far the largest creature in its own domain."[4]

BRITISH COMPLACENCY:
WHEN SECURITY IS MEASURED IN SHIPS AND GOLD

As the Great War approached, Pitt considered the British strategic position invulnerable and believed that the initial conflicts were only a temporary disturbance of the post-1783 peace. Presenting his budget on February 17, 1792, the prime minister assured Parliament that, given the situation in Europe, England would enjoy peace for fifteen years and, accordingly, proposed cutting 2,000 sailors and 5,000 soldiers. Thus in 1792 the Royal Navy was reduced to 16,000 servicemen, and the regular army was reduced to 18,000. The spending cuts also affected the defense of the colonies. In Jamaica, for example, in early 1792 the garrison was cut back from 1,868 to 800, to the level of the years of peace, 1764-1775.[5]

This assessment conforms to a rational estimate of the military and economic power balance in Europe at the onset of the revolutionary wars. By early 1793, when France declared war on Britain, the British government signed formal treaties of mutual assistance with Austria, Prussia, the Netherlands, Spain, and Russia. Of these countries, the first two were already at war with France. The Netherlands entered the war in February 1793, at the same time as Britain. Russia and Spain were on the sidelines but formally pledged to fight against France. France thus found itself confronted by all the other great powers of Europe, united in what was termed the First Coalition. The odds of France winning a war against this group, even without counting the capabilities of Spain and Russia, were very low. In February 1793, Britain, the Netherlands, Austria, and Prussia could together field an army exceeding that of France by more than three times, and had three times as many warships. These First Coalition powers produced four times as much pig iron and cotton as France and had a total population that was two and one-half times larger. Even after the mass mobilization (*levée en masse*) of summer 1793, this balance remained little changed, except that the French army gained a marginal superiority in size (still only 1.8 percent) over these four members of the First Coalition. With Spain and Russia added to the Coalition, French prospects looked even bleaker. In August 1793, France's army was still only one-third the size of the combined armies of the anti-French alliance. If the balance of these capabilities were relied on, the probability of a rational decision maker launching a war on Britain, the Netherlands, Prussia, and Austria in 1793 would be less than one in three.[6] The odds of France winning with Russia and Spain in the First Coalition would be less than one in four. The paradox is that these same odds, while making Pitt and the British government feel secure allowed the French revolutionary decision makers to see an opportunity for challenging the status quo in battle. In subsequent years this paradox was illustrated by the France's invasion of Ireland: this was attempted not in 1793, when French odds of succeeding in a one-on-one contest with Britain were more than 41 percent, but in 1798, when the odds of winning had dropped to 37 percent.[7]

Even after the British government learned of the coming rupture with France on November 26, 1792, precautionary measures were largely limited to drafting 9,000 naval personnel the following month. The total number of naval servicemen still stood at about half the level of 1790.[8] With respect to long-term strategy, Pitt failed to see how, after three years of internal strife, France could pull itself out of the bankruptcy into which it had sunk during the financial crisis of 1788. The information that Pitt had on the state of France's economy and finances only confirmed the Cabinet's view that France had "neither money, credit, nor government."[9] The foreign secretary, Lord Grenville, wrote to Ambassador Auckland in The Hague, "The security we feel respecting the comparative state of our preparations with those of France . . . is very great indeed."[10] This confidence was based on knowledge of Britain's global sea-power superiority and sound finances, reorganized during the economic and administrative reforms of the 1780s. In a *Times* interview on January 20, 1793, Lord Loughborough, then recently appointed Lord Chancellor, explained the government position:

Pitt saw it [war] was inevitable, and that . . . we were in much greater forwardness than the French. They had only six ships of the line in the Mediterranean—we upwards of twenty; that he had two millions ready, and that he trusted the surplus of the permanent revenue would be 600,000 1. a-year. That the Dutch were quite right, and in earnest; that Russia was willing to go all lengths; that Spain was ready to join, and that all the little Powers only waited our giving the signal.[11]

Other evidence concurs that Pitt placed the calculations of the major European powers' composite military capabilities at the center of strategic threat assessment. Before deciding on a strategy, Pitt took the time to re-view reports by his ministers, painstakingly tallied the numbers of avail-able troops, and calculated military balances.[12] In Lefebvre's opinion, the attention devoted to numbers and calculations was so strong that it some-times thrust Pitt into "a world of dreams." Yet whether Pitt got things right or wrong, the resulting strategies followed the logic of capability-based threat assessment.

Consistent with that logic, intelligence on French military buildup in the Low Countries, including the invasion of Belgium on October 27, 1792, and the reopening of the Scheldt River for navigation, was critical to Britain's estimate of an increasing strategic threat from France.[13] The deci-sive impact that the French buildup in the Low Countries had on threat assessments was conditioned by the long-term association of Britain's strong position in the United Provinces with global leadership. The British sys-tem of government was also associated with Holland through William of Orange and the Constitutional Settlement of 1688-1689. Edmund Burke told the House of Commons on March 29, 1791, that "Holland might justly be considered as necessarily a part of this country as Kent."[14] Accord-ing to T. C. W. Blanning, "When Burke laid claim to Holland as part of England, he was expressing a conviction that was as common as it was deep. It was also well founded. Given their geographical location, if the United Provinces ever fell under the control of a hostile power, then British commerce, British prosperity and British security would all be in jeopardy. Once that threat appeared, then even the most land-locked booby squire roused himself to take an interest in continental affairs."[15]

The British foreign secretary, Lord Grenville, also addressed the long-term significance of this position by sending a warning to the French Na-tional Convention in December 1792: "This [British] government, *adhering to the maxims which it has followed for more than a century* [emphasis added], will also never see with indifference, that France shall make herself, either directly or indirectly, sovereign of the Low Countries, or general arbitress of the rights and liberties of Europe."[16]

The reopening of the Scheldt River in Belgium by an invading French naval squadron in early December 1792 was concrete evidence of France's threat to the long-term interests of Britain and Holland. The Scheldt had been closed under the Treaty of Westphalia (1648), a condition that Britain regarded as essential for its commercial and naval leadership, as well as for the maintenance of a network of treaties underlying the leadership status quo. The reaction from London was unequivocal. In a statement to the National Convention issued on December 27, 1792, barely more than a month before France declared war, Grenville wrote: "England never will consent that France shall arrogate the power of annulling at her pleasure, and under the pretence of a pretended natural right, of which she makes herself the only judge, the political system of Europe, established by solemn treaties, and guaranteed by the consent of all the powers."[17]

In October 1792 Pitt's government considered the degree of the threat and possible British responses. Significantly, chief British decision makers concluded that the most potent indicator would be the France's annexation of Belgium. In Pitt's view, such a move by France—as opposed to any kind of feisty revolutionary proclamations—should automatically activate Britain's entry into war on the Continent.[18] The four major considerations were the geographic proximity of Belgium to the British Isles, the capacity of Belgian ports to handle concentration of naval power, the French naval capacity for potential deployment at Belgian ports, and the opening of the Scheldt River by France, enabling an increased delivery of supplies to the port of Antwerp. All these factors relate to tangible naval capabilities and the impact of their distribution on Britain's control of major sea routes, security, and global trade—a perfect case of capability-based threat assessment.[19]

The British government's view that the war threat was increasing was distinctly linked to a combination of French military advances and a propaganda decree issued in November 19, 1792. Adopted in response to an appeal for help from the supporters of the French Revolution in the German duchy of Zweibrucken, this decree pledged to lend "fraternity and assistance" to all peoples who wished to gain liberty from monarchical rule. At the forefront of those seeking to qualify for French military assistance were the supporters of revolutionary activist groups, such as the ones led by Cloots in Holland, or by Bayonne, Marchena, and Hevia in Spain. That the propaganda decree promised military assistance to specific groups threatening to topple the governments of Holland and Spain signaled to Britain that France was ready to launch its expansionist strategy. The prospect of French control over the maritime capabilities of the United Provinces and Spain directly threatened British sea power. Although the November 19 decree was only one in a series of official pronouncements of France's expansionist intentions, the direct linkage it implied between the forced annexation of territories in Belgium and Holland and domestic political groups supporting the French revolution raised the level of the estimated strategic threat to Britain. Whitehall became further alarmed when tangible evidence of French territorial expansion became available— barely a week after the decree was passed. On November 27, France annexed the Duchy of Savoy and began requisitioning the property of wealthy citizens in Belgian cities and in the countryside. These operations in Belgium were supervised by Danton's *commissaires* who, protected by French bayonets, declared "war on the castles, peace to cottages!"[20]

Indicators of threat based on less tangible aspects of power were also present in Britain's selection of strategy toward France, but these were mitigated by material considerations and therefore failed to thrust Whitehall into panic. Indeed, the British government regularly monitored specific indicators of rising domestic political resistance inspired by the French Revolution, such as the rapidly increasing membership in radical societies in the first half of 1792; sales of a cheap edition of Tom Paine's *The Rights of Man;* the Irish rebellion and the public celebration in Scotland of French military victories in autumn 1792; and the reception by the French envoy, Chauvelin, in November 1792, of deputations from the Norwich Revolution Society, the Manchester Constitutional Society, the London Independent Whigs, and the London Corresponding Society.[21]

Yet even while proposing measures in Parliament to restrict freedom of assembly, speech, and association, the British government was cautiously optimistic. The popularity of French revolutionary ideas, as measured by these specific indicators, was deemed limited and the foundations of the political establishment secure. Pitt and his ministers shrewdly associated the growing popular protest with a mightier cause than "Continental lunacy": after a typical British summer in 1792, the country was "in a vortex of mud, clay, and water," with poor harvests contributing to soaring prices, a fall in trade, and a rapidly increasing number of bankruptcies. Correspondence among the leading members of the British government at the time suggests that they were confident of the essential loyalty of the British public to their political establishment and their private property. Lord

Auckland, writing in confidence to Sir Robert Murray Keith, the British ambassador in Vienna, expressed the government's confidence in domestic public support: "The bulk—under which word I comprise *nineteen-twentieths* of this nation, is contented and decidedly anti-Gallican; and against all levelling or innovating ideas, and duly and fully sensible of their own unexampled prosperity. With such materials, and so vigilant a government, I feel no uneasiness, though the times are *very mad.*"[22]

Maintaining popular confidence in political stability after the bad harvest of 1792 required additional measures: the key instrument was the Association for the Preservation of Liberty and Property against Republicans and Levellers (APLP). Founded by a police official, John Reeves, on November 20, 1792, and sponsored by the government, the association's task was to disrupt radical meetings and publications and to assist authorities in the prosecution of sedition, in particular that associated with riots and royalist propaganda. Though planted by the government, the APLP grew quickly, a seed sown in the fertile soil of supportive public opinion. Just after it was established, the APLP enjoyed an outburst of grassroots support and its ranks swelled, greatly outpacing those of the pro-French radical societies nationwide. Within ten days, the APLP had a branch in every parish in London and was spreading to other parts of the country. About 2,000 branches were soon established. A great number of other loyalist and Gallophobic associations emerged, opening the floodgates of national sentiment seeking to avenge France's success in helping Britain's American colonies gain independence a decade before. The stunning success of these associations and their rapid proliferation gave the British government a direct quantitative measure of the public's loyalty.[23] This indicator had also escaped the attention of French intelligence and decision makers.

Thus, at both the military and political levels, the assessment of the French strategic threat was conducted along the lines of what one author described as "a characteristically British obsession with property."[24] Unlike French revolutionary assemblies and committees, proceedings in the British Parliament were more decorous, less demagogic, and further removed from populist passions. William Pitt demonstrated consistently that speeches and policies well grounded in level-headed, factual estimates had the best chance of carrying the "aye" vote. Within this context, Pitt presented his war strategy against France as one aimed primarily at offsetting French military gains in geographic locations deemed vital to Britain's naval and commercial interests worldwide and, consequently, to the well-being of the proverbial English "booby squire." A consistent focus on material interests and on defining political issues in terms of property proved successful for Pitt within the context of the British Parliament: not only did his motions win approval, but in the course of debates the Whig opposition, led by Charles Fox, a sympathizer of the French Revolution, split. The more ardent of the France-friendly Foxites were increasingly marginalized. By adopting a war strategy proportionate to specific French threats affecting British material interests, Pitt relied on the resolute support of the great majority of the propertied classes, whose interests underlay the political and economic structure in Britain and were anchored firmly in almost a century of global leadership.[25] The security of the Low Countries and the closure of the port of Antwerp were linked to the emergence and endurance of Britain's naval and commercial superiority. The evolution of Britain's global leadership strategy included fighting major wars on these same issues at the start of the One Hundred Years' War against France, against Spain in 1585-1609, against Louis XIV, and once again in 1914 and 1940.[26]

This logic fit well with the traditional "British way in warfare," which minimized continental commitments and emphasized global reach capabilities, financial support of French adversaries, and the accumulation of colonies, while envisaging a short and successful war. For Britain, the priority of naval preponderance and commerce management worldwide, coupled with a popular drive for budget economies, the gradually rising legislative power of the purse, and the constraints of due process on decision making established a context favoring intelligence on tangible capabilities, quantitative analysis, and a naval/global focus. In this manner, a combination of global and domestic conditions favoring Britain's claim to global leadership in the late eighteenth century was generally conducive to rational capability-based assessments of strategic threats and opportunities.

THE FRENCH CHALLENGE:
"WE NO LONGER COUNT THE NUMBER OF OUR ENEMIES"

France's strategy for war against Britain and its European allies was constructed out of several information streams, in which comprehensive assessments of army and naval strength and economic factors were relegated to a secondary role. Assessments of France's own military and economic capabilities, as I have shown, emphasized the superior mobilization and the resolve to fight of a revolutionary nation-at-arms, as well as the prospects for industrial growth in the wake of abolishing the "feudalist rubbish." It was taken for granted, as Kersaint proudly stated in his keynote address preceding the declaration of war, that France's potential, drawn from the energy of a liberated and united nation, would be "infinitely greater than any expenses" and that France would instantly mobilize as many soldiers as were required for victory.[27] Consequently, the critical intelligence sought by French policy makers concerned the revolutionary loyalty of the army and the navy, support for the French Revolution in major European states, the political intentions and conspiracies of the European monarchies, and the prospects for strategic surprise.

The leading politicians at the National Convention in late 1792 and early 1793 argued passionately for a grand strategy based on revolutionary idealism. In the rising spirit of nationalism, every Frenchman was seen as a potential soldier. Estimates of the potential size of the French army ran from Philippe-Jacques Ruhl's 4 million to Jacques-Pierre Brissot's 6 million, whereas Charles Charlier counted every single inhabitant: "What is the army? It is the entire population." French military capabilities never achieved these astronomical levels; even at the peak of revolutionary mobilization in August 1793, according to the war ministry, the size of the French army was 732,474. The fantastic and unsubstantiated projections of army's size that underlay the war strategy were based in great part on the elite view of rising nationalism as a uniquely French power multiplier. When Brissot called for war on England at the Convention on January 12, 1793, the gap between reality and idealistic rhetoric was as wide as at the time of his famous speech in December 29, 1791. The deputies supported him no less enthusiastically, neglecting the estimates of tangible military capabilities: "I do not compare here our military forces with those of our secret and avowed enemies: if we want to remain free, we should ask, as the Spartans did, *where* are our enemies, not how many are there of them (Applause). . . . And where is the power on earth, where is the Genghis Khan, where is the Tamerlaine, even with clouds of slaves in his train, who could hope to master six million free soldiers?"[28]

Characteristically, the debate at the Convention on the organization of the army for war focused on intangibles, such as the unity, energy, discipline, resolve, and heroism of the French military forces. Of the several plans submitted for army reorganization, the blueprint advanced by the Military Committee chairman, Edmond Dubois-Crancé, was selected. Central to this plan was the amalgamation of the volunteer *armée révolutionnaires* with the regular army. This idea proved the most resilient in the prolonged and acrimonious debates at the Convention; various factions became convinced that it was the best method to promote a revolutionary fighting spirit among the soldiers. This reasoning prevailed over the argument that mixing units of different size (for example, regiments and companies), organizational structure, and personnel would disrupt the effective operations of the army. The voice of St. Juste was critical in illustrating the emphasis on revolutionary values: "Victory will attend you not just because of the number and discipline of the soldiers. You can only achieve it to the extent that the *republican spirit* [my emphasis] makes progress spreading in the army. Nothing seems to me to be more capable of inspiring it than the plan presented by Dubois-Crancé."[29]

Battlefield defeats and loss of territory immediately after the declaration of war on the emerging First Coalition was later attributed to inadequate capability estimates by French policy makers.[30] This is also corroborated by the timing of national mobilizations. The first *levée* to draft 300,000 into the army was launched on February 24, 1793, almost a month after France's declaration of war on Britain and Holland (February 1, 1793). At the time war was declared, the French line army numbered 178,000 men, including artillery (10,000 men) and cavalry (35,000). Approximately 75,000-95,000 trained militia were theoretically available, bringing the estimated total to 250,000-270,000 by mid-February 1793.[31] Debates on the campaign plan and organization of the French army began in earnest only on January 11, 1793, however. And after declaring war on Britain and Holland, the National Convention was still debating for nearly a month the issues of amalgamating the volunteer *armées révolutionnaires* with the regular army and the national conscription of 300,000 men. It took four sessions of the Convention, on February 14, 19, 20, and 21, to complete voting on these measures.[32] Their strategic inadequacy was soon demonstrated by French defeats at Aix-la-Chapelle and Neerwinden, as well as by General Dumouriez's defection following a failed coup. These developments brought about increased political repression at home and the drive for a new *levée en masse* (implemented in August of 1793) to compensate for losses and bring the army size to over 650,000.[33]

By autumn 1792, French sea power had been considerably undermined as a result of the revolutionary drive for introducing the principles of *liberté, égalité, et fraternité* in the navy. Beginning in 1789, sailor mutinies broke out, and senior officers who tried to suppress them were arrested and removed by the *représentants en mission*. The majority of the ablest captains resigned their command. In all ports, according to E. H. Jenkins, officers were commonly insulted, gallows were erected next to their houses, and during the 1792 mutiny at Toulon, some were hanged from streetlamps. Supporters of the naval officer corps in Paris, which included a former ambassador to Britain, La Luzerne, failed to convince the National Assembly that maintenance of stocks, equipment, discipline, and organization were more important than *égalité*, and that the election of captains and the wholesale abolition of class distinctions diminished the navy's capabilities. As a result, most naval officers, who were drawn primarily from the lesser aristocracy, emigrated. By November 1791, the chief naval base at Brest was 30 captains and 160 lieutenants short, reflecting the lack of officers at other ports. In 1792 civil administrators were put in charge of ports and ship movements within them. Despite appeals by naval officers throughout 1791-1792, the Legislative Assembly failed to understand that replacement officers drafted from the merchant marine were poorly prepared to handle fleet maneuvers, gunnery, signals, and combat discipline. Neglect of the navy's special requirements continued in 1793, as the strategy of universal mobilization was applied almost indiscriminately to operations both on land and at sea.[34]

The lessons of a failed invasion of a much weaker Sardinia in autumn 1792 went unheeded as the National Convention continued to disregard information on France's diminishing naval capabilities. The committees on marine affairs and the colonies were asked to produce the first report to the Convention on the state of the French navy only after hearings on the British intentions on December 31, 1792. Those were in turn delayed by highly politicized debates on the execution of the royal family. The same day, Minister Monge sent a circular to revolutionary clubs in the port cities, urging them to recruit personnel for the navy. His report to the marine committee on January 11, 1793, emphasized the superior revolutionary spirit of France and assured his audience that "as far as the hostile disposition of certain maritime powers is concerned, I have redoubled the care, the zeal, and the activism . . . all the measures have been taken." The committee rejected suggestions that France would be unable to provide naval resistance and disregarded information on British superiority in warships, matériel, and equipment, and in the training of new officers.[35] Instead, Jeanbon Saint-André, Rochegude, Taveau, Breard, Rouyer, and Marec, who represented the naval committee at the Committee on General Defense (which evolved into the terror-wielding Committee of Public Safety), spent the month of January trying to apply the strategy of rapid revolutionary mobilization in the navy. The committee's zealous work was taken as evidence of imminent success, but the reality was different. Four days after the declaration of war, Breard reported on behalf of the committee that it had proved impossible in such short time to reorganize the navy "on the sacred basis of equality that entitles all men to have an equal share of the responsibilities and benefits of a society." The "void occasioned by the emigration of officers" was acknowledged.[36]

Revolutionary principles, however, were to be maintained. Instead of concentrating on the lack of capabilities and trained personnel, the committee attributed the problems to insufficient enforcement of the very same egalitarian measures which that to the deterioration of naval power in the first place. Jeanbon Saint-André, who chaired the committee, declared it fortunate that so many naval officers had emigrated, delivering France from the most irreconcilable enemies of *égalité*. The naval strategy would rely on the wholesale recruitment of merchant-seamen and emphasize the ideal French national character at the expense of practical naval skills, such as "the knowledge of mathematics acquired in the course of long studies." According to Saint-André:

> Courage and audacity are things that will animate your sailors; these are, if not the only, at least the primary qualities that are going to distinguish them. It is necessary to bring back the times of Jean Bart and Duguay-Trouin who were certainly not great geometers, but who had that hotness of the soul and the quick eye that constitute true naval talent and solely provide for victory; they must profit from the French impetuousness and the enthusiasm of freedom to triumph over their enemies. Perhaps they should disdain the spirit of reflection and the calculations of naval evolutions, but deem it more expedient and of higher utility to combat the enemy by boarding in which the French have always been victorious.[37]

The grand strategy continued to emphasize the promotion of revolutionary ideas and the French national spirit in the navy. On February 6, 1793, all captains were ordered to procure the certificates of *civisme* (devotion to the revolution) that were to be signed by the general council of their communes of origin. The decrees of March, June, and July 1793 ruled to "get any officers who are at all suitable," further de-emphasizing special naval training. In October an extraordinary "purification" decree was adopted by the Committee of Public Safety. It ordered that lists of naval officers be posted in the officers' ports and hometowns. Anyone suspecting an officer's *civisme* was obligated to denounce him. In the assessment of E. H. Jenkins, many were denounced to give way to "the Pistols of the service—the strutting noisy types who could shout loudest 'égalité, la nation, et la patrie.'" Jeanbon Saint-André also persuaded the Convention to abolish the corps of seamen-gunners, which he described as the aristocracy of the sea. For the sake of equality, gunners from land artillery units without any experience in operating cannons mounted on moving platforms were recruited to man and fight the batteries.[38]

The lack of realistic data on France's naval capabilities relative to Britain and the disproportionate emphasis on revolutionary spirit were further exemplified by Dubois-Crancé in a keynote speech to the Convention on January 25, 1793, in which he proposed to attack Holland and invade Great Britain. In this address, Dubois-Crance insisted that France could succeed in war *precisely because* deficiencies in material capabilities would encourage the pride of a nation liberated from the monarchy. This view echoed Kersaint's January 1, 1793, estimate: "Our position is such that we no longer must count our enemies; they have put us in a position of this glorious necessity of defeating them or perishing ourselves."[39]

Successive revolutionary governments relied on optimistic projections of French economic potential, discounting for the existing shortcomings. The stage was set in early 1792, when the Legislative Assembly's financial expert, Cambon, in the absence of credible economic intelligence, argued that France's resources were inexhaustible and its money supply virtually limitless.[40] Although ministry officials withheld negative economic data for fear of political repercussions, the alienation of regional governments from Paris disrupted reporting from the provinces; the abolition of feudalism and redistribution of property further complicated accountability and data analysis.

The *conventionnels* also lacked reliable information on the British economy, finances, and commerce. Voicing the widely accepted assumptions underlying French assessments of the British threat, Kersaint's address interpreted the rise of capitalism and financial markets in late eighteenth-century Britain as the proliferation of "financial aristocracy and the numerous agents of the government" serving only "one or two people who rule England." According to Kersaint, Britain therefore had more aristocracy than France had had in 1789. Moreover, Kersaint wishfully claimed that the British people had experienced greater oppression and were readying themselves for revolution. The Scots and the Irish in particular were seen as certain to "refuse paying new subsidies to make a war on us [France]." The nature of economic exchanges between Britain and its colonies was also misinterpreted on the basis of mirror imaging: Kersaint argued that

Britain's colonies were an economic liability, as in the case of France. There-fore, even if Britain overcame local resistance inspired by French revolu-tionary ideas and "rendered itself master of your [French] colonies, it would be forced to guard them incurring a surcharge that would weaken it, while your [French] disposable forces would provide ample compensation else-where."[41]

French victories at Valmy and Jemappes in early autumn 1792 signaled to the leaders in Paris that France was in an increasingly better position to promote revolutions against all the monarchies of Europe. The grand strategy was modified to step up propaganda and expansion. Brissot ar-gued that war would be easy, and Danton pushed through a resolution in the Convention proclaiming that France must declare war on the kings. The deputies applauded Danton's call to have the National Conven-tion serve as a "committee of general insurrection against all the kings in the universe."[42]

Within this context, French policy makers were seeking information to confirm their rising expectations about "the awakening of oppressed peoples of feudal Europe." Reports of this kind began to arrive in autumn 1792—an appeal for help by a group of French Revolution supporters in the Duchy of Zweibrucken, a request for military protection by a newly established revolutionary club in Mainz, and information on public opinion in Bel-gium supporting the extension of the French Republic to the Rhine. The latter coincided with Dumouriez's promises to establish his winter quarters in Brussels.[43]

A substantial portion of this stream of reports concerned Great Britain. A large and vocal British expatriate colony of radicals in Paris drew atten-tion to the increasing popularity of their supporters back home. This colony was joined in September 1792 by Thomas Paine, who had a seat on the National Convention. The Convention was also receiving an increasing number of congratulatory addresses from radical societies in Britain, along with some symbolic shipments of money, arms, and ammunition to help France in war. The Society of Constitutional Information asserted that "in a much shorter space of time than can be imagined the French should send addresses of congratulation to a national convention of England." Reports on insurrection in Ireland and celebrations for French military victories in Scotland were exaggerated, as were the political fortunes of Charles Fox, who was considered destined to replace Pitt as prime minister and whose pronouncements in Parliament in support of French victories against Prussia and Austria were well known in Paris.[44]

French policy makers consistently assessed the degree of support for the French Revolution in Britain from impressionistic reports. One searches official records in vain to establish whether Lebrun, Danton, Kersaint, Dubois-Crancé, Brissot, or other officials actually attempted to quantify the impact of the British radical societies or the nationalist uprisings in Ireland and Scotland on Britain's political stability. War opportunity assessments were correspondingly made with disregard for hard data, leading to vastly exaggerated estimates of the prospects for revolution in Britain. The self-congratulatory reports and addresses of British radical societies and émigrés were salient because they fit the political expectations of the French elites, who needed to assert their power by denouncing monarchies. There was little time for careful deliberation, especially considering that the Convention was almost entirely preoccupied with the question of Louis XIV's trial until late December 1792. Moreover, in the political climate of the Convention, the lack of deliberation was directly proportionate to the excesses of oratory. The revolutionary fervor turned even the cooler heads, including Robespierre. The decrees on propaganda and pan-European political fraternity made key French politicians prisoners of their rhetoric. Brissot captured the spirit, proclaiming on November 26, 1792, "We cannot be calm until Europe, the whole of Europe, is on fire."[45]

Major figures in National Convention committees and government departments all argued that Britain was predisposed to attack France sooner or later. These policy makers insisted that France must therefore preempt hostile British designs by attacking first, at the earliest opportunity. Evolving out of centuries of repeated conflicts with Britain, this view was enhanced by the revolution and was in the ascendance, following the overthrow of the monarchy and the radicalization of the revolutionary regime.[46]

Conspiracy theories promoted a persistent direct assessment of British intentions as hostile throughout the late 1780s and into 1793, when war was declared, while they discounted the material evidence necessary to verify such assessments. Prior to 1789, French policy makers had viewed Britain as fomenting an antiroyalist conspiracy; in 1789-1792, Britain was seen as a source of designs to subvert French constitutional monarchy. Since September 1792, London had come to be viewed as the center for royalist plots against the French revolutionary government and, by extension, the French nation. Intelligence from England further reinforced the shifting conspiracy theories. La Luzerne, ambassador to England in 1789-1790, regularly referred to the "malevolence" and "infernal intrigue" of the English government, without providing much tangible evidence. La Luzerne's successor, Barthelemy, in the same manner accused the British Cabinet of "the most perfidious machiavellianism" and portrayed Pitt as an anti-French revanchist who had plotted the 1789 revolution with a small group of French nobles in retaliation for France's support of the American colonies. Britain's hostility was even attributed to a plan to avenge Richelieu's intrigues against Charles I a hundred and fifty years earlier—as if late eighteenth-century British policy makers seriously believed and deeply cared that the civil war of 1642-1649 was nothing but a French plot.[47]

Strategic surprise and deception were also considered in the comparative power estimates of French strategists. Dumouriez was preparing for a strike against Holland that would be so unexpected and so rapid that the British would have no time to intervene. The strategic surprise factor was to be enhanced by the innovative tactics of "shock and fire." According to the plan, the speedy conquest of the Dutch navy would demoralize Britain at sea, make France safe against maritime retaliation, and furnish France with a springboard for attacking the British colonies and naval communications worldwide. To enhance the impact of surprise and divert attention from these preparations, French representatives in London and The Hague kept insisting that France wanted peace. Thus, Chauvelin continually made this point to foreign secretary Grenville in a series of letters, messages from Foreign Minister Lebrun, and informal meetings held at Chauvelin's request. A French diplomat, de Maude, held secret negotiations at The Hague, with Lord Auckland and the Dutch presenting a plan for general peace on the part of France. De Maude reported that reluctance to engage in war was a sign of their opponents' feebleness and nervousness. Lebrun and his colleagues became even more convinced of British weakness and French strength. Emboldened by these reports, Lebrun stepped up pressure on Britain to abandon Holland without a fight and threatened Grenville on December 27 with a direct appeal to the British people if Britain continued its "interference in Dutch affairs." The idea to consider direct revolutionary propaganda as a power multiplier in the war against Britain was institutionalized on January 1, 1793, when the National Convention, after Kersaint's presentation, adopted an address to be read by French admirals to servicemen of the Royal Navy when confronted at sea. Britain's superiority in tangible naval power was discounted, as the British seamen were expected to be revolutionized by appeals like this: "Not a single grievance, not a single motive could justify in your eyes the war into which you are being drawn; and now your blood and ours will merge in our two navies through which we must pass peacefully in order to enrich our common fatherland and upon which we must embrace one another as brothers, and you will extend to us the helping hand."[48]

Kersaint, along with other architects of France's war strategy, argued that the outbreak of hostilities would whip up revolutionary ferment in England and bolster French fighting spirit. The deputies were brought to their feet in support of Kersaint, who evoked the image of Cortez burning his boats in view of the army on the shores of Mexico, as if France could do the same and defeat Great Britain.[49]

INTELLIGENCE OBJECTIVES, SOURCE LOCATIONS, AND DECLARATIONS OF WAR

In the decade preceding the outbreak of the Great War, the asymmetric threat assessment patterns of Britain and France relied on systematically divergent intelligence. According to Alfred Cobban's study of all major French and British archival documents, the British government focused its intelligence collection in 1784-1792 on the military capabilities—principally, the navies and naval support systems—of France and other European powers. Reviewing the data assembled by Cobban (Table 6.1), I found that the British government in the late 1780s and early 1790s was concerned with forty-four intelligence topics or objectives regarding assessment of the threat posed by France. Of these, thirty-two (or 73 percent of the intelligence topics) dealt with sea power, and five others with land power capabilities. Altogether, this "hard" intelligence on military capabilities accounted for 84 percent of Britain's strategic intelligence objectives.[50] Among the chief intelligence targets were the movement of French ships sailing for India and the East Indies, the position of the Swedish fleet in the Baltic, the state of the Spanish navy, and the condition of shipyards and magazines, as well as detailed accounts of ships at major French ports (for example, Marseilles, Dunkirk, Gravelines, and Toulon), descriptions of socioeconomic conditions in the French maritime provinces, and the state of the magazines and encampments to be used by the French army attacking the Netherlands.

Table 6.1 shows that with the exception of Paris and Liege, all intelligence was collected in ports and coastal provinces, or from spy vessels (*Narcissus, Zebra, Fury, Hound, Melampus, Alert*) cruising along the French coast. In other words, more than 85 percent of Britain's intelligence sources and observation platforms were located close to the areas of French naval activity, in Brest, Brussels, Corsica, Dunkirk, Gravelines, Marseilles, Nice,

Table 6.1
British Sources of Intelligence on France, 1784-1792

Location and Source of Intelligence	Time period	Intelligence Topics
Brest		
"X"	March 1786:	-- intelligence from the port of Brest
Cpt. Dumaresq	1787-88:	-- data on ships and troops preparing to sail from Brest to India
Brussels		
Richard Oaks, merchant and Nepean's informant	1787-90:	-- reports on ships sailing for the East Indies
Chevalier Floyd, agent to minister Lord Torrington	1777-91:	-- variable, undetermined information, possibly from ports -- "news bulletins from Paris" (1789) - soon discontinued
Colonel Gardiner, minister at Brussels	1789-92:	-- developments in the Austrian Netherlands
Corsica		
Masseria	1789-90:	-- support for the movement of Corsican patriots, French views
Dunkirk		
Lt. Monke	September 1787:	-- report about the port of Dunkirk
Gravelines		
Lt. Monke	September 1787:	-- report about the port of Gravelines
Liege		
William Miles	October 1787:	-- excursion to Givet "to watch the motions of the French army"
	August 1787:	-- formation of magazines and potential use of encampments at St. Omens to "facilitate the march of the French army into the United Provinces"
	September 1787:	-- journey to Cologne to check formation of magazines on the Rhine
	1787-88:	-- support/bribery of editor of the Journal General de l'Europe
Marseilles		
Lt. Monke	September 1787:	-- report about the port of Marseilles
Nice		
John Birkbeck, British consul	1780s:	-- intelligence on the port of Toulon
Cpt. Phillips	March 1785:	-- data on ships at Toulon
Paris		
de St Marc	February 1785:	-- copies of all materials dispatched by French court to India -- correct number and distribution of ships at Rochefort
de la Fond, artillery captain, resident at Versailles	October 1787:	-- proposed disposition of troops on Atlantic and Channel coasts -- charts of the coast of Normandy -- manuscript volume, Reconnaissance Militarie de la Normandie -- memorial on French plans in India by M. de Brasseur
Eden	June 1786:	-- "nature and progress of the works" at the new port of Cherbourg
Richard Oakes, merchant and Nepean's informant	1790:	-- information about French attitude on alliance with Spain
Dalrymple, merchant and Nepean's informant	1785:	-- dispatch of 60 prisoners by France to form a settlement in New Zealand
	1780s:	-- data on Spanish trade and navy
Major-general Dalrymple	1787-88:	-- information about five regiments sent to the East Indies
Miles-Elliot mission to the National Assembly	1790:	-- to sound out and influence members of the Comite Diplomatique with a view of preventing activation of the Family Compact between France and Spain over the Nootka Sound dispute

(Continued on next page)

(Continued from previous page)

Toulon

"X"	March 1785:	-- intelligence respecting the port of Toulon
Lt. Monke	October 1787:	-- detailed account of ships at Toulon
	September 1788:	-- follow-up report on the ships at Toulon
	February 1789:	-- follow-up report on the ships at Toulon
Cpt. H. Warre	September 1788:	-- data on the port of Toulon

St Malo

Cpt. Dumaresq	1790:	-- data on the Spanish fleet
		-- "mutinous conditions in the French fleet at Brest"

Channel provinces

Philip d'Auvergne	1784:	-- description of the maritime provinces
	1792:	-- information about the French navy
		-- development of information sources in chief French ports

Frigate *Narcissus*

Philip d'Auvergne	1787-88:	-- reconnaissance of French coasts between St Malo and Le Havre
		-- progress of the works at the new port of Cherbourg

Small scouting vessels

Sloops *Zebra* and *Fury*	1790:	-- watch for deployment of Spanish squadrons off Cadiz and Ferrol
Sloop *Hound*	1790:	-- watching for movements of Swedish fleet in the Baltic
Melampus	1790:	-- information on the number and fitness of French ships at the port of Brest (reported by cutter to England); watch for any squadron leaving port
Cutter *Alert*	Mid-1790:	-- observations of the port of Ferrol for naval deployments

Source: Alfred Cobban, *Aspects of the French Revolution* (New York: W.W. Norton, 1968), 202-223.

Toulon, St. Malo, and the Channel provinces. Although the largest number of intelligence reports from any given location—one-third—came from Paris, the overwhelming majority of them (over 85 percent) concerned French ports, naval capabilities, or colonial operations.[51] This evidence confirms that the gathering of strategic information on France by the British government prior to the outbreak of the Great War seems "with very few exceptions to have been directed to one object—intelligence about the situation and distribution of the French Navy."[52]

In the context of the British parliamentary politics detailed in chapter 3, the economy drive by Pitt's administration and constraints on executive power made the government cautious about spending on intelligence that did not relate to tangible military or economic capabilities. Even in the case of Holland, Britain's key maritime ally, King George III was very circumspect about authorizing Civil List funds to support pro-British Orangists, as he was only too aware of the unpleasantness of parliamentary scrutiny with regard to spending on "soft" or political intelligence: "I now reluctantly consent to it from the fatal experience of having fed the Corsican cause, and Ministry never having, as they had promised, found means of its being refunded to me, which made me consequently appear afterwards in an extravagant light to Parliament."[53]

The marginalization of information not dealing with naval deployments is illustrated by the termination after 1785 of such long-trusted British secret agents as Mrs. Wolters and Mr. Hakes, stationed in Rotterdam. The British government cut the annual funding for the Wolters-Hakes spy ring from about 1,370 to 710 pounds, chiefly due to lack of information on French naval preparations. On the possibility of restoring the cut payments, the Foreign Office informed its station chief in The Hague that only "a correct and minute account of the state of the French fleet . . . would be a proof that these channels of former intelligence may be recovered."[54]

Since parliamentary accountability was conducive to a concentration on specific collection targets and capability data, annual outlays of the British Foreign Office for Secret Service were kept steady and relatively low, averaging slightly above 24,000 pounds from 1784 to 1792.[55] Spending in 1793 (21,165 pounds) and in 1794 (29,334 pounds) was consistent with the average. Only two years into the war, with the increasing commitment of national resources by major powers, did intelligence outlays rise to 90,232 pounds (1795), averaging a wartime high of 127,355 per year between 1795 and 1800.[56]

In the late 1780s, one notable exception to this spending pattern further confirmed the predominant intelligence focus on tangible targets directly affecting British proprietary interests. Secret service operations in the Dutch Republic consumed nearly 60,000 pounds in 1787 and at least 185,000 pounds in 1788. More than 76 percent of the increase, however, went to subsidize the Zeeland East India Company, considered critical by British policy makers for maintaining global naval and commercial superiority over potential challengers, such as France.[57]

In contrast, French intelligence topics regarding Britain in autumn 1792 centered primarily on politics. Key intelligence questions focused on the prospects for revolution and the collapse of government in Britain. Thus, Lebrun, the French foreign minister, who was in charge of external intelligence collection, gave this guidance to his agents in London on November 11, 1792: "It is very certain that our principles will penetrate everywhere sooner or later of their own accord, precisely because these principles are those of sound reason, for which the larger part of Europe is now ready."[58]

French agents, working in Britain illegally or under diplomatic cover, hastened to provide confirming evidence to Lebrun and the government of the National Convention. Their intelligence reports concentrated on incidents of unrest in Great Britain and Ireland, public expressions of opposition to the government, rumors of the imminent dismissal of Pitt,

Table 6.2
Names and Location of French
Intelligence Sources in Great Britain, 1787–1793

Year	Names of Agents	Primary Location
1787	Barthelemy	London
	Adhemar	Unknown (London)*
	La Luzerne	London
1788	Barthelemy, ch. d'affaires	London
	La Luzerne, ambassador	London
1789	La Luzerne, ambassador	London
	le duc d'Orléans, mission chief	London
1790	La Luzerne	London
	le duc d'Orléans, mission chief	London
	Barthelemy, ch. d'affaires	London
1791	Barthelemy	London
	La Luzerne	London
1792	Chauvelin, minister	London
	Hirsinger, ch. d'affaires	London
	Herman, consul general	London
	Noel	Unknown (London)*
	Talleyrand	London
	Benoist, mission chief	London
1793	Chauvelin, minister	London
	Miles, mission chief	London
	Forster, commissaire	Unknown (London)*
	Petry, commissaire	Unknown (London)*
	de Menneville, mission chief	London
	Mitchell, secret agent	Unknown
	Mathews, secret agent	Unknown
	Oswald, secret agent	Unknown

Source: Archives du Ministére des Affaires Etrangéres, État numerique des fonds de la correspondance politique de l'origine à 1871 (Paris: Imprimerie Nationale, 1934), 43-44.

* Indicates the most probable primary location for that person.

rumors of the imminent appointment of the Francophile Charles Fox as prime minister, "financial panic in the City," a naval mutiny at Shields (and, possibly, other mutinies), the size of radical societies' membership, public celebrations to mark French victories, and fraternal addresses sent to the National Convention.[59]

French intelligence collection and analysis on Britain thus centered on political targets. Little wonder that, in stark contrast to Britain, at least 73 percent of French intelligence sources were located precisely where such political information was most likely to be obtained—in London (Table 6.2).

Given the intelligence collection priorities set by the French government, it is also hardly surprising that estimates of Britain's capabilities and intentions were couched in intuitive language. Data on the incidence of unrest or the size of radical societies were not quantified in a fashion that made it possible to estimate their impact on British political establishment as a whole. Moreover, the primary intelligence questions posed by the French government failed, by definition, to focus decision makers' attention on indicators of political and socioeconomic stability in Britain. But since in the more open British polity plenty of evidence suggesting popular dissatisfaction with the political status quo was likely to be found, intelligence consumers in the French government set themselves up for self-delusion. Thus, Noel, a well-connected agent in London, having collected enough information on antigovernmental and pro-French sentiment in Britain, reported in late 1792, "To the eyes of an outside observer, England offers precisely the same prospect as France did in 1789."[60] This intelligence found a ready audience in Lebrun, Brissot, Dumouriez, and other key makers of French strategy. Based on these reports, Lebrun estimated that the strategic threat to French war plans from Britain was low. Lebrun explained his view in a November 29, 1792 report: "If the cabinet of St. James adopts a policy of severity and resistance, it will provoke inevitably an insurrection, if not on a national, then at least on a partial scale, including all the towns surrounding the capital. The results would be fatal for the monarchy and the government."[61]

Danton presented exactly this assessment in his famous speech on January 31, 1793, that propelled France into war. The power of the British navy, the First Coalition's overwhelming preponderance in manpower and arms, the dynamism of the British economy, and the superior wealth of Britain's coffers were no longer seen as a threat to the French challenge:

> The limits of France are marked by nature. We shall reach them at four corners of the horizon: at the Ocean, by the Rhine, at the Alps and in the Pyrenees. . . . No human power can stop us. In vain do they threaten us with the anger of kings. You have thrown them the gauntlet. This gauntlet is the head of a king. This is a signal of their future death. They threaten us with England, but the tyrants of England are dead; the people will be free. They will be our friends. You [the people of France] have plenty of national power. The day when the Convention nominates the Commissaries to go into all the communes and claim men and the arms, the entire France will attack your enemies.[62]

This asymmetry in key indicators of threat assessment between Britain and France prior to the outbreak of the Great War comes through with striking clarity in the war declarations exchanged by the two powers in early 1793. Following the French declaration of war on England and Holland issued by the National Convention on February 1, 1793, Prime Minister Pitt announced the British declaration of war on France in a speech in the House of Commons on February 12, 1793.[63]

The government in Paris and "the cabinet of St. James" both emphasized precisely what the other discounted in their reasons for going to war. Thus, of the 18 motives to go to war in the French war declaration, 13 (72 percent) focused on the political intentions of foreign powers. The conclusion was that France perceived the political intentions of the major European powers—mainly, their dislike and fear of the French Revolution—as serious enough to warrant the initiation of hostilities. Part of the sad irony was that these hostile political intentions, attributed to Britain, were gravely misconstrued. For example, France was alarmed by England's political "attachment to the coalition of crowned heads" directed against France. Conversely, Pitt emphasized that Britain only entered alliances to prevent a territorial expansion by France in Europe and that Whitehall was not in the business of mobilizing Britain's continental allies to invade France and crush the French Revolution. In London, the official position was that the revolutionary developments in France should be left to run their course, for as long as they did, France would be weakened and less capable of challenging British global interests. For its part, the National Convention considered Britain's embargo of corn and arms shipments to France part of a grand and deadly antirevolutionary design; to Pitt, however, such measures were confined to curbing French expansion in selected parts of the Low Countries.[64]

Another act of hostility ascribed to Britain against France was Westminster's prohibition against circulating the *assignat,* the new revolutionary currency. In fact, British policy makers banned the *assignat* for legal and economic reasons, aiming chiefly to protect the British economy and markets from this quasi currency which, in Britain's view, was "worth nothing." The British government, as well as the leaders of industry and finance, considered the introduction of this new French tender—intended to bolster the collapsed French economy—"a gigantic system of swindling." The French government also accused Britain of "considerable naval armament," most likely referring to Britain's drafting 9,000 naval personnel in late 1792. Yet the French declaration failed to specify why this rather marginal increase in the European balance of manpower at arms would seriously challenge France. From the British viewpoint, these concerns were overstated, since Whitehall economically proportioned this naval armament to the task of preventing France from opening the Scheldt River for navigation and commerce.[65]

The additional grievances, both general and specific, stated in France's war declaration were overwhelmingly political: the King of England continued to give "the French nation proofs of his malevolence"; England refused to recognize the Provisional Executive Council and the National Convention—key political institutions created by the French revolutionaries; the British government "discontinued its correspondence with the French ambassador in London" and refused to acknowledge the representatives of the French Republic;" the British Parliament passed the requirement that all French subjects be registered with the British authorities, an act perceived as "most inquisitorial, most vexatious and most dangerous;" the British government welcomed French monarchists with open arms and maintained correspondence with "the rebels who have already fought against France;" the British Parliament openly admitted that naval armaments were being directed against France; the government of St. James "prosecuted with fury those who were supporting the principles of the French Revolution in England;" Britain, in some unspecified ways, allegedly employed "every possible means . . . of heaping ignominy upon the French Republic and of inspiring against it the execration of the English nation and of all Europe;" and Britain supposedly formed a secret coalition with Prussia in January 1793 (a coalition that most probably existed only in the imagination of French intelligence agents and leading decision makers).[66]

Conversely, out of the 17 reasons to declare war on France emphasized by Prime Minister Pitt, 14 (more than 82 percent) concerned very specific military, economic, and legal assessments: France had violated the compact "not to intervene in the government of any neutral country" and "not to pursue any system of aggrandizement," specifically, by annexing the Duchy of Savoy and taking possession of Flanders; France had seized British vessels in the British ports "without any preparation on our [Britain's] part for war;" French authorities had imposed an embargo on "all the vessels and persons of his Majesty's subjects who were then in France;" France had violated the 1787 Commerce Treaty with Britain providing that "in each case of rupture . . . time shall be given for the removal of persons and effects" from each other's territory, and France thus had behaved aggressively toward Britain's global trade; the French government had therefore threatened "the continuance and safety of that commerce which is a source of so much opulence" and the "high state of prosperity" in Britain; and, finally, France had amassed troops in the north and thus "while brandishing freedom, threatened Holland with invasion."[67]

In this way, Britain and France ran on separate decision tracks, a race ending in the Great War of 1792-1815. In this case of asymmetric threat assessment, British policy makers gave priority to collecting intelligence about military and economic power in Europe and throughout the world. Based on such indicators as the number of French, Spanish, and Swedish naval ships in the north Atlantic and the Mediterranean; the conditions in French ports and coastal provinces; the state of French global maritime traffic; and the economy, the finances, and the manpower available to the armies of France versus the armies of Britain and the First Coalition (especially Austria, Prussia, and the Netherlands), William Pitt's government developed a high level of confidence in Britain's military and economic superiority over France. British intelligence was organized in line with these collection objectives: more than 85 percent of Britain's intelligence sources were placed at the key centers of French naval activity, and nearly 84 percent of all intelligence topics concerned French military capabilities. Documents on Britain's spy ring at Rotterdam suggest strongly that funding for intelligence agents was linked tightly to their ability to provide detailed and up-to-date information on the French navy.

The decision of the French government to pursue an aggressive challenge against Britain and its allies derived almost exclusively from internal political considerations, especially since these considerations were projected onto the British government. The emphasis was on political stability in Britain. According to debates in the National Convention, French decision makers seriously considered challenging Britain's naval dominance on a global scale. The opportunity for such a risky challenge was measured not in terms of ships of the line or the aggregate weight of broadsides, but in the courage and audacity of the French sailors. French decision makers were most receptive to intelligence reports indicating that the British navy could be defeated after French sailors met their British counterparts at sea and read to them revolutionary proclamations adopted by the National Convention. Little wonder that almost all French intelligence sources were concentrated in London, where they could zealously focus on what the French government deemed crucial intelligence tasks. These tasks centered on incidents of political unrest in Britain and Ireland, public expression of opposition to the government's policies toward France, rumors of Pitt's dismissal, and other perceived indicators of British political vulnerability. In this context, public celebrations of French military victories in Britain acquired strategic significance. Intelligence reports on these topics gave the

French decision makers glaringly misconstrued and self-deluding notions of Britain's war capacity as well as British public sentiment. Accordingly, when calling on France to go to war against Britain, Kersaint argued that France would defeat Britain by burning boats (rather than building boats). Danton proclaimed that executing the French king would give France more power than Britain could ever rely on with all its superior navy and massive coalition armies.

This asymmetry of strategic threat and opportunity estimates thus shows why the British government did not believe Britain was sufficiently threatened to warrant a preemptive military strike at France in 1792-1793, and why France, for its part, persisted with a revolutionary war strategy that discounted the low probability of long-term success against militarily and economically superior opponents.

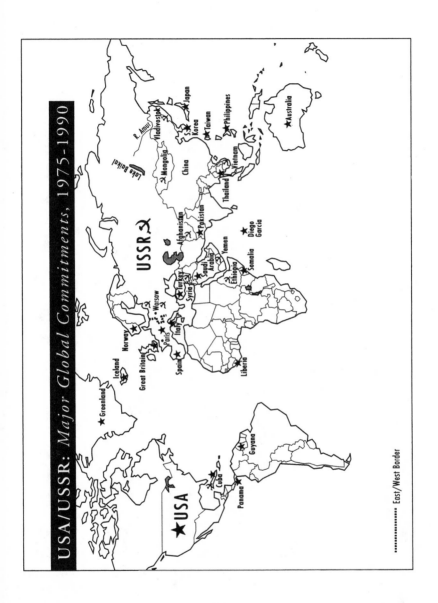

USA/USSR: *Major Global Commitments, 1975–1990*

Greenland
Iceland
Norway
Great Britain
Paris
Spain
Italy
Warsaw
Syria
Turkey
Saudi Arabia
Yemen
Liberia
Ethiopia
Somalia
Diego Garcia

USSR
Lake Baikal
R. Amur
Vladivostok
Mongolia
China
Afghanistan
Pakistan
Thailand
Vietnam
Korea
Japan
Taiwan
Philippines
Australia

USA
Cuba
Panama
Guyana

·········· East/West Border

Chapter 7

CIA and KGB: Separate Tracks to the "New Cold War," 1975–1985

In the late 1970s a series of events disrupted the Soviet-American rapprochement of the previous decade, and once again, "each superpower found itself compelled to view the other as a threat that called for maximum attention to military power and strategic security."[1] What became known as the "New Cold War" peaked around 1983 vivid vilifications of one adversary by the other, played out on a global stage: President Ronald Reagan cast the Soviet Union as "the evil empire" and "the focus of evil in the modern world"; the Soviet leaders called the United States a hotbed of "ultra-reactionary adventurist forces, bent on turning history backward."[2]

Conventional realist and rationalist explanations of this rapid aggravation of outright hostility between the superpowers focused on diplomatic conflict over the deployment of new intermediate nuclear forces (INF) in Europe and the security dilemmas it evoked on both sides, as well as on proxy wars in the Third World, especially in Afghanistan and Nicaragua. Changes in domestic politics, and especially the rise of Ronald Reagan, whose unabashed and colorful anti-Soviet rhetoric was bound to insult the ideological sensitivities of the Kremlin, can be cited as another obvious factor. As these events slip further into the past, so grows the temptation to explain them as a bump on the road in U.S.-Soviet relations or just another twist in the global competition for power and ideological influence.

At some level, the conventional view has much going for it: the diplomatic wrangling over the Soviet SS-20s and American Pershing IIs and Cruise missiles in Europe saw each party overemphasizing the capabilities of the opponent while downplaying their own—a typical bargaining game in arms control. The United States, for example, argued that Soviet SS-20 missiles could hit targets within a 5,000-kilometer range, whereas Moscow insisted that their new missile could only be effective within 4,000 kilometers. Disagreements such as this one, particularly given the absence of joint testing of the SS-20 missile, may easily be explained in terms of a classical security dilemma—each side portrayed as a rational actor seeking, in the ongoing arms control negotiations, to maximize the adversary's zone of reduction and withdrawal and minimize one's own zone of reduction and withdrawal of military capabilities.[3]

Major conceptual problems surface, however, when this logic is extended to the military balance between the Soviet Union and NATO in Europe in the early 1980s. For one thing, realist and rationalist assumptions that international actors have uniform access to all available information (either complete or restrained only by cost) is confounded by the staggering asymmetry between the accounting methods used by Washington and Moscow to assess the balance of intermediate nuclear forces between the Soviet bloc and NATO. Briefly, in 1981 the official U.S. view held that the Soviet Union had 3,825 intermediate nuclear systems (mostly missiles and bombs) deployed in Europe, whereas the United States had only 560 such systems. According to the Kremlin, the USSR was disadvantaged, albeit marginally, with an estimated 975 Soviet INF systems facing NATO's 986. And whereas Moscow regarded SS-20s as an equitable replacement of the older SS-4 and SS-5 missiles, Washington saw SS-20s as a qualitatively improved intermediate-range system that destabilized the global power balance. Thus, explaining the New Cold War in terms of the security dilemma is possible only ex post facto, assuming the accounting asymmetry as a given.

Such rationalization, however, overlooks an interesting theoretical puzzle: Why did these widely divergent assessments of the power balance in Europe suddenly become so politically "hot"? As late as 1979, the United States and the Soviet Union signed SALT II, a treaty that was based on the assumption of approximate strategic nuclear parity between the superpowers and was a logical extension of earlier U.S.-Soviet arms control agreements underlying the 1970s detente. In other words, how could a symmetric, parity perception of the global power balance, still underlying SALT II even after the Soviet deployment of SS-20s in 1977, suddenly become so asymmetric?

This problem is even more challenging to conventional interpretations, if one applies the supposedly objective indexes of national power, such as the index used in the Correlates of War (COW) project. When measured this way, any power balance between two international actors may only change one way—favoring or disfavoring either actor. And when this power balance shifts, how can both actors feel either more secure or more threatened simultaneously? The overall balance of U.S. and Soviet gross national capabilities, including strategic nuclear forces, GNP, and population changed only slightly in favor of the Soviet Union from 1975 to 1982, if one measures this balance by applying the COW method and thus discounts the path breaking qualitative improvements in U.S. military technology during that time. The realist model fails to specify why U.S. and Soviet perceptions of or accounting schemes for global power balance should have changed so dramatically from detente to the New Cold War.

Another conundrum is that the asymmetry between continental and sea-based forces, as described in chapter 6, has been a persistent feature of U.S.-Soviet competition, from the Kennedy era to the Gorbachev days. Hence the relevant question is if power asymmetries persist and if shifts in the power balance affect only one side, why would *both* sides suddenly feel more threatened? With regard to the New Cold War, the deficiency of the realist and rationalist explanation becomes evident: If the Soviet Union increases the number of its intercontinental ballistic missiles already armed with thousands of warheads, and while the U.S. retains its twofold preponderance in naval and air power relative to the Soviet Union, what would the deployment of a few hundred intermediate-range nuclear missiles in Europe make the Soviet leaders think? That is, would they estimate that the United States is about to launch a nuclear missile attack? Or is the Western bloc so fearful because it is internally weak, ready to collapse from within? Or is there nothing to worry about, since the global power balance is not substantially altered? The realist and rationalist paradigms offer little guidance to address such questions systematically, which goes a long way toward explaining why the dominant international relations theories were so confounded by the rapid improvement in U.S.-Soviet relations under Gorbachev, the Soviet collapse, and the end of the Cold War.

A conventional perspective emphasizing deterrence theory also fails to explain the rise of the New Cold War. From this perspective, by introducing new SS-20 missiles into the western USSR and Eastern Europe, Moscow undermined, if not ruined, the credibility of extended deterrence. This strategy envisioned American ICBMs taking off from the Great Plains and striking Soviet targets in the event of a conventional Soviet attack on Western Europe. Assuming, however, that Moscow strongly doubted that Washington would risk starting a global nuclear war to save Paris or London from a Soviet conventional attack, the proponents of extended deterrence argued that increases in Soviet power should be counterbalanced in Europe. This would give the Kremlin a clear signal of NATO's resolve to retaliate without holding the United States hostage to the risks of an intercontinental nuclear shootout.

The problem with this theory is that nothing like the New Cold War materialized when extended deterrence was dealt a much more massive blow in the early 1970s. At that time the United States was surprised to discover a large-scale Soviet buildup of intercontinental ballistic missiles that gave Moscow virtual parity in intercontinental nuclear forces. But precisely when the rationale for a U.S. nuclear umbrella over Western Europe was undermined, relations between Moscow and Washington took a sharp turn for the better. Fear gave way to trust, summit meetings took place, path breaking SALT I and anti-ballistic missile (ABM) treaties were signed, and postwar disputes in Europe were finally settled with the approval of the Helsinki Final Act. The crews of the U.S. Apollo and Soviet Soyuz craft sealed their docking in space with a handshake, an ultimate symbol of global goodwill. If a shift in the balance of most lethal nuclear capabilities during the 1960s in Soviet favor was followed by detente in the 1970s (and during an initially hawkish Nixon administration), why should a relatively limited change in a military balance in Europe in the late 1970s, from a deterrence theory perspective, trigger off a new superpower standoff?

These puzzles suggest that the deterrence framework, though it dominated U.S. government thinking on security, appears to be a poor predictor of threat assessment. Hence, using government strategy as social theory to explain developments in world politics may undermine the theory by making explanations applicable only to one side. In real life, as Raymond Garthoff has demonstrated, Moscow's conception of deterrence differed greatly from Washington's, because the Soviets regarded nuclear deterrence as only a necessary interim safeguard rather than a central concern in the quest for security.[4]

Finally, the data on which most conventional explanations rely come from media accounts and the diplomatic record. Although such data yield valuable insights into the bargaining process on such issues as arms control, these information sources hardly allow one to address two principal issues: Are negotiating tactics a good measure of underlying threat assessments? If anything, the diplomatic record is not specifically designed to reflect institutional preferences for information collection and analysis—before diplomats sit down to talk, they usually rely on information that was collected and analyzed beforehand.

The record of the intelligence services provides a window on what governments want to know and which threat indicators should be monitored, and thus a window on information selection preferences, which has confounded mainstream international relations thinking. In the New Cold War case, insight into information selection preferences may be gained by systematically comparing the content of the National Intelligence Estimates of the Central Intelligence Agency that were declassified after the end of the Cold War and the KGB instructions from the Moscow Center on worldwide intelligence collection. The main point is not whether these or any other intelligence estimates are right or wrong, accurate or inaccurate, timely or untimely, biased or objective, but that they were made, that they represented a concerted effort of hundreds of professional workers, and that they left us with a telling sample of what both Washington and Moscow wanted to learn about external threat.

"INFORMATION HIGHWAYS" OF THREAT ASSESSMENT

In the United States, the NIEs originated in a document that helped shape strategy and institutions throughout the Cold War—the National Security Act of 1947. Designating the production of NIEs as one of the three principal tasks of the Director of Central Intelligence, under the direction of the National Security Council, the act charged the agency to "correlate and evaluate intelligence relating to the national security, and provide for the appropriate dissemination of such intelligence within the Government."[5] In this sense, according to Sherman Kent, whose *Strategic Intelligence for America's World Policy* (1949) soon became CIA analysts' chief guide, the NIEs were truly "national" and truly "estimates."

Kent also described the institutional mechanism by which the U.S. government coordinated intelligence collection among the agencies involved in the production of NIEs. This mechanism is evidence that the estimates indeed reflected what policy makers or intelligence consumers wanted to know. These consumer requirements were transmitted to the intelligence community through a system of Priority National Intelligence Objectives, encompassing such instruments as *terms of reference* (TRs) and their institutional equivalents. Drafted first by the Office of National Estimates and then its successors, the terms of reference, for example, defined the subject matter of the estimate, its scope, and timeframe. The purpose of TRs was, as described by Kent, "to focus the forthcoming estimate on the new major points which were discerned as the principal concern of the requestor; it aimed to ask those questions (*irrespective of anyone's ability to supply factual answers*) which would direct research and cogitation to the general area of these major points. In a word, it was a statement of precisely what was wanted and a polite message to the community's expert research analysts, telling what was wanted of them" [emphasis added].[6]

In the Soviet Union of the 1970s and 1980s, the Communist Party conveyed the Soviet leaders' information collection priorities for external threats to the KGB's First Chief Directorate (responsible for foreign intelligence). The Kremlin's requirements, set by a narrow circle of collegiate leadership, were translated within the First Chief Directorate (FCD) into intelligence collection instructions known to Soviet agents abroad as "instructions from the Center." With the limits of the known world thus established, the FCD analyzed and disseminated within Soviet government agencies intelligence collected by KGB stations abroad, published a daily summary of events for the Politburo, and forecast future world developments.[7]

The Kremlin's priorities were conveyed to the KGB hierarchy in no uncertain terms. As head of the FCD, Vladimir Kryuchkov instructed his subordinates in 1984 to organize their intelligence work abroad "in strict accord with the decisions of the 26th Party Congress, the November (1982) and June (1983) plenary sessions of the CPSU Central Committee, and the program directives and fundamental conclusions contained in the speeches of the Secretary General of the CPSU Central Committee, Comrade Yu. V. Andropov, as well as the requirements of the May (1981) All-Union Conference of the Heads of the Service."[8] Instructions from the Center were similarly conditioned by the political agenda of the Communist Party.

Thus, despite a major difference—the CIA's NIEs were explicitly designed to abstain from politics, whereas the KGB's instructions were explicitly made part of the Communist Party's political agenda in foreign affairs—the process on both sides in the Cold War reflected what each government wanted to know about the outside world. Both processes also represented a broad consensual view of the intelligence community—the NIEs by design, and the KGB instructions through Soviet institutional arrangements and norms.[9]

Finally, neither the NIEs nor the instructions were set by default to deal exclusively with military and economic capabilities or political intentions, plans, doctrines, and ideology. Thus, the House Committee on Foreign Intelligence in a 1980 study considered NIEs "a thorough assessment of a situation in the foreign environment which is relevant to the formulation of foreign, economic, and national security policy, and which projects probable courses of future development."[10] This was clearly the case with the 11-3 and 11-4 series of NIEs, which routinely focused on Soviet strategic capabilities, politics, doctrines, and socioeconomic factors.[11] KGB instructions, according to Nikolai Leonov, who headed the Analysis and Assessments Directorate from 1973 to 1984, targeted political developments as they related to military and strategic issues, including "the organization of the armed forces of foreign states and . . . both military and political aspects of international conflict." Leonov complained that the scope of foreign intelligence collection tasks was too wide, or, as he said, "unembraceable."[12]

In this capacity—as mirrors of consumer requirements and institutional information highways, both NIEs and KGB instructions are a useful documentary source for testing the hypothesis linking intelligence outputs and the broader political contexts in which the outputs emerge. As I will show, the magnitude of threat estimated by the CIA and KGB regarding each superpower's aggression against the other peaked in 1980-1984 and then leveled off prior to Gorbachev's accession to power.

VULNERABILITY MEASURED IN MISSILES

National Intelligence Estimates evoke an image of threat assessment as an accounting enterprise, when assessing the likelihood of Soviet aggression or war initiation and when tracking specific threat indicators. Conforming to the bean-counter pattern, the CIA estimated the likelihood or threat level of Soviet aggression in terms of set probability ranges, expressed in denotative language. This system of language markers for probability levels was designed and introduced by Sherman Kent. For example, a statement such as "chances are good that the Soviet Union will expand its military presence in the Middle East" would signal to alert readers of the estimate that Soviet expansion was within a 60-84 percent range of certainty. A qualifier such as "almost certain" or the phrase "we believe" applied to the same statement would raise the estimated likelihood of Soviet attack to 85-99 percent. Conversely, the phrase "is not expected" would reduce the estimated probability to 15-39 percent. No language markers referred to the 100 percent probability level. Several phrases, including "it is possible that," "may" or "might," and "could have," were reserved for situations in which the CIA regarded evidence as inconclusive. This system of probability estimates, implicit in every NIE, became an enduring part of the estimating process.[13]

Twenty-three declassified NIEs produced in 1975-1984 tell an unambiguous story: beginning in 1980, the CIA saw both Soviet aggression in the Third World and a Soviet intercontinental attack on the United States (a description implying a global nuclear war) as more likely. The estimated probability of Soviet aggression in China, as well as in Europe—the latter despite Soviet deployment of SS-20s—was unchanged. Though the likelihood of Moscow initiating an intercontinental nuclear war was considered a remote possibility, the language markers assessing the threat shifted one notch up the Kent probability scale. The watershed estimate was NIE 11-3/8-80, issued in late 1980. The language marker for intercontinental attack was "unlikely," instead of the previously used "almost certain than not" and "we do not believe," signifying an upward adjustment in probability levels from one in nine to one in three. This estimate persisted through the last declassified NIE for the 1975-1984 period.

The same NIE 11-3/8-80 also struck an alarmist note, in line with the assumptions of extended deterrence theory. The estimate predicted that once "decoupled from intercontinental theater"—in other words, once confident that the United States would not risk a Soviet nuclear attack on the White House to save Bonn—the Kremlin "would press on with offensive against Western Europe aimed at seizure." (Such conditional statements are considered inconclusive, however.) With regard to the Third World, the CIA in 1976 estimated that active Soviet intervention directly challenging Western vital interests was "likely to continue"—a language marker for the 64-80 percent probability range on Kent's scale. In 1981 a change in the operative words raised the level of certainty to 85-99 percent, with an estimate that the USSR was not merely "likely" to continue its challenge in the Third World but "will attempt" and "will continue" its aggressive intervention.[14]

A perception of a mounting red scare is also implicit in the changing titles of the 11-4 NIE series. While conveying the same information and meaning, "the change in title implied a shift in the intellectual climate in which the estimates were made." Hence the differences in titles: *Soviet Strategic Objectives* (NIE 11-4-77), *Soviet Goals and Expectations in the Global Power Arena* (NIE 11-4-78), and *The Soviet Challenge to US Security Interests* (NIE 11-4-82). A rather subtle shift from neutral "objectives" in 1974 to proactive "expectations" in 1978 is followed in 1982 by a more explicit modification—"challenge to US security interests," with the word *challenge* implying "contention, contest, struggle, belligerency, pugnacity, combativeness, competition, rivalry."[15]

What indicators did the CIA monitor when assessing Soviet threat levels? And more critically, changes on which indicators were associated with the rising red alert? I examined these questions through content analysis of thirteen NIEs in the 11-3/8 and 11-4 series published in 1975-1984, in five broad categories of Soviet threat indicators:

1. The balance of strategic capabilities between the Soviet Union and the United States, based on the number and throw weight of intercontinental and submarine-launched ballistic missiles, the number of reentry vehicles and long-range bombers, the survivability of missile silos, and the capacity of antiballistic missile (ABM) defenses;

2. the state of the Soviet economy, including agriculture, energy, manpower, productivity and growth rates, hard currency supply, and the impact of economic cooperation in the Soviet bloc;

3. the impact of Soviet economic conditions on development of strategic programs;

4. political aspects of Soviet power, such as the political stability and proclivities of the Soviet leadership, especially assessments of the post-Brezhnev leadership changes;

5. ideological aspects bearing on Soviet foreign policy and military doctrine, such as Soviet approaches to relations with the United States in the light of long-term systemic competition between the capitalist and socialist systems.

These five categories define the limits of the known world in the NIEs, which systematically evaluated each indicator. Not all indicators, however, were considered in every estimate, giving the first measure of their relative weight.

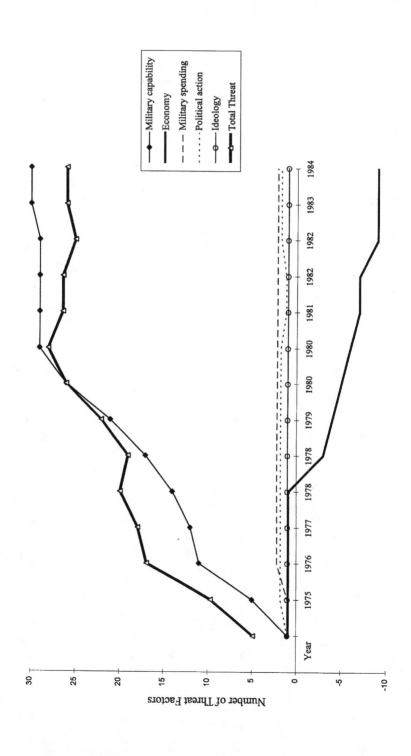

As institutional attention getters, indicators of Soviet military capabilities occupied center stage. Chief among these indicators was the ability of Soviet ballistic missile silos to survive a U.S. nuclear strike and the capacity of Soviet ABM systems to strike down incoming U.S. missiles. Of the thirteen NIEs I analyzed, missile silos and antiballistic missile systems were featured in twelve, closely followed by other indicators of Soviet military might: intercontinental ballistic missiles figured in eleven estimates, submarine-launched missiles in ten, reentry vehicles in nine, and strategic bombers in eight. Soviet ideology was mentioned in eight estimates, military spending in seven, and GNP growth in five. Other measures of Soviet threat appeared in three or fewer estimates.

The frequency with which different indicators appeared in the overall threat picture is only part of the story, however. The key question is what changes in which indicators cued the estimated levels of Soviet threat and how? The NIEs systematically evaluated changes on each indicator with respect to both the balance of U.S.-Soviet military power and the political aggressiveness of the Soviet state. From this perspective, the NIEs clearly followed the bean-counter method by linking threat levels mainly to changes in power balance indicators.[16]

Evidence in support of this claim is strong and unambiguous. The NIEs systematically described positive, negative, or zero change in each indicator's impact on either the power balance or the political proclivity for aggression. For example, the estimates discussed whether the introduction of new technology increased survivability of the Soviet missile silos relative to existing or projected U.S. capabilities, whether problems in the Soviet energy sector affected Soviet economic capacity negatively, or whether leadership changes after Brezhnev's death would make the Soviet posture more or less aggressive. By coding these statements and aggregating them for 1975-1984, I was able to chart trends in each indicator's impact on Soviet threat levels (see Figure 7.1).[17]

The data in Figure 7.1 show why the U.S. intelligence community and policy makers operating within these limits of the known world feared Soviet aggression more in 1980 than in 1975 or 1977, setting the stage for rising superpower tensions. This trend is evident in the line labeled in this chart "Total Threat," which represents the sum of all indicators analyzed in NIEs for every given year. To draw an analogy, the "Total Threat" line will be to the CIA and U.S. policy makers what the Dow Jones Index is to market analysts. This line rises sharply in 1975-1977, then levels off in 1977-1978 (paving the way for SALT II in 1979), then sharply rises again

Table 7.1
Correlation of Soviet Threat Factors

Threat Indicators	Pearson Correlation Coefficient: Indicators, by Category, with Aggregate Threat Level (TOTAL THREAT line)
1. Military capabilities	0.963
2. Economy	− 0.809
3. Military Spending/Production	0.843
4. Politics	0.160
5. Ideology	n/a (0 value change)

Source: Author's calculations based on indices aggregated in Figure 7.1.

until the end of 1980, then levels off again. Following this trend line, the estimated Soviet threat looms larger, then lingers, then soars, then stays the same.

The trend lines also show that these changes in Soviet threat levels are associated strongly and positively only with changes in indicators of Soviet military capabilities (the correlation scores in Table 7.1). The perception of rising Soviet aggressive propensity from 1975 to 1980 builds explicitly on estimates that Soviet missile silos were less vulnerable to U.S. attack, that the accuracy of Soviet re-entry vehicles was increasing, that nuclear submarines of the Typhoon class would shift the balance of sea-based nuclear forces in the Soviets favor, and that new phased-array radars would give the Soviets much better antimissile coverage against the offensive capabilities of the United States. From 1976 to 1980, five NIEs consistently reported that the Soviet Union could by the early 1980s achieve "marginal advantages in a central strategic conflict" based on "gains in relative offensive capabilities."[18] These capability trends, showing that the USSR was gaining ground on the United States, were seen as giving the Soviet Union a window of opportunity to confront the United States globally. The United States, in contrast, would be facing a more dangerous situation, or window of vulnerability.[19]

Table 7.1 tells yet another story: had estimated threat levels been driven by "soft" indicators—related, for example, to ideological shifts in Soviet leadership—the "Total Threat" line would run low and flat, consistent with the lines representing changes in political and ideological indicators.

Perhaps even more interesting is the contrast between the estimated negative changes in Soviet economic power and the increase in the overall level of Soviet threat: the "Economy" line turns downward precisely when the "Total Threat" line turns sharply upward. In other words, estimates of

Soviet threat are associated strongly and negatively with Soviet economic conditions. Whereas the overall trend of Soviet economic decline is projected correctly, the impact of economic factors is diminished when all indicators of Soviet threat are aggregated. Economic factors, however, were played down for a reason: the CIA struggled all through the Cold War trying to develop reliable measures of the Soviet economy and failed, but so did the Soviet leaders. If anything, Soviet military expenditures were intractable, and the official figure of 17 billion rubles a year in the late 1970s was a ruse. Applying its own techniques, the CIA in its estimates put Soviet military spending in 1975-1980 at 11-15 percent of GNP, approximately two times lower than the actual figures, as only became evident after the Soviet collapse.[20]

Without a reliable index of Soviet economic indicators and wary of the Kremlin feeding statistical "red herrings" to outsiders, U.S. policy makers and intelligence producers filtered direct statements of political and economic intentions by the Soviet government out of the NIEs. For this reason, the CIA grossly underestimated a massive Soviet ballistic missile buildup in the late 1960s, a development that could have been deduced from statements of high-ranking Soviet officials—including defense minister, Marshal Malinovskiy. General secretary Leonid Brezhnev, responding to the publication of NIE data in *The New York Times,* warned as early as July 1965 against underestimating the Soviet buildup: "Any attempt at aggressive acts against our country [USSR] on the basis of such evaluations of our military potential [NIEs] will be fatal for its initiators." Stringent data requirements forcing the intelligence community to provide these permanently erroneous, independent dollar estimates of Soviet economy were hardly a bureaucratic aberration of the CIA but rather an institutional requirement embedded in the strong congressional power of the purse. Former Director of Central Intelligence Robert Gates said he abolished these dollar estimates right after his appointment because, in his view, they did not make sense and had been proven inadequate repeatedly. Gates, however, had to cave in under pressure from the Defense Department and Congress, whose members immediately complained that without the dollar estimates they would be unable to draft and pass the U.S. defense budget.[21]

The decisive role of capability-based threat assessments in the U.S. case can also be illustrated by evoking historical antecedents. Thus, the period 1980-1984 was projected to be "the threat years" in NIEs of the mid- to late 1970s, according to the same conceptual blueprint, "an information

processing pattern," as in the depths of the Cold War. In 1950, CIA estimates identified 1954 as "the threat year," a projection extrapolated from
available data on Soviet A-bomb stockpiles. These 1950 estimates played a
critical role in the U.S. government adopting NSC-68, a directive that
toughened containment strategy and set the tone for the chilliest years of
the "First Cold War" (1950-1954). In a similar fashion, CIA estimates of
the widening window of vulnerability, based on perceived improvements
in the Soviet capability to survive a nuclear first strike, are linked with
President Carter's presidential directive (PD-59) that set the tone for U.S.
strategy in the early 1980s. PD-59 ordered massive new forces built to
fight a prolonged but geographically limited nuclear war and, in retrospect, was the first chapter in the massive military spending program
launched in the early 1980s by the Reagan administration.[22]

Although domestic political considerations did play a part in exagger-
ating the threat levels—a game in which Reagan ultimately gained the
upper hand over Carter—it is questionable whether the underlying political debates and shifts in strategy, coming both with NSC-68 and PD-59,
could have occurred in the absence of steady institutional flows of information presenting an increasingly menacing picture of Soviet strategic capabilities. Moreover, the similarity in the policy-making background leading
to both PD-59 and NSC 68 suggests that Soviet political and ideological
considerations and direct intention assessments were subsumed by capability analysis or were misinterpreted.

Thus, the estimate of 1954 as a "threat year" excluded the possibility of
massive changes in Soviet policy in the wake of Stalin's death. In fact, after
the death of the Soviet leader, Moscow became more cooperative in efforts
to end the war in Korea and abandoned the fundamental Soviet concept of
"the historical imminence of war between capitalism and socialism."[23]
Considering the thawing in U.S.-Soviet relations, the start of disarmament
talks, and the Soviet relinquishment of Austria in mid-decade, the designa-
tion of 1954 as a "threat year" was at best an exaggeration.

Similarly, the preoccupation with military capabilities in the case of
PD-59 made the prospects of leadership change amid a stagnating economy
and incipient political and nationalist dissent appear frightening to Carter,
who concluded: "It may be that the thermodynamic law of entropy has
finally and fully caught up with the Soviet system. . . . We could be seeing
a period of foreign movement at a time of internal decay."[24] Although the
Soviet invasion of Afghanistan fits this assessment, a closer look at Soviet
political intentions reveals that at the global level, the Soviet challenge was

becoming increasingly moribund. Particularly after the invasion into Afghanistan—although a costly and dangerous debacle, it was hardly a massive geostrategic push to warm water ports—further aggression was seen by the Kremlin as politically damaging. As Kremlin insiders later reported, these developments only strengthened Moscow's focus on their last potent symbol of political legitimacy—"a historical achievement of nuclear parity with the West"—whereas wholesale military expansion in the Third World, very soon after the Afghanistan invasion, was increasingly viewed as damaging. The Politburo's reluctance to invade Poland after the rise of the anticommunist Solidarity movement in the early 1980s signaled the beginning of the end of the Soviet empire.[25]

Could there have been a reverse causality at work in the CIA's estimates? In other words, could the estimates of threat levels simply have been a reflection of political and ideological changes in Washington following the advent of the more hawkish Reagan administration? The adoption of a more hawkish PD-59 well before the power transition in the White House poses a major argument against this view. Several others merit consideration.

For one thing, if the NIE-assessed threat levels relied *predominantly* on domestic political pressures coming from Reagan's "princes of Darkness," such as Richard Perle, one would expect the "Total Threat" line in Figure 7.1 to have risen after 1981 at least at the same rate as in 1975-1980. One would also have expected more alarming reports on the growing Soviet preponderance in the intercontinental theater to have poured into the Oval Office from supposedly sycophantic analysts, anxious to serve the "evil empire" bashers. From an ideological perspective, such reports would have been politically beneficial to the administration in power. This also would have been a serious anomaly in relation to the main hypothesis advanced in this book. The data indicate, however, that precisely during the evil empire years, the cumulative index of threat indicators stayed at approximately the same level as before the arrival of Reagan.

In like manner, I observed no reported increase in political and ideological indicators of a Soviet threat. Such an increase would again have played well with the domestic political imperatives of the Reagan administration and should have been observed, if the "Reagan factor" were decisive. The NIEs also continued to provide estimates of declining Soviet economic power following Reagan's arrival, which appears to have been politically disadvantageous for defending sharp increases in U.S. military spending.

This is not to say that U.S. estimates of the Soviet threat were immune to partisan politics. The scope of the debates, however, was constrained by the limits of the world known to the key players. Those limits were set in the first place by established institutional information flows, including the NIEs. Confined to those limits, ideological differences between hawks and doves fall within a narrow range when the entire scope of threat indicators is considered. After all, none of the three U.S. administrations in the period 1975-1984 instructed the CIA to assess the Soviet threat *primarily* on the basis of noncapability indicators, such as popular support and respect for political leaders, worker resolve to sustain high levels of production in the face of a decaying industrial base, the willingness of young Soviet males to serve in the armed forces, or changes in the ideological prescriptions of the Communist Party's Central Committee. Had these factors been considered *over and above* Soviet strategic capabilities, the imminent decline and collapse of the Soviet system would have been more plausible and the New Cold War of the early 1980s might not have ensued. Paradoxically, had that happened and had the United States pursued a more cooperative policy toward the USSR, the latter could plausibly have survived much longer and still exist today.[26]

An emphasis on capabilities for intercontinental attack, especially in addressing political and ideological factors, also accounts for U.S. policy makers' failure to discern critical shifts in Soviet strategy in the early 1980s. The NIEs consistently argued that "changes in Soviet strategic policy would not be likely under a post-Brezhnev regime" and that "any changes would likely be in the direction of increases in strategic capabilities, especially if SALT TWO fails to produce an agreement."[27] These views are indicative of the assessment, or rather lack of it, of the independent impact of Soviet leaders' political intentions and the ideological transformations underway among the Soviet elites.

An example of how the CIA estimates neglected ideological shifts having a direct impact on the Soviet security outlook is provided by the assessments of the potential for Soviet intervention in the Third World. The NIEs measured this threat by focusing on a stable set of indicators, such as shipments of military equipment, the volume of arms trade, the number of Soviet bloc technicians in developing countries, the size of pro-Soviet communist parties, and even the number of Third World students in the USSR.[28] Precisely at this time—the early 1980s—the Soviet leadership was reconsidering its strategy of "fraternal assistance to the developing countries," a euphemism that when translated from Moscow's political jargon referred to Soviet policies in the less developed countries (LDCs) around the world. Emphasizing that these developing states must commit to the "socialist choice," the Communist Party leadership reduced the number of the developing countries worthy of "fraternal assistance." This shift was reflected in keynote party documents and justified ideologically by arguments that choice of government was an internal matter for LDCs. Whereas the official report of the Twenty-fifth Congress of the Communist Party in 1976 listed 18 developing countries as "sharing fundamental aspirations" with the Soviet Union, the Twenty-sixth Congress report in 1981 listed only 11. A change in the report's section titles also suggested that priority in "fraternal assistance" would be given to states showing firmer commitment to a "socialist orientation," as opposed to a broader "world revolutionary process." This trend increased with the arrival of Gorbachev: in the Twenty-seventh Congress report (1986), the special section on fraternal assistance to Third World states, entitled "Developing Relations with the Liberated Countries," was no longer present.[29]

Finally, the preponderance of capability-based assessments of the Soviet threat comes through even in the way the CIA criticized its own products during the so-called A Team/B Team experiment in competitive estimates in 1976. Harvard professor of Russian history, Richard Pipes, led the B Team, a specialized study group of outside experts working on the 1976 CIA estimate. He noted that the same tendency in the structure of intelligence collection and analysis preferences as has been presented in this book led to a misperception of Soviet strategy: "This misperception has been due in considerable measure to concentration on the so-called hard data, that is data collected by technical means, and the resultant tendency to interpret these data in a manner reflecting basic U.S. concepts while slighting or misinterpreting the large body of 'soft' data concerning Soviet strategic concepts."[30]

Yet the B Team's analysis followed precisely the same path of extrapolating Soviet intentions from capabilities, albeit in a different way, arguing that the Soviet Union was seeking to develop war-fighting capabilities, as opposed to a deterrent. Soviet concerns and priorities, as I shall show later, were of a different nature.

VULNERABILITY MEASURED IN POLITICAL INTENTIONS

Viewed retrospectively, NIEs and KGB instructions share the perception of increased threat in the early 1980s, exactly at the time of the New Cold War. Yet their timing of the rising threat estimates was different. Whereas the CIA announced an emerging window of vulnerability five years in advance, the KGB appears to have been content with the Soviet position in world affairs in the second half of the 1970s, until in a panic discovery of a window of vulnerability in 1983, the KGB sent reports of an impending nuclear attack on the USSR, causing grave alarm in Moscow.

Instructions from the Center rarely mentioned changes in external threats to Soviet interests from 1975 to 1982. KGB Instruction No. 551/PR in March 1977, by stating that China "remained a serious and dangerous adversary," only implied that the threat of Chinese aggression stayed the same. A weak, indirect suggestion of increased threat came in a KGB instruction on the European Economic Community (EEC), issued in April 1977; increasing integration among the EEC members was giving the Kremlin cause for alarm.[31]

Yet beginning in 1983-1985, KGB instructions and supporting documents began to warn of an increasing possibility of conflict between the Soviet Union and "the capitalist world." On February 17, 1983, the instructions conveyed to KGB stations abroad cited the "growing urgency of discovering promptly any preparation by the adversary for a nuclear missile attack on the USSR," and on November 21, Moscow Center urged its agents to note "the increase in tension" characterizing the international situation. On February 1, 1984, "increasing tension" was diagnosed by KGB instructions "in literally all sectors of the struggle between the two opposed social systems," whereas *the threat of outbreak of a nuclear war* was reaching *"dangerous proportions."* The same instruction also stated that the growing threat of war was "creating a new situation in the world"—a testimony to profound changes in Moscow's outlook on the Soviet global posture. On July 10, 1994, the KGB introduced a heightened combat alert procedure under the code name KOSTYOR 1 (Campfire 1) with an unambiguous reference to the mounting danger of global nuclear conflagration. References to the "dangerous development in the world situation" persisted in the instructions issued on December 17 of the same year. The assessment of February 13, 1985, was milder yet grave, still characterizing the situation in world politics as "increasingly tense."[32]

This system of threat indicators used by the KGB hardly resembles an accounting scheme, and the language markers are as flexible and as contingent on the party line as statements in *Pravda* editorials. With the limits of the known world set by these instructions, threat assessments, to use a popular Soviet colloquialism, are bound to "fluctuate with the party line." In contrast to the CIA estimates, which are not entirely immune from some political pressures either, fluctuation with the party line was the KGB's principal norm in threat assessment. In the examples just cited, KGB stations were requested to find information after the fact to fit preset threat levels, rather than deduce the numeric probability levels of NATO's aggression from meticulous comparisons of the alliance's military and economic power relative to the Soviet Union.

This indexing of intelligence targets to party prescriptions implies that Soviet estimates, starting in May 1981, assumed an increasing probability of global war when the ailing general secretary, Leonid Brezhnev, denounced Reagan's policies in a secret speech to the All-Union Conference of the Heads of Service. The Central Committee plenum in November 1982 marked a further rise in the estimated war threat levels: Yuri Andropov, the KGB Chairman and Brezhnev's successor, declared that the new American administration was actively preparing for nuclear war.[33] According to the last KGB chairman, Vadim Bakatin, the Soviet leaders believed that communist theory would be the best guide to threat assessment, even in the event of a nuclear war. When visiting a vast underground command and communications center east of Moscow, maintained by the KGB and designed to run the Soviet Union in the event of a nuclear war, Bakatin immediately spotted "signs of ideological servitude": the only thing on the bookshelves in the bunker, from which the Soviet leaders were supposed to command military operations in the aftermath of a nuclear attack, was a complete collection of works by Lenin, the founder of the Soviet state.[34]

Whereas in NIEs, estimated threat levels fluctuated according to indicators of the U.S.-Soviet military balance (Pearson's R = 0.963), in KGB instructions, threat assessment was linked first and foremost with indicators of political motives, plans, strategies, intentions, and ideology. Content analysis of eight KGB instructions issued in 1977-1984 shows that these soft indicators constituted almost two-thirds of Moscow's collection requirements (0.647 percent in the data sample, as shown in Table 7.2).[35] An illustration is the KGB's *Priority Questions of Military Strategy,* published in December 1984. In this document, questions targeting political intentions (38) outnumber questions dealing with capabilities and economic issues (23).

As a further illustration, consider Moscow Center's instructions on intelligence collection regarding the potential military uses of the space-shuttle system. The KGB requested information on five key issues [emphasis added]:

Table 7.2
**War Threat Factors in KGB Collection
and Analysis Requirements, 1977–1984**

Year/Document	Number of War Threat Factors by Category and Region					Share (1=100%)	
	MIL	ECON	MIL-ECON	POL	IDEOL	MIL	POL & IDEOL
1. 891/PR/52 (3/77): Plan of Requirements on Chinese Subjects for 1977	2	4	2	20	3	.065	.742
2. No. 2121/PR/52 (4/78): On the Activities of the West in the Arctic	1	3	0	5	0	.111	.555
3. No. 1967/PR (11/82): Plan for Work on the Problem of the World's Oceans, the Arctic and the Antarctic, 1982-1985	1	0	0	7	1	.111	.889
4. --/PR draft (12/82): Plan for Work of the PR Line of the London Residency of the KGB for 1983	4	6	1	30	0	.098	.732
5. No. 2126/PR (11/83): Kryuchkov's instructions on planning and organization of work of the Service abroad in 1984	4	1	0	10	0	.267	.667
6. 1025/PR/61 (4/84): Guidance-Requirements for carrying out our work with regard to the European Economic Community	2	4	0	15	0	.095	.714
7. No. 2106/PR (12/84): List of Priority Questions of Military Strategy on Which the Intelligence Service Abroad is Required to Throw Light	16	4	3	38	1	.258	.629
8. No. 337/PR, Attachment (2/85): American Policy on the Militarization of Space	6	0	0	16	0	.273	.727
AVERAGE:						.160	.647

Sources: Christopher Andrew and Oleg Gordievsky, eds., Comrade Kryuchkov's Instructions: Top Secret Files on KGB Foreign Operations, 1975-1985 (Stanford: Stanford University Press, 1993), 18-19, 110-12, 114-15, 121-23, 164-67, 198-203; Christopher Andrew and Oleg Gordievsky, eds., "More 'Instructions from the Center': Top Secret Files on KGB Global Operations, 1975-1985," Intelligence and National Security 7 (January 1992), 16-24, 57-58, 61-62.

1. Specific contents of *plans* to use the 'Shuttle' craft in a strike variant to destroy targets in space and on the ground (in the air, on water and on land).
2. The *attitude* of Congress, political parties, public and academic organizations to these plans.
3. The *degree of involvement* of the USA's West European allies in NATO in *implementing* these plans and their *attitude* towards them.
4. Possibility of the Americans including the question of the 'Shuttle' as a subject in the forthcoming *talks* with the Soviet Union on space and nuclear weapons.
5. *Content of the experiments* carried out during the 'Shuttle' flight on 25-28 January this year [1985].[36]

In this typical example, the KGB instructions list only one collection requirement—the content of experiments on board the shuttle—that directly addresses the capability aspects of the shuttle program. This collection target is listed last. Other questions zero in on attitudes, plans, and intentions to discuss the shuttle in talks on space and nuclear weapons, and a very ambiguous degree of involvement of the European NATO states in the U.S. space program. Apparently, the KGB requested its stations to do a great deal of political palm reading.

This evidence reflects the Politburo's well-known obsession at the time with the U.S. Strategic Defense Initiative (SDI) and alleged American plans for the militarization of outer space. It has since been established that Moscow's concerns ran contrary to technical assessments and were largely based on the Kremlin's "faith in the ability of American technology to achieve apparent miracles (paradoxically, greater than among many Western politicians and scientists)."[37]

The tone for these eight KGB instructions (listed in Table 7.2) on intelligence collection and analysis worldwide was set in annual KGB briefs, "Chief Conclusions and Views Adopted at the Meeting of Heads of Service." One of these annual briefs, issued in March 1983, has been made public.[38] The "Chief Conclusions" closely reflected the positions of key policy makers in the Kremlin and illustrated vividly the traditional priorities of the Moscow Center in the global arena.[39]

The main theme in the 1984 "Chief Conclusions" was that Ronald Reagan, the U.S. President most hated and feared by Moscow since the grimmest years early in the Cold War, had openly embarked on a course of global confrontation with the Soviet Union and seriously considered a nuclear first strike. The language of the "Conclusions," a top-secret government document, could have been taken straight out of the most vitriolic anti-American editorials in Soviet newspapers at the time: "The fantastic idea of world domination has become the initial basis of the Pentagon's plans for a preventive, 'limited,' 'protracted,' 'cosmic,' and other conceptions of conducting a nuclear war. The White House is advancing in its propaganda the adventurist and extremely dangerous notion of 'survival' in the fire of a thermonuclear catastrophe."[40]

The KGB took Reagan's vehement anti-Soviet rhetorical escapades as "nothing else but psychological preparation of the [American] population for nuclear war." This KGB document leaves the impression that when Reagan joked in 1983, albeit in an unstatesmanlike manner, about nuking the evil empire in five minutes, the Center could have easily drafted a report saying that the American president was about to push the nuclear button. Another important criteria used in the KGB's assessment of the alleged U.S. plans to initiate a global nuclear showdown was "the unwillingness of the United States government to follow the example of the Soviet Union and accept the undertaking not to be the first to use nuclear weapons."[41] These assessments illustrate clearly the significance Moscow attached to symbolic political pronouncements, both of American leaders and its own. In contrast, none of the NIEs (at least among those released so far) explicitly based their assessments of Soviet threat on public statements of Soviet (or U.S.) leaders.

While taking these largely rhetorical and symbolic political acts as incontrovertible evidence of a rising nuclear war threat, Moscow Center also searched for deeper, intrinsic reasons, with a clearly Marxist-Leninist bent. The KGB argued that global war was closer at hand due to the alleged "deepening social and economic crisis in the capitalist world," a sure sign that "American monopolies would like to recover the positions they have lost in recent decades and conquer fresh ones."[42]

Startling as it may be to a rational observer, the KGB reports backed allegations like this one with no hard evidence but rather took these threat assessments as starting points to target ever more elusive "intentions," "plans," and "plots" that would comfortably fit with the image of increasingly aggressive imperialism. Speaking at a meeting of KGB heads, recorded in the "Chief Conclusions," the Soviet foreign intelligence chief, Vladimir Kryuchkov, pointed out that "in our [KGB's] information-gathering activity the main emphasis was put on obtaining secret documentary information giving us early warning of the main adversary's military policy and strategic plans revealing his preparations for war against the Soviet Union, or any crisis which may be developing." Desperately needed was "*political information* [original emphasis] about the emergence and development of pre-crisis and crisis situations." In addition to the aggressively inclined governments of imperialist powers, the KGB saw other plotters and schemers lining up against Soviet interests—ordinary Americans supporting the immigration of Soviet Jews to the United States, undisclosed "subversive emigre, nationalist and Zionist organizations and associations," "reactionary Muslim organizations," and a number of mysterious "anti-Soviet diversionary and terrorist counter-revolutionary organizations of various shades in developing countries."[43]

Primary intelligence collection targets were those that could furnish such revelations—"confidential and special unofficial contacts" in the

United States, Western Europe, Japan, and China. Lamenting a shortage of secret information from these locations, Kryuchkov urged KGB stations to cultivate, using more sophisticated covers and approaches, "prominent figures in politics and society [chiefly, the U.S.], and important representatives of business interests and science." Characteristically, Kryuchkov underscored that businesspeople and scientists were important not only because they could provide valuable information in their fields but also because they could actively influence the "foreign and domestic politics of target countries in a direction of advantage to the USSR."[44]

Somehow, Moscow Center believed that an intelligence breakthrough illuminating the dark political intentions of imperialist powers and their henchmen was critical to preserving the balance of strategic nuclear forces and to deterring the United States and its allies from launching a nuclear first strike against the Soviet Union. Hardly surprising, then, that Lenin's works were considered the best guide to action in the event of a nuclear war and were the only books on the shelves of the emergency command and communications center. Hence, a logical answer to one vexing question in international relations theory—"what deters?"—is Lenin in the bunker.

Operation RYAN

Documents in the Gordievsky-Andrew collection of KGB instructions tell the story of Operation RYAN, an obvious case of Soviet intelligence estimating the threat of global war from indicators of political intentions.[45] RYAN is an acronym for the Russian *raketno-yadernoye napadenie,* meaning nuclear missile attack.[46] Operation RYAN refers specifically to the KGB "program for monitoring a sudden nuclear missile attack on the USSR," as defined by the last KGB chairman, Vadim Bakatin. Bakatin took credit for dismantling the program in 1991. Calling RYAN "an atavism of the Cold War," Bakatin indicated that it was a long-term intelligence community effort representing the way Soviet institutions were set up to conduct war threat assessments: "Almost the entire foreign intelligence apparatus of the KGB and GRU of the General Staff of the Soviet Armed Forces carried out this program for decades with various degrees of intensity. Consuming a vast amount of public funds, the program was highly inefficient, a sort of window dressing, and boiled down to compilation of regular reports stating that any given country was not intending in the next few days to drop a nuclear bomb on the USSR."[47]

Although the GRU (Soviet military intelligence) regularly provided information to Soviet chiefs of staff on the military capabilities of the United

States and NATO, it took second place to the KGB both within the Soviet political hierarchy and the intelligence community. The structure of inter-agency collection priorities in Operation RYAN as a whole was defined and cued by the KGB, with the FCD, the foreign intelligence service, play-ing the lead in this structure. In addition, the FCD had a broad mandate, including responsibility for intelligence on both political and military in-dicators of war threats. KGB documents also explain Soviet leaders' ratio-nale for giving priority to indicators of political intentions. According to the accepted view within the Kremlin, all U.S. land-based intercontinental missiles, 70 percent of U.S. naval facilities, and 30 percent of strategic air force were permanently on duty throughout most of the Cold War. Thus, the main task was not to acquire technical information on what the Krem-lin believed a priori were superior U.S. capabilities but "to discover signs of [U.S. and NATO's] preparation for a nuclear missile attack at a very early stage, before the order is given to use nuclear weapons."[48]

One critical piece of evidence showing that political intentions took center stage when it came to uncovering these ominous "signs" is that Brezhnev and Andropov personally addressed the KGB rather than the GRU on the need to intensify—and, in Gordievsky's view, to launch Op-eration RYAN. In the Soviet political system, it must be noted that the personal attention of the top leader was probably the most decisive institu-tional act signaling the importance of specific programs or policies. The intensive stage of Operation RYAN began with secret addresses by Brezhnev and Andropov to a conference of the KGB heads of service in May 1981. Andropov, who later succeeded Brezhnev in the Kremlin after fifteen years as KGB chairman, declared that the new Reagan administration was "ac-tively preparing for a nuclear war" and that there was "the possibility of a nuclear first strike by the United States." Ironically, according to the CIA view, Moscow must have estimated the Soviet global posture as much more secure precisely at this time, due to an increased capability to survive a first nuclear strike. But in 1982-1984, "the Center's fear of the Main Adversary was greater than at any time since the Cuban Missile Crisis of 1962."[49]

The KGB instructions and the testimony of Oleg Gordievsky, a high-ranking KGB officer stationed in London, enable us to identify threat in-dicators that were pivotal in the KGB's decision to inform the Center in November 1983 about NATO's imminent nuclear first strike against the Soviet Union. This was arguably the highest point in the Kremlin's nuclear panic, not only in Operation RYAN but also in the entire history of the Cold War since the Cuban Missile Crisis.

When briefed in June 1982 about RYAN requirements before taking a post as a KGB officer at the Soviet Embassy in London, Gordievsky was struck "by the comparatively low priority accorded to intelligence on new developments in Western missile technology." This was particularly puzzling, since the United States was considering the deployment of new intermediate-range missiles in Europe, Pershing II and Cruise missiles. Instead, the permanent operational assignment (POA) on RYAN, issued in February 1983, was "to organize a continual watch to be kept for *indications of a decision* [emphasis added] being taken to use nuclear weapons against the USSR or immediate preparations being made for a nuclear missile attack."[50]

All seven of the immediate information-collecting tasks for KGB residencies that were listed in the POA centered on soft targets: places where government officials and members of their families were to be evacuated; preparedness of Civil Defense shelters; increased purchases of blood from donors, the prices being paid for it, and extension of the network of reception centers; changes around individual Civil Defense installations; places most frequently visited outside working hours by employees of institutions and installations connected with taking and implementing decisions regarding RYAN; any changes from the ascertained normal level of activity of the most important government institutions, headquarters, and other installations (cars parked after hours, an increase in the number of lighted windows at night, increased activity on nonworking days); and finally, any significant changes in the police administration system and the activity of the special (i.e., security and intelligence) services regarding Soviet citizens and institutions.[51]

This pattern of selecting intelligence priorities has a historical antecedent in a similar nuclear crisis situation. During the Cuban Missile Crisis, the KGB's Washington, D.C. residency targeted the same types of threat indicators as the London residency did during Operation RYAN. Aleksandr Feklisov, who was in charge of the KGB residency in Washington, D.C., in 1960-1964 describes the crisis indicators monitored by his agents:

> Starting October 21 [1962], the personnel of the USSR Embassy was on the job 24 hours a day. The [KGB] residency employees spent every night driving around the White House, the Pentagon, the State Department, the FBI and the CIA Headquarters and making observations: the lights still on in the windows, too many agency cars in the parking lots meant that the frenetic activity in the top echelons of power continued. Anticipating an attack on the embassy we posted guard reinforcements, installed additional locks

on the doors . . . checked the alarm system and the equipment for destroying secret documents.[52]

Similar threat indicators were also part of the "principal prospective directions for the residency to discover adversary's preparations for RYAN," which had been set for the longer term in the 1983 POA. The requirement to monitor "increased purchases of blood and a rise in the price paid for it" reflected the Center's woefully inadequate understanding of Western society (British blood donors are unpaid). This bizarre intelligence collection target, however, fit the Soviet ideological construction of capitalism as "a society where everything can be bought and sold." The explicit adherence to Soviet communist ideology by the KGB facilitated the assignment of collection and analysis requirements based on Marxist-Leninist notions of power in the capitalist system. Projecting those notions onto contemporary Britain, the Center instructed the London residency that advance warning of a nuclear holocaust could be obtained from "heads of national churches and international church organizations" and from "heads of international and the larger national banks."[53] One almost imagines the Archbishop of Canterbury being followed by men in trench coats looking for indications of a decision by NATO to launch a nuclear attack on the Soviet Union.

With a paucity of data on tangible strategic capabilities, the Center inaccurately claimed in RYAN instructions that the Pershing IIs, after deployment in West Germany, needed only 4-6 minutes' flying time "to reach long-range targets in the Soviet Union." The actual flying time was about double that. Some other major technical aspects of Pershing II missiles, which in the minds of U.S. authorities made the missiles "nonprovocative," fell flat on the KGB and the Soviet government. Thus, in KGB reports, Pershing II comes through as a superfast, long-range monster. In reality, Pershing II's design explicitly emphasized survivability, useful especially in response to a crisis (such as a Soviet conventional attack on Western Europe). Despite the increased range over its predecessor, even Pershing IIs stationed in West Germany—unless upgraded—would be unable to reach Moscow or vital command-and-control centers east of the Soviet capital, from which a global nuclear war would be directed. Only Western parts of the Soviet Union were vulnerable.[54] In other words, Lenin in the bunker was safe, except in KGB estimates. And unlike the CIA struggles over the Bomber Gap and the Missile Gap in the 1950s, basic technical information on Pershing II was available to the KGB, much of it from open sources.

Technical aspects, however, were overshadowed by the primary KGB collection target concerning NATO's military preparations—the state of NATO's alert system. Particular attention was directed to implementation procedures regarding military alert and a battle alarm system ("Orange" alert and "Scarlet" alert), as well as activation procedures of the official alarm system.[55]

Estimates of war probability peaked in autumn 1983, following Andropov's warning at the June Central Committee plenum of "an unprecedented sharpening of the struggle" between East and West after the shooting down of Korean airliner KAL 007 in September. The highest threat point was in November 1983, during the NATO command-post exercise Able Archer '83, which was held November 2-11 to practice nuclear release procedures. According to Gordievsky, then KGB deputy station chief in London, "In the tense atmosphere generated by the crises and rhetoric of the past few months, the KGB concluded that American forces had been placed on alert—and might even have begun the countdown to nuclear war."[56]

Able Archer '83 triggered a heightened sense of nuclear war threat in Moscow because the exercises focused on procedures *prior to attack,* thus activating threat indicators to which the Soviet intelligence and policy-making establishment were particularly sensitive. Instructions from the Center at that time did not question the technical feasibility or military utility of a NATO nuclear missile attack, given the balance of strategic capabilities between the West and the Soviet bloc in Europe or globally. Rather, the established causes of Moscow's paranoia were chiefly related to direct intention assessment.

First, using military exercises as a cover for a real offensive was envisaged in Soviet contingency plans for a surprise nuclear attack on the West, and therefore Moscow projected this stratagem onto Able Archer '83. Second, the procedures and message formats employed in the transition from conventional to nuclear warfare during Able Archer differed from past NATO exercises. Third, the imaginary NATO forces during this exercise were moved through all alert phases to general alert. The KGB permanent operation assignment on RYAN, which was issued nine months prior to Able Archer '83, emphasized the importance of monitoring NATO's alert systems, and thus the movement through all alert phases during NATO exercises was deemed highly significant. Fourth, surveillance teams reporting to the KGB around American bases in Europe recorded changes in patterns of officer movement and the observation of one hour's radio silence between

1800 and 1900 hours, Moscow time, by some bases. This radio silence, according to Gordievsky, was the last straw, leading the KGB to issue strong warnings to Moscow of an impending war. An additional reason for alarm was that these apparently significant signals reached the Kremlin when Andropov's health had seriously deteriorated after a prolonged illness (leading to his death on February 9, 1984). Andropov's advisers considered that the United States was counting on "the weakening of the levers of governance in the Kremlin" and assumed that the United States was aware of Andropov's condition—a perfect opportunity to carry out an imperialist plot for a surprise missile attack on the Soviet Union.[57]

As the operation went on and war refused to erupt, Chairman Kryuchkov of the FCD was dissatisfied with the lack of information on NATO's preparations for a nuclear attack. When the RYAN scare began to diminish after the Able Archer exercise and Andropov's death, Kryuchkov informed KGB stations worldwide that "all the diverse intelligence assignments against the USA" could not succeed unless there was a "radical improvement in agent recruitment." In other words, the KGB considered that RYAN failed not for the lack of actual NATO plans for a surprise nuclear first strike on the Soviet Union but for the lack of highly placed secret agents.[58] In this context, the recruitment of Aldrich Ames in 1985 should have calmed the KGB leadership, resulting in fewer panic assessments.

The real failure of RYAN was more conceptual than operational. As the Soviet strategy of challenging world capitalism was anachronistically inadequate in tangible economic resources and strategic capabilities, so the ambitious goals of Operation RYAN exceeded available intelligence means. In the London residency, for example, the tiresome detailed observations required by the Center were conducted by a junior officer who did not even have the use of a car. But even if he did, he would have been unable to travel outside London without Foreign Office permission, a factor that was not considered by Moscow.

All in all, the deployment of Cruise and Pershing II missiles—marking a key shift in the capability balance in Europe—consumed far less energy and caused nowhere near as much tension in the KGB as did Operation RYAN during Able Archer '83. And in 1984, following the deployment, the Kremlin was more likely to receive information on the London residency's main immediate priority—field exercises of Cruise missiles based at Greenham Common—from the Tass News Agency than from the residency itself. The residency's flash telegram on the first such exercise, held

March 9, 1984, was based on British press reports after the *rezident,* Arkadi Guk, heard the news on the BBC.[59]

Chapter 8

Intelligence, Threat Assessment, and the End of the Cold War

The United States took the lead in extricating itself from the threat assessment trap of the New Cold War. By the time the KGB's Operation RYAN generated reports of the mounting threat of a NATO nuclear first strike on the Soviet Union, U.S. decision makers began to receive estimates suggesting that America no longer faced a window of vulnerability for a Soviet attack. The first such reassessment came out in April 1983, in a report of a conservative bipartisan group chaired by Brent Scowcroft (the Scowcroft Commission), established under pressure from congressmen and local politicians opposed to Reagan's proposal for deploying 200 MX intercontinental ballistic missiles. The commission concluded that America was less vulnerable to Soviet nuclear attack than was previously believed, a reassessment extrapolated largely from existing military capabilities.

Soviet political intentions, assumed to be hostile and immutable, were given no independent role in the Scowcroft report's reassessment. No allowance was made for the Soviet threat diminishing as a result of the Kremlin abandoning "aggressive totalitarianism" for any kind of political, economic, or ideological reasons. Though it acknowledged that "deterrence is a set of beliefs in the minds of the Soviet leaders, given their own values and attitudes," the report provided no independent assessment of these beliefs.

Instead, Soviet intentions were explicitly interpreted as a function of capabilities: "The overall military balance, including the nuclear balance, provides the backdrop for Soviet decisions about the manner in which they will try to advance their interests. This is central to our understanding of how to deter war, how to frustrate the Soviet efforts at blackmail, and how to deal with the Soviets' day-to-day conduct of international affairs" [emphasis added].[1]

Representing a combined executive and legislative effort to assess the procurement requirement for intercontinental ballistic missiles, the Scowcroft report is a sensitive gauge of the priorities set by U.S. decision makers for war threat assessment. In the report, the reassessment of the degree of America's vulnerability to a nuclear missile attack was not attributed to major political developments, either in the Soviet leadership cadre or in political ideology following Brezhnev's death. The reassessment was based on playing out macabre-sounding scenarios of the United States responding to a Soviet nuclear attack, given the strategic balance of forces between the two sides:

> For example, if Soviet war planners should decide to attack our bomber and submarine bases and our ICBM silos with simultaneous detonations—by delaying missile launches from close-in submarines so that such missiles would *arrive* at our bomber bases at the same time the Soviet warheads (with their longer time of flight) would arrive at our ICBM silos—then a very high proportion of our alert bombers would have escaped before their bases were struck. . . . If the Soviets, on the other hand, chose rather to *launch* their ICBM and SLBM attacks at the same moment (hoping to destroy a higher proportion of our bombers with SLBMs having a short time of flight), there would be a period of over a quarter of an hour after nuclear detonations had occurred on U.S. bomber bases but before our ICBMs had been struck. In such a case, the Soviets should have no confidence that we would refrain from launching our ICBMs during that interval after we had been hit. It is important to appreciate that this would not be a "launch-on-warning" or even "launch under attack," but rather a launch *after* the attack—after massive nuclear detonations had already occurred on U.S. soil."[2]

Concluding that the three components of the U.S. strategic nuclear triad were more survivable together than each would be alone, the Scowcroft report, in the words of Raymond Garthoff, helped "to quietly bury the lingering thesis that the United States faced a 'window of vulnerability' in its deterrent force that might open a 'window of opportunity' for the Soviet attack."[3]

This refutation of the window of vulnerability concept was hardly a one-time act. Reassessments took place incrementally against the background of NIEs in 1983 and 1984 that showed that the threat—and, hence, probability—of a Soviet intercontinental attack had stopped increasing. (In contrast, the CIA estimates from 1975 to 1982 indicated that the Soviet threat was constantly on the rise.)[4] Nonetheless, the CIA's Deputy Director for Intelligence at the time, Robert Gates, points out that in early 1983, for the first time, the intelligence community reported that the growth rate in Soviet military procurement had leveled off and that Soviet military spending had posted no real growth since 1976.[5] In September 1983, as the anti-Soviet mood swelled in the wake of the Soviet Union shooting down a Korean airplane with 269 passengers on board, Gates presented a quantitative reevaluation of earlier intelligence on the scale of the Soviet military effort, in open testimony before the Subcommittee on International Trade, Finance and Security Economics of Congress Joint Economic Committee. In his briefing paper, Gates reiterated new intelligence findings that from 1976 through 1983, Soviet defense outlays had increased at an average of just 2 percent per year, or at less than half the rate given in the previous estimates. These intelligence estimates effectively delegitimated the "spending gap," a notion that had been one of major building blocks of the window of vulnerability assessment.[6]

Also striking, particularly in comparison to the Soviet system, was that such reassessments were made openly in a legislature, even though they contradicted the conventional wisdom within the administration. Gates notes that he was "treated to repeated lectures at Defense and the White House on the problems we [the CIA] were creating with this analysis." Gates was also upset by what he considered misuses and abuses of the estimates in Congress; yet admittedly, he "never backed off one iota" from the statutory mandate to seek methodologically rigorous—that is, demonstrably quantifiable—assessments of Soviet military and economic capabilities.[7]

It is not that Gates was anywhere near dovish toward the Soviet Union or that the data stream correcting past errors was automatically accepted by all key decision makers. But these new estimates provided grounds for debate at the highest levels. And in the competitive information selection environment characteristic of America's political institutions, these well-documented and rationally argued reassessments of the window of vulnerability proved viable. They began to affect decisively Reagan's whole strategy toward the Soviet Union, particularly when accompanied by evidence of major shifts in public opinion. For example, in 1981, the majority of those polled by Gallup—51 percent—believed that Washington was spending too little on defense and military purposes, whereas only 15 percent considered military outlays excessive. In a sharp turnaround, by 1982 only 15 percent of respondents in the same poll thought the United States spent too little on defense, whereas 36 percent believed U.S. military spending was too high. Furthermore, a 53 percent majority in a summer 1982 Harris poll rated the president's strong posture on arms-control talks with the Soviet Union negatively, whereas only 17 percent in a May 1982 Associated Press and NBC survey supported the administration's proposition that limited nuclear war would be both possible and winnable.[8]

THE UNITED STATES:
FROM SOVIET THREAT TO SOVIET BREAKDOWN

By summer 1983, in the context of these new information inputs, President Reagan and his administration showed signs of what John Lewis Gaddis describes as "new moderation:" even when presented with a perfect opportunity by the Soviet shooting down of KAL 007, Reagan did not revive his evil empire rhetoric; instead, he called for continuing arms control negotiations and in early 1984 asserted that the United States was "in its strongest position in years to establish a constructive and realistic working relationship with the Soviet Union." For Garthoff, "the fearful 'window of vulnerability' depicted in 1980 was closed not by enhanced American defense capabilities or diminished Soviet ones but by the sober realism of the Scowcroft Commission in 1983. The real military relationship remained stable. The United States was not so weak in 1980 as pictured, nor so much stronger by 1984 or 1988; what changed was the official rhetoric and the public impression."[9]

The paradox of the U.S. government's transition from the evil empire scare to the grand reconciliation of the late 1980s was that the closure of this symbolic window of vulnerability did more to ease the perception of the Soviet threat than the regular stream of intelligence reports in later years about profound political, social, economic, and cultural malaise in the Soviet Union. In retrospect, it is indeed remarkable that less than a year after his evil empire speech, following the window of vulnerability reassessment, President Reagan made an unexpectedly pacifist television address, in which he announced that the time was ripe for "a constructive and realistic working relationship with the Soviet Union." The president went so far as to visualize a typical Russian couple, Ivan and Anya, and a typical American couple, Jim and Sally, deciding that "they were all going to get together for dinner some evening soon."[10] No less remarkable is that after the arrival in power of Mikhail Gorbachev, who boldly pushed the agenda for dismantling Cold War arsenals, and despite years of CIA reports describing the deadly ills of Soviet society, the Reagan and then the Bush administrations drifted warily in their relations with the Soviet Union in the late 1980s, thereby relinquishing the reconciliation initiative to the new Soviet leader.

These paradoxes are further compounded by the contradictory nature of CIA estimates of the Soviet military threat. As the 1980s unfolded, the Soviet Union was coming through in the U.S. intelligence reports as a formidable military power continuing to enhance its strategic forces, while its populace—apparently spending most of its time in endless lines for scarce goods that were getting scarcer—was becoming alienated from and deeply resentful of the Soviet system. Making sense of the Soviet Union was akin to making sense of phantasmagoria—as if one had slipped into a magic lantern show where, by optical illusion, objects rapidly change size, coalesce, or splinter into millions of sparks. Translating this phantasmagoria into intelligence assessments made the Soviet Union look increasingly like what it was—an Upper Volta, or perhaps an Argentina, with intercontinental missiles and nuclear submarines. In the context of American political institutions, making inferences about the magnitude of military threat and the essence of political intentions from this highly contradictory portrayal required some kind of equitable quantification of strengths and weaknesses. Being in principle impossible, especially given the consistent effort of the Soviet government to muddy the evidence of any problems, the institutionally mandated rational quantifications of Soviet threat factors made U.S. intelligence estimates gravitate toward observable data, primarily on military capabilities, while discounting softer, conceptual evidence.

The only declassified NIE of the Gorbachev era, entitled *Domestic Stresses on the Soviet System* and issued in November 1985, as well as other declassified assessments of the CIA's Office of Soviet Analysis, illustrate the logical confusion arising from the clash of qualitative and quantitative information on which America's policy was supposed to be based. Although the qualitative information flow portrayed mounting political and socioeconomic challenges to the Soviet regime (albeit lucidly and incisively), the quantitative information flow continued to portray the Soviet military as powerful and modernizing and the Soviet economy as still growing, albeit at a slower rate.

Little of what later proved fatal to the Soviet system escaped the CIA's attention: the stifling political legacy of the moribund party leadership (three Soviet leaders died in office between 1982 and 1985), the economic stagnation, the social pathologies, the dissident and opposition movements, the shifts in the popular mood, and the growing exposure of Soviet people to life in the "decadent" West (which triggered unfavorable comparisons to life at home). With great clarity the CIA detailed massive, if as yet in abeyance, problems facing the Soviet political leadership: an entrenched and increasingly change-averse bureaucracy "relieved of pressures for innovation needed to improve economic performance;" leaders moving at a leisurely pace despite their technical and managerial incompetence for handling an increasingly complex economy; cynicism, careerism, and selfish interests coming "almost openly to dominate the actual values of the ruling elite;" and pervasive corruption "in the form of bribery and shady dealings on the underground economy," which was reaching "epidemic proportions." The CIA correctly saw these ills transforming the party-state apparatus "from a mobilization tool into an obstacle to progress on all fronts."[11]

By all accounts, in the CIA's estimate the Soviet Union had turned into an economic sloth: the average annual growth of the Soviet GNP had decreased at least twofold between the late 1960s and the early 1980s; public consumption growth had ground to a halt; shortages of food staples and lines in Soviet stores were legendary; Soviet public health was decaying due to sparse funding, sloppy execution of public programs, mounting environmental problems, and a slackening control over communicable diseases; life expectancy and birthrates were declining; housing shortages—often with three generations under the same roof in squalid one-bedroom apartments—had "deleterious effects" on family life; endemic alcoholism and work absenteeism were rising; and significant numbers of Soviet youth were increasingly rejecting home and family life, engaging in violent crime, draft dodging, drifting, and trafficking on the black market in foreign goods. As a result, the CIA claimed, "many Soviet citizens have had the impression that their standard of living deteriorated in this period."[12]

This pessimistic outlook was compounded by "a wholesale theft of time and goods" in and out of the workplace; a "pernicious and massive" erosion of standards of honesty and accountability; declining police effectiveness due to corruption and nepotism; and the world's highest per capita alcohol consumption (even though one in seven Soviet citizens were Muslim). Drug abuse—quite a novelty in the Soviet context—was identified by the CIA as a nascent but mounting problem, associated with thousands of young Soviet soldiers' exposure to drugs in Afghanistan.[13]

The U.S. intelligence community argued that these growing social pathologies were engendering "politically and morally conscious forms of dissent," including the rise of anti-Russian nationalism and "resentment of the Muscovite rule throughout the multinational Soviet empire;"[14] a resurgence, albeit "faintly discernible," of Russian nationalism due to a "conscious belief that communist rule has subverted Russia's values and despoiled its substance;" growing discontent among ethnic Russians that non-Russian regions were profiting at Russia's expense; an "observable growth" of adherence to Orthodox Christianity, Catholicism, Protestant denominations, and Islam serving as "the most widespread manifestation of rejection of the official values of the avowedly atheistic Soviet system."[15] From 1970 to 1985, the CIA also documented some 300 visible "jolts" to a generally secure Moscow leadership in the form of demonstrations, strikes, riots, and protests. Overall, the CIA concluded that despite arrests, expulsions, exile, and emigration, "dissenting attitudes—that is, conscious adherence to moral, political, or social beliefs the state opposes—are probably more widespread in the USSR today than at any time since Stalin's death."[16] This weakening of the regime's "political and psychological leverage" was aggravated by Soviet elites exhibiting weaker commitment to public service; middle- and lower-level officials fearing that "the economy is played out;" the ruling Politburo turning into a "geriatric group" lacking a problem-solving strategy; top party officials defecting increasingly to the West; and even members of the KGB and the Soviet military—"the ultimate custodians of coercive power in the system"—becoming "particularly disgruntled and pessimistic" about the Soviet future in the mid-1980s.[17]

Could Gorbachev's arrival rescue the USSR? As someone who lived through the entire Gorbachev era as both a Soviet citizen and a political correspondent covering the Kremlin at that critical time in Soviet history, I find the CIA's qualitative estimate of Gorbachev's dilemmas remarkably foresightful. Issued in late 1985, *Domestic Stresses on the Soviet System* portrayed Gorbachev as facing a no-win situation in the long run. Reverting to Stalinist totalitarianism was precluded because "Stalin-style controls over the population have seriously weakened and to reassert them in the old form would conflict directly with the avowed goals of growth and modernization in contemporary conditions." Systemic liberalization of the Soviet economy and political institutions would be watered down and resisted effectively by political elites brandishing the specter of "political chaos, economic collapse, and possibly a revolution." Gorbachev's only remaining option—"a balance between controls and dynamism"—would be hard, if not impossible, to achieve due to the overwhelming culture of passivity, the lingering system of pervasive control over what people do, know, and think, and the party's parasitic imperviousness to change. In this manner, the CIA estimates identified with astonishing clarity a problem that would develop into a malignant tumor and metastasize in the late 1980s: the more Gorbachev publicly encouraged the rank and file to boldly challenge corrupt elites through administrative and Communist Party institutions forged by Stalin, and the more these challenges were crushed by the deeply entrenched ruling *nomenklatura* resistance, the more the initial enthusiasm gave way to an even deeper disenchantment of the Soviet people than the one Gorbachev had inherited from Brezhnev's times, known as "the stagnation era."[18]

Nevertheless, the quantitative information stream in the same NIE set up quite a few hedges against anyone concluding that the Soviet Union was on a course leading to a meltdown. Thus, its description of manifold socioeconomic illnesses notwithstanding, the estimate still argued that the Soviet GNP grew by an average of 2.3 percent in 1980-1984 and would "probably be in the range of 2.5 to 3.0 percent."[19] Predictions of a possible slowdown and decline of the Soviet economy, in contrast, were not accompanied by quantitative data. Retrospectively showing the importance of governance by numbers in the American political context, these few figures—rather than descriptive evidence of profound Soviet malaise—were placed at the center of academic and public debates in the United States about the CIA's performance at the end of the Cold War. Herbert Meyer, a former economic editor of *Fortune* magazine who served as a special assistant to CIA's director William Casey in the early 1980s, argued that these numbers were counterintuitive.[20] A Swedish economist, Anders Aslund, who later advised the Russian government on post-communist economic reform, contended: "If the CIA assessments had been reasonably accurate, the Soviet economy would be a maturing industrialized economy . . . there would be little need for economic reform; Gorbachev's urgency would be incomprehensible; and most internal criticism in the USSR would be unfounded."[21]

Paradoxically, both the CIA and its critics were right, implicitly documenting the absurdity of quantitative estimates of growth in a centrally planned economy. "Dear Comrades," the manager addresses his workers in one of the tell-all-about-the-real-USSR jokes of the 1980s, "our glorious factory produced one million shoes this year. Hurray! Next year we'll make shoes for the left foot!" Metaphorically speaking, CIA estimates of the Soviet economy reported both the number of shoes and that the shoes fit only one foot. But if a hypothetical Soviet factory made one million shoes for the right foot only, how many shoes should it be credited for in a CIA estimate—zero, half a million, a million, or some other number? Such analytical transposition was essentially made impossible by the very design of the Soviet system, combined with the information processing habits of America's political institutions. The CIA indirectly acknowledged this analytical conundrum by noting in the "Scope Note" to the *Domestic Stresses on the Soviet System* that the estimate suffered "from severe data problems, particularly the lack of statistics on [Soviet] social trends and pathologies," and more importantly, from a lack of good social theory for describing Soviet behavior.[22]

The CIA took no risk, however, to evaluate the quantitative impact of Soviet social and political pathologies on Moscow's military might. (For example, how many years would it take for Soviet factories making shoes for one foot only to diminish Soviet war-fighting capacity by X percent?) *Domestic Stresses on the Soviet System* had a special insert labeled "The Exceptional Sector: The Soviet Military-Industrial Complex" at the beginning of the estimate that was separate from the narrative text. The USSR was seen as having fielded about 200 new or modernized military systems and ordered approximately $640 billion worth of military hardware during 1975-1985. (Here the CIA used the building-block method described earlier to present Soviet expenditures in terms compatible with U.S. Department of Defense practices.) The USSR reportedly "scored major military and technology advances in solid-propellant strategic missiles, surface-to-air and air-to-air missiles, long-range cruise missiles, fighters, bombers, transport aircraft, tanks, command-and-control systems, and reentry vehicles." Though it acknowledged that the Soviet military-industrial complex was "not isolated from the problems of the surrounding society," the estimate ventured no quantitative projections of the impact of these problems on the Kremlin's defense procurements in the rest of the 1980s and beyond. In this fashion, U.S. intelligence estimates clearly separated quantitative assessments of Soviet military strength from descriptive evidence of political and socioeconomic malaise.[23]

As is suggested even by selectively declassified CIA papers, this bifurcation in intelligence reporting—portraying the Soviet Union as both a military superpower by quantitative measures and a political dinosaur/economic wreck by descriptive evidence—persisted through the second half of the 1980s. In March 1986, a CIA-DIA presentation to the Joint Economic Committee of Congress contended that even though Gorbachev's reforms to boost consumer goods production would "certainly involve increased competition with the defense sector . . . the production capacity required to support the Soviet force modernization over the next 5 to 6 years" was in place. At about the same time, a CIA paper, "Gorbachev's Modernization Program: Implications for Defense," evaluated Gorbachev's first year in office: "Gorbachev can coast a few years on the basis of the USSR's past investment in its military industrial complex." The paper also implicitly suggested that Gorbachev's modernization efforts—albeit not without overcoming massive socioeconomic obstacles and tensions between the civilian and military sectors—may actually "pay off in greater numbers of more advanced, high-quality [military] equipment and in substantially increased productivity." These assessments are directly related to the stream of quantitative data on Soviet production capacity (primarily GNP) and defense spending, which was the mainstay of flagship NIEs on Soviet military capabilities (the 11-3/8 series). A declassified CIA memo disagreeing with the April 1986 NIE on Soviet force projections indicates that the coordinated U.S. intelligence community view saw Moscow as capable of increasing its "procurement spending on strategic mission" (that is, capabilities for intercontinental attack) by at least 11 percent annually. The CIA's objection, omitted from the NIE, was not followed by an alternative quantitative estimate, however, nor were Gorbachev's political intentions a primary reason for the CIA's dissenting view.[24]

During 1987-1989, the CIA's Office of Soviet Analysis continued to draw attention to major political and socioeconomic pathologies obstructing Gorbachev's reforms; yet once again, estimates of the quantitative impact of these challenges on Soviet defense outlays was explicitly absent. For example, a February 1987 report suggested only that "there will be a time in the next year or two, we think, when the question of cutting tools for the next generation of weapons systems will be a serious issue, and when the debates begin on the next Five Year Plan. It is clear that the military is going to have to be dealt with insofar as its share of investments is concerned." In July, another CIA paper saw no signs of slackening in what was perceived as Gorbachev's military modernization program. In April 1988, while reporting troubles for Gorbachev with "too few investments chasing too many needs," the CIA testified to Congress that "military expenditures remained at the generally low rate of growth but they remained at an extremely high absolute level," a conclusion that generally fits the quantitative pattern outlined in the declassified NIEs for 1983-1984 (see chapter 7) and in Robert Gates's briefing of the Joint Economic Committee in 1983.[25]

In June 1988, the Office of Soviet Analysis produced an assessment explaining the rationale for this view: "Even if [economic] growth is constrained, *the present high level of military spending ensures a continuing large input of new weapons* that should keep the defense constituency mollified, as long as the military does not sense a serious deterioration of the Soviet side of the military balance" [emphasis added]. The paper also illustrates how the CIA extrapolated Soviet political intentions, as well as policies, from the balance of military capabilities rather than weighing the Soviet leadership's programmatic statements as an independent factor: "Because so much of the USSR's superpower status rests on military power, however, resistance to any efforts to slacken appreciably the defense effort will not be confined to the military. Indeed, what Soviet military writers tout as the Western thrust into high-technology hardware will continue to be a basis for arguing to increase defense resources. All this suggests that we will *see a prolongation of the trend of the past decade—continued high but flat or slowly growing defense spending"* [emphasis added].

Seemingly contradicting this assertion, the paper argued that Gorbachev might initiate unilateral defense cuts by the end of the 1980s. But this assessment was not derived from Gorbachev's now well-documented political intention to transcend the Cold War rivalry and build a lasting East-West partnership. Rather, the paper concluded that Gorbachev had enough leeway to ensure that Moscow's "defense spending could be cut at the same time the effectiveness of the Soviet military is improved." In this sense, defense spending cuts would affect only the outdated sectors of the military-industrial complex, whereas spending in competitive high-technology sectors could conceivably increase. Thus, no room was left for the possibility that Gorbachev might intentionally and unilaterally reduce Soviet military power.[26]

Concurrently, the CIA painted a bleak picture of Soviet society plagued by political and socioeconomic problems. In September 1988, a CIA paper saw widening divisions over policy within the Kremlin elites, burgeoning ethnic unrest unleashed by greater political openness, and lack of significant progress concerning the proverbial Soviet shopper waiting in line for hours for a solitary stick of butter. These developments, however, were viewed through the prism of the leadership crisis facing Gorbachev and its impact on personnel changes in the ruling Politburo, providing no assessment of any quantitative impact on the Soviets' capabilities and proclivity for intercontinental attack. In a similar fashion, CIA reports about Gorbachev's housecleaning of the top party echelons in September 1988— including the expedited retirement of the durable foreign minister, Andrei Gromyko, which paved the way for Gorbachev's UN speech the same year offering massive unilateral force reductions—were confined to the issue of Gorbachev's political survivability. Only an unqualified general statement was made suggesting that "the prospects for advancing 'new thinking' on national security issues have increased." A March 1989 CIA analysis of the Soviet economy from a global perspective not only concluded that Soviet consumption and trade patterns were more like those of Egypt or Mexico than those of major industrial states, but also acknowledged no link to quantitative estimates of Soviet military might.[27]

These intelligence flows reflecting what U.S. administrations preferred to know about the multiple dimensions of Soviet threat explain Reagan's and Bush's reluctance to share Gorbachev's enthusiasm about burying the Cold War until, essentially, the collapse of communism in Eastern Europe in late 1989. The record of the Reagan and Bush administrations' dealings with Gorbachev during 1985-1991 leaves little doubt that American strategy changed primarily in response to reported changes in estimated Soviet military capabilities rather than in response to changes in the description of Soviet socioeconomic pathologies, political malaise, or ideological shifts under Gorbachev.

In a policy paper on the national security strategy of the United States, issued in January 1988, Ronald Reagan still referred to the "global challenge posed by the Soviet Union" as the "most significant threat to U.S. security interests." The U.S. government stated that this assessment was based on the realist approach—"a strategy without illusions, based on observable facts." Therefore, the fundamental transformation of Soviet ideology in the mid-1980s, which placed universal human values above class struggle as the foundation of Soviet international behavior, was given short shrift in the policy paper: "In the Soviet Union we hear talk of 'new thinking' and of basic changes in Soviet policies at home and abroad. We will welcome real changes, but we have yet to see any slackening of the growth of Soviet military power, or abandonment of expansionist aspirations." Explicitly pledging to "judge the Soviets by actions, rather than words," the paper suggested why Gorbachev's leadership was still suspected of ex-

pansionism: "For decades the Soviet Union has allocated a disproportionately high share of its national income to military expenditures and has
created technologically sophisticated forces far in excess of any plausible
need for self-defense." While calling Soviet external propaganda and support to communist parties and insurgent movements "equally threatening," the paper did not link the possible softening of American strategy to
Soviet reversal of these practices.[28]

Considering that Soviet global propaganda and clandestine financial
assistance to communist parties worldwide, including the U.S. Communist Party, continued even after the fall of communism in Eastern Europe
and the signing of major arms reductions treaties, the U.S. government's
embrace of Gorbachev in late 1989 would have been unlikely if these softer
aspects of Soviet expansionism were as decisive in assessing the Soviet threat
as military power.[29]

At the same time, the position of principal U.S. decision makers during 1985-1989 was very much in line with the cautious approach outlined
in Reagan's national security paper of January 1988 and consistent with
the priority given to intelligence on Soviet military capabilities and expenditure. Reflecting the consensus within the Reagan administration, Robert
Gates, then deputy director of Central Intelligence, implied in his speech
to the Dallas Council on World Affairs that Gorbachev's reform program
could, in fact, succeed. In such a case, Gates said, "the United States will
face in the 1990s and beyond a militarily powerful, domestically more
vital and politically more adroit Soviet Union whose aggressive objectives
abroad and essential totalitarianism at home remain largely unchanged."[30]
Even as persistent an advocate for closer contacts with Moscow as Secretary of State George Shultz argued that the Soviet Union, given a realistic
appraisal, was unlikely to switch from intimidation to dialogue as the ultimate goal in its dealings with other states in any foreseeable future. And
despite a heartwarming exchange of televised New Year addresses between
Reagan and Gorbachev, the American president, still deeply skeptical about
Gorbachev's sweeping proposals on disarmament and global cooperation,
held back from signing a strategic arms reduction treaty.[31]

Even after Gorbachev's speech to the United Nations in late 1988, in
which he proposed to cut Soviet armed forces unilaterally by 500,000 men
in the next two years, pull out and disband six tank divisions from East
and Central Europe, and make large troop withdrawals from Mongolia,
Reagan indicated that the real change in the assessment of Soviet threat
levels would occur when these cuts and a complete Soviet pullout were

implemented and verified. In the meantime, the U.S. president defined the proposed Soviet unilateral force reductions as "redeployments" that would still leave the Warsaw Pact with "a large conventional advantage."[32] Also accentuating U.S. decision makers' preoccupation with observable military capabilities was that in evaluating Gorbachev's UN speech, the U.S. government focused predominantly on proposed force reductions (that is, on only one half of Gorbachev's speech). Considerably less attention was devoted to the other half of Gorbachev's speech, which addressed major conceptual shifts in the Soviet policy outlook—and was precisely the part of the speech that Gorbachev considered the most significant.[33]

The arrival in the White House of George Bush, who was much less of a political visionary than Reagan, brought Soviet military capabilities even more to the fore in decision making. Bush had to take into account the position of such hard-liners as Vice President Dan Quayle, who argued—even in late 1989—that Gorbachev remained a "refined Stalinist" attempting to win breathing space for the Soviet Union to regroup and beat the United States in global competition. In Bush's view, when he was inaugurated in January 1989, the jury was still out on Gorbachev's intentions, and passing the verdict required demonstrable evidence. For the moment, the United States would abstain from seeking or expecting further major improvements in relations with the Kremlin. Thus, soon after taking office, Bush issued National Security Review 3 (NSR-3) to study the implications of Gorbachev's policies on U.S.-Soviet relations. The NSR-3 report, issued on March 14, 1989, cautioned that Moscow retained enough capabilities to emerge as a "more competitive superpower" if Gorbachev's perestroika succeeded.[34]

Unsatisfied by that assessment, Bush, Scowcroft, and Baker requested a national security directive (NSD-23) to reassess the U.S. policy of containment. The document was drafted in May 1989 by Robert Blackwill and Condoleeza Rice, the National Security Council's experts on Europe and the Soviet Union, but it was not signed by Bush until September 22, 1989—caution was still the operative concept in the U.S. administration's dealings with the Soviet Union. If changes were to occur in the U.S. position, the Soviet Union would need to make demonstrable reductions in its global reach capabilities. In a May 12, 1989, speech at Texas A&M University, in which he laid out much of the NSD-23 text, Bush declared the containment strategy successful and announced the need to "move beyond containment to a new policy . . . that recognizes the full scope of change taking place around the world and in the Soviet Union itself." This new policy envisaged "integration of the Soviet Union into the community of nations" and a "broader economic relationship" with the United States. To benefit from this new U.S. approach, however, the Bush administration set specific benchmarks requiring the Soviet Union to reduce the military and economic capabilities that could pose a challenge to America's global interests. These demands included further reductions of the Soviet military, termination of military and economic support to Cuba and Nicaragua, "abandonment of the Brezhnev doctrine" (meaning essentially an agreement to withdraw Soviet forces from East and Central Europe), cooperation with the United States in regional conflicts (primarily on American terms), and the lifting of emigration restrictions.[35]

Seen by U.S. decision makers in the context of a "broader national security strategy," even this humanitarian push for liberalizing Soviet emigration laws was explicitly linked to military competition with Moscow. Issued on October 2, 1989, after Gorbachev had allowed tens of thousands of émigrés to leave the country, National Security Directive 27 (NSD-27) provided for the granting of special passage rights to America over five years for as many as 150,000 Soviet citizens deemed of "special foreign policy interest" (that is, intelligence interest) to the United States.[36]

The fundamental downward reassessment of the level of Soviet threat to America's national security began in late 1989, as Moscow allowed Soviet-style regimes to collapse all across Eastern Europe, and continued through 1990. By early 1990, President Bush's policy paper, "National Security Strategy of the United States: 1990-1991," in contrast to Reagan's national strategy papers, identified no single state as posing a "global challenge" to the United States. The issue of the Soviet Union was addressed in the section entitled "Regional Challenges and Responses." While still looking for "fundamental alterations in Soviet institutions that can only be reversed at great economic and political cost," the policy paper implicitly gave a rationale for relegating the challenges posed by the Soviet Union from a global to a regional level: "With [strategic arms reduction] agreements in place—and weapons destroyed, production lines converted, and forces demobilized—any future Soviet leadership would find it costly, time-consuming, and difficult to renew the pursuit of military supremacy and impossible to attempt without providing ample strategic warning." The paper also implied that Soviet capabilities for intercontinental attack, even after all the arms reduction treaties, remained the primary focus of threat in U.S. national security strategy assessments. Relations with the Soviet Union, despite a profound internal crisis of the communist system and possible breakup of the "evil empire," were declared "a strategic priority because that country remains the only other military superpower."[37]

The visible shift in the global balance of capabilities in late 1989-1990 validated those who had argued for years that Gorbachev's adherence to interdependence and radical arms reduction proposals had been genuine, and that domestic political and socioeconomic conditions made the Soviet Union much less likely to pursue expansionist policies. Whereas Reagan's 1989 national security strategy paper attributed Gorbachev's "new think-ing" to a modification of "style," Bush's 1990 policy paper finally acknowl-edged as fact that Moscow had "repudiated its doctrines of class warfare and military superiority and criticized major tenets of its own postwar policy."[38]

In the context of U.S. political institutions, this validation of trust in Gorbachev required rigid scrutiny of intelligence estimates by Congress. The open testimony of top intelligence officials to Congress Joint Eco-nomic Committee allows one to go inside the institutional information process that shaped threat assessment criteria and the reevaluation of So-viet strategic intentions at the close of the Cold War. In an opening state-ment to the Subcommittee on Technology and National Security on April 20, 1990, Senator Jeff Bingaman summarized intelligence reports on the Soviet Union. Referring to these reports, the senator announced that the hearing marked a milestone in Gorbachev's drive to reform the Soviet Union. After citing among the good news that the Soviet Union had become "a more open society, more tolerant of diversity of views at home, more re-spectful of human rights, and less confrontational abroad," Senator Bingaman explicitly identified the main reason for taking Gorbachev's tran-sition for real: "Perhaps the best news is that the Soviet military spending is going down. . . . The Soviet forces are being restructured along less threat-ening lines. In the past, we have seen a slowdown in the rates of growth in defense outlays. Now we see real cutbacks, and substantial reductions across the board. There is, at last, concrete evidence of a shift in priorities and resource allocations away from the defense sector. If these trends continue we may actually see a significant slowing of the arms race."[39]

The congressional committee scrutinized intelligence reports and offi-cial testimony.[40] Intelligence officials were hard pressed to furnish concrete evidence and quantitative data, or to explain their methodology. Two months after discussing the evidence, the Joint Economic Committee requested a consolidated intelligence community response on the principal points of interest to U.S. policy. In June 1990, Senator Bingaman, presiding at the hearings, sent a list of twenty questions to the CIA's deputy director for intelligence, John Helgerson. The questions represent precisely what the policy community wanted to know in order to make informed judgments about the level of Soviet threat to U.S. national security. Seventeen of the twenty questions (85 percent) addressed Soviet military capabilities directly. Thirteen questions addressed the central issue—the extent of Soviet military spending and modernization of forces, especially strategic offensive capabilities: Could the intelligence community give specific examples of Moscow's continued modernization of strategic forces (such as intercontinental missiles)? Was the Pentagon's 1989 assessment that this modernization had "extraordinary momentum" still accurate in 1990? Did Moscow continue apace the with modernization of tank forces? Was it accurate to say that the decline in defense spending did not necessarily affect force modernization? Was it possible to measure modernization rates in the past several years for Soviet strategic and conventional forces? What was the effect of military spending as opposed to force modernization on the level of the Soviet military threat? Was there sufficient evidence in recent military and economic developments to back up claims that the Soviet Union spent as much as 20-25 percent of its GNP on the military, rather than 15-17 percent, as the CIA estimated at the time? Was Gorbachev correct claiming in an April 27 speech that military spending amounted to 18 percent of Soviet GNP? Was the Pentagon report *Soviet Military Power* still correct in claiming that the defense industry was the fastest-growing sector under Gorbachev in 1990? Could the CIA specify exactly which Soviet military production lines had been cut? What would be the size of the Soviet peace dividend from defense cutbacks, and how much of this dividend could be reinvested? What quantitative data, if any, were available on the extent and significance of the conversion of Soviet production from the military to the civilian sector? Did Moscow cut down its military deployments in the Far East and the Pacific Ocean, reducing the threat to Japan and China?[41]

The intelligence community portrayed a measurable sea-change in the U.S.-Soviet global military balance. With regard to Soviet intercontinental attack capabilities, intelligence assessments still regarded Soviet forces as likely to be "extensively modernized by the late 1990's" and "more capable, diverse and survivable." This, however, was a fuzzy and distant prospect, yet to be tested and verified. The reality at hand, acknowledged even by the traditionally more hawkish Defense Intelligence Agency (DIA), was that the numbers and the throw weight of Soviet missiles targeted at the United States and its allies were being reduced.[42] Moreover, in the coordinated intelligence community's view, conveyed to U.S. Congress by the CIA's director of congressional affairs: "The [Soviet] strategic force modernization currently underway is not . . . as robust as in the 1960s and 1970s—current modernization patterns indicate that the Soviets do not plan to replace older systems on a one-for-one basis, or to keep aging systems."[43] Some other principal indicators of Soviet military power were reassessed at the time as well. For example, the classification of the Soviet Tu-22M Backfire medium bomber as intercontinental was quietly recognized as a mistake. Also corrected was an earlier technical intelligence error that resulted in the overestimation of the SS-19 missile's accuracy, which had contributed to the window of vulnerability scare in earlier years.[44]

Modernization of Soviet ground forces, with an emphasis on tanks, had loomed on Western Europe's doorstep for over four decades, but no longer continued apace. According to the intelligence community, the USSR produced only 1,700 tanks in 1989, as compared with 3,500 tanks in 1988, and would produce between 1,300 and 1,400 tanks in 1990. Furthermore, intelligence analysts judged this "dramatic decline in tank production" as hampering modernization of the entire Soviet forces in the 1990s, since the Soviet military would "receive newer equipment at a slower pace than in the past." Moreover, with large holdings of conventional weapons, Moscow would have to reduce its vast weapon stockpiles if modernization rates were to be maintained "in an era of defense cuts."[45]

After several years of caution, the intelligence community could finally present to Congress what, in John Helgerson's view, were the first fruits of Gorbachev's military reduction program. After estimated real-term increases of about 3 percent annually in 1986-1988, overall Soviet defense spending fell by 4-5 percent in 1989, according to intelligence calculations. Furthermore, Moscow's military procurement outlays the same year dropped even more sharply—by an estimated 6-7 percent. The intelligence community also suggested that the growth in Soviet GNP, national income, and defense spending in the several years prior to this dramatic reversal could have been lower than the numbers implied. On the basis of these data, the congressional committee concluded that not only was the defense industry no longer the fastest-growing sector of the Soviet economy, but it was not even growing after 1989. The USSR also reportedly cut its uniformed military personnel by 200,000, thus making good on much of Gorbachev's 1988 pledge to reduce the number of servicemen by 500,000 before the end of 1991. Dennis Nagy of the DIA testified that the Soviet Union most probably had completed at least half of the promised tank reductions as well as three-fourths of the artillery and combat aircraft cutbacks in the Atlantic to the Urals zone. Nagy mentioned reductions in Soviet air forces, stationed along the Sino-Soviet border and said that the DIA believed the USSR would withdraw 75 percent of its ground forces from Mongolia by late 1990, thus substantially lessening the Soviet military threat in the Far East and the Pacific region. As summarized by Senator Bingaman at the hearings, these intelligence community findings "paint a different picture from the one we get from certain administration officials who have argued that the Soviet defense spending is still growing, or that certain military capabilities are still increasing. Also this is a very different picture from that which we received last year in the DOD [the Pentagon] publication, 'Soviet Military Power.' The fact that outlays were being reduced for offensive strategic weapons, as well as for conventional weapons, indicates the seriousness of Soviet efforts to cut back on overall armaments."[46]

Recognizing "the substantial uncertainties and the basic difficulty in attempting to estimate data that the Soviets attempted to keep secret until at least 1989," the intelligence community stood firm by the CIA's estimate that the Soviet Union allocated 15-17 percent of its GNP to defense, rather than the 25 percent suggested by some critics. At the same time, the intelligence community implicitly acknowledged in the same response that the Soviet leadership was becoming much more open and trustworthy in their own public estimates of Soviet defense burden—a conceptual breakthrough perhaps far more important than the correctness of the CIA's own assessments of Moscow's military spending. Translating from Soviet to Western economic concepts, the intelligence community reported that Politburo member Yegor Ligachev's estimate of the Kremlin's defense spending at 100-115 billion rubles for 1985 was "very close to the Intelligence Community's range (in current prices), and well above the revised official Soviet defense budgets for the late 1980s." To CIA analysts, Gorbachev's statements also implied that defense consumed 15 percent of the Soviet GNP in 1990—perfectly consistent with the CIA's assessment.[47] Given this solid quantitative substantiation of increasing Soviet transparency, Gorbachev's promise to cut defense spending by 14.2 percent by 1991 appeared increasingly credible.

Congress also obtained quantitative data signaling that the conversion of Soviet industrial production from the military to the civilian sector was in fact underway. The intelligence community could account roughly for 100 Soviet plants involved in conversion, as well as for an 11 percent increase in the defense industry's production of consumer goods in the first four months of 1990, compared with the same period in 1989. At the same time, even if the Soviet Union reduced its defense spending by as much as Gorbachev had promised, the peace dividend would still amount to as little as 2 percent of the Soviet GNP in 1989—hardly a number that could sustain any kind of a secret crash modernization of the Soviet economy and military, as some hard-liners suspected was Gorbachev's true goal. In addition, the intelligence community provided more compelling quantitative data of Soviet economic decline, in comparison to the 1985 NIE, *Domestic Stresses on the Soviet System*. According to a joint CIA-DIA paper on the Soviet economy, in 1989 the annual growth of per capita GNP approached zero; the state budget deficit exceeded 10 percent of the GNP (rising 2.5 times since 1985); total energy production declined in absolute terms for the first time since the 1940s (with oil output falling 2.5 percent); crude steel production dropped by 2 percent; state quotas for aluminum, copper, lead, and zinc remained unfulfilled; output of chemicals declined sharply; machinery output posted no growth; output of processed foods (excluding alcoholic beverages) and soft goods rose by only 1 percent; the 1-2 percent increase in farm output failed to make a dent in retail food shortages; the number of thefts and violent robberies rose 70 percent; the number of strikes jumped from two dozen in 1987-1988 with a few thousand workers participating to more than 500 in the first seven months of 1989 involving several hundred thousand workers; only 50 of about 1,200 basic consumer goods were readily available to most Soviets; 7 million days were lost to strikes and ethnic unrest; the trade balance registered a $1.4 billion deficit; and net hard currency debt rose from $11 billion in 1984 to $32 billion, exceeding the entire Soviet gold reserve (valued at $28 billion) and making Western bankers tighten credit and charge higher interest rates.[48]

A striking example of the marginalization of political factors in U.S. intelligence analyses of the Soviet threat in the late 1980s was the lack of integration of intelligence on nationalism and ethnic problems (even though individual analysts, intelligence officers, and decision makers were keenly aware of Soviet nationality problems). What we know about the intelligence provided to U.S. decision makers suggests that riots in Kazakhstan, pogroms in Azerbaijan, human chains formed in support of independence in the Baltic republics and the Ukraine, irredentist clashes in Moldova, and the rise of Yeltsin in Russia—all, ultimately, playing a key part in the self-destruction of the "evil empire"—were marginal to the intelligence flows to assess the strategic threat posed by the Soviet Union.

While deputy CIA director, Robert Gates implicitly admitted as much. For example, Gates found that U.S. intelligence "seismographs" were ill designed to register the quakes of massive unrest in the mountainous enclave of Nagorno-Karabakh in the Caucasus, in retrospect, "the final act of the seventy-year-old Soviet tragedy." Ultimately, in 1988, despite its best efforts, the CIA's best source of information on Nagorno-Karabakh was the Cable News Network (CNN). Gates gave this explanation:

> Our efforts had long been focused on events in Moscow, and we were only beginning to realize how small and inadequate were our collection capabilities and expertise on the non-Russian republics and ethnic groups. For the first time, the press in places like Yerevan and Baku was important as a source of information, and yet it took us weeks to get copies of newspapers. We had virtually no human sources and, apart from monitoring military actions, our technical collection systems were of marginal value. We had countless pictures of demonstrators, but that wasn't much help in learning about or understanding the decisions and actions being taken on the ground.

Having established a secret study group to examine the potential consequences of widespread turmoil in the Soviet republics in autumn 1989, Gates could keep the president and his senior advisers "current and well-warned" on events in the Baltics and the Caucasus, mainly through the president's *Daily Brief.* "But, in truth," writes Gates, "the nationalities problem was not high on the White House agenda. The problems in the Caucasus were seen in 1989 and 1990 primarily as interethnic conflict, with Moscow trying to maintain order, prevent additional bloodshed, and bring calm."[49]

Given the preponderance of capability-based threat assessments, this White House view is quite understandable. As the CIA's chief Soviet analyst, George Kolt, testified to Congress in mid-1990, the agency believed that Soviet disintegration posed no "significant risk at all of nuclear weapons getting into the hands of insurgents or groups not controlled by Moscow." The DIA's Dennis Nagy added that even assuming the worst, the use of nuclear weapons would be "extremely difficult" for anyone outside the KGB and military elite, "because of the codes and other safeguards that the Soviets have built into the system."[50]

In light of this threat assessment paradigm, the U.S. intelligence establishment and policy makers in 1990 and for most of 1991 backed Gorbachev and Moscow's retention of the still-evil empire to ensure the KGB's safeguarding of Soviet nuclear weapons. By then, Gorbachev had acquired a solid record of delivering on promises: the withdrawal of intermediate nuclear forces from Europe, unilateral cutbacks in the Soviet military and signing of the Conventional Forces in Europe Treaty, an agreement to exclude British and French nuclear forces from U.S.-Soviet negotiations, a pledge to dismantle a radar installation in Krasnoyarsk that could be used for missile defense, and the signing of the Strategic Arms Reduction Treaty that provided for a disproportionately large cut in the intercontinental land-based missiles targeting the United States. Through these actions, Gorbachev lowered the readings on the major indicators of Soviet threat embedded in the U.S. intelligence assessment process. The foe-to-friend transformation was complete. As Robert Gates explained, "There was also a widely held view at senior levels of the administration that Gorbachev was doing what we wanted done on one major issue after another—from his willingness to let Germany be reunified in NATO to his partnership with us in taking on Iraq. There was no desire to jeopardize that. There also was growing worry that fragmentation of the Soviet Union other than whatever might be worked out politically and by agreement would provoke civil war and dangerous instability in a country with tens of thousands of nuclear warheads."[51] In this manner, with the Cold War extinguished, the continuing existence of the Soviet Empire was regarded as much less threatening than its collapse.

THE KGB: SHORT-CIRCUITED

The Kremlin's intelligence alert of a NATO nuclear first strike against the Soviet Union began withering away in early 1984 under the impact of political changes in Moscow that had little, if anything, to do with the assessment of the East-West military balance or with threat estimates. At the time, the balance of strategic forces between the Soviet Union and the West was still relatively stable. The political changes began on February 9, 1984, with the death of Yuri Andropov, the party's general secretary and former KGB chairman. Andropov's successor, the visibly moribund Konstantin Chernenko, was much less suspicious of the West's intention to launch a nuclear attack on the Soviet Union, a view conveyed to the KGB's London agents in February and March 1983 by Ambassador Viktor Popov and Nikolai Shishlin, a visiting international affairs specialist from the Central Committee staff. By July 1983, the KGB's acting resident in London missed filing several fortnightly reports on NATO's preparation for nuclear attack. As the summer rolled on, growing numbers of KGB officers were returning from their leave in Moscow and conveying to residencies abroad their growing sense that the priority of monitoring the signs of a surprise first strike by NATO was declining. The impetus for sustaining the intelligence alert was further weakened in autumn 1984 by the absence of the two principal Operation RYAN supporters in the Soviet military—the ouster of Marshal Ogarkov, chief of the general staff of the Soviet Armed Forces, and the death of the defense minister, Marshal Ustinov.[52]

Moreover, Chernenko's deteriorating health in the second half of 1984 left a black hole at the very top of the ruling hierarchy. According to Mikhail Gorbachev, who succeeded Chernenko, the ailing Soviet leader even neglected to appoint acting chairs of the weekly Politburo meetings until just fifteen to twenty minutes before the meetings were scheduled to start. In his memoirs, Gorbachev notes, "By the end of the year [1984], this problem reached dramatic proportions, as Chernenko was totally out of circulation. . . . Things got even worse when Konstantin Ustinovich [Chernenko] was hospitalized. Everyone tried to validate their position by making references to a conversation with Chernenko. Often, two people would be arguing completely different things with both referring to the General Secretary. Discord set in among the leaders and in the party apparatus." The KGB must have been aware, however, that the person consistently asked to chair Politburo meetings in Chernenko's absence was Mikhail Gorbachev. Still a junior member of the Politburo during the heyday of Operation RYAN in 1982-1983, Gorbachev was seen as a reformer favoring a return to detente with the West. The time was ripe for the intelligence alarm, associated squarely with the late Brezhnev and Andropov eras in Soviet politics, to be deactivated.[53]

In addition, by December 1984, deep resentment against the Center's Operation RYAN had accumulated within the KGB's ranks. Since 1981, when Moscow first issued the special intelligence alert, KGB agents and analysts had become weary and deeply resentful of filing fortnightly nil returns. Reading speeches by bankers and church leaders for signs of nuclear attack plans struck even hardened KGB operatives as futile and outlandish. In addition, political changes in the Kremlin after the deaths of Andropov and Chernenko left room for slack attitudes toward this increasingly detested task. Thus, the KGB's many briefings of Gorbachev in the critical months of his rise to power, including briefings in London by Gordievsky and the KGB residency in December 1984 during a visit to Great Britain, happened precisely when Operation RYAN was being discredited and intelligence assessments were growing less alarmist.[54]

This shift in the KGB's threat assessment practices also occurred when party and military leaders' conceptualization of the Soviet role in world politics had begun to change. This reevaluation of the Soviet Union's international role, which evolved through a secret and lengthy process, was remarkable, for it happened mostly outside the stream of vital quantitative data on Soviet military and economic capabilities, especially since these capabilities could affect the proposed changes.

One of the first major focal points in this search for new thinking was President Reagan's Strategic Defense Initiative (SDI), popularly known as "Star Wars." Announced on March 23, 1983, the program envisioned an antimissile space-based astrodome that would make nuclear weapons obsolete. This dream made a profound impression on Moscow. Challenging as it sounded, Reagan's space astrodome vision resonated well with the communist leaders, whose rise to power and whole lives were shaped by a political system dependent on the population mobilizing to translate the Kremlin's daring "visions" into reality. Conditioned to blur distinctions between a desirable dream and reality, the Soviet leaders started contingency assessments, as if American x-ray guns capable of knocking down Soviet missiles were already being deployed. Marshal Viktor Kulikov, commander-in-chief of the Warsaw Pact forces at the time, saw the United States as soon being capable to defend itself against Soviet missile forces. The chief of staff of the Warsaw Pact forces, General Anatoly Gribkov, remembers that the Soviet leaders perceived SDI "with a great degree of anxiety" from the start and shortly "began to scare one another more and more about this program." In the view of Georgi Arbatov, a member of the Central Committee and the director of the USA-Canada Institute in Moscow, the Kremlin felt shudders of existential fear—Star Wars made all Soviet "efforts to create deterrence against Americans" go down the drain. The feasibility of Star Wars was not assessed against demonstrable American capabilities (those were assumed to be sufficient to implement SDI) but against projected Soviet industrial and scientific potential. "And it became clear," concluded General Makhmud Gareev, deputy chief of the Soviet General Staff during 1984-1988, "that it was beyond our power." The Star Wars idea, in KGB general Leonov's view, "played a powerful psychological role" at a time when, according to Gareev, years of economic stagnation and senseless competition with the West had changed the psychology and consciousness of the Soviet leadership. General Sergei Kondrashev, chief foreign policy adviser to the KGB chairman during 1978-1991, believes in retrospect that SDI "was the issue that influenced the situation in the country [USSR] to such an extent that it made the necessity of seeking an understanding with the West very acute."[55]

In this convoluted fashion, it took Reagan's "virtual adventurism" to make the Soviets face reality. But there was much more to this critical phase in the Soviet transition to the Gorbachev era than the realization that the Soviet Union had run out of gas. The masters of the Kremlin could face reality only through the prism of institutions explicitly designed to promote Soviet policies that were themselves typical manifestations of virtual adventurism—the idea of building a global society in which all people would be entitled to whatever remuneration they desired for whatever work they did. New thinking was an offshoot of this forced reality testing through the conceptual lenses innate to Soviet political institutions. Thus, Gorbachev came to believe that the arms race was humanity's conventional trap and that his best bet, as a true Marxist-Leninist, would be to end the arms race. Extricating the USSR—and with it, all of civilization—from what Gorbachev saw as a historical dead end would be credited to socialism's peace-loving nature. Such a towering achievement would ensure Moscow's paramount role in world politics for as long as people preferred peace over the destruction of the planet. The USSR, then, could live up to the Marxist-Leninist tenet that a socialist society is ultimately wiser than and superior to any other form of human organization. Consequently, socialism's triumph over capitalism would no longer require a successful worldwide socialist revolution along Bolshevik lines, a doctrine implicit in the entire Soviet approach to world politics since Lenin. The Cold War, kept alive by the West's "military-industrial complex" and Soviet policies originating in the old thinking, was to be buried, not capitalism as a social system or the United States as its prime exponent. In this way Gorbachev sincerely believed he could be *both* a champion of global interdependence—a liberal idea, even in the Western tradition—and a herald of true and renewed communism as a viable and increasingly attractive component of a world "united in its diversity."[56]

In the context of Gorbachev's new thinking, the Cold War as the key organizing principle of world politics was effectively obsolete. The major threat to Soviet security would come first and foremost from ideas, intentions, and policies perpetuating the Cold War as a trend in world politics, subsuming the threat of imperialism's intentions to wage war against the Soviet Union or to develop new and deadlier military capabilities. The timing of this shift has been well established. In a sense, calling off the Cold War was framed as an official Soviet strategy in 1986—in Gorbachev's

January announcement of the Soviet program to achieve universal nuclear disarmament, in the Twenty-seventh Communist Party Congress report in March, and in Gorbachev's address to a closed session of top foreign ministry officials in May. In his memoirs, Gorbachev specifically names this foreign ministry session, held in late May 1986, as "the starting point for comprehensive efforts to translate 'new thinking' into reality."[57] All this strongly suggests that the downward reassessment of the "imperialist threat" on the Soviet side happened at least three years prior to major the downward reassessment of the Soviet threat in the U.S. government.

This new thinking reassessment was vigorously presented by Gorbachev in his report to the Twenty-seventh Congress and induced tangible shifts in the KGB's threat assessment priorities. At the congress, Gorbachev articulated startling changes in Soviet global political intentions, ones that Gorbachev hoped would send a powerful signal to the United States that the Cold War era was passé. (As I observed earlier, however, such changes in Soviet political intentions were not critical to changes in threat assessment by the U.S. intelligence community.) The key political task was no longer to discredit capitalism and undermine its allegedly rotten edifice from within but to ensure international security. In turn, political will was seen as critical in implementing this new security concept, whereas the doctrines of deterrence and intimidation by military force were now regarded as hopelessly out of date.

The triumph of communism over capitalism became secondary to "establishing a *constructive, creative interaction among states and peoples on the scale of the entire world* . . . in order to prevent a nuclear catastrophe, so that civilization would survive." The breakthrough to a "Sinatra Doctrine"—allowing states formerly under Soviet control to do it "their way"—was discernable in the new Soviet position on the Third World: "Fueling revolutions from outside, and doubly so by military means, is futile and inadmissible." This new ideological position was clearly supported by the political emphases embedded within the structure of Gorbachev's report. In contrast, Brezhnev's report to the Twenty-sixth Party Congress in 1981 contained a separate section on Soviet relations with "national liberation movements" and "nations that gained independence" in the Third World. Comprising thirty paragraphs, the 1981 report mentioned more than a dozen countries by name and suggested strengthening "the union of world socialism and the national liberation movement." The 1986 report had no section on this issue, and only three sentences briefly acknowledged "anticolonial revolutions and national liberation movement" as part of "basic trends in the contemporary world," without mentioning any country by name or promising assistance. The long section on the world communist movement was reduced to three short paragraphs.[58]

Gorbachev was therefore conceptually predisposed to reinterpret specific security threats along the lines of the new thinking. Star Wars became an especially poignant symbol, not so much of Soviet technological weakness (Gorbachev was convinced that the Soviet military could quickly develop much cheaper "asymmetric countermeasures" against space-based weapons), but of the world still treading the dangerous path of arms race, war, and mistrust. Gorbachev's memoirs tell us that at the time he considered SDI primarily as "testimony that the United States do not trust us." Star Wars signified "continuation of the arms race in a different and more dangerous sphere," as a result of which "suspicions and mistrust would be growing and each side would fear to be overtaken by the other." Steeped in a typically Marxist interpretation of capitalist politics, Gorbachev believed that the pressure to develop SDI was coming exclusively from America's sinister military-industrial complex against the deeper wishes of the overwhelming majority of the common people in the United States and around the world.[59]

And yet the new thinking made Gorbachev intensively look for signs that Western leaders and governments could rise above these sinister "class" influences and agree to keep pace with Gorbachev's efforts to rid the world of the deadly nuclear arms race. Gorbachev increasingly saw such signs, beginning with Margaret Thatcher's characterization of him as a man she could "do business" with and continuing with Reagan's willingness to persist with bilateral discussions on disarmament, despite the failure to reach breakthroughs at the first summit in Geneva in November 1985. And the Reykjavik summit, in October 1986, was a turning point in Gorbachev's perception of the United States: the old "imperialist threat" that for decades had loomed over the Soviet Union could now be buried. Gorbachev's foreign policy adviser, Anatoliy Cherniayev, who accompanied the Soviet leader in Reykjavik and helped formulate the Soviet position at the talks, believes that the conceptual breakthrough happened after Reagan, for a brief period of time, accepted Gorbachev's idea to cut U.S. and Soviet strategic nuclear weapons by half and even contemplated getting rid of all nuclear stockpiles. As Cherniayev explains in his memoir, the arms reduction proposals advanced at Reykjavik were seen by Gorbachev as "momentous and unprecedented":

> [The proposals] epitomized Gorbachev's political and ideological evolution in his one and a half years at the helm of a nuclear superpower. The [arms reduction] formula comprised everything that

was necessary for the fundamental transformation of world politics—
realization that nuclear confrontation was inadmissible, breaking
with the arms race, readiness to activate disarmament process, a
revision of the entire Soviet foreign policy that for decades had focused on international class struggle, rejection of the "enemy images,"
new approaches to security issues, and, ultimately, a recognition that
the Soviet Union no longer faced the "imperialist threat."[60]

According to Cherniayev, prior to Reykjavik, Gorbachev sometimes
characterized the U.S. administration as "a bunch of unpredictable political scumbags." In his memoir, Gorbachev acknowledges that after the
Geneva summit in late 1985, he told members of the Soviet delegation
that "politically speaking, Reagan was not just a conservative, but a veritable 'dinosaur.'" But after October 1986, Cherniayev reports that he never
again heard such assessments of U.S. leaders from Gorbachev. At Reykjavik,
Gorbachev "became convinced that things would 'work out' between
Reagan and him, and that the U.S. President—never keen on grasping the
technicalities—intuitively sensed 'the call of the times.'" At the summit,
Cherniayev says, "a spark of mutual understanding lit up when they talked,
as if they winked at one another in anticipation of future agreements. At
least Gorbachev emerged from the meetings trusting him [Reagan] as a
person. After Reykjavik Gorbachev changed the way he spoke to his entourage about Reagan."[61]

This conceptual shift at the summit of the Soviet hierarchy deeply affected the KGB's threat assessment priorities. With his new thinking in
place, Gorbachev was increasingly less interested in war threat estimates
derived from traditional indicators of imperialism's hostility. Since the KGB
chiefs insisted that the agency must tailor information collection and analysis
priorities to the prescriptions of the Communist Party's congresses and
plenums, the turn to new thinking, codified in the resolutions of the Twenty-
seventh Congress, in effect invalidated the traditional KGB conception of
threat indicators. Yuri Andropov saw this traditional system of threat indicators as falling into four "concentric circles" corresponding to state security priorities. At the center—the core "security circle"—was the "internal
unity, economic well-being, and moral health" of the Soviet Union; the
second circle encompassed the "reliability of our ideological and military
allies" (that is, other socialist states, from Poland to Vietnam to Cuba); the
third circle included the "international communist movement" (mainly
communist and other leftist parties); the fourth, outer, circle comprised
"the rest of the world." According to Leonov, Andropov insisted that "as

long as we are certain that the first three circles [comprising the 'socialist world system'] are solid and reliable, we should not be afraid of any threat coming from the fourth circle [dominated by the capitalist West]."[62] This set of threat assessment priorities, outside the core security circle, perfectly matched the thematic structure of the section entitled "On the International Policy of the Communist Party of the Soviet Union" in the Twenty-sixth Congress report.[63] As noted earlier, however, in Gorbachev's report to the Twenty-seventh Congress, this entire section was replaced with one entitled "The Contemporary World: Basic Trends and Contradictions," based entirely on the new thematic structure.

Instead of ideological divisions, this radically revised section emphasized peaceful coexistence and competition in a closely interdependent world. In the context of Soviet institutions, Gorbachev was implicitly pushing the KGB to internalize the new vision of world politics sanctioned by the party, to jettison the concentric circles concept of Soviet security, and to devise a new, as yet unspecified, system of threat indicators. If anything, Gorbachev made sure to remind the KGB, soon after his arrival in power, that the party was the boss. The new Soviet leader also signaled that a critical reassessment of the KGB's system of reporting to Soviet decision makers was afoot. In December 1985, Gorbachev sent a note to the KGB chairman, Viktor Chebrikov, admonishing the agency "on the impermissibility of distortions of the factual state of affairs in messages and informational reports sent to the Central Committee of the CPSU [Communist Party of the Soviet Union] and other ruling bodies."[64] This note serves as an unambiguous indication that Gorbachev believed some serious "distortions" had occurred. The KGB hierarchy quickly responded to Gorbachev's note, pledging to take Gorbachev's instructions "for unswerving execution by all *chekists* [KGB officers]." Vladimir Kryuchkov, then head of the First Chief Directorate, was tasked by the KGB chairman to convey this instruction to all officers in KGB residencies around the world.[65] Although Gorbachev's notes—he reportedly issued several others of the same nature—were not specific or far-reaching enough to induce any significant transformation of KGB practices, they demonstrate clearly that the KGB was beholden to the Communist Party, new thinking or old.

Yet the impact on the KGB's reporting of war threats was substantial. Recently declassified annual reports of the KGB chairman to Mikhail Gorbachev covering 1985, 1986, 1988, and 1989 (each report was submitted early in the following year) suggest that several key indicators of hostile imperialist intentions used by the KGB in prior years were considerably devalued after the rise of the new thinking in 1986. Thus, the 1985 and 1986 reports to Gorbachev, entitled "On the Work of the Committee for State Security of the USSR," explicitly cite "indications of [the West's] preparations for a possible surprise unleashing of nuclear-missile war" or "information in the interests of timely warning of a surprise nuclear-missile attack on the USSR" as principal concerns. Consistent with KGB instructions on global operations for the early 1980s, declassified by Gordievsky, the political intentions of the Western powers—namely, "information on the military-strategic plans of the opponent, his [NATO's] designs for achieving military superiority over the USSR"—took precedence in the KGB's surprise attack watch. There was a strong indication, however, that the significance of this topic diminished from 1985 to 1986. In 1985, the KGB chairman considered it politically viable to report to the Soviet leader that the monitoring of NATO intentions for a nuclear first strike received the "highest priority attention" of Soviet foreign intelligence. In contrast, the report covering 1986 just stated briefly that the KGB continued to direct "significant forces and means" to acquiring intelligence on a surprise nuclear strike against the USSR.[66]

A more decisive break with past threat assessment priorities happened after 1986. In its reports to Gorbachev for 1988 and 1989, the KGB no longer sought credit for watching NATO's intentions regarding a surprise attack and failed even to mention the subject. (The 1987 report has not been made available.) Regarding "active measures," such as the use of propaganda, front groups, deception, forgery, bribery, or blackmail to influence public opinion and political decisions abroad in favor of the Soviet Union (accounting for up to 25 percent of Soviet foreign intelligence activities), the report for 1985 takes credit for tarnishing the public's perception in the West of Reagan's Star Wars program. In a clear sign that this program was considered less of a threat by early 1987, the report for 1986 dropped the reference to active measures against the SDI. In assessing the intentions of potential enemies in 1985, the KGB still took pride in providing the Kremlin with information about policies and "practical actions" of the United States, NATO, Japan, and China "undermining the international position of our country and peaceful initiatives of the Soviet state." In the 1988 report, fine-tuned to Gorbachev's new thinking, the KGB claimed instead to have "adjusted its activity with the aim of making a greater contribution to resolving the tasks of creating a universal system of international security, and favorable conditions for deepening the processes of perestroika in the country."[67]

This vague, Gorbachevian newspeak also reflects the KGB's many headaches and confusion caused by party instructions to redefine threat indicators. General Leonov, promoted in 1984 from head of the Analysis and Assessments Directorate to chief of intelligence operations for the entire Western Hemisphere, keenly sensed the contradiction between Gorbachev's right-sounding promises and symbolic actions, and the forbidding reality facing the Soviet leadership and the KGB. In his memoir, Leonov says that his high-ranking KGB colleagues had long and frustrating debates about the meaning of Gorbachev's reform program known as perestroika, or restructuring: "Until the program's tragic finale, none of us could explain how our life and our economy were supposed to change as a result of this restructuring. . . . *Perestroika* turned out to be a hollow concept, devoid of practical meaning."[68] The KGB's problem was that it had to continue making threat assessments according to the new party instructions derived from this "hollow concept." In this respect, the KGB's dilemma reflected very much that of Soviet society as a whole: most people had a sense that life was getting increasingly unbearable yet had no idea about how to change things for the better.

In the context of Gorbachev's new thinking, the main threat was now associated not with the hostile imperialist bloc but with groups within the Western states that opposed Gorbachev's proposals for peace and disarmament. The extent of this type of threat was to be assessed by gauging the political weight of those in the West who supported Gorbachev's ideas against the political weight of those who opposed Soviet initiatives. In this sense, the fullest possible political intelligence on Western responses to the increasingly far-reaching Soviet initiatives was, in Gorbachev's view, the priority for KGB foreign operations. There were also signs that those who furnished positive intelligence to Gorbachev—showing that the Soviet leaders' initiatives met with increasing support among the Western public, politicians, and business leaders—could expect rapid promotion in the changing ideological climate. For example, briefings to Gorbachev in December 1984 suggesting prospects for improved relations with Britain helped Gordievsky's appointment as KGB's London resident. In April 1987, Leonid Shebarshin, who had served as deputy head of the Analysis and Assessments Directorate (regarded as less prestigious than operations directorates), leapfrogged over several more senior KGB officials to the position of deputy head of the FCD. In 1988 Shebarshin was placed in charge of the FCD. In Andrew's and Gordievsky's view, Shebarshin's rapid rise through the KGB hierarchy was "a certain indication that his efforts in the previous few years had greatly impressed the Politburo. And for them to have impressed the Politburo, they must have dealt with such major issues as the West's response to the 'new thinking' of the Gorbachev era."[69]

Shebarshin's own comments to the Soviet media, as well as the fact that he was the first Soviet foreign intelligence chief who spoke to the press and whose name was declassified, suggest that he was a perfect fit for Gorbachev's glasnost and new thinking blueprint. Just as Gorbachev had argued that communism—in its humanized, cleansed version—was a positive development in human history and deserved a legitimate place in the world system, Shebarshin argued the KGB's traditional monitoring of "the real [i.e., secret] plans and designs of the leading Western countries" could greatly contribute to dismantling the Cold War by "uncovering all the positive elements of world politics, all the possibilities for further improvement of international relations and for reaching mutually acceptable agreements."[70]

Nevertheless, the mobilization of hundreds of KGB officers to collect and analyze responses to Gorbachev's domestic and foreign policy initiatives in the West was a confusing endeavor for a massive intelligence apparatus built for entirely different purposes. In this sense, Gorbachev's new thinking was a time bomb under the KGB. According to Vadim Bakatin, the last head of the KGB appointed after the 1991 anti-Gorbachev coup: "Without a clear-cut enemy—as identified by the Politburo—the KGB could not exist."[71] As Gorbachev reached new, groundbreaking agreements with the West, the KGB received progressively less guidance from the Kremlin on who or what exactly were the principal Soviet enemies. As the KGB attempted to fill the vacuum with new threat indicators, all the while severely constrained by an institutional design based on the more traditional Soviet ideology, the entire KGB threat assessment system was short-circuited: not only was Moscow Center increasingly chasing nonexistent threats but the KGB also found itself increasingly distanced from its intelligence consumers and political masters, to an extent unprecedented before Gorbachev.

As early as January 1986—barely a month after Gorbachev's note critical of KGB's reports—the FCD old-timers were surprised and displeased by the announcement of Gorbachev's initiative to dismantle all nuclear weapons worldwide by the year 2000. That the Soviet Communist Party was taking a bold step in the global peace offensive was hardly a new development; moreover, it quite befitted the traditional Soviet claim that socialism was superior to capitalism because it offered perpetual peace. Nor was the direct appeal to world public opinion, ultimately expected to influence the intentions of decision makers in Western capitals, a surprise, either. Yet learning about such a momentous initiative from the press was most upsetting for the top officials in Soviet foreign intelligence: the KGB had not been asked to sound out the possible reactions to this initiative in the Western capitals. It was also unclear whether the Soviet leadership considered defense of the USSR—covering one sixth of the earth's surface—feasible without a nuclear deterrent. (For a true believer like Gorbachev, this was not such an outrageous idea, however, as a possible means of convincing the rest of the world that war was obsolete.)[72]

At the same time, the FCD's workload in staging Gorbachev's summit meetings was increasing. To General Leonov's chagrin, however, starting with Reykjavik in October 1986, this increase in workload primarily affected the KGB's "bodyguard" functions. The KGB was increasingly shut out of the loop on the substantive issues of the summit talks. The KGB's key tasks at Reykjavik were to maintain reliable, 24-hour communications with Moscow for Gorbachev, ensure the Soviet leader's personal security, and select a summit location (for political reasons, it had to be held on neutral territory) where public protests against Soviet policies and its human rights record would be least likely. The latter was particularly important, for Gorbachev was vigorously promoting disarmament initiatives as a champion of universal human values. According to Leonov, the KGB was seeking to protect Gorbachev from "irritating and noisy demonstrations of paid and volunteer freedom and human rights activists who would take turns picketing our embassies and missions abroad and protest at the summits featuring Soviet leaders." The KGB was happy to have the summit in Iceland, a small and remote state where, according to Moscow Center estimates, only eighteen people were "Zionists" (that is, likely to support publicly the plight of Soviet Jewish refuseniks). The KGB also estimated that most of the remaining citizens of Iceland were "direct descendants of the Vikings and therefore silent, restrained, and dignified types." At the same time, Gorbachev and members of his Reykjavik delegation requested no intelligence reports from the FCD and left unanswered several proposals on summit issues that the FCD had submitted on its own initiative.[73] Representatives of the KGB were also conspicuous by their absence among the twenty-eight advisers who developed Gorbachev's strategy for the summit and accompanied him to Iceland.[74]

To be informed on disarmament issues, Gorbachev set up an interdepartmental commission comprising what was known as "the Big Five": a Central Committee secretary, and the heads of the KGB, the Ministry of

Foreign Affairs, the Defense Ministry, and the Military-Industrial Commission (subordinate to the Soviet Council of Ministers and the CPSU Central Committee). The commission usually held its meetings at the Central Committee, in the office of the Central Committee secretary, Lev Zaikov. The commission's documents were prepared by a working group of experts, "the Little Five." This expert group convened at the General Staff Headquarters, in the office of the deputy chief of the general staff of the Soviet Armed Forces. Representing the KGB on the Little Five and participating in the sessions of the interdepartmental commission was General Leonov, "an involuntary witness of how the highest ranking officials of the Soviet state and the communist party made decisions."[75] Leonov was thus placed precisely at the interface between intelligence production and policy making, just the vantage point from which to document the formulation of threat assessment tasks and priorities.

The commission apparently ran up against the same conceptual problem in translating Gorbachev's disarmament initiatives into specific proposals as did the FCD officers in debating the specific implications of Gorbachev's perestroika for Soviet society and the KGB. As the KGB representative, Leonov came to "an iron-clad conclusion" that, in 1986, the Soviet leaders had "no clear conception—to say nothing of a detailed program—regarding disarmament." One new concept advanced by Gorbachev to guide the development of Soviet military strategy—"reasonable sufficiency" (*razumnaya dostatochnost'*)—would have been critical in the KGB's reevaluation of threat assessment priorities. And yet, as one of the key players in Soviet foreign intelligence, Leonov found Gorbachev's new formulation of the military doctrine "nothing but a verbal formula." The discussions at the Big Five and Little Five sessions must have frustrated the KGB representative: "None of the Soviet political and military leaders at the time could make any sense how to translate the concept of 'reasonable sufficiency' into the language of quantitative indicators regarding the weapons, the size of the armed forces, and economic costs."[76]

This conceptual difficulty was exacerbated by bureaucratic infighting between the ministries of foreign affairs and defense, as well as by Gorbachev's personal efforts to publicize the disarmament initiative before consulting the Big Five. In the end, the political imperative of "ensuring the success of the negotiating process" with the United States consistently prevailed over reasoning by numbers. According to Leonov, at the Big Five meetings, Shevardnadze was consistently able to override even the united opposition of the defense ministry, the General Staff, the KGB, the Council of Ministers, and the Central Committee, disregarding quantitative estimates of the disarmament treaties' impact on the U.S.-Soviet military balance and the economic costs of weapons elimination and troop withdrawals: "Whenever discussions in the Big Five got deadlocked—most often with the foreign ministry chief in the minority of one—Shevardnadze would say: 'All right, let us put this matter aside, I'll talk it over with Mikhail Segeyevich [Gorbachev].'"[77]

Thus brought into the group's discussions, Gorbachev usually took Shevardnadze's side, which reflected his position better, in any event, and left the interdepartmental commission out of the loop. Thus, despite being at the hub of the institutional decision process on disarmament, as well as receiving information through the KGB pipeline, Leonov never knew "when and where Gorbachev agreed with the Americans to eliminate the most advanced Soviet missile complex, 'Oka' [SS-23], with a range under 500 kilometers." Although he was a member of the Little Five, which was tasked by Gorbachev with working out the specifics of Soviet disarmament proposals, Leonov was unaware that weapons of this type were even subject to U.S.-Soviet arms reduction talks. The interdepartmental commission and the KGB also had no input into Gorbachev's concession at Reykjavik giving the United States an option to keep one heavy bomber (armed with multiple nuclear-tipped short-range attack missiles and nuclear bombs) for each eliminated ballistic missile warhead. And in early February 1990, Leonov was surprised to find out that the expert group was not consulted on Shevardnadze's agreement to consider each U.S. heavy bomber as capable of carrying ten rather than twenty air-based Cruise missiles.[78] Whatever the arguments may be on the accuracy of these quantitative estimates, the Kremlin was definitely not a decision-making environment in which war threat assessment would be derived from the numbers debate.

This was increasingly frustrating for the KGB hierarchy as the Gorbachev era unfolded. On the one hand, Soviet intelligence officers had to fulfil Gorbachev's demands for more "objective facts." On the other hand, when the KGB presented what it believed were facts, they were ignored. Ironically, at the root of such frustrations was the very system of one-party rule, of which the KGB was the ultimate "sword and shield" and which Gorbachev naïvely trusted to serve as the prime mover of his reforms. According to Leonov, "Once the [communist] party general secretary agreed to something [at the talks], we considered it impossible to modify our position. We considered all general secretaries infallible, at least until they died or were ousted."[79] Such institutional uncertainty and confusion, feeding directly into the reassessment of Soviet intelligence priorities to match the new thinking, was typical of the Big Five's sporadic work pattern. Without a regular meeting schedule, the interdepartmental commission was convened either "in response to Gorbachev's initiatives that hit the press, or in response to American proposals which were usually more detailed and concrete."[80]

The KGB's confusion over threat assessment priorities was also evident in a remarkable mixture of the old and new thinking in a speech given by Vladimir Kryuchkov at a Soviet Foreign Ministry conference in summer 1988, shortly before his promotion from Soviet foreign intelligence chief to KGB chairman. That Kryuchkov decided to publish the speech was evidence of the new intellectual climate in Gorbachev's USSR. No less startling was the optimistic view of the intentions of the Soviet Union's arch-enemies: "Statesmen, public figures, but also ordinary people abroad are today reflecting on the processes taking place in our country. The 'enemy image,' the image of the Soviet state as a 'totalitarian' 'half-civilized' society, is being eroded and our ideological and political opponents are recognizing the profound nature of our reforms and their beneficial effort on foreign policy." Based on this assessment of the West's political intentions, Kryuchkov argued that "disarmament, achievement of a non-nuclear world and removal of the threat of major military conflict" were now "fully realizable" objectives. Kryuchkov also explained that this major shift in reassessing Western intentions was due to changes in the KGB mindset under the strict guidance of the Communist Party: "A number of Party documents and material from the 19th Party Conference have provided us with a new methodology for looking at the world." In the past, Kryuchkov acknowledged, Soviet intelligence mistakenly believed that "the whole of America, apart from a few judicious-minded people" (especially communists) would oppose Moscow's disarmament moves. "But now it is evident," Kryuchkov asserted, "that those who admit the possibility of conflict are in the minority, and the majority are people who are confused by propaganda, and they are not thinking about war."[81]

At the same time, the old thinking still remained in the KGB mindset and in Moscow's policies in general, reflecting Gorbachev's fear of a conservative backlash against his reforms. At the end of his speech, Kryuchkov reminded his audience that "right-wing circles in NATO countries" worked hard to "undermine confidence in the Soviet proposals on disarmament;" that "the whole potential of the CIA and other intelligence services" was still doing "serious damage to our country;" that in the first half of 1988 the West carried out more than 900 "provocation operations," such as shootings, explosions, and anti-Soviet demonstrations; and that the United States continued to develop unspecified but "highly dangerous forms of weapons, outside the generally known program of the SDI." For these reasons, many "former responsibilities [had] not been removed from the agenda" of Soviet intelligence; principal among them, according to Kryuchkov, was "not to overlook the immediate danger of nuclear conflict being unleashed." In other words, it is most likely that the FCD foreign residencies still continued, through inertia, to file fortnightly reports on the prospects of nuclear attack against the Soviet Union, but these were now more of an afterthought to the KGB's intelligence priorities.[82]

Adding to this confusion about the priorities arising from the old and new thinking was a paradox that few at the KGB understood with Gorbachev's arrival: the more Soviet intelligence succeeded in helping Gorbachev dismantle Moscow's enemy image worldwide, the less Gorbachev needed the KGB. This was particularly so since the Soviet leader, at least privately, did not share Kryuchkov's position that Western intelligence operations posed a major threat to Soviet security. When George Shultz complained to Gorbachev during talks in Moscow in April 1987 that the KGB packed American diplomatic quarters in the USSR with listening devices, Gorbachev replied, "We are political leaders, we are not babes. We know why the CIA was set up and what it does. You gather intelligence on us, we gather intelligence on you. I'll say even more: the fact that you know a lot about us introduces an element of stability. It's better to know a lot about one another than a little. . . . Intelligence, the way it is normally understood, plays a constructive role by helping to avert precipitous political or military acts." Gorbachev then went on to say that the Soviet ambassador in Washington, Yuri Dubinin, and the U.S. ambassador in Moscow, Jack Matlock, were, in this sense, "our intelligence chiefs, thank God"— leaving the KGB and the CIA out of the picture.[83]

With the political significance of old imperialist threats fading away and the usefulness of dismantling the Soviet enemy image close to being exhausted, KGB intelligence officers were increasingly feeling abandoned by the Kremlin. According to Leonov, starting in late 1986, the intensity of intelligence work rapidly began to wane: "Often I handled files on very interesting cases, for which, in the past, we would petition that intelligence officers be decorated. Now the interest in such cases was declining. The intelligence lost its consumers, and the consumers lost interest in intelligence. A thought haunted me that our political leaders were acting like wood-grouse [*gluhari,* Russian slang for stone-deaf]—singing their own song without paying attention to anything around them." By 1991, Leonov believed that "foreign intelligence was no longer in the focus of government's attention. Testifying to this most acutely were my office telephones that almost never rang. I could not help thinking, that a state in retreat, like an army in retreat, can't care less about foreign intelligence—they retreat over native land, trample native interests, and will not turn attention to the lands of others." Vadim Bakatin, who carried out the autopsy of the KGB after the 1991 Moscow coup, found that the KGB had become alienated from political decision making because it was wired to the old, ideologically correct information channels: "The information that the KGB provided to the Soviet political leadership did not help to curb the arms drive, or to enhance trust between states. The KGB's contacts outside the USSR centered on intelligence services of the 'friendly' [socialist or 'socialist-oriented'] countries. Meanwhile, contacts within advanced democracies were sporadic and limited to some very peculiar specifics." Bakatin also concluded that despite easing the obsession with political dissidents at home and the "imperialist threat" abroad, the KGB failed "to master analysis" and, perhaps even more critically, did little to reform its institutional structure and operations.[84]

Inextricably linked to the mounting turmoil and confusion in Soviet society in the late Gorbachev era was the Kremlin's growing neglect of foreign intelligence and the KGB's lack of internal reform, which demoralized the intelligence ranks. Leonid Shebarshin, appointed head of the FCD in early 1989, reported on the debilitating paralysis at the KGB all across the Soviet Union. After an inspection tour of KGB offices in the Baltic republics, Krasnodar in southern Russia, and Vladivostok in the Russian Far East, Shebarshin observed: "Massively staffed local KGB committees had no idea what their objectives were, what problems they were supposed to solve, what kind of information to collect, and to whom report this information. They generated plenty of chaotic mechanical movement (reminding one of a beheaded chicken running around and flopping its wings), but it was only an illusion of active work. . . . Emptiness, futility, and despair ruled in the KGB and communist party offices."[85]

This description is consistent with Shebarshin's account of his meeting with Gorbachev on January 24, 1989, prior to the new intelligence chief's formal appointment. According to Shebarshin, Gorbachev was dry, formal, and strict, "displaying not the slightest interest" in the person about to become responsible for the Soviet Union's global intelligence collection. Gorbachev's instructions were very terse and vague: "The Soviet Union was on the path to serious disarmament treaties. It was important to make sure we would not be put at a disadvantage." Upon returning to his intelligence chief's office, Shebarshin eyed the eight telephones on his desk and wondered which one would ring if Gorbachev were to get in touch.[86] But the FCD's line to the Soviet leader remained silent.

Kryuchkov's own communication as KGB chairman with key Kremlin players provided poignant indications of the KGB's declining political clout. According to Shebarshin, Kryuchkov complained in 1990 that administrative assistants taking his calls on the closed-circuit Kremlin phone line number one *(pervaya "Kremlevka")* no longer could identify the KGB chief by name. A receptionist's innocent oblivion—"Where are you from, Comrade Kryuchkov?"—was worse than a death knell to the perpetually most feared and venerated Soviet institution.[87]

Just as the KGB was becoming moribund, so was the concept of the main adversary, which had been at the heart of the KGB's system of threat assessment for decades. From the 1920s until 1945, this label had been assigned both to Great Britain and after 1945, to the United States—for being the most powerful exponents of capitalism. (In the military context, the term *forces of the main adversary* also sometimes referred to NATO forces, or forces of the capitalist states collectively.) Judging from Shebarshin's account, from 1987 through 1990, top Soviet intelligence officials debated the utility of applying the term *main adversary* to the United States. That the debate took place at all testified to remarkable changes in the Soviet political climate toward greater openness. The lack of institutional rules guiding this debate was yet another sign of KGB's glasnost blues. But since the debate concerned the core threat-related concept used by Soviet foreign intelligence, the arguments of the KGB's high-level insiders for and against scrapping the main adversary concept reveal the KGB's lasting threat assessment priorities. All the key reasons, based on the account of the then-FCD chief, Leonid Shebarshin, related directly to estimates of U.S. political intentions, rather than to quantitative shifts in U.S. and Soviet military capabilities or to economic data.

Supporters of abolishing the main adversary concept argued that U.S.-Soviet relations were no longer confrontational, that the Cold War was over, that bilateral contacts and exchanges were expanding exponentially, and that the United States and its allies were disposed to provide economic assistance and humanitarian aid to the Soviet Union. Those in favor of clinging to the main adversary notion contended that Vice President Dan Quayle, Defense Secretary Dick Cheney, and even President George Bush repeated in their official speeches "with depressing regularity" that the Soviet Union remained America's main adversary, that the U.S. intelligence community had "doubled and tripled" its efforts to recruit agents among Soviet citizens, that the increasing participation of the United States and its Western allies in resolving Soviet domestic problems, including economic aid and humanitarian assistance, stemmed from subversive intentions, and that U.S.-financed radio broadcasts to the Soviet Union were aimed at fanning ethnic conflicts, labor unrest, and resistance to the Communist Party's reform drive. In the end, the "main adversary" concept was scrapped, most likely in late 1990, as the KGB's top officials realized that the Soviet center would not hold. As Shebarshin observed, "Confrontation [with the West] made no sense once the party-state system in the Soviet Union collapsed."[88] Even in its death throes, the KGB's overpowering emphasis on direct intention assessment was unabated.

Increasingly left out in the political vacuum and, by 1990, mistrustful of Soviet leadership, Kryuchkov made one final mistake: the grave misreading of Western political intentions and the failure to grasp the complexity of democratic free-market societies were projected domestically onto the most liberalizing aspects of Gorbachev's reforms. A new Analysis Directorate for assessing threats to internal stability was established close to the KGB's central headquarters in downtown Moscow, on Pushechnaya Street 1/3. General Leonov was appointed the new directorate's chief. His mission was to collate reports, mostly "negative, but realistic," from all of the KGB's directorates and departments (which traditionally resisted such in-house intelligence sharing), so that Kremlin consumers could get a panoramic view of multitudinous domestic problems. The directorate kept track of the dwindling meat, milk, and sugar deliveries in major Soviet cities; monitored public speeches and actions of the new chairman of Russia's Supreme Soviet, Boris Yeltsin; processed hundreds of "informational cables arriving daily from all corners of the USSR and from abroad;" took stock of key participants, crowd size, slogans, and speech content at public protests staged by opposition movements all over the Soviet Union; analyzed transcripts of Gorbachev's meetings with top Central Committee members (most likely without sharing the results of the analyses with Gorbachev); monitored the rise of dissenting factions within the Central Committee, such as the Movement for Democracy, led by Shevardnadze and Yakovlev; canvassed the public mood in the run up to the March 17, 1991, referendum on the preservation of the Soviet Union and the June 12, 1991, presidential election in the Russian Federation; monitored Gorbachev's efforts to conclude a power-sharing agreement with the leaders of nine non-Russian republics (the Novo-Ogarevo process); and even arranged barter deals with collective and state farms to improve food supplies to KGB employees.[89]

Established for blanket surveillance of society in order to eradicate anticommunist dissent, the KGB turned out to be incapable, however, of assessing broader and more diverse social tendencies and public opinion bursting the floodgates of Gorbachev's glasnost. For all the last-ditch analytical efforts concerning domestic problems, the top KGB hierarchy failed to realize that their agency not only had little public support but—in what was the final irony—that most people also regarded the KGB as a greater threat than whatever threats the KGB considered paramount. Limited in its perception of the new political reality by an institutional setting designed for an era slipping irretrievably into the past, the KGB committed the ultimate error of trying to play savior in a society in which the majority of people considered the KGB as the root of all evil. Few, if any, intelligence agencies in history have made a threat assessment lapse as disastrous as Kryuchkov did in August 1991. In helping to mastermind the coup against Gorbachev, Kryuchkov was counting on a restoration of the old order. Instead, three days after tanks were sent into the streets of Moscow, the KGB's Lubyanka headquarters was under siege and the statue of the KGB's founder, Felix Dzerzhinski, was ripped from the heart of Moscow; Kryuchkov was on his way to a high-security KGB jail, and the Soviet Union was on its way to collapse.

The hypertrophied perception of a mounting war threat during the New Cold War of the early 1980s eroded so thoroughly by the end of the decade that the Manichean confrontation was turning into a strategic partnership. This threat erosion was, if anything, an asymmetric and complex process. Each side fought its own Cold War, and each Cold War ended on a separate track, and at different times. In the end, it took someone like Mikhail Gorbachev, a visionary capable of abandoning conventional thinking and uniquely endowed with near-dictatorial powers by the Soviet Communist Party to translate his vision into policy, to generate enough creative destruction of old stereotypes and hasten the end of both Cold Wars.

As it happens, the U.S. intelligence community and principal decision makers, including the president, abandoned the window of vulnerability notion with regard to the Soviet Union at the very height of the New Cold War and the anti-evil empire crusade. Also, this reassessment of war threat came when the Soviet Union had been politically stagnant and repressive for decades, and when neither the rise of Gorbachev nor his economic and political reforms, perestroika and glasnost, were evident. Conversely, from 1985 to 1989, as Gorbachev revised the fundamentals of Soviet ideology, abandoning the imperative of global class struggle in favor of global interdependence, U.S. intelligence estimates suggested that the Soviet Union posed the same level of threat as before, and American decision makers coasted from one treaty and initiative to the next, wary of moving beyond containment. And by 1990, in an ultimately paradoxical turnaround from the evil empire years, the U.S. intelligence establishment and policymakers took the view that backing Gorbachev and preserving the Soviet Union was less threatening than helping the old evil empire fall to pieces.

For the Soviet part, Gorbachev's assessment that the West posed less of a war threat than his predecessors in the Kremlin believed is also puzzling: at Gorbachev's arrival, the United States was implementing a major arms buildup; it had also introduced intermediate nuclear forces in Europe, invaded Grenada, and sent money and arms to the Contras in Nicaragua and the *mujahedin* resistance fighters in Afghanistan. Yet precisely at this time when—even in the view of the alarmist Reagan administration—the United States was gaining ground on the Soviet Union in military terms, Gorbachev increasingly saw the West as less of a threat and more of a potential strategic partner. The incredibly strong fixation of Soviet decision makers on the war threat emanating from the Strategic Defense Initiative, even if confined to a never-never world of demo videos, also opened a window on the Soviet pattern of threat assessment.

Paradoxically, the Soviet fear of Star Wars as a grand vision had a greater impact on the Kremlin than Star Wars as a research and development program. In this fashion, the Soviet threat assessment in the Cold War end game confounds realist, rational interpretations of international relations. If Gorbachev had played exclusively by the rules of realpolitik, the Soviet Union would probably have shed some military and economic burdens by withdrawing from Afghanistan and reducing "fraternal assistance" in the Third World, but Moscow would have been highly unlikely to relinquish its military and political hold on Eastern Europe, disband the Warsaw Pact, agree to German unification within NATO, and reduce its disproportionately large number of intercontinental ballistic missiles. These paradoxes and a look inside the intelligence streams shaping Soviet and American decisions suggest that highly asymmetric threat assessment, though instrumental in triggering past global wars, also played a major role in averting global military confrontation and in bringing the Cold War—that is, each of the two Cold Wars—to a close.

Conclusion:
Global Problems, Intelligence, and Post–Cold War Threats

Then suddenly he was struck violently. By nothing! A vast weight, it seemed, leapt upon him, and he was hurled headlong down the staircase, with the grip at his throat and a knee in his groin. An invisible foot trod on his back, a ghostly patter passed downstairs.[1]

This attack on Colonel Adye by a maniacal chemist in H. G. Wells's *The Invisible Man* is emblematic of the global wars described in this book: a challenger, whose threats initially resonate no more than a ghostly patter, unexpectedly strikes at the incumbent world power with full force. Eventually, as in Wells's story, the community mobilizes and defeats the challenger aspiring to rule the world by terror. By the close of the novel, the invisible man's chance to escape, let alone prevail, grows dim. The unseen threat is defeated. For the most part, however, *The Invisible Man* describes a less comforting dynamic: an ambitious and zealous experimenter, unable to prove his theory within his scientific discipline, evolves into an aggressive challenger to the scientific community and world order yet remains undetected within the society he hates until blood is spilled, havoc is wreaked, and the community recognizes the challenger's invisibility as a clear and present danger.

Asymmetric threat assessment is part and parcel of this pattern, be it in Wells's classic story or in the three case studies of global leadership competition: threats and opportunities apparent to one side were unnoticed or incomprehensible to the other. The confluence of such asymmetric interpretations of threat in the end produced momentously surprising outcomes. That obscure, "barbaric" tribes from the Mongol steppes would launch successful campaigns against the world's most populous and developed empires was not at all obvious right up to Genghis Khan's invasion of Chin China in 1211. That the rise of revolutionary France in armed revolt against the world's richest and most powerful nations was a prologue to more than two decades of global warfare would easily have been regarded a loser's bet in 1793. That the abandonment of global class warfare as the guiding principle of Soviet foreign policy after 1986 meant that the Kremlin de facto called off the Cold War was something the White House still tested as late as 1989. And few expected that the "evil empire" year, 1983, would witness two turning points in threat assessment that paved the way for the end of the Cold War: the Scowcroft report closing "the window of America's vulnerability" in Washington and Reagan's Star Wars salesmanship inducing Moscow to seek understanding with the West, precisely when Mikhail Gorbachev, the Soviet leader-in-waiting, was on his first visit to an advanced capitalist state—Canada.

Like Wells's invisible man, the challengers in the global leadership competitions analyzed in this book were aware of their inferior strategic capabilities. They too sought to compensate for their vulnerabilities in military and economic power by exploiting the perceived political and organizational weaknesses of their adversary. They too believed that a reign of terror was a superior form of social organization. With each challenger—the Mongols, revolutionary France, and the USSR—the lack of institutional checks and balances and the means of free expression and assembly was reflected in their emphasis on exploiting political intentions, interpersonal elite relationships, and ideological rifts. These inputs played a crucial role in the war initiation strategies of Genghis Khan and the leaders of revolutionary France. Genghis Khan correctly identified windows of opportunity when his more numerous and better equipped opponents, the Chin Empire and the Sultanate of Khwarazm, experienced leadership crises, diminishing war resolve, and growing internal dissent, all of which eroded the political authority necessary to assemble forces for decisive battles. From Genghis Khan's standpoint, intelligence suggesting that the new Chin leader was "an imbecile" and that the Khwarazm-shah and the Caliph of Baghdad were irreconcilably split was central to the decisions to launch aggressive campaigns in China and Central Asia. For the Mongols, carrying out the divine plans expressed in the khan's *yasa* was more important than comparing military capabilities and estimating the probability of victory. If capability balances were unfavorable, ways to circumvent them had to be found. This explains the enormous intelligence efforts the Mongols deployed to sustain their troops along such avenues of approach as deserts and mountains, where the adversary would least expect them. Had Genghis Khan acted as a rational power maximizer assessing the number of enemy troops and his adversaries' economic potential, he would have seen no glimmer of hope and the Mongol world empire would have never materialized.

The aggressive French strategy leading to the Revolutionary and Napoleonic Wars was keyed in part by intelligence focused on preserving the revolutionary government of France, its potential for resistance to external and domestic subversions, and its prospects for inspiring revolutions against all the crowned heads of Europe. The impact of British naval power and wealth were discounted. So deeply was the National Convention in the throes of revolutionary idealism that French decision makers believed the British navy could be defeated if French sailors read a standard revolutionary proclamation to British sailors encountered at sea. Moreover, such apparently naïve faith was exhibited in Paris when France's ablest seamen were likely to be hanged on lampposts in major French ports—suspected, because of their social origins, of nursing counterrevolutionary intentions. French decision makers who initiated the Great Terror on behalf of the nation considered every French citizen a potential soldier and interpreted the political situation in Britain in the context of the narrow limits of their known world: Britain's third estate, they believed, would storm the Tower of London and erect on its ruins the "Bastille on the Thames," a French-style national assembly to displace the monarchy and the administration of William Pitt. The deterioration of France's navy and the sorry state of its finances were downplayed, and war on England and Holland was declared. This considerable and deadly negligence of military and economic capabilities was later replicated by Napoleon, leading to disastrous geostrategic moves, such as the continental blockade against Britain and the invasion of Russia.

The Kremlin's preoccupation with hostile imperialist intentions and competing ideologies in the global power arena set the stage for an unprecedented intelligence alert (Operation RYAN) in 1983 over the possibility of a NATO surprise nuclear attack. The declining health of top Politburo members, along with the loss of socialism's popular appeal amid growing apathy and economic and political stagnation, made ailing Brezhnev and his moribund Politburo more reclusive and fearful of the West's ploys to undermine the historic value of Soviet achievements by brandishing capitalism's superior military and economic strength. In the absence of public debate and alternative information sources, Soviet leaders fell prey to conspiracy theories of NATO's preparations for a nuclear missile attack. Yet Moscow's focus on the Soviet Union's own ideological vitality—increasingly deflated in the late 1970s and early 1980s—prepared the ground for the abandonment of global competition with the West just when the U.S. National Intelligence Estimates were most alarmist about Soviet expansionism.

Like the local community upon which Wells's invisible man was trying to force his demented vision, the incumbent world powers missed many signs of challengers' aggressive intentions and failed to take preemptive action. In this sense, the status quo powers were as cautious, and for much the same reasons, as the owners of the Coach and Horses Inn at Iping, who were debating whether to inspect the Invisible Man's room: "The Anglo-Saxon genius for parliamentary government asserted itself; there was a great deal of talk and no decisive action. 'Let's have facts first,' insisted Mr. Sandy Wadgers. 'Let's be sure we'd be acting perfectly right in bustin' that there door open. A door onbust is always open to bustin', but ye can't onbust the door once you've busted en.'"[2]

In all the case studies, some degree of political pluralism, the separation of civilian and military authority, and especially the rise of representative institutions holding the power of the purse were conducive to evaluating threats and opportunities in the light of available resources. The threat of the Mongol's drive for universal empire, with all its brutal and uncompromising intensity, was virtually invisible to the Sung Court: decision makers saw the "northern barbarian slaves" as realist, rational actors who would exchange poverty, backwardness, an uncertain way of life, and aggressive conquests for a fraction of the Sung's riches.

In Britain, particularly owing to pressure from Parliament during the economic reforms of the 1780s, the government instituted a more rigorous monitoring of expenses and the evaluation of policy costs in monetary terms. Consistent with this trend, the potential threat from revolutionary France was assessed by comparing the size of the army and navy, budget revenues, the state of manufacturing (especially military procurement), and control over the geographical areas providing access to British-controlled sea-lanes. Thus, the 1789 revolution was primarily seen in London as beneficial to Britain's security, because it weakened France's economy and military capabilities. Britain's confidence in its strategic superiority in the face of the French challenge can be directly traced to intelligence that emphasized French naval and military capabilities, economic power, and potential for global commercial operations. British intelligence sources were predominantly located in or around the ports of France and its neighbors. Indicative of this trend, the pay of Britain's secret agents depended primarily on intelligence about French navy and port facilities.

In the case of the United States, the increase in the estimated level of global war probability in 1980 was explicitly linked in National Intelligence Estimates to a steady increase in the Soviet capabilities for intercontinental attack relative to the United States. Transcending three presidential administrations, U.S. intelligence reporting in 1975-1979 on the emerging window of vulnerability provided a steady flow of information that set the boundaries for policy debates on the extent of the Soviet threat. Conflicting information on the weakening economic position of the USSR was addressed by all sides in the debate but downplayed in the face of uncertainty and domestic political pressures that could not be translated into reliable quantitative data. Notably, even the most consistent congressional critics of the CIA favored continuation of the NIEs on the Soviet strategic capabilities while arguing that other NIEs could be terminated. As late as 1991, however, when the director of Central Intelligence made a unilateral move to abolish quantitative dollar estimates of Soviet military and economic capabilities, the pressures of the congressional budget process (involving both Pentagon and Capitol Hill players) prompted the reversal of those decisions. The impact on the Soviet proclivity for war from changes in the Kremlin's ideological outlook, such as limiting the definition of "states with socialist orientation" and, later, Gorbachev's "new thinking," were all but invisible in the estimates. The potential for change with the advent of post-Brezhnev leadership was misjudged on the assumption that the decline of Brezhnev's moderating influence was likely to result in a more assertive and aggressive Soviet posture. But Brezhnev's demise heightened the Kremlin leaders' vulnerability, uncertainty, and search for understanding with the West. The virtual invisibility of such major political intention shifts in U.S. intelligence estimates of Soviet war strategy suggests that had the Kremlin really been determined to wage war against the West, the United States would have been unlikely to detect the rising threat.

A trend may be observed across the three case studies that was not apparent when each was examined separately: asymmetric competition was unfolding in a world system of increasingly greater complexity that was also undergoing "a prolonged process of explicit organization that had grown as part of the global leadership system."[3] The systemic environment at the time of the Mongol challenge was characterized by interactions among powers that possessed mainly challenger-type characteristics. The only major power that displayed some characteristics of global leadership, the Southern Sung, did not engage in proactive leadership and institution-building in Eurasia. Coupled with disastrous alliance policies, this shortcoming facilitated the Mongols' conquest of Sung China after 1237. Lacking systemic leadership structures with corresponding institutions, the Mongols attempted to reach cooperative and peaceful accommodation with their wealthier and more advanced neighbors; these transient attempts were indistinguishable from stratagems, and were easily abandoned in favor of massive military campaigns. Diplomacy was rare, diplomatic mail exchanges and missions took weeks and frequently months, routes of communication were not secure, and chances for misinterpretation and mixed signals were plentiful. (Translation problems alone were often enough.) Domestic conditions were too volatile and violent to allow much room for maneuvering during the wait for tangible results from negotiations. The impulse toward war and quick-gain strategies based on direct intentions assessment best addressed these domestic and systemic conditions, prompting Genghis Khan's aggressive expansion of the Mongol Empire.

In the case of the French Revolutionary Wars, the lineage of global leadership was well established and represented by Great Britain's preponderance in sea power and in lead economic sectors. Although military conflicts with France persisted throughout the eighteenth century, so did attempts to arrive at a peaceful settlement by accommodating at least some of the French concerns. Although the 1783 Paris Treaty and the 1786 Commerce Treaty failed to live up to French expectations, thus contributing to the French Revolutionary Wars, France was in a markedly improved position after its defeat in the Revolutionary and Napoleonic Wars. The Congress of Vienna (1814-1815) included France in the Concert of Europe and paved the way for French participation with Britain in the alliance of 1914-1918. In this respect, the higher degree of democratic and free market development in France in comparison to the other two challengers helped integrate France into the global leader alliances. In turn, the openness and free market elements in French society were further enhanced in the process, and France today is hardly associated with aggressive challenges to world peace.

In the post–World War II period and by the 1970s in particular, the Soviet Union was striving to promote its position in major global institutions, such as the United Nations and the Council for Security and Cooperation in Europe. Of the utmost importance to Soviet elites, as evidenced by Brezhnev personally taking charge, was participation in the U.S.-Soviet summit meetings with U.S. presidents. International arms control agreements were also pursued; several test-ban treaties and the 1968 Nuclear Non-Proliferation Treaty were signed. Recently declassified National Security Council documents suggest that the unraveling of the Cold War rivalry was facilitated by U.S. pressure to improve communications with the Soviet leaders and outreach to the Soviet people; the timely increase in U.S. interest after 1985 in negotiating issues relating to a greater Soviet role in the world economy, including the Soviet Union's application to participate in trade negotiations under the General Agreement on Tariffs and Trade (currently the World Trade Organization); the Soviet Union joining the International Monetary Fund and the World Bank; settlement with the United Kingdom on defaulted czarist bonds and the first-time participation in a Eurobond syndication; talks between the European Community and the Council for Mutual Economic Assistance; the increase in Soviet international financial market transactions; the Soviet international economic security initiative; and Soviet proposals for joint ventures involving Western corporate management and on-site participation.[4] Competition between the Soviet Union and the United States meant playing much more to global audiences and global institutions than did the competition for leadership in thirteenth-century Central and East Asia or in the eighteenth-century Eurocentric world system.

Although the increased integration of world powers and their challengers in transnational institutions is a positive trend, human society is yet to develop a threat assessment system that can detect and prevent global war in a timely manner. After all, in the past 500 years, global wars have recurred about once every century. Today, half a century after World War II, we may simply be in the midst of one such interwar time span.

This book suggests that the Cold War ended peacefully chiefly because the challenger-state, the Soviet Union, had lost its ideological determination by the time it had acquired sufficient capabilities for an intercontinental attack on its main adversary, the United States. Substantial changes in the Kremlin's predisposition for aggressive behavior in the 1970s and 1980s could not be perceived through the prism of threat assessment embodied in U.S. intelligence estimates. Therefore, as the twentieth century comes to a close, intelligence communities have yet to pass the real test of detecting and successfully frustrating an aggressive challenger determined to unleash—and capable of unleashing—a global war. Although in the present context the prospects of facing such a test appear remote at best, the possibility of a global war cannot be ruled out entirely. In addition, it is as yet unclear whether the recent security challenges—terrorism, ethnorebellion, major regional conflicts, or "bombs in the basement"— signal a permanent fragmentation of the global war threat or underlie a global dynamic that may aggravate a combustible rivalry among some mix of states, alliances, and transnational nonstate actors in the years to come.

THREATS UNDER GLOBALIZATION AND GLOBAL PROBLEMS INTELLIGENCE

The self-destruction of the principal potential challenger to America's global leadership in 1991 called for a redefinition of the U.S. intelligence community's mission. U.S. intelligence services find themselves after the Cold War in a position somewhat similar to Soviet intelligence agencies in the era of Gorbachev's new thinking. Resources were shifted from the old Soviet target, declining from 60 percent of the U.S. intelligence community budget in the 1980s to about one-third in the mid-1990s, but the process of channeling the "peace dividend" toward new targets has run into multiple obstacles.[5] The U.S. intelligence community has essentially been asked "to do the world." Meanwhile, studies of U.S. intelligence organization, conducted by Congress, the Twentieth Century Fund, and by academics and practitioners, describe America's spasmodic search for a new set of first principles. The nation's centralized intelligence organizations must adjust to the new challenges of post–Cold War globalization: What are the manifest threats to U.S. national security? What are the criteria for defining such threats? What are the best forms of intelligence collection and analysis to measure these threats? Who are the appropriate immediate consumers of a much more fragmented—and increasingly compartmentalized—analytical product? How does one integrate these increasingly diversified and compartmentalized assessments? The traditional priority assigned to capability analysis, deeply embedded in America's intelligence-decision-making-political institutions nexus, looms as a major problem in coping with post–Cold War confusion. (In many ways, this dilemma is similar to the shock that the KGB received when Gorbachev eliminated "hostile imperialist intentions" as the KGB's number one threat assessment target.) In a report by Allan Goodman to the Twentieth Century Fund Task Force on the Future of U.S. Intelligence, the dissipation of an overriding security threat such as that posed by Soviet power will result in "the conundrum that foreign policy will inevitably involve winning domestic political support for 'a vision of a future that cannot be demonstrated when it is put forward. . . .' Nowhere is the demonstration of such vision more important or more difficult than in the case of framing U.S. intelligence requirements to pass the scrutiny of the budgetmakers."[6]

Post–Cold War threat assessment by the U.S. intelligence community seems to replicate the same dichotomy implicit in assessments of the Soviet threat in the mid-1980s: policy makers whose decisions intelligence estimates are designed to support will face a conflicting stream of quantitative versus qualitative data. On the one hand, the November 1995 national intelligence estimate (NIE 95-19) on nuclear proliferation reportedly calculated that no countries other than the major nuclear powers will have the capability to develop ballistic (intercontinental) missiles for the next fifteen years. Moreover, with the United States possessing increasingly more advanced satellites, the warning time for ballistic missile deployment will increase, making the acquisition of long-range missile capability much harder for any potential U.S. adversary. The missile threat to the United States therefore will be virtually eliminated, even though regional missile threats, according to NIE 95-19, will most likely increase (for example, in the Korean peninsula or in South Asia and the Middle East).[7]

On the other hand, intelligence community reports on multiple developments, new and not so new, increasingly challenge the U.S. security in world politics. The problem of evaluating a shifting mix of security threats is already daunting. These threats include the spread of ethnic conflict and militant nationalism; proliferation of weapons of mass destruction to states and to nonstate actors; the ability of "rogue states" (most notably, the so called Club MAD, which includes North Korea, Libya, Iran, Iraq) to destabilize regional security; environmental degradation, such as ozone depletion, tropical deforestation, climate changes, greenhouse emissions, ocean dumping of hazardous substances, water scarcity, and degradation; transnational criminal and terrorist groups; and, refugee flows.

Hearings and inquiries held by the U.S. Senate's Permanent Subcommittee on Investigations, chaired by Senator Sam Nunn, suggest that these threats are genuine. For example, in December 1995 a man allegedly related to survivalist groups was charged with attempted smuggling into the United States of 130 grams of ricin, a powerful toxin that causes almost immediate death when inhaled or absorbed through skin, for use as weapon. (A ricin-daubed 1.7-mm pellet, fired from an umbrella, killed a Bulgarian dissident, Georgi Markov, in London in 1978.) In November 1995, Chechen resistance fighters threatened to blow up a radiological device (conventional explosives laced with some radioactive material) in Moscow. In November 1995, sophisticated guidance systems taken from disassembled Soviet intercontinental ballistic missiles turned up in Jordan and Iraq. In May 1995, Larry Wayne Harris, a former member of the Aryan Nations, was arrested after successfully ordering through the mail for a mere $240 three vials of freeze-dried bubonic plague bacteria from the world's largest distributor of microorganisms, the American True Type Collection. In March 1995, twelve people were killed and more than 5,000 hospitalized after the Japanese doomsday cult, Aum Shinrikyo, released sarin nerve gas into the Tokyo subway.[8]

On aggregate, the problem is that demonstrable, quantifiable, and clear threats of global war are fewer; whereas fuzzy, fragmented, and less quantifiable—hence, less "visible"—threats are legion; the combined impact of the former and the latter on U.S. security is unfathomable. Moreover, the "invisibility" of security threats has also been heightened by the coming together of previously distinct issues, such as terrorism, proliferation, organized crime, arms control, and violent extremism. Although these issues merge in reality, they are considered separately in the threat assessment process. For example, the Nunn hearings revealed that the federal government was doing little research or intelligence collection on the roles of organized crime and corruption in weapons proliferation. The Aum Shinrikyo case indicates the problems involved in giving strategic warning about such muted, qualitative threats. The Senate subcommittee on found that several warning signals had not been interpreted effectively: Aum's strong anti-American and anti-Western preaching; the cult's extensive global search for chemical and biological weapons; its procurement networks in Japan and Russia; its high-level connections in the Russian government and elsewhere, as reported in the press; and its New York network, which had been established in 1987. According to Sam Nunn's legal counsel, John Sopko, "Every U.S. intelligence and law enforcement official interviewed admitted to the subcommittee that Aum Shinrikyo 'were not on anyone's radar screen.'"[9]

At the level of threat recognition, the end of the Cold War also meant a shift in intelligence's stock and trade from puzzles or questions that could be answered definitively given the necessary information to mysteries or questions that cannot be answered with certainty no matter what information is received. The U.S. intelligence community, in the course of the

Cold War, addressed such questions as how much does Moscow spend on the military, or how many missiles do the Soviets have, or whether these missiles had been launched. Although the intelligence capability for solving such puzzles is and will be vital to threat assessment, intelligence consumers of the post–Cold War era are increasingly interested in new questions, most of them mysteries: Will Russia be an enemy or an ally—and on which issues? Will China become more aggressive toward Taiwan, Vietnam, Malaysia, or Indonesia now that Deng Xiaoping is gone and Hong Kong is back under Beijing's rule. Will North Korea cheat on nuclear agreement with the United States? Will market reforms hold in Latin America and Eastern Europe? If France bribed Brazil to land a $1.4 billion radar contract, will France persuade China to beat Boeing in competition for aircraft orders? If Chechnya secedes from Russia, how will that affect relations between Moscow and its provinces as well as with the former Soviet republics?[10]

In designing new missions for the U.S. intelligence community, senior lawmakers sounded rather utopian, given the magnitude of the conceptual, organizational, and political challenges facing the entire U.S. foreign policy process. In 1993, then chairman of the House Permanent Select Committee on Intelligence, Representative Dan Glickman of Kansas, praised the intelligence community for giving policy makers ample warning of "hostile intentions or of the development of dangerous situations" regarding terrorism, narcotics trafficking, regional and ethnic hostilities, economic challenges to U.S. interests, and "the rapidly changing political atmosphere in the former Soviet Union."[11]

In practice, however, while conveying "a palpable sense of threat," the intelligence community in fact became mired in the conceptual uncertainties of defining threats in post–Cold War world politics. One clear illustration of these uncertainties is the emergence of a wide range of views on a seemingly straightforward subject: how many armed conflicts take place in the world, and how does one define these conflicts in the first place? For 1996, the CIA counted 28 "conflicts," whereas the National Defense Council Foundation, a Virginia-based think tank, registered 64 "hot spots," and the more liberal Center for Defense Information identified 20 "active wars." At the organizational level, according to Allan Goodman, "The uncertainty has led many policy officials to respond to intelligence community surveys about what it is they might need by saying that they need as much information from as many different sources as possible about all the things that could go wrong or precipitate crises in which the nation might have to be involved." Another element adding to the confusion is that the number of major consumers in the policy community posing such intelligence tasks has approximately doubled during 1991-1995.[12]

Caught in these "do-the-world" dilemmas, as well as in revelations about past and current scandals, from plots to overthrow foreign governments and assassinate leaders to the discovery of CIA's Russian double agents, such as Aldrich Ames and Harold Nicholson, large numbers of younger clandestine operatives and intelligence analysts have quit since the end of the Cold War. In late 1996, CIA spokesman Mark Mansfield implied that the "disproportionate number of resignations" was considered serious enough by the agency to set up an investigation under CIA Inspector General Frederick Hitz into "reasons for [employees] leaving [and to] see if more can be done to retain people with core competency and . . . skills."[13]

My analysis suggests that after the Cold War, the potentially destabilizing asymmetry between the palm-reading and bean-counting threat assessment paradigms of competing global powers is further complicated by identifying national priorities amidst security challenges that have simultaneously fragmented and gone global. As Robert Steele has put it, this new asymmetry in threat assessment may be described as one between focusing predominantly on monolithic "high-tech brutes" (for example, China acquiring space-based laser weapons) and complex combinations of threats posed by "low-tech brutes" (that is, low-intensity conflicts), "high-tech seers" (such as terrorists targeting government computer and communications networks), and "low-tech seers" (ethnic or religious extremists).[14]

Therefore, if in the past, asymmetric assessments systematically reflected military, economic, and political differentiation in world politics among major global powers, then the globalization of threats, the fragmentation of national political power centers, and the rise of transnational actors should also be reflected in emergent global intelligence organizations. The complex political power game at the global level should naturally spawn complex intelligence institutions, alliances, partnerships, networks, coalitions, teams, and missions targeting global problems and serving a wider range of national and international consumers. To revisit the Aum Shinrikyo example, the puzzle pieces that had to be assembled to generate a timely warning of the cult's sarin attack in Tokyo were widely dispersed around the world and among different institutional jurisdictions. Putting these pieces together would require a very complex transnational coordination framework. Agencies as diverse as the anti-organized crime department of the Moscow police, Russian federal bodies overseeing religious organizations, the Tokyo city police, and nongovernmental organizations monitoring international criminal activities in the United States and Australia (where Aum tested nerve gas on sheep) could have regularly provided information on the cult to an international terrorism data analysis center, possibly under the UN auspices interfacing with U.S. intelligence services. (Leaks of classified information could be discouraged by the threat of losing a good civil service job or criminal prosecution under host country—the United States—laws.) As an intelligence clearinghouse with proper information safeguards, such a center could have verified local reports with U.S. intelligence experts and have fed integrated intelligence assessments back to the localities where Aum was active. This—or anything else—still would not make the world safe from such attacks. But Aum's efforts to procure toxic stockpiles would have been more visible to the agencies best positioned to take swift and decisive action to seize the deadly chemical gas before it was used.

In other words, the complex, globalized dangers of the post–Cold War era should not discourage specialists working on intelligence reforms in various nation-states, and in especially the United States. Rather, these dangers suggest that reformers must consider the globalization of intelligence, while retaining streamlined core national functions, more boldly and more creatively. In this sense, the confusion besetting the U.S. intelligence community after the Cold War is a positive development: it offers more creative opportunities than the rigid if brilliant unified blueprints for the post–Cold War intelligence mission. A more concerted effort is needed to forge meaningful and flexible global institutions capable of dealing with classical security problems such as interstate aggression and with transnational weapons proliferation, ethnic conflicts, organized crime, environmental terrorism, and peacekeeping.

Mirroring world politics as a whole, the post–Cold War reorganization of intelligence services embodies two competing trends, one with the potential to lessen and the other to enhance destabilizing threat assessment asymmetries.

Just as many threats have arisen from the shadows the former Soviet Empire, a network of global intelligence institutions to tackle global threats emerged in the 1940s. In spring of 1941, Britain and the United States, the two states with the strongest characteristics of global leadership in this century, fostered cooperation in global signals intelligence and ocean surveillance. At that time, four American representatives delivered a model of the Japanese PURPLE cipher machine to British code-breakers at Bletchley Park and received in return the Marconi-Adcock high-frequency direction finder, along with other advanced cryptological equipment.[15] After World War II, the intelligence relationship between Australia, Britain, Canada,

New Zealand, and the United States became institutionalized under the 1947 UK-USA Security Agreement (UKUSA Agreement). These states adopted international regulations on SIGINT, synchronizing code words and procedures for handling and disseminating intelligence obtained from signals intercepts. Global ocean surveillance became a major area of cooperation, involving the multilateral deployment of surface ships, submarines, ground stations, and satellites. Intelligence output from these collection stations has been channeled directly into the U.S. Naval Ocean Surveillance Information System—a perfect system for fusing globally decentralized collection and globally coordinated analysis. The United States and Britain also divided the world for the wholesale monitoring of foreign radio broadcasts between the CIA's Foreign Broadcast Information Service (FBIS) and the British Broadcasting Corporation's (BBC) Monitoring Service. By the mid-1980s, the UKUSA security and intelligence community employed more than a quarter of a million full-time personnel with a total budget of $16-18 billion. While becoming one of the world's largest bureaucracies, the UKUSA security and intelligence community also evolved into "a truly multinational community, with its numerous organizations and agencies bound together by an extraordinary network of written and unwritten agreements, working practices and personal relationships."[16]

By the early 1980s, several structures emerged within the U.S. intelligence community as a possible model of interagency collection and analysis, able to interface with international organizations such as the UN as well as to diversify the UKUSA and NATO intelligence sharing. Among these structures, which rose to prominence with the decline in importance of Cold War threats, are special study centers devoted to global problems, such as the Arms Control Intelligence Staff (ACIS), the Counterterrorism Center (CTC), and the Nonproliferation Center (NPC). While initially disliked by the DIA, the NSA, and the INR (State Department's Bureau of Intelligence and Research), the oldest and most successful of those study centers, ACIS (established in the mid-1970s), came to be considered a model for intelligence community cooperation. ACIS's role was substantially expanded in the 1980s as the Reagan administration increased its efforts to constrain Soviet mobile missile developments through effectively verifiable treaties. The rise of ACIS was also part of a new phase of intelligence support for arms control in connection with the 1988 intermediate nuclear forces (INF) treaty. The clustering and further expansion of the new centers occurred in 1989, when the Treaty Monitoring Center and the conventional forces component of the Office of Soviet Analysis (SOVA) were incorporated into a "super-ACIS." In the early 1990s, ACIS began providing information on global arms control problems to a wider range of political institutions and decision makers. That included support for U.S. discussions with the former Soviet republics on nuclear disarmament, disposal, safety, and security; providing various data and monitoring judgments to the U.S. Congress for treaty ratification; dissemination of periodic monitoring reports to policy makers in the administration and Congress; and support for treaty compliance monitoring through on-site consultations and coordination of monitoring and inspection. After 1991, the focus of U.S. intelligence priorities shifted to the proliferation threat. The NPC, created in 1991 to support policy in this area was modeled on ACIS. Thus, with respect to post–Cold War global problems, centers such as NPC and ACIS "would likely continue to be the model for existing centers and future cooperative mechanisms of this nature."[17]

The case studies also suggest that the growing use of national intelligence services in global arms control and treaty verification is likely to produce fewer asymmetric threat assessments, in part due to a greater value being placed on strategic information about tangible capabilities obtained by the "national technical collection means" (such as reconnaissance satellites). Such efforts will help to form a common "global data universe" on critical security issues that transcend national limits of the known world. These activities of intelligence organizations as well as the complexity and scope of arms control agreements have been on the increase ever since the advent of the space age. The Nuclear Non-Proliferation Treaty alone, signed in 1970, comprised more than 80 percent of the world's countries by 1990.[18]

One encouraging development is that postwar international intelligence cooperation crossed the divide between the incumbent world power (the United States) and potential challengers, particularly Russia, albeit gingerly. Despite the high-profile spy scandals of the early 1990s, Washington and Moscow have cooperated on global counternarcotics and counter terrorism campaigns and, to some extent on nonproliferation threats. In November 1995 NATO and Russia signed an information security agreement, paving the way for integrating Russia's Federal Security Service into a network of NATO-Russia information exchanges. The United States had provided the Chinese government with intelligence data on Soviet troops during the Sino-Soviet border disputes in 1969-1970 and also provided the know-how for setting up China's population census service. Since the Cold War, the international community has been focusing more specifically on establishing an efficient UN early warning system with the principal purpose of increasing the effectiveness of peacekeeping operations. In autumn 1995, senior intelligence, military, and political officials of the United States, NATO, Japan, Europe, and Russia agreed on the joint use of highly classified reconnaissance spacecraft for peacekeeping operations and crisis monitoring around the world. To coordinate intelligence collection and analysis, work was started on establishing one or more international reconnaissance data fusion centers.[19]

Another post–Cold War sign of intelligence globalization is that national intelligence missions have been conducted in support of UN military commanders and multinational forces in regional conflicts. In this newly emergent partnership, UN member nations contribute the intelligence collection and analysis machinery, from analysts to satellites, while the UN integrates intelligence input and distributes essential information to its agencies and departments responsible for specific operations. The concept of UN intelligence is a radical departure from traditional principles. According to Hugh Smith, "Intelligence will have to be based in information that is collected primarily by overt means, that is by methods that do not threaten the target state or group and do not compromise the integrity or impartiality of the U.N." Sir David Ramsbotham, a former British army general specializing in UN peacekeeping operations, suggests that national contingents in such operations will be responsible for collecting intelligence from their own human sources and acting "as information exchanges for U.N. Agencies and NGOs [nongovernmental organizations] operating with them, and with whom mutual operation, because it is locally focused, is often easier and closer."[20]

Counterbalancing these developments, however, are persistent conditions in world politics—among them, proud East Asian autocracies, especially China, enjoying phenomenal economic growth—that may again give rise to asymmetric threat assessments. China, for example, has entered the post–Cold War era with an autocratic political system and an economy heavily relying on sweatshop socialism—both typical challenger characteristics.[21] According to Feng Baoshing, a former Chinese diplomat who defected to the West, the direct assessment of political intentions commands disproportionately much attention from China's policy makers. One of Beijing's major intelligence activities in the 1990s has been to identify and keep under surveillance Hong Kong residents suspected of opposing the return of the former British colony to China's rule in 1997, and especially political activists insisting on the retention of democratic governance after the Hong Kong handover. In 1992, China's public security minister, Tao

Siju, stated that Beijing would judge friends and foes in the global arena on the basis of their utility for "promoting Chinese patriotism."[22]

Intelligence sharing with international organizations dealing with globally dispersed threats remains a sensitive subject for nation-states, including democracies, that are concerned about their sovereignty and competitiveness. For example, during Operation Desert Storm against Iraq in 1991, several partners in the anti-Saddam Hussein coalition that were denied certain intelligence information by the United States became resentful and suspicious. In 1995, Republican legislators in Congress increased their opposition to sharing intelligence with the United Nations for fear of security leaks after the discovery of sensitive U.S. documents abandoned in Mogadishu, Somalia. These lawmakers proposed tough congressional checks in the form of authorization and independent contracts on all intelligence sharing. In 1996, the chairman of the Senate Committee on Foreign Relations, Jesse Helms, argued that the United Nations must dramatically scale down its activities or be abolished. In the House, Rep. Joe Scarborough, a Florida Republican, introduced legislation for the United States to withdraw from the United Nations and replace it with a league of democracies. Jesse Helms also led a successful campaign to oust Secretary General Boutros Boutros-Ghali, an outspoken champion of enhancing the UN's role in early warning of international conflicts and crises.[23]

For its part, the UN's Lessons Learnt Unit, designed to enhance the organization's early warning framework, has had difficulties publishing material that would implicate UN Secretariat officials or member states with mistakes or wrongful actions. The United Nations has yet to take the initiative in and acquire a mandate for proactive intelligence procurement in international conflicts: its secretary generals, at this writing, have invoked Article 99, empowering them to alert the Security Council about threats to international peace, in regard to only three cases of armed conflict (Congo 1960, Iran 1979, and Lebanon 1989); the UN has yet to purchase a spy satellite photo for its military operations—at the UN gets satellite intelligence only on a need-to-know basis, determined by nation-states.[24]

Intelligence cooperation among potential challengers to US global leadership would also signal an ongoing differentiation between these two historical lineages in world politics. Some elements of such intelligence collaboration have been evident. In 1992, Russia was aiding Chinese nuclear, missile, and space programs and strengthening arms trade through intelligence exchanges that may have violated international nonproliferation treaties, especially given China's record of transferring military technology to third countries. Thus, U.S. intelligence sources said that in February 1996 China sold 5,000 ring magnets used for weapon-grade enriched uranium production to Pakistan. China also was suspected of selling C-802 Cruise missiles to Iran in violation of a 1992 weapons nontransfer pact. In June 1996, U.S. intelligence sources reported that Pakistan secretly acquired M-11 ballistic missiles from China. Such sensitive trade in weapons of mass destruction and related technology implies high-level contacts between China and Pakistan's military and intelligence services. Greater intelligence exchanges among Russia, Iran, China, and India outside the broader international community will also emerge from the jointly operated Asian Fund for Thermonuclear Research, established in 1996. Under this fund's auspices, atomic scientists from the four countries would collaborate in the construction of a new, experimental thermonuclear reactor.[25]

Meanwhile, a study of causes underlying the increase in nuclear proliferation after the 1970 Nuclear Non-proliferation Treaty found that the International Atomic Energy Agency, a UN branch charged with safeguarding the treaty, has no efficient intelligence capability to uncover many national nuclear programs. Even treaty member countries were willing to compromise on the original nonproliferation standards.[26]

In postcommunist Russia, against a backdrop of mounting economic and social problems associated with the transition to democracy and free markets, the KGB-successor services struck a tough position on NATO's eastward enlargement and argued for expanding Russia's political and economic leverage in the former Soviet republics.[27] In 1993, for example, the Russian Defense Ministry designated three intelligence satellites to closely monitor events and communications in the Commonwealth of Independent States and bolster the ministry's authority in the region.[28] In 1996, Yeltsin replaced the foreign minister, Andrei Kozyrev, who was identified with Russia's efforts to become part of the global community and a strategic partner of the United States, with the former head of the Foreign Intelligence Service (SVR), Yevgeny Primakov, who consistently argued that accommodations with the West should take second place to the reassertion of Russia's control in the former Soviet republics.[29] Making these issues a priority will distract the attention and resources of Russia's intelligence services from developing new forms of cooperation with global intelligence networks and institutions.

Finally, increasing global organization in the form of transnational political and economic institutions, coupled with the arrival of the information age in the world economy, may indicate that intelligence services, while reflecting national priorities, will also become more integrated into the framework of international political institutions such as the United Nations and the global leader's alliances, such as NATO. From the perspective of world system's evolution over the long term, it is unlikely that the trend toward global organization will be reversed. It is also unlikely, however, that major actors in world politics—from states to alliances of states and transnational nonstate actors—would abandon efforts to aggressively reshape a world order in which they may perceive their position as disadvantaged. Increasing global political and economic transactions, supported by flexible global intelligence institutions or "virtual intelligence teams," may minimize the challengers' incentives to play a greater part in the world system by pursuing aggressive military strategies, while possibly encouraging more peaceful and cooperative forms of global participation. The present world power, the United States, by having unrivaled military capabilities of global reach, the lead sector intensive economy, and the most advanced intelligence institutions, will play a decisive role in shaping world politics in such a way as to discourage future aggressive challengers. Extending U.S. economic and military leadership to global intelligence institutions-building will go a long way toward making many otherwise invisible post–Cold War threats visible. Such integration of critical threat assessment tasks and resources at the global level will help major players in world politics push wider their limits of the known world—in time, perhaps, to avoid asymmetric decision paths leading to global war.

Notes

Notes to Chapter 1

1. Philippe Baumard, "From Noticing to Making Sense: Using Intelligence to Develop Strategy," *International Journal of Intelligence and Counterintelligence* 7: 1 (1994), 37.

2. V. P. Lukin and A. I. Utkin, *Rossiya i zapad: Obshchnost' ili otchuzhdeniye* [Russia and the West: Commonality or estrangement] (Moscow: SAMPO, 1995), 29-30. The conference, hosted by the Battelle Research Laboratories (Seattle), in which the author participated, was held in May 1990.

3. Ellery Eels, *Rational Decision and Causality* (New York: Cambridge University Press, 1982), 5.

4. On deterrence effects in conditions of "opaque proliferation," see Devin T. Hagerty, "Nuclear Deterrence in South Asia: The 1990 Indo-Pakistani Crisis," *International Security* 20 (Winter 1995- 96), 79-114.

5. Kenneth N. Waltz, *Theory of International Politics* (New York: Random House, 1979), argued that measures taken to enhance security by one state will inevitably lead to a shift in systemic power balances that would endanger others (64), hence the "security dilemma." For a more recent presentation of the argument, see Joseph M. Grieco, *Cooperation among Nations: Europe, America, and Non-Tariff Barriers to Trade* (Ithaca: Cornell University Press, 1990), 28-29.

6. See Robert J. Art and Robert Jervis, *International Relations: Enduring Concepts and Contemporary Issues,* 3d ed. (New York: Harper Collins, 1992), 2; Farid Zakaria, "Realism and Domestic Politics," *International Security* 17 (1992), 177-98.

7. Stephen A. Kocs, "Explaining the Strategic Behavior of States: International Law as System Structure," *International Studies Quarterly* 38 (December 1994), 536.

8. Richard K. Ashley, "The Poverty of Neorealism," in *Neorealism and Its Critics,* ed. Robert O. Keohane (New York: Columbia University Press, 1986).

9. Richard L. Merritt and Dina A. Zinnes, "Alternative Indexes of National Power," in *Power in World Politics,* eds. Richard J. Stoll and Michael D. Ward (Boulder: Lynne Rinnai Publishers, 1989), 11-28.

10. J. David Singer and Paul F. Diehl, eds., *Measuring the Correlates of War* (Ann Arbor: University of Michigan Press, 1990); Melvin Small and J. David Singer, *Resort to Arms: International and Civil Wars, 1816-1980* (Beverly Hills: Sage, 1982). For other research programs testing multivariate indexes of power, see Wilhelm Fucks, *Formeln zür Macht* [Formulas of Power] (Stuttgart: Deutsche Verlags-Anstalt, 1965); F. Clifford German, "A Tentative Evaluation of World Power," *Journal of Conflict Resolution* 4 (1960), 138-44; Ray S. Cline, *World Power Assessment: A Calculus of Strategic Drift* (Boulder: Westview Press, 1975); Klaus Knorr, *Military Power and Potential* (Lexington, Mass: D. C. Heath, 1970).

11. J. David Singer, Stuart Bremer, and John Stuckey, "Capability Distribution, Uncertainty, and Major Power War, 1820-1965," in *Peace, War, and Numbers,* ed. Bruce M. Russett (Beverly Hills: Sage, 1972), 25-26.

12. On the autocorrelation problem, see Zeev Maoz and Bruce Russett, "Normative and Structural Causes of Democratic Peace, 1946-1986," in *American Political Science Review* 87 (1993), 631-32. On conceptual problems typical of the realist view of world system transformation, see Richard Rosecrance and Arthur A. Stein, "Beyond Realism: The Study of Grand Strategy," in *The Domestic Bases of Grand Strategy,* eds. Richard Rosecrance and Arthur A. Stein (Ithaca: Cornell University Press, 1993), 10-11. For the classic example of neorealism's failure to explain global wars based on system-level distribution of power, see William R. Thompson, *On Global War: Historical-Structural Approaches to World Politics* (Columbia: University of South Carolina Press, 1988), 9-14.

13. Singer et al., "Capability Distribution," 28.

14. Jacek Kugler and Marina Arbetman, "Choosing Among Measures of Power: A Review of the Empirical Record," in *Power in World Politics,* eds. Stoll and Ward, 75.

15. Waltz, *Theory of International Politics,* chap. 4.

16. Richard C. Eichenberg, Brigitta Widmaier, and Ulrich Widmaier, "Projecting Domestic Conflict Using Cross-Section Data," in *Quantitative Indicators in World Politics: Timely Assurance and Early Warning,* eds. J. David Singer and Richard J. Stoll (New York: Praeger, 1984), 11-34.

17. See, for example, Ted Robert Gurr and Thomas Irving Lichbach, "Forecasting Domestic Political Conflict," in *To Augur Well: Early Warning Indicators in World Politics,* eds. J. David Singer and Michael D. Wallace (Beverly Hills: Sage, 1979), 153-94.

18. Michael Howard, "Reassurance and Deterrence: Western Defense in the 1980s," *Foreign Affairs* 61: 2 (1982-83), 315.

19. Quoted in Charles W. Kegley, Jr. and Eugene Wittkopf, *World Politics: Trends and Transformation* (New York: St. Martin's Press, 1995), 407.

20. Paul K. Huth, *Extended Deterrence and the Prevention of War* (New Haven: Yale University Press, 1988), 57-71.

21. Arkady N. Shevchenko, *Breaking with Moscow* (New York: Ballantine Books, 1985), 144-45; Raymond L. Garthoff, *Assessing the Adversary: Estimates by the Eisenhower Administration of Soviet Intentions and Capabilities* (Washington, D.C.: The Brookings Institution, 1991), 42-43.

22. Huth, *Extended Deterrence,* pp. 71-72.

23. Frank A. Zagare, "Classical Deterrence Theory: A Critical Assessment," *International Interactions* 21 (1996), 377-79.

24. Ibid., 377-79.

25. Jacek Kugler, "Terror Without Deterrence," *Journal of Conflict Resolution* 28 (1984), 479.

26. Paul K. Huth and Bruce M. Russett, "Deterrence Failure and Crisis Escalation," *International Studies Quarterly* 32 (March 1984), 29.

27. Richard K. Betts, *Nuclear Blackmail and Nuclear Balance* (Washington, D.C.: Brookings Institution, 1987), 20.

28. For the exposition of rational choice theories, see Graham T. Allison, *Essence of Decision: Explaining the Cuban Missile Crisis* (Boston: Little, Brown, 1971); Michael Nicholson, *Formal Theories in International Relations* (New

York: Cambridge University Press, 1989); Bruce Bueno de Mesquita, *The War Trap* (New Haven: Yale University Press, 1981). A critical discussion of the expected utility theory is provided in Robert Jervis, "Realism, Game Theory, and Cooperation," *World Politics* 40 (1988), 317-49.

29. Bueno de Mesquita, *War Trap,* chap. 4.

30. Zagare, "Classical Deterrence Theory," 373.

31. Stephen van Evera, "The Cult of the Offensive and the Origins of the First World War," *International Security* 9 (1984), 58-107.

32. Robert Jervis, *Perception and Misperception in International Politics* (Princeton: Princeton University Press, 1976), 50, 101.

33. Ibid., 51.

34. Ibid., 128-201, offers an extended analysis of cognitive closure and related concepts. For a comprehensive insider's account of the evolution of Gorbachev's perception about the nature of the confrontation between communism and capitalism on the world stage, see Anatoly S. Chernyayev, *Shest let s Gorbachevym: Po dnevnikovym zapisyam* [Six years with Gorbachev: According to the diary record] (Moscow: Izdatel'skaya gruppa "Progress," "Kul'tura," 1993), 65-301.

35. Joe D. Hagan, "Domestic Political Systems and War Proneness," *Mershon International Studies Review* 38 (1994), 183.

36. Quincy Wright, *A Study of War* (Chicago: University of Chicago Press, 1942), 847, noted the propensity of democratic governments to favor the conciliatory type of leader personality. For comprehensive review of more recent studies, see George Modelski, "Democratization: A Global Evolutionary Process" (paper presented at the annual meeting of the American Political Science Association, San Francisco, 1990); Steve Chan, "Democracy and War: Some Thoughts on Future Research Agenda," *International Interactions* 18 (1993), 205-13; William J. Dixon, "Democracy and the Peaceful Settlement of International Conflict," *American Political Science Review* 88 (1994), 14-32; James Lee Ray, "Wars between Democracies: Rare, or Nonexistent?" *International Interactions* 18 (1993), 251-76; Bruce M. Russett, *Grasping the Democratic Peace: Principles for a Post-Cold War World* (Princeton: Princeton University Press, 1993).

37. See Steven Rosen, "War Power and the Willingness to Suffer," in *Peace, War, and Numbers,* ed. Russett (Beverly Hills: Sage Publications, 1972), 167-83; George Kennan (X), "The Sources of Soviet Conduct," *Foreign Affairs* 25 (July 1947), 566-82; A. F. K. Organski and Jacek Kugler, *The War Ledger*

(Chicago: University of Chicago Press, 1980); Alan C. Lamborn, *The Price of Power: Risk and Foreign Policy in Britain, France, and Germany* (Boston: Unwin and Hyman, 1991); eds. Richard Rosecrance and Arthur A. Stein, *The Domestic Bases of Grand Strategy* (Ithaca: Cornell University Press, 1993); Jack Snyder, *Myths of Empire: Domestic Politics and International Ambitions* (Ithaca: Cornell University Press, 1991); Jack S. Levy, "The Diversionary Theory of War: A Critique," in *Handbook of War Studies,* ed. Manus I. Midlarsky (Boston: Unwin Hyman, 1989); John Vasquez, *The War Puzzle* (New York: Cambridge University Press, 1993).

38. See Randolph M. Siverson and Harvey Starr, "Regime Change and the Restructuring of Alliances," *American Journal of Political Science* 38 (February 1994), 145-61.

39. Hagan, "Domestic Political Systems," 192.

40. Joshua S. Goldstein, *International Relations* (New York: HarperCollins, 1996), 181.

41. Based on the data in Jack S. Levy, *War in the Modern Great Power System, 1495-1975* (Lexington: University of Kentucky Press, 1983).

42. Thompson, *On Global War.*

43. David L. Sills, ed., *International Encyclopedia of the Social Sciences,* vol. 8 (New York: Free Press, 1968), 62.

44. This refers to the traditional distinction between strategic and tactical intelligence. Strategic intelligence is used for the solution of political, military, and economic problems of a long-range character at the level of a nation-state. Tactical intelligence is applied to the problems of daily operational necessity of particular government departments and agencies.

45. Michael C. Fry and Miles Hochstein, "Epistemic Communities: Intelligence Studies and International Relations," *Intelligence and National Security* 8 (July 1993), 25.

46. Wesley K. Wark, "The Study of Espionage: Past, Present, Future?" *Intelligence and National Security* 8 (July 1993), 4.

47. On the Japanese and Western connotations of the terms information and intelligence, see Mindy L. Kotler, "Information Perception: A Strategic Gap" (paper presented at the Third International Conference on Japanese Information Science, Technology and Commerce, Nancy, France, May 15-18, 1991). For the meaning of the Russian *razvedka,* its connotations and idiomatic usage, see S. I. Ozhegov and N. Yu. Shvedova, *Tolkovyy slovar'*

russkogo yazyka [Explanatory dictionary of the Russian language] (Moscow: Az", 1992), p. 662-63; for the meaning and connotations of its root, *vedat'*, see ibid., p. 70.

48. *Webster's Third New International Dictionary*, rev. ed. (1990), s.v. "Intelligence."

49. Baumard, "From Noticing to Making Sense," 30.

50. George Modelski and William R. Thompson, *Leading Sectors and World Powers: The Coevolution of Global Politics and Economics* (Columbia: University of South Carolina Press, 1996).

51. Tomonori Morikawa, John M. Orbell, and Audun S. Runde, "The Advantage of Being Modestly Cooperative," *American Political Science Review* 89 (September 1995), 601-11.

52. Ken Osterkamp, "Evolutionary Game Theory with Genetic Algorithms: Stability and Structural Change in Complex Political Systems" (paper presented at the Evolutionary Paradigms in Social Sciences Workshop, Seattle Battelle Research Center, May 26, 1995).

53. For the first quote, see Organski and Kugler, *The War Ledger,* 23; the second quote is in Robert Gilpin, *War and Change in World Politics* (New York: Cambridge University Press, 1981), 209.

54. Fernand Braudel, *The Perspective of the World* (London: Collins, 1982), 17-18.

55. George Modelski, "The Evolution of Global Politics," *Journal of World-Systems Research* 1 (1995), 8. In Modelski, "Is World Politics Evolutionary Learning?" *International Organization* 44 (Winter 1990), 1-24, this sequence of processes is defined as the four-stage ACME learning cycle, consisting of agenda-setting (global problems), coalition-building (core alliance formation), macrodecision making (global war), and execution (rise of the world power and challenger). For a book-length treatment of these issues see George Modelski, *Long Cycles in World Politics* (London: MacMillan, 1987). For a structural realist approach to the leadership succession in world politics see Gilpin, *War and Change.* A less flattering view of global leadership is provided in Immanuel Wallerstein, *The Capitalist World Economy* (New York: Cambridge University Press, 1984). The latter two studies, however, emphasize the phenomenon of the leading powers or hegemons in world politics.

56. See Modelski, "Democratization."

57. For the latest data on the first two conditions for global leadership, see Modelski and Thompson, *Leading Sectors.*

58. Modelski, "Evolution of Global Politics," 21-22.

59. See note 47 to this chapter.

60. On the difference in national patterns of strategic intelligence and its institutions, see Abram N. Shulsky, *Silent Warfare: Understanding the World of Intelligence*, 2d ed. (Washington, D.C.: Brassey's, 1993), especially 177-97. Also see Adda B. Bozeman, *Strategic Intelligence and Statecraft* (Washington, D.C.: Brassey's, 1992).

61. Sherman Kent, *Strategic Intelligence for American World Policy* (Princeton: Princeton University Press, 1953), 30-65.

62. Shulsky, *Silent Warfare*, 177-88.

63. Kent, *Strategic Intelligence*, 62-63. In this work, considered a classic in intelligence studies in the United States, Kent suggests that when the context of estimating probable causes of action is war, the nonmilitary elements of grand strategy are converted into "quasi-military instruments." Therefore, he explained, "our side will be calculating the courses of action open to the enemy in terms of our estimate of his capabilities."

64. Shulsky, *Silent Warfare*, 177-88.

65. David Kahn, *The Codebreakers* (New York: Macmillan, 1973), 1-67.

66. Federal'naia sluzhba bezopasnosti Rossii [Federal Security Service of Russia], Sluzhba vneshnei razvedki Rossii [Foreign Intelligence Service of Russia], Mosckovskoe gorodskoe ob'edinenie arkhivov [City of Moscow Archives Administration], *Sekrety Gitlera na stole u Stalina: Razvedka i kontrrazvedka o podgotovke Germanskoy agressii protiv SSSR, mart-iyun', 1941—Dokumenty iz tsentral'nogo arhiva FSB Rossii* [Hitler's secrets on Stalin's desk: Intelligence and counterintelligence on German preparations for aggression against the USSR, March-June 1941—documents from the Central Archive of the FSB of Russia] (Moscow: Mosgorarkhiv, 1995), 3-17.

67. Christopher Andrew and Oleg Gordievsky, *Inside the KGB: The Inside Story of Its Foreign Operations from Lenin to Gorbachev* (New York: Harper Perennial, 1991), 259-69.

68. See John B. Hattendorf et al., eds., *British Naval Documents, 1204-1960* (Aldershot, U.K.: Scholar Press for the Navy Records Society, 1993), 746, 754-55; William J. Perry, "Defense in the Age of Hope," *Foreign Affairs* 75 (November–December, 1996): 73.

69. See, for instance, Wallerstein, *World Economy*.

70. Michael I. Handel, "Strategic Surprise: The Politics of Intelligence and the Management of Uncertainty," in *Intelligence: Policy and Process,* eds. Fared C. Maurer, Marion D. Tunstall and James M. Keagle (Boulder: Westview Press, 1985), 239.

71. On adapting strategy to the existing and emerging weapons systems (i.e., material capabilities), see Michael Howard, *War in European History* (New York: Oxford University Press, 1979); J. F. C. Fuller, *The Conduct of War, 1789-1961: A Study of the Impact of the French, Industrial, and Russian Revolutions on War and Its Conduct* (London: Methuen, 1972); Brian Ranft, ed., *Technological Change and British Naval Policy, 1860-1939* (New York: Holmes & Meier, 1977).

72. Shulsky, *Silent Warfare,* 178.

73. Modelski, "Evolution of Global Politics," 15.

74. Robert A. Dahl, *Democracy and Its Critics* (New Haven: Yale University Press, 1989), 186-87.

75. The countries are Australia, Austria, Belgium, Canada, Denmark, Finland, France, Federal Republic of Germany, Greece, Iceland, Ireland, Italy, Japan, Luxemburg, Netherlands, New Zealand, Norway, Portugal, Spain, Sweden, Switzerland, Turkey, United Kingdom, and the United States.

76. Dahl, *Democracy and Its Critics,* 221.

77. Meyers v. United States, 272 U.S. 52, 292 (1926).

78. John W. Kingdon, *Agendas, Alternatives, and Public Policies* (New York: Harper Collins, 1984), 95-99.

79. David McLellan, *Ideology* (Minneapolis: University of Minnesota Press, 1986), 3.

80. Harry S. Eckstein and Ted Robert Gurr, *Patterns of Authority: A Structural Basis for Political Enquiry* (New York: Wiley-Interscience, 1975). Democracies thus can be distinguished from autocracies as political systems "in which some kind of assent is required, whether by especially prestigious minorities . . . numerical majorities, or virtually all of them" (ibid., 375).

81. Dahl, *Democracy and Its Critics,* 187.

82. Allen Dulles, *The Craft of Intelligence* (New York: Harper & Row, 1963), 22.

83. See Bozeman, *Intelligence and Statecraft;* Ernest R. May, *Knowing One's Enemies: Intelligence Assessments before the Two World Wars* (Princeton: Princeton University Press, 1986); Andrew and Gordievsky, *KGB.*

84. See, for example, Richard E. Morgan, *Domestic Intelligence: Monitoring Dissent in America* (Austin: University of Texas Press, 1980); Frank J. Donner, *The Age of Surveillance: The Aims and Methods of America's Political Intelligence System* (New York: Vintage Books, 1981); Richard Gid Powers, *Secrecy and Power: The Life of J. Edgar Hoover* (New York: Free Press, 1987).

85. For example, the U.S. Commission on CIA Activities within the United States, *Report to the President* (Washington, D.C.: U.S. Government Printing Office, June 1975); *The Watergate Hearings: Break-in and Cover-up. Proceedings of the Senate Select Committee on Presidential Campaign Activities as Edited by the Staff of* The New York Times (New York: Bantam Books, 1973).

86. See Jay Miller, *Lockheed U-2* (Austin: Aerofax Inc., 1983); Clarence L. Johnson, "Development of the Lockheed SR-71," *Lockheed Horizons* 9 (Winter 1981-82), 2-7; Merton E. Davis and William R. Harris, *Rand's Role in the Evolution of Balloon and Satellite Observation Systems and Related U.S. Space Technology* (Santa Monica: Rand Corporation, September 1988).

87. For the requirements of the comparative case study method, see Alexander L. George, "Case Studies and Theory Development: The Method of Structured Focused Comparison," in *Diplomacy: New Approaches in History, Theory and Policy,* ed. Paul G. Lauren (New York: Free Press, 1979), 54-66; Arend Lijphart, "Comparative Politics and Comparative Method," *American Political Science Review* 65 (September 1971), 682-93; Alexander L. George calls the method focused because it deals with a limited number of critical aspects of a historical case, in this instance, selection of strategic information in global conflicts, and structured because a uniform set of general questions is asked to generate data collection, analysis, and inferences.

88. Christopher H. Achen and Duncan Snidal, "Rational Deterrence Theory and Comparative Case Studies," *World Politics* 41 (January 1989), 143-69.

89. George, "Case Studies and Theory Development," 60.

90. Thazha V. Paul, *Asymmetric Conflicts: War Initiation by Weaker Powers* (Cambridge: Cambridge University Press, 1994) 35-36.

91. James A. Caporaso, "Research Design, Falsification, and the Qualitative-Quantitative Design," *American Political Science Review* 89 (June 1995), 458.

92. Modelski, "Evolution of Global Politics," 25.

93. The focus on the leading world powers and their main challengers as opposed to other types of actors in world politics is designed to maximize variation on all main variable indicators.

Notes to Chapter 2

1. Douglas S. Benson, *The Mongol Campaigns in Asia: A Summary of Mongolian Warfare with Governments of Eastern and Western Asia in the Thirteenth Century* (Ashland, Ohio: BookMasters, 1991), 13.

2. Paul Ratchnevsky, *Genghis Khan: His Life and Legacy,* trans. and ed., Thomas Nivison Haining, (Oxford: Blackwell, 1992), 115; H. Desmond Martin, "The Mongol Army," *Journal of the Royal Asiatic Society* (April 1943), 61.

3. Janet L. Abu-Lughod, *Before European Hegemony: The World System* A.D. *1250-1350* (New York: Oxford University Press, 1989), 198-203.

4. Martin, "Mongol Army," 46-49.

5. Ibid., 84.

6. Meng Hung, *The Meng Ta Pei-lu,* quoted in Martin, "Mongol Army," 52.

7. Ratchnevsky, *Genghis Khan,* 93.

8. For example, in pursuit of the Khwarazmian prince Jalal ad-Din in September 1221, Genghis Khan's cavalry crossed about 130 miles of the highest and roughest mountain terrain in Afghanistan, traveling from Bamian to Ghazni via Kabul in two days, during which the Mongols "did not even have time to cook their food." Baron C. D'Ohsson, *Histoire des Mongols, Depuis Tchinguiz-Khan jusqu'à Timour Bey ou Tamerlan* (The Hague: Les Frères van Cleef, 1834), 305. See also Martin, "Mongol Army," 51.

9. Martin, "Mongol Army," 52.

10. Sir Henry Yule, ed. and trans., *The Book of Ser Marco Polo the Venetian and Marvels of the East,* 3d ed. (New York: Scribner, 1903), vol. 1, 331.

11. Ibid., 331; D'Ohsson, *Histoire,* 244.

12. Martin, "Mongol Army," 52.

13. Ibid., 53; the remaining gear consisted of a helmet made of steel or leather, a file for sharpening arrows, a rope for pulling wagons, two leather bottles for food or drinks, a leather bag with a thong for clothes and equipment when crossing rivers, and a cooking pot made of baked clay or sometimes of iron.

14. Martin, "Mongol Army," 54; Igor de Rachewiltz et al., eds. *In the Service of the Khan: Eminent Personalities of the Early Mongol-Yuan Period, 1200-1300* (Weisbaden, Germany: Harrassowitz Verlag, 1993), xvii.

15. George Modelski and William R. Thompson, *Leading Sectors and World Powers: The Coevolution of Global Economics and Politics* (Columbia: University of South Carolina Press, 1996), 168-69.

16. Joseph Needham, *Science and Civilization in China* (Cambridge: Cambridge University Press, 1954), 242-43.

17. L. S. Stavrianos, *A Global History: From Prehistory to the Present,* 6th ed. (Englewood Cliffs, NJ: Prentice Hall, 1995), 162-63; George Modelski and William R. Thompson, *Seapower in Global Politics, 1494-1993* (Seattle: University of Washington Press, 1988), 62; Paul Kennedy, *The Rise and Fall of the Great Powers: Economic Change and Military Conflict from 1500 to 2000* (New York: Vintage Books, 1989), 7.

18. Jung-pang Lo, "China as a Sea-power," *Far Eastern Quarterly* 14 (August 1955), 491; Modelski and Thompson, *Seapower,* 30; Ernst Dupuy and Trevor Dupuy, *The Encyclopaedia of Military History* (New York: Harper and Row, 1977), 221; Yoshinobu Shiba, "Urbanization and the Development of Markets in the Lower Yangtze Valley," in *Crisis and Prosperity in Sung China,* ed. John Winthrop Haeger (Tucson: University of Arizona Press, 1975), 15-18.

19. Modelski and Thompson, *Coevolution,* 153.

20. Quoted in Will and Ariel Durant, *The Story of Civilization,* vol. 7: *The Age of Reason, 1558-1648* (New York: Simon and Schuster, 1961), 39.

21. Based on data in Modelski and Thompson, *Seapower,* 119-21.

22. Duke of Newcastle to the Earl of Hardwicke, September 6, 1749, British Library, Add. MSS 35410, ff. 153-4 (Hardwicke Papers) quoted in *British Naval Documents, 1204-1960* (Cambridge: Scolar Press for the Navy Records Society, 1993), p. 326.

23. Modelski and Thompson, *Seapower,* 207.

24. Ibid., 70, 111, 121; Karen A. Rasler and William R. Thompson, *The Great Powers and Global Struggle, 1490-1990* (Lexington: University of Kentucky Press, 1994), 197, 221; the whale and the elephant analogy is made in Kennedy, *Rise and Fall,* 124.

25. Jenkins, *French Navy,* 198-99.

26. Memorandum by Lord Sandwich, First Lord of the Admiralty, December 31, 1781, National Maritime Museum, SAN/F/29/108 (Sandwich Papers) quoted in *British Naval Documents,* 337-38. For the scale of the Royal Navy's presence around the world, see J. Holland Rose, A. P. Newton, and E. A. Benians, *The Cambridge History of the British Empire,* vol. 2: *The Growth of the New Empire, 1783-1870* (Cambridge: Cambridge University Press, 1940), chap. 1.

27. Rose et al., *British Empire,* 1.

28. Kennedy, *Rise and Fall,* 89-90.

29. Rose, et al., *British Empire,* vol. 2, 36-38. The data on the number of battles are based on Quincy Wright, *A Study of War* (Chicago: University of Chicago Press, 1942), 626.

30. Alfred T. Mahan, *The Influence of Sea Power upon History, 1660-1783* (New York: Holland Wang, 1890); Modelski and Thompson, *Seapower,* 70, 111, 121. For a tally of sea power indicators, see Rasler and Thompson, *Global Struggle,* Appendix B; Alfred T. Mahan, *The Influence of Sea Power upon the French Revolution and Empire, 1793-1812,* 2 vols. (Boston: Little, Brown, and Company, 1898), vol. 1, 75.

31. Mahan, *French Revolution and Empire,* 74.

32. Ibid., 71.

33. See Rasler and Thompson, *Global Struggle,* 194-95; Kennedy, *Rise and Fall,* xv-xvii, 98-100; George Lefebvre, Raymond Guyot, and Philippe Sagnac, *La revolution française* (Paris: Librairie Felix Alcan, 1930), 184, 223.

34. Rasler and Thompson, *Global Struggle,* 43; Kennedy, *Rise and Fall,* 99.

35. Mahan, *French Revolution and Empire,* 36; *Archives parlementaire,* vol. 36, 607.

36. Mahan, *French Revolution and Empire,* 36.

37. Modelski and Thompson, *Seapower,* 85-96; Kennedy, *Rise and Fall,* 347-437; see also Michael Mandelbaum, *The Nuclear Revolution: International Politics Before and After Hiroshima* (Cambridge: Cambridge University Press, 1981); Albert Carnesale, Paul Doty, Stanley Hoffmann, Samuel P. Huntington, Joseph S. Nye, Jr., and Scott D. Sagan, *Living with Nuclear Weapons* (Toronto: Bantam Books, 1983); Dietrich Schroeer, *Science, Technology, and the Nuclear Arms Race* (New York: John Wiley, 1984); Bruce G. Blair, *Strategic Command and Control* (Washington, D.C.: Brookings Institution, 1985).

38. International Institute for Strategic Studies (hereafter cited as IISS), *The Military Balance, 1975/76* (London: IISS, 1976), 71-73; idem, *The Military Balance, 1988-1989* (London: IISS, 1989), 230.

39. IISS, *The Military Balance, 1974/75* (London: IISS, 1975), 75-77.

40. Kennedy, *Rise and Fall,* 511. These measurements of the global reach capability shares are corroborated by more sophisticated comparisons of the relative position of the United States and the Soviet Union. Indicators of global naval capabilities that are based in equal proportion on the number of

aircraft carriers, nuclear attack submarines, equivalent megatonnage (EMT) and accuracy of sea-based nuclear missile warheads (counter military potential, or CMP) translate into highly compatible scores: the average share of American global naval capabilities is estimated at 0.736 in 1962, 0.770 in 1965, 0.714 in 1970, 0.707 in 1975, 0.648 in 1982, 0.645 in 1985, and 0.620 in 1988 (with 1.000 = 100 percent). See Modelski and Thompson, *Seapower,* 86-92.

41. Rasler and Thompson, *Global Struggle,* 198.

42. Kennedy, *Rise and Fall,* 511.

43. Paul Dibb, *The Soviet Union: The Incomplete Superpower* (London: Macmillan, 1985), 171; Jonathan Steele, *Soviet Power: The Kremlin Foreign Policy—Brezhnev to Chernenko* (New York: Simon and Schuster, 1977), 33-36; Andrew Cockburn, *The Threat: Inside the Soviet Military Machine* (New York: Vintage Books, 1984), chap. 15; Kennedy, *Rise and Fall,* p. 511.

44. Nikolai Leonov, *Likholet'ye* [The stormy years] (Moscow: Mezhdunarodnye otnosheniya, 1994), 141-43.

45. Kennedy, *Rise and Fall,* 512-13.

46. James Bamford, *The Puzzle Palace: A Report on America's Most Secret Agency* (New York: Penguin Books, 1983), 241; Dino A. Brugioni, *From Balloons to Blackbirds: Reconnaissance, Surveillance and Imagery Intelligence: How It Evolved* (McLean, Va.: Association of Former Intelligence Officers, 1993), 44-45.

47. Desmond Ball, *Soviet Signals Intelligence (SIGINT)* (Canberra: Australian National University, 1989), 119-21; Bamford, *The Puzzle Palace,* 250.

48. Ronald J. Diebert, assistant professor of political science, University of Toronto, personal communication, Seattle Battelle Research Center, May 25, 1995.

Notes to Chapter 3

1. B. D. Grekov and A. Yu. Yakubovsky, *Zolotaya orda i yeë padeniye* [The Golden Horde and its downfall] (Moscow: Izdatel'stvo Akademii Nauk SSSR, 1950), 42.

2. In the traditional Mongolian explanation, widespread in the thirteenth and fourteenth centuries, Temuchin received his name because he belonged to a family of smiths *(temurchi).* Other chronicles also suggest that Temuchin's cradle was made of iron *(temur)*—hence the names of Temuchin's brother—

Temuge, and his sister—Temulun, all deriving from the same root. See Paul Ratchnevsky, *Genghis Khan: His Life and Legacy*, trans. and ed. Thomas Nivison Haining (Oxford: Blackwell, 1991), 16-17.

3. V. V. Barthold, "Svyaz' obshchestvennogo byta s hozyaystvennym ukladom u turok i mongolov" [Linkage between social lifestyle and economic conditions among the Turks and the Mongols], in *Izvestiia Obshchestva arkheologii, istorii i etnografii pri Kazanskom universitete* 34 (vyp. [no.] 3-4, 1919), 3; S. A. Kozin, *Sokrovennoye skazaniye. Mongol'skaya khronika 1240 g. pod nazvaniyem Mongol-un niguca tobciyan. Yuan chao bi shih. Mongol'skiy obydennyy izbornik.* [Secret history. Mongol chronicle of the year 1240 under the title Mongol-un niguca tobciyan. Yuan-Ch-Ao Pi-Shih. Mongol Domestic Chronicle] (hereafter *Secret History*) (Moscow: Izdatel'stvo Akademii Nauk SSSR, 1941), vol. 1, para. 118; V. V. Barthold, "Obrazovaniye imperii Chingiz-khana" [The formation of the Genghis Khan Empire] in *Zapiski vostochnogo otdela Russkogo arheologicheskogo obshchestva* 10 (1897), 111; Secret History, para. 118.

4. For a comprehensive semantic analysis of the word 'Genghis,' see Ratchnevsky, *Genghis Khan*, 89-90.

5. Henry H. Howorth, *History of the Mongols: From the Ninth to the Nineteenth Century*, part I: *The Mongols Proper and the Kalmuks* (London: Longmans, Green, and Co., 1876), 62.

6. Baron C. D'Ohsson, *Histoire des Mongols, Depuis Tchinguiz-khan Jusqu'à Timour Bey ou Tamerlan* [History of the Mongols, from Genghis Khan to Timur Bei or Tamerlaine], 4 vols. (The Hague: Les Frères van Cleef, 1834), vol. 1, 98. Representing the entire range of ethnic and social groups of the empire, these assemblies were convened at the most important points in the initial period of the Mongol expansion: the first *khuriltai* (1203) endorsed Temuchin's campaign plan for Mongol unification, after some intensive debate; the second (1206) declared Genghis Khan supreme ruler of the newly established empire; the third (1211) endorsed the Mongol campaign against the Chin; and the fourth (1219) approved of the attack on Khwarazm.

7. B. Vladimirtsov, *Gengis-khan* [Genghis Khan] (Paris: Librairie d'Amérique et d'Orient Adrien- Maisonneuve, 1948), 54.

8. *Secret History,* paras. 202-34.

9. Eugene Weber, *The Western Tradition: From the Ancient World to Louis XIV* (Lexington, Mass.: D. C. Heath, 1990), 211-18.

10. The 1206 *khuriltai* endorsed Genghis Khan as emperor and rubberstamped the appointments of the commanders of the units of One Thousand, the administrative structure of the empire, and the composition of Genghis Khan's guard. Harsher measures against political dissenters were approved and the murder of the influential Shaman, Teb-tengri, by Genghis Khan's guards was condoned and justified. In 1211, the *khuriltai* accepted the pledge of loyalty by the Uighurs, approved a 20,000- strong security force to quell domestic rebellions, and adopted an appeal to the Mongol national spirit. The 1219 *khuriltai* approved new administrative laws, issued orders for war with the Sultanate of Khwarazm, and approved Genghis Khan's choice of Ogodei as his successor. See Ratchnevsky, *Genghis Khan,* 89-101, 108-9, 125-29; *Secret History,* paras. 202-34; Rashid ad-Din, *Sbornik letopisey* [Collected chronicles], vol. I/2, trans. O. I. Smirnova, ed. A. A. Semenov (Moscow: Akademiya nauk SSSR, 1952), 150, 162-79, 197; *Istoriya pervykh chetyrekh khanov iz doma Chingisova* [A history of the first four khans of the house of Genghis, based on *Yuan Shi*], trans. Monk Iakinf [Hyacinth] (St. Petersburg: Karl Kray, 1829), 35-40, 45-53, 97-103.

11. Howorth, *History of the Mongols,* 62. The high drama of the 1203 *khuriltai* was also reflected in the *Secret History:* describing the policy debate, the author switched from prose to poetic narrative. *Secret History,* para. 190.

12. Further distancing himself from the commoners and, hence, alternative sources of information, Genghis Khan, in his known speeches, conversations, edicts, ordinances, and laws never addressed the common people but only the princes of the blood (*noyons* and *bahaturs*). Vladimirtsov, *Gengis-khan,* 56.

13. A combatant private of the guard ranked higher than the chief of a regiment in the regular army, while non-combatant members outranked chiefs of squadrons. The families of the guardsmen were to be held superior to all others and any outsider quarrelling with a guardsman was to be punished. Making inquiries about the day of duty of the guard or their numbers on duty was punishable by a fine of a saddled horse and clothing. Barthold, *Turkestan,* 94, 384; Martin, "Mongol Army," 56-7; *Secret History,* paras. 224-25.

14. Barthold, *Turkestan,* 385.

15. *Secret History,* para. 245.

16. Ibid., para. 216.

17. ad-Din, *Sbornik letopisey,* vol. I/2, 163.

18. The sons of the leaders of Tens brought with them one kinsman and three companions. See Barthold, *Turkestan,* 384.

19. "If the men of any city or country do not do what these *bastarki* [*basqaqs*] wish, the latter accuse them of being unfaithful to the Tartars [Mongols], and consequently that city or country is destroyed and the inhabitants put to death by a strong force of Tartars who, summoned by the governor to whom the land is subject, arrive, unknown to the inhabitants, and suddenly rush upon them." John of Plano Carpini, "History of the Mongols," in *The Mongol Mission,* ed. Christopher Dawson (London: Sheed and Ward, 1955), 40.

20. Ibid.

21. Ratchnevsky, *Genghis Khan,* 180-86. The top-heavy character of this type of administration and information collection and analysis is documented in the chronicles of the Mongols and the Yuan dynasty, translated and preserved by Rashid ad-Din. Even on minor missions, the *elchi* customarily took escorts numbering 200-300, and higher-ranking officials could be accompanied by 500-1,000 men. See Rashid ad-Din, *Sbornik letopisey,* trans. A. K. Arends (Moscow: Izdatel'stvo Akademii Nauk SSSR, 1952), vol. 3, 251-52, 264-65.

22. Ratchnevsky, *Genghis Khan,* 103, 250n.; e.g., the Uighur, Tata-tonga, served as Keeper of the Great Seal *(ulugh tamgha)* and together with other secretaries *(bichechi)*—predominantly Uighurs— controlled the day-to-day running of the empire. Their responsibilities embraced recording and translating edicts and instructions; they set tax guidelines for tax collection and managed income and expenditure accounts, thus controlling the financial system almost completely. See ad-Din, *Sbornik letopisey,* vol. 3, 275, 298.

23. Barthold, *Turkestan,* 386; Martin, "Mongol Army," 56; *Secret History,* par. 223; ad-Din, *Sbornik letopisey,* vol. I/2, 260.

24. The surviving written record of the Mongol law consists of the orders, instructions, and commands *(bilik)* of Genghis Khan (and his successors) inscribed in scrolls and bound in volumes. These volumes are known as the "Great Book of the Yasas" *(Yasa nama-i buzurg)* in the Arab sources or "The Great Yasa" *(da zhasa)* in Chinese sources. See Juvaini, *The History of the World Conqueror,* vol. 1, 25; *Yuanshi,* ed. Sung Lien et al. (Beijing, 1976) quoted in Ratchnevsky, *Genghis Khan,* 187.

25. N. I. Berezin, "Ocherk vnutrennego ustroistva ulusa Dzhuchieva" [A sketch of the internal organization of the Jochi *Ulus*], *Trudy vostochnogo otdeleniya Moskovskogo arkheologicheskogo obshchestva* 8, (1864), 405. See also Valentin A. Riasanovsky, *Fundamental Principles of Mongol Law* (Bloomington: Indiana University Press, 1965); V. A. Riasanovsky," Velikaya yasa Chingis-

Hana," [The Great Yasa of Genghis Khan], *Izvestiya Harbinskogo yuridicheskogo fakul'teta* 10 (1938); George Vernadsky, "O sostave velikoy Yasy Chingis-khana" [On the content of the Great *Yasa* of Genghis Khan], in *Studies in Russian and Oriental History,* ed. George Vernadsky (Brussels: Edition Petropolis, 1939), vol. 1, 13; Vladimirtsov, *Gengis-khan,* 63.

26. Klaus Lech, *Das mongolische Weltreich: al-'Umari's Darstellung der mongolischen Reich in seinem Werk Marsalik al-absar fi mamlik al-amsar,* Asiatische Forschungen [Asiatic Studies], (Wiesbaden, 1968), vol. 22, 95, quoted in Ratchnevsky, *Genghis Khan,* 189.

27. H. G. Raverty, *Tabakat-i-nasirt: A General History of the Muhammadan Dynasties of Asia by the Maulana, Minhaj-al-Din, Abu-'Umart-'usman* (London, 1881), vol. 2, 953, quoted in Ratchnevsky, *Genghis Khan,* 196.

28. ad-Din, *Sbornik letopisey,* vol. I/2, 135.

29. Plano Carpini, "History," 25; ad-Din, *Sbornik letopisey,* vol. I/2, 260.

30. C. P. Fitzgerald, *China: A Short Cultural History* (London: The Cresset Press, 1942), 381, 393.

31. John Winthrop Haeger, "Introduction: Crisis and Prosperity in Sung China," in *Crisis and Prosperity in Sung China,* ed. John Winthrop Haeger (Tucson: University of Arizona Press, 1975), 3; Fitzgerald, *China,* 378.

32. L. S. Stavrianos, *A Global History: From Prehistory to the Present* (Englewood Cliffs, NJ: Prentice Hall, 1995), 215.

33. Ho Ping-ti, *The Ladder of Success in Imperial China* (New York: Columbia University Press, 1967), 74.

34. Haeger, "Introduction," 5. Perhaps even more significantly, in this political climate the "ever-widening sectors of society sought to improve themselves by learning." The impact of this Sung Enlightenment on social life is vividly described by Fang Ta-tsung, one of the flourishing men of letters of the Southern Sung: "In my own county every family is adept at music and the chanting of texts. People know the laws; and this is true not only of the scholars—every peasant, artisan, and merchant teaches his son how to read books. Even herdsmen and wives who bring food to their husbands at work in the fields can recite the poems of the men of ancient times. Jacques Gernet, *Daily Life in China on the Eve of the Mongol Invasion, 1250-1276* (New York: Macmillan, 1962), 128. Fang Ta-tsung, *Tieh-an Fang-kung weh-chi* [Literary works of Ts'ai Hsiang], chuan [vol.] 29, quoted in Shiba, "Urbanization and the Development of Markets," in ed. Haeger, *Crisis and Prosperity,* 44.

35. Fitzgerald, *China,* 381, 403.

36. Ibid., 376, 381, 388.

37. Quoted in Stavrianos, *Global History,* 129, 136.

38. Igor de Rachewiltz, Hok-lam Chan, Hsiao Ch'i-ch'ing, and Peter W. Geier, eds., *In the Service of the khan: Eminent Personalities of the Early Mongol-Yuan Period, 1200-1300* (Wiesbaden: Harrassowitz Verlag, 1993), 462, 490-91.

39. Charles A. Peterson, "First Sung Reactions to the Mongol Invasion of the North, 1211-1217," in *Crisis and Prosperity,* ed. Haeger, 219.

40. To a close circle to comrades, Genghis reportedly said, "Man's greatest good fortune is to chase and defeat his enemy, seize his total possessions, leave his married women weeping and wailing, ride his gelding, use the bodies of his women as nightshirt and support, gazing upon and kissing their rosy breasts, sucking their lips which are as sweet as the berries of their breasts." See Ratchnevsky, *Genghis Khan,* 153.

41. For the entire period of more than 100 years between the Glorious Revolution Settlement of 1688 and the Great Wars of 1793-1815, England's constitutional law was based on the Bill of Rights adopted in 1689, whereas in France the constitution of the ancien régime was replaced four times between 1789 and 1795 (once every year and a half), counting the *Declaration of the Rights of Man and the Citizen* (August 26, 1789); the 1791 Constitution (September 3, 1791); the Constitution of Year I (June 24, 1793); and the Constitution of Year III (August 22, 1795).

42. R. K. Webb, *Modern England: From the Eighteenth Century to the Present,* 2nd. ed. (New York: Harper & Row, 1980), 44.

43. Quoted in Roger Price, *A Concise History of France* (Cambridge: Cambridge University Press, 1993), 82-83.

44. Paul Kennedy, *The Rise and Fall of Great Powers: Economic Change and Military Conflict from 1500 to 2000* (New York: Vintage Books, 1989), 82. Alfred Cobban, *Aspects of the French Revolution* (New York: W.W. Norton, 1968), 79-80.

45. Jenkins, *French Navy,* 198-99.

46. See Great Britain, Laws, Statutes, etc., *The Bill of Rights. An Act for Declaring the Rights and Liberties of the Subject, and Settling the Succession of the Crown, 1689* (Boston: Directors of the Old South Work, 1896), 3. Many of the subsequent acts on constitutional delineation are excerpted in Neville E. Williams, *The Eighteenth-Century Constitution 1688-1815: Documents and*

Commentary (Cambridge: Cambridge University Press, 1960). On the structure of political institutions in France, see Jacques Godechot, *Les Institutions de la France sous la Révolution et l'Empire* (Paris: Presses Universitaires de France, 1951); the quoted passage is from ibid., 75.

47. *Bill of Rights*, 3; *Declaration of the Rights of Man and the Citizen*, quoted in John Hall Stewart, *A Documentary Survey of the French Revolution* (New York: Macmillan, 1951), 113-15; Godechot, *Les Institutions*, 36-39.

48 *Bill of Rights*, 3; *Declaration of the Rights of Man*, quoted in Stewart, *Documentary Survey*, 113-15; Godechot, *Les Institutions*, 37.

49. Bernard S. Silberman, *Cages of Reason: The Rise of the Rational State in France, Japan, the United States, and Great Britain* (Chicago: University of Chicago Press, 1993), 89-90; Ran Halevi, "La révolution constituante: Les ambiguités politiques," in *The French Revolution and the Creation of Modern Political Culture*, vol. 2: *The Political Culture of the French Revolution*, eds. Keith Baker, Francois Furet, and Colin Lucas (Oxford: Pergamon Press, 1988), 74-75.

50. Colin Jones, *The Longman Companion to the French Revolution* (London: Longman, 1988), 70-74; Stewart, *Documentary Survey*, 398.

51. Jones, *French Revolution*, 2-60, 70-71, 96-98, 102; Clive H. Church, *Revolution and Red Tape: The French Ministerial Bureaucracy, 1770-1850* (Oxford: Oxford University Press, 1981), 70-71.

52. Lord Thomas B. Macaulay, *History of England from the Accession of James II*, ed. T. F. Henderson (1895), vol. 1, 698.

53. The appointments to the key positions of House Speaker and Chairman of Ways and Means also followed a regular pattern, strongly tied to the convocation of new parliaments. Sir Lewis Namier and John Brooke, *The House of Commons, 1754-1790*, vol. 1: *Introductory Survey, Constituencies, Appendices* (London: HMSO, 1964), 535-37.

54. John L. De Lolme, *The Constitution of England; or, an Account of the Government: In Which It Is Compared Both with the Republican Form of Government and the Other Monarchies of Europe* (London: Henry G. Bohn, 1853), 67.

55. David H. Willson, *History of England* (New York: Holt, Rinehart and Winston, Inc., 1967), 487.

56. See *Wordsworth Dictionary of British History*, J. P. Kenyon, ed. (Ware, Eng.: Market House Books, 1981), 277-78, 282, 323, 353-54. On William Pitt the Younger, see Namier and Brooke, *House of Commons*, vol. 1, 89. Other

authoritative works on the subject include J. H. Plumb, *Sir Robert Walpole,* 2 vols. (London: Cresset Press, 1956, 1960); J. Holland Rose, *William Pitt,* 3 vols. (London: G. Bell, 1911, 1912); Donald G. Barnes, *George III and William Pitt, 1783-1806* (Stanford: Stanford University Press, 1931).

57. Webb, *Modern England,* 94-95; The King to Lord North, Queen's House, March 27, 1782, Sir J. Fortescue, *The Correspondence of George III* (1927-8), No. 3593; The King to Lord Shelburne, Queen's House, April 12, 1782, ibid., No. 3648; Memorandum by the King (1783), ibid., No. 4268; Great Britain, Laws, Statutes, etc., Crewe's Act, 1782, in Pickering, *Statutes,* vol. 34, 48; Great Britain, Laws, Statutes, etc., *An Act for Restraining Any Person . . .,* in Pickering, Statutes, vol. 34, 56; Great Britain, Laws, Statutes, etc., *Civil Establishment Act, 1782,* in Pickering, *Statutes,* vol. 34, 143; Great Britain, Laws, Statutes, etc., *An Act for Appointing Commissioners . . .,* in Pickering, *Statutes,* vol. 35, 44; Great Britain, Laws, Statutes, etc., *An Act for Better Examining and Auditing the Publick Accounts of this Kingdom,* in Pickering, *Statutes,* vol. 35, 225, all quoted in Williams, *Constitution,* 91-94, 99-103, 198-207. Also see an account of the economical and administrative reforms and their political origins in John Norris, *Shelburn and Reform* (London: Macmillan, 1963). A fine historical twist, highlighting the contrast between institutional preferences in Britain and France when dealing with the American wars, is that economical reforms were pushed by Edmund Burke, who later wrote *Reflections on the Revolution in France.*

58. P. G. M. Dickson, *The Financial Revolution in England: A Study in the Development of Public Credit, 1688-1756* (London: Macmillan, 1967), 198.

59. Will and Ariel Durant, *The Story of Civilization,* vol. 9: *The Age of Voltaire* (New York: Simon and Schuster, 1965), 71-73.

60. Jones, *French Revolution,* 115, with reference to Donald Greer, *The Incidence of the Terror during the French Revolution: A Statistical Interpretation* (Cambridge: Harvard University Press, 1935).

61. Quoted in Williams, *Constitution,* 385.

62. Lord Thomas B. Macaulay, *The history of England from the accession of James II* (London: Routledge, 1895), 5 vols., vol. 2, 503.

63. Thus, the juries were not allowed to decide on whether any given piece of writing was a libel but only on the fact of the publication and whether the subject matter of the writing matched the indictment. The English lawyers, especially in the earlier part of the century, considered any inauspicious comment on the government as libelous. See Williams, *Constitution,* 397-98.

64. Ibid., 397-98; Webb, *Modern England,* 60-61; Great Britain, Laws, Statutes, etc., *Libel Act, 1792: An Act to Remove Doubts Respecting the Functions of Juries in Cases of Libel,* in Pickering, *Statutes,* vol. 37, 627, quoted in Williams, *Constitution,* 407. An increasing number of social groups were exploiting the diverse political information channels in the eighteenth century England. Following the Toleration Act of 1689, which allowed freedom of worship to Protestant Dissenters, the second half of the eighteenth century saw a religious revival with the growing popularity of Methodism and the Evangelical movement. The latter included William Pitt's close friend, William Wilberforce, who joined Evangelicalism in 1785 and gave it an important voice in Parliament eventually carrying through the abolition of slave trade in 1807. This period also saw the rise of activism and intellectualism on the part of women, such as religious writer and social reformer Hannah More and those in the Blue Stockings Society. Also apparent was the increasing diversity of denominations, with many English Presbyterians turning Unitarian, and Congregationalists and Baptists discarding their Calvinistic heritage in favor of experiential religion expressed through good works. Despite the fact that most Dissenters still considered themselves to be branded socially inferior, their denominational vicissitudes contributed to a growing diversity of ideas being exchanged in society at large and permeating political discourses. This only better illustrates the fact that the prevailing code of churchmanship was anti-sectarianism combined with toleration and moderation in worship known as Latitudinarianism. The culture of moderation and deliberative conservatism accounted for the massive popularity of the late seventeenth-century preacher, Tillotson, whose sermons became best-sellers in the second half of the 1700s. See Webb, *Modern England,* 126-27; Williams, *Constitution,* 330-31.

65. The younger Pitt was also a subject of public ridicule which even today might appear too forthright. On one notable occasion, Gillray portrayed the prime minister as "an upstart fungus, springing suddenly out of the hot-bed of royal favor" in a print descriptively entitled "An excrescence—a fungus,—*alias,* a toad-stool upon a dung-hill." See Wright, *Caricature History,* 463, 467.

66. A. Aspinall, "The Reporting and Publishing of the House of Commons Debates, 1771-1834," in *Essays Presented to Sir Lewis Namier,* eds. R. Pares and A. J. P. Taylor (London, Macmillan, 1956); Charles Abbot, *Diary and Correspondence of Charles Abbot, Lord Colchester, Speaker of the House of Commons, 1802-1817* (London: J. Murray, 1861), vol. 1, 421.

67. Williams, *Constitution,* 423-29.

68. Ibid., 209; The French Revolution sparked off another wave of reform enthusiasm and saw the emergence of English Jacobins and radical societies such as Major Cartwright's Society for Constitutional Information and the London Correspondent Society. More than 200,000 copies of Thomas Paine's *Rights of Man* were printed in cheap editions and circulated around Britain as a response to the more conservative *Reflections on the Revolution in France* by Burke. Edward Smith, F.S.S., *The Story of English Jacobins: Being an Account of the Persons Implicated in the Charges of High Treason, 1794* (London: Cassell, Peter, Galpin & Co., 1881); Webb, *Modern England,* 130.

69. Webb, *Modern England,* 45. Data on petitions is from Great Britain, *Parliament, Report from the Select Committee on Public Petitions* (London, 1832), 10.

70. Durant, *Age of Voltaire,* 266-67; on the impact of *lettres de cachet* during that period on literature and the press, see Friedrich Melchior Grimm, Denis Diderot, Abbé Raynal et al., *Correspondance litteraire, philosophique, et critique,* (Paris: Nendeln, Garnier frères, Kraus reprint, 1968), vol. 8.

71. Jones, *French Revolution,* 255-59.

72. Based on the author's analysis of the newspapers listed in Jones, *French Revolution,* 266-70.

73. J. Michael Waller, *Secret Empire: The KGB in Russia Today* (Boulder: Westview Press, 1994), 13.

74. Quoted in Cobban, *Aspects of the French Revolution,* 198-99, from the chapter entitled "British Secret Service in France, 1784-1792," which details Cobban's study of all relevant departmental archives in Britain.

75. These asymmetries are well established in the political science literature: cf., for example, Alexis de Toqueville, *Democracy in America,* trans. Henry Reeve (New York: Oxford University Press, 1947); Robert Dahl, *Democracy and Its Critics* (New Haven: Yale University Press, 1989); Tatu Vanhanen, *The Emergence of Democracy: A Comparative Study of 119 States, 1850-1979* (Helsinki: Finnish Society of Arts and Letters, 1984); Zbigniew Brzezinski and Samuel P. Huntington, *Political Power: USA/USSR* (New York: Viking Press, 1968); Merle Fainsod, *How Russia Is Ruled* (Cambridge: Harvard University Press, 1963); Michael S. Voslensky, *Nomenklatura: The Soviet Ruling Class* (Garden City, N.Y.: Doubleday, 1984); and Adam Ulam, *A History of Soviet Russia* (New York: Holt, Rinehart and Winston, 1976). See also *Constitution (Fundamental Law of the Union of Soviet Socialist Republics* (Moscow: Novosti Press Agency, 1977), chap. 1 (esp. article 6), 6-7.

76. In the Soviet Union, the study of politics was largely confined to the Marxist philosophy, political economy, "scientific communism," and the history of the Soviet Communist Party, without any regard to the methods of scientific inference that are so much a focus of attention in the American political science.

77. Ted Robert Gurr, Keith Jaggers, Will Moore, *Polity II Handbook* (Boulder: University of Colorado Press, 1989). The *Polity II* dataset measures degrees of democracy or autocracy based ·on competitiveness of political participation; regulation of participation, openness and competitiveness of political recruitment, especially in the executive branch; and constraints on the chief executive. Freedom House annual reports on the state of civil rights and political freedoms worldwide documented a substantial U.S. lead over the Soviet Union in the development of the due process of law and the exercise of human rights and freedoms. Using 25 indicators of political rights and civil liberties and scoring each country on a scale of one (most free) to 7 (least free), the USSR was ranked as "not free," with average scores for 1973-1986 of 6.5 on both political rights and civil liberties; the average U.S. score was 1.0 in both categories. Raymond D. Gastil, *Freedom in the World: Political Rights and Civil Liberties, 1986-87* (New York: Greenwood Press, 1987), 40-41, 64-65. Other comparative studies that employed indicators such as freedom of group opposition and number of religious groups confirmed this asymmetry along the democracy-autocracy continuum between the United States and the Soviet Union and suggested that the United States had a greater political distance from the USSR in the early 1970s than even China, Albania, or Mongolia. See R. J. Rummel, "U.S. Foreign Relations: Conflict, Cooperation, and Attribute Distances," in *Peace, War, and Numbers,* ed. Bruce Russett (Beverly Hills: Sage, 1972), 104.

78. Soviet leaders could, theoretically, be replaced in a legal manner, if a party congress voted in a new general secretary of the Soviet Communist Party, replacing the current (and still living) leader—a provision of the party rules that never worked in practice; after Stalin made the position of the general secretary supreme in Soviet politics, none of the incumbent Soviet leaders, including the embattled Gorbachev in 1990, lost a congress reelection.

79. Richard Niemi et al., *Trends in Public Opinion: A Compendium of Survey Data* (New York: Greenwood Press, 1989), 61.

80. *The Harris Survey,* August 8, 1974.

81. U.S. Congress, Senate, *Select Committee to Study Government Operations with Respect to Intelligence Activities* (Church Committee), Final Report. Book III: Supplementary Detailed Staff Reports on Intelligence Activities and the Rights of Americans (Washington, D.C., April 26, 1976), 942.

82. Oleg Kalugin, *Vid s Lubyanki: "Delo" byvshego generala KGB* [A view from Lubyanka: The "case" of a former KGB general] (Moscow: PIK, 1990), 45. As deputy KGB chief of the Leningrad *oblast* (region), Kalugin had a blanket authorization to wiretap phone conversations. For the list of exceptions, see Filipp Bobkov, *KGB i vlast'* [KGB and power] (Moscow: Veteran MP, 1995), 256. A 45-year veteran of the KGB, Bobkov served as first deputy chairman of the KGB and was responsible for domestic surveillance.

83. Hence, the Church Committee, which convincingly stated its preference for very specific, legalistic approach to the investigation, and vouched to protect the necessary secrets, quickly gained access to the intelligence community staff and hundreds of thousands of pages of documents. In contrast, the Otis Pike Committee, suspected of having their minds made up to dismantle the CIA prior to conducting the investigation, was less successful in obtaining specific evidence, provoking a "hardball" response in the administration. Alerted to Pike's political motivation, President Ford more closely monitored Pike's demands for documents and information, consulted with the attorney general and withheld any requested materials, when the attorney general said no. In the end, the House Select Committee was plagued by internal rivalries and failed to finish its report. See John Ranelagh, *The Agency: The Rise and Decline of the CIA* (New York: Simon and Schuster, 1987), 594-95.

84. William Colby and Peter Forbath, *Honorable Men: My Life in the CIA* (New York: Simon and Schuster, 1978), 403-4.

85. U.S. Congress, Church Committee, *Alleged Assassination Plots Involving Foreign Leaders: Interim Report of the Select Committee to Study Government Operations with Respect to Intelligence* (New York: W. W. Norton, 1976), 281.

86. Quoted in *The Intelligence Community: History, Organization, and Issues,* Tyrus G. Fain, comp. and ed. (New York: R. R. Bowker Company, 1977), 144. The Church Committee suggested that the intelligence community should not be given a free hand in inflating any categories of the budget.

87. U. S. Constitution, Art. I, Sec. 9, Cls. 7.

88. Quoted in *The Intelligence Community,* 145.

89. Quoted in *The Intelligence Community,* 805-6, 807.

90. Colby and Forbath, *Honorable Men,* 406; Ranelagh, *The Agency,* 598.

91. A detailed description of the direct costing method, including mathematical formulas for price estimates, based on conventional Laspeyres and Paasche indices) is provided by Steven Rosefielde, *False Science: Underestimating the*

Soviet Arms Buildup—An Appraisal of the CIA's Direct Costing Effort, 1960-80 (New Brunswick, NJ: Transaction Books, 1982); CIA ruble prices data is in William T. Lee, *CIA Estimates of Soviet Military Expenditures: Errors and Waste* (Washington, D.C.: American Enterprise Institute, 1995), 11-12.

92. Dr. Robert Gates, presentation in a series of talks, "The New Structures of European Security," sponsored by the Pacific Northwest Colloquium on International Security, University of Washington, March 10, 1995, from author's notes.

93. Nikolai S. Leonov, *Likholet'ye* [The stormy years] (Moscow: Mezhdunarodnye otnosheniia, 1994), 167.

94. Waller, *Secret Empire,* 14-17. In addition, the author directly experienced the effects of most of these KGB information control mechanisms in the 1970s and 1980s while a citizen of the Soviet Union.

95. Leonid V. Shebarshin, *Ruka Moskvy: zapiski nachal'nika sovetskoi razdveki* [The hand of Moscow: Notes of a Soviet foreign intelligence chief] (Moscow: Tsentr-100, 1992), 271; Leonov, *Likholet'ye,* 132-33.

96. Daniel O. Graham, *Confessions of a Cold Warrior: An Autobiography* (Fairfax, Va.: Preview Press, 1995), 86.

97. Ranelagh, *The Agency,* 620.

98. Waller, *Secret Empire,* 217.

99. The Stepashin commission report is quoted in the memoirs of the last KGB chief, Vadim Bakatin, *Izbavleniye ot KGB* [Getting rid of the KGB] (Moscow: Novosti, 1992), 48. The commission chairman, Sergei Stepashin, later served as head of the Federal Counterintelligence Service (FSK) from 1993 to 1995. The commission directly attributed KGB unaccountability to the absence of control on behalf of the Supreme Soviet (legislature) and the USSR State Procuracy (the judiciary).

Notes to Chapter 4

1. Abu-Lughod, *Before European Hegemony: The World System, A.D. 1250-1350* (New York: Oxford University Press, 1989), 355; George Modelski and William R. Thompson, *Leading Sectors and World Powers: The Coevolution of Global Economics and Politics* (Columbia: University of South Carolina Press, 1995); William R. Thompson, "The Evolution of Political-Economic Challenge in the Active Zone" (paper presented at the Second Workshop on Evolutionary Paradigms in the Social Sciences, Seattle, May 27, 1995).

2. Abu-Lughod, *Before European Hegemony*, 154. The "strategic crossroads location" refers to the junctions of trans-Eurasian silk roads and particularly to the intersections of major land and sea trade routes.

3. William of Rubruck, "The Journey of William of Rubruck," in *The Mongol Mission*, ed. Christopher Dawson (London: Sheed and Ward, 1955), 103.

4. John of Plano Carpini, "History of the Mongols," in *The Mongol Mission*, ed. Christopher Dawson (London: Sheed and Ward, 1955), 18.

5. G. Jenkin, "A Note on Climatic Cycles and the Rise of Cinggis Khan," *Central Asiatic Journal* 18 (1974), 217-26.

6. I.e., *qara qumys, bal,* and *terracina.*

7. Rubruck, "Journey," 175.

8. The demise of Karakorum was as swift as its rise. The palace did not survive, and only an austere Erdene Dzuu Monastery built in later years and a lonely granite sculpture of a turtle are at this site today to break the monotony of windswept hills and the vast emptiness of the steppe. Paul Ratchnevsky, *Genghis Khan: His Life and Legacy*, trans. and ed. Thomas Nivison Haining (Oxford: Blackwell, 1992), 200-1.

9. H. Desmond Martin, "Mongol Army," *Journal of the Royal Asiatic Society* (April 1943), 51.

10. H. Desmond Martin, "Chingiz Khan's First Invasion of the Chin Empire," in *Journal of Royal Asiatic Society* (October 1943), 211.

11. Domestic lead industries included iron, cotton, timber, paper.

12. For example, "Guyuk Khan's Letter to Pope Innocent IV (1246)," in *The Mongol Mission*, ed. Christopher Dawson (London: Sheed and Ward, 1955), 85-86.

13. B. Ya. Vladimirtsov, *Obshchestvennyy stroy mongolov. Mongol'skiy kochevoy feodalizm* [Social system of the Mongols. Mongol nomadic feudalism] (Leningrad, 1934), 98-99, quoted in G. A. Fedorov-Davydov, *Obshchestvennyy stroy Zolotoy Ordy* [Social system of the Golden Horde] (Moscow: Izdatel'stvo Moskovskogo universiteta, 1973), 43.

14. Fedorov-Davydov, *Obshchestvennyy stroy*, 48.

15. Ibid., 50. Under this new *ulus* system, Jebe and Subodei were granted authority to combine in their regiments captured warriors from different tribes and regions; Korchi's regiment was drawn from 3,000 Ba'arin, as well as Chinos, To'olas, and Telenggut from the Adarkin tribe. According to

Ratchnevsky's survey of primary sources, "Tribal unity was only preserved in those few cases in which Genghis was sure of their loyalty." He recorded only seven such cases for Genghis Khan's reign from 1206 to 1227. Ratchnevsky, *Genghis Khan*, 92-93.

16. Baron C. D'Ohsson, *Histoire des Mongols, Depuis Tchinguiz- Khan Jusqu'à Timour Bey ou Tamerlan* [History of the Mongols, from Genghis Khan to Timur Bei or Tamerlaine], 4 vols. (The Hague: Les Frères van Cleef, 1834), vol. 1, 404-6; Fedorov-Davydov, *Obshchestvennyy stroy;* L. I. Duman, "Nekotorye problemy sotsial'no-ekonomicheskoy politiki mongol'skih hanov v Kitaye v XIII-XIV vv." [Some problems of socioeconomic policy of the Mongol Khans in China in the 13-14th centuries], in *Tataro-Mongoly v Azii i Yevrope* [Tatar-Mongols in Asia and Europe], ed. S. L. Tikhvinskiy (Moscow: Nauka, 1970), 311-51. *Secret History,* paras. 234, 279, 274; John P. Powelson, *Centuries of Economic Endeavor* (Ann Arbor: University of Michigan Press, 1994).

17. *Secret History,* para. 234.

18. Herbert Schurmann, review of *Steuergerechtsame der chinesischen Kloster unter der Mongolenherrshaft,* by Erich Haenisch, *Harvard Journal of Asiatic Studies* 14 (1951), 291-306; Herbert Schurmann, "Mongolian Tributary Practices of the Thirteenth Century," *Harvard Journal of Asiatic Studies* 18 (1956), 304-89; N. I. Berezin, *Ocherk,* 427, 465, quoted in Ratchnevsky, *Genghis Khan,* 180-87.

19. *Yuan-shi,* quoted in N. Ts. Munkuyev, "Novye materialy o polozhenii mongol'skih aratov v XIII- XIV vv." [New materials regarding the state of the Mongol arats in the thirteenth to fourteenth centuries], in *Tataro-Mongoly v Azii i Yevrope,* ed. S. L. Tikhvinskiy, [Tatar-Mongols in Asia and Europe] (Moscow: Nauka, 1970), 386-402.

20. Modelski and Thompson, *Coevolution,* 160-70.

21. Mark Elvin, *The Pattern of the Chinese Past* (Stanford: Stanford University Press, 1973), 171-72; On the role of Sung China in the formation of the modern world system, see William McNeill, *The Pursuit of Power* (Chicago: University of Chicago Press, 1982). For more detailed accounts of China's manufacturing industries and the evolution of market instruments, see Robert Hartwell, "A Revolution in the Chinese Iron and Coal Industries during the Northern Sung, 960-1126 A.D.," *Journal of Asian Studies* 21 (1962), 153-62; and Robert Hartwell, "Markets, Technology, and the Structure of Enterprise in the Development of the Eleventh-Century Chinese Iron and Steel Industry," *Journal of Economic History* 26 (March 1966), 29-58.

22. Modelski and Thompson, *Coevolution,* 160.

23. Joseph Needham, *The Great Triation: Science and Society in East and West* (Toronto: University of Toronto Press, 1969), 65.

24. Modelski and Thompson, *Coevolution,* 167-68.

25. Ibid., 173.

26. Haeger, "Introduction," 5.

27. Rondo Cameron, *A Concise Economic History of the World* (New York: Oxford University Press, 1989); David Landes, *The Unbound Prometheus: Technological Change and Industrial Development in Western Europe from 1750 to the Present* (London: Cambridge University Press, 1969); E. J. Hobsbawm, *Industry and Empire* (New York: Penguin Books, 1969). Also included among the critical factors behind the Industrial Revolution is long-distance trade, for its impact on the raising of capital, incentives for innovation, and the scale and sophistication of industrial development. For a concise summary of these arguments, see George Modelski and William R. Thompson, "Kondratieff Waves, the Evolving Global Economy, and World Politics: The Problem of Coordination" (paper presented at the N. D. Kondratieff Centenary Conference, Moscow, March 17-19, 1992), 14-15. See also P. Bairoch, "International Industrialization Levels from 1750 to 1980," *Journal of European Economic History* 11 (Spring 1982), 290n., on the role of the mechanization of spinning in the industrialization of the British economy.

28. Walt W. Rostow, *The World Economy: History and Prospect* (Austin: University of Texas Press, 1978). See ibid., 369, for the quote. Also, Robert Gilpin, *U.S. Power and the Multinational Corporation* (New York: Basic Books, 1975), 67. An in-depth analysis of the leading sector indicators is available in William R. Thompson, *On Global War: Historical-Structural Approaches to World Politics* (Columbia: University of South Carolina Press, 1988), 131-45.

29. See Bairoch, "International Industrialization;" Paul Kennedy, *The Rise and Fall of the Great Powers: Economic Change and Military Conflict from 1500 to 2000* (New York: Vintage Books, 1989), chap. 4.

30. Thompson, *On Global War,* 140. In 1750 the world manufacturing output share was 0.019 for Britain and 0.040 for France, but the population of France (21.5 million) was more than twice the population of England (10.5 million), making per capita output shares about equal. Kennedy, *Rise and Fall,* 149.

31. Thompson, *On Global War*, 140.

32. Kennedy, *Rise and Fall*, 149.

33. Paul Butel, *L'économie Française au XVII Siècle* (Paris: Sedes, 1993), 88.

34. Ibid., 105.

35. Willson, *A History of England*, 586-87; Kennedy, *Rise and Fall*, 130.

36. Author's estimate based on Butel, *L'économie Française*, 70; C. Knick Harley, "Reassessing the Industrial Revolution: A Macro View," in *The British Industrial Revolution: An Economic Perspective*, ed. Joel Mokyr (Boulder: Westview Press, 1993), 196-97.

37. Joel Mokyr, "Editor's Introduction: The New Economic History and the Industrial Revolution," in *British Industrial Revolution*, ed. Mokyr, 16-131; Butel, *L'Économie Française*, 67; Bernard S. Silberman, *Cages of Reason: The Rise of the Rational State in France, Japan, the United States, and Great Britain* (Chicago: University of Chicago Press, 1993), 304-9; Jean-Charles Asselain, "Movement des salaires réels (1789-1815) et modèle de croissance économique francaise après la révolution," in *État, finances et économie pendant la révolution française* (Paris: Comité pour l'Histoire Économique et Financière de la France, 1991), 495-520. For a case study, see A. P. Wadsworth and J. De Lacy Mann, *The Cotton Trade and Industrial Lancashire* (Manchester: Manchester University Press, 1931).

38. Mokyr, "New Economic History and the Industrial Revolution," 16-131; Eric J. Hobsbawm, *Industry and Empire*, diagram 38; Roger Price, *A Concise History of France* (Cambridge: Cambridge University Press, 1993), 74-77; Kennedy, *Rise and Fall*, 129-33; Jean-François Belshoste, "Le financement de la guerre de 1792 a l'an IV," in *État, finances et économie*, 320-39; Colin Jones, *Longman Companion to the French Revolution* (London: Longman, 1988), 276, 281, 298-94, 302-6.

39. Henry Birse, *Engineering at Edinburgh University: A Short History, 1673-1983* (Edinburgh: University of Edinburgh, School of Engineering, 1983), 16.

40. Claude Fohlen, "The Industrial Revolution in France," in *Essays in French Economic History*, ed. Rondo Cameron (Georgetown, Ont.: Richard D. Irwin, 1970), 204-5; George Naquet, "La régie des droit d'enregistrement, du domaine et autres y réunis ou la naissance d'une administration moderne sous la période révolutionnaire, in *État, finances et économie*, 113-14.

41. Kennedy, *Rise and Fall*, 80.

42. Ibid., 83.

43. The leading sectors in this sequence are cotton textiles, iron, railroads, steel, chemicals, electricity, and motor vehicles. See Gilpin, *U.S. Power and the Multinational Corporation;* Landes, *The Unbound Prometheus;* and Rostow, *World Economy,* 365-560.

44. Rostow, *World Economy,* 379-435.

45. Thompson, *On Global War,* 136-40; ed., Christopher Freeman, *Long Waves in the World Economy* (London: Frances Pinter, 1983); ed. Tibor Vasko, *The Long Wave Debate* (Berlin: Springer Verlag, 1987); and Joshua Goldstein, *Long Cycles* (New Haven: Yale University Press, 1988). For a discussion of the emerging new leading sectors in the global economy, see Modelski and Thompson, "Kondratieff Waves," 25-30.

46. Edward N. Luttwak, *The Grand Strategy of the Soviet Union* (New York: St. Martin's Press, 1983), 170. Although the Soviet GNP could not be estimated precisely, these "guesstimates" are still useful as a general illustration of the U.S.-Soviet economic power balance in the long perspective.

47. Kenneth A. Oye et al., eds., *Eagle Defiant: United States Foreign Policy in the 1980s* (Boston: Little, Brown, 1983), 8.

48. See, for example, Kennedy, *Rise and Fall,* 488-500; Alec Nove, *An Economic History of the USSR, 1917-1991,* 3d ed. (London: Penguin Books, 1992); E. H. Carr, *Foundations of a Planned Economy, 1926-29,* vol. I (London: Pelican, 1974); Pavel Dembrinski, *The Logic of the Planned Economy: The Seeds of Collapse* (Oxford: Oxford University Press, 1991).

49. Gastil, *Freedom in the World,* 72-78.

50. USSR Kommunisticheskaya partiya Sovetskogo Soyuza, *Programma Kommunisticheskoy partii Sovetskogo Soyuza: Novaya redaktsiya. Prinyata XXVII s" ezdom KPSS* [The program of the Communist Party of the Soviet Union: New edition. Adopted at the Twenty Seventh Congress of the CPSU] (Moscow: Politizdat, 1988), 17-22.

51. E.g., a university textbook definition of capitalism: "An economic system in which the means of production are privately owned and the allocation of goods and services is decided by the marketplace rather than by government planning." See John J. Harrigan, *Politics and the American Future,* 3d ed. (New York: McGraw Hill, 1992), 502.

52. Stephen E. Hanson, "The Leninist Legacy and Institutional Change," *Comparative Political Studies* 28 (1995), 306-14.

53. Open Media Research Institute, *OMRI Daily Digest,* part I, no. 9 (January 12, 1996).

54. See David Holloway, *Stalin and the Bomb: The Soviet Union and Atomic Energy, 1939-1956* (New Haven: Yale University Press, 1994).

55. To trace the long-term impact of repressions against the developers of the Soviet jet aircraft, see Howard Moon, *Soviet SST: The Technopolitics of the Tupolev-144* (New York: Orion Books, 1989); among some good sources on the influence of Lysenko, the anticosmopolitanism purges, and other adverse consequences of Stalin's rule on the Soviet economy, are Robert Conquest, *The Great Terror: A Reassessment* (New York: Oxford University Press, 1990) and Roy Medvedev, *Let History Judge: The Origins and Consequences of Stalinism,* ed. and trans. George Shriver (New York: Columbia University Press, 1989).

56. Nikolai Ryzhkov, *Perestroika: Istoriya predatel'stv* [Perestroika: A history of betrayals] (Moscow: Novosti, 1992), 72.

57. Richard Sakwa, *Gorbachev and His Reforms, 1985-1990* (New York: Prentice Hall, 1990), 268.

58. Kennedy, *Rise and Fall,* 514; for gross world product shares, see Oye et al., *Eagle Defiant,* 8. Another comparative assessment of economic problems facing the United States and the USSR by the early 1980s concurred that "the Soviets found themselves much worse off than the Americans." See Walter LaFeber, *America, Russia, and the Cold War, 1945-1990,* 6th ed. (New York: McGraw-Hill, 1991), 316.

59. Canadian Institute for Strategic Studies, *Airwar 2,000,* ed. B. MacDonald, Proceedings of the Canadian Institute of Strategic Studies Spring Seminar (Toronto, 1988), 60.

60. The author's personal experience with photocopying documents as an employee of Soviet government institutions.

61. R. Amann and J. Cooper, eds., *Industrial Innovation in the USSR* (New Haven: Yale University Press, 1982); author's personal experience.

62. LaFeber, *America, Russia, and the Cold War,* 318.

63. Kennedy, *Rise and Fall,* 498-503.

64. Ibid., 489.

65. Mikhail Gorbachev, *Zhizn' i reformy* [Life and reforms], 2 vols. (Moscow: Novosti, 1995), vol. 1, 237-38.

66. Nikolai Leonov, *Likholet'ye* [The stormy years] (Moscow: Mezhdunarodnye otnosheniia, 1994), 345.

67. Gavriil Popov, *Snova v oppozitsii* [Again on the opposition's side] (Moscow: Galaktika, 1994), 31-32.

68. Stephen E. Hanson, *Time and Revolution: Marxism and the Design of Soviet Institutions* (Chapel Hill: University of North Carolina Press, 1997), 124-28.

69. Quoted in Hanson, *Time and Revolution,* 128. By the 1980s, this storming of economic fortresses was mired in nepotism, red tape, neglect of innovation, and widespread corruption. Perhaps the biggest corruption case, the so-called Uzbek affair of the 1980s, was especially emblematic of the woes affecting the Soviet system. The case involved top party and government officials in the Soviet Central Asian republic of Uzbekistan who received billions of rubles in bribes for reporting higher than actual cotton production data to Moscow. This was the ultimate case of what was known to most Soviet managers as *pripiski* (upward distortions of achieved results), a widespread Soviet practice effectively denying the state-planning agencies data that could be used in designing economically proportionate strategies. In a market economy such as that of the United States, by contrast, taxpayers have an incentive to underreport their taxable income. In the absence of central planning, these downward distortions are no threat to the economic system, however. If anything, these distortions are even less likely to result in government economic strategies that would bankrupt the state and its population.

70. *Ogonyok,* 3 (January 1990).

71. Leonov, *Likholet'ye,* 129.

72. Ibid., 309-10.

Notes to Chapter 5

1. Paul Ratchnevsky, *Genghis Khan: His Life and Legacy,* trans. and ed. Thomas Nivison Haining (Oxford: Blackwell, 1992), xiii and 284-85; George Modelski, "The Evolution of Global Politics," in *Journal of World Systems Research,* 1: 7 (1995), 3.

2. Robert O. Keohane, "Realism, Neorealism and the Study of World Politics," in *Neorealism and Its Critics,* ed. Robert O. Keohane (New York: Columbia University Press, 1986), 7.

3. Ratchnevsky, *Genghis Khan,* 170-71.

4. See Batu's (Genghis Khan's grandson and ruler of the Golden Horde) interpretation of this prediction of Genghis Khan in John of Plano Carpini, "History of the Mongols," in *The Mongol Mission,* ed. Christopher Dawson (London: Sheed and Ward, 1955), 30.

5. The data on the size of the Mongol and Chin armies and populations were obtained from H. Desmond Martin, "Chingiz Khan's First Invasion of the Chin Empire," *Journal of the Royal Asiatic Society* (October 1943), 190; and Martin, "Mongol Army," 46-48. Even after their initial defeat in 1211, the Chin continued to underestimate Mongol power and in 1212 launched another attack on the Sung, despite the potentially grave implications of fighting a war on two fronts.

6. Martin, "Chingiz Khan's First Invasion," 192; ibid., 191-92.

7. Joseph Mullie, *Les Anciens villes d'empires des Grandes Leao au Royaume Mongol de Barin* (T'oung Pao, 1922), quoted in Martin, "Chingiz Khan's First Invasion," 191-92.

8. ad-Din, *Sbornik letopisey,* vol. I/2, 263; Douglas S. Benson, *The Mongol Campaigns in Asia: A Summary of Mongolian Warfare with the Governments of Eastern and Western Asia in the Thirteenth Century* (Ashland, Ohio: BookMasters, 1991), 73.

9. For the quotation, see Abu-Lughod, *Before European Hegemony,* 178; other information in W. Barthold, *Turkestan Down to the Mongol Invasion,* 2 ed., trans. and revised by the author with H. A. R. Gibb (London: Oxford University Press, 1928), 84-88.

10. Henry H. Howorth, *History of the Mongols: From the Ninth to the Nineteenth Century, Part I: The Mongols Proper and the Kalmuks* (London: Longmans, Green, and Co., 1876), 8.

11. Martin, "Mongol Army," 46; Howorth, *History of the Mongols,* 8.

12. Ala' ad-Din 'Ata-Malik Juvaini, *The History of the World Conqueror,* 2 vols., trans. John Andrew Boyle (Manchester, 1958), vol. I, 116, 117, vol. II, 375.

13. I. P. Petrushevskiy, "Pohod mongol'skih voysk v Srednyuyu Asiyu v 1219-1224 gg. i ego posledstvia" [The Mongol army campaign in Central Asia in 1219-1224 and its consequences], in S. L. Tikhvinskiy, ed., *Tataro-Mongoly v Azii i Yevrope* [Tatar-Mongols in Asia and Europe] (Moscow: Nauka, 1970), 108.

14. Muhammad an-Nasawi, *Zhizneopisaniye sultana Dzhalal ad-Dina Mankburny* [The life story of Sultan Jalal ad-Din Mankburny], trans. and ed.

S. M. Buniyatov (Baku: "Elm," 1973), 53, 78. Muhammad an-Nasawi (Nisawi), whose dates of birth and death are unknown, was the personal secretary to Sultan Muhammad's son Jalal ad-Din and took part in the campaign against the Mongols.

15. I. P. Petrushevskiy, "Pohod mongol'skih voysk," 117, with reference to an-Nasawi.

16. See the chapter on Genghis Khan and Subodei (Sabutai) in Basil H. Liddell Hart, *Great Captains Unveiled* (Edinburgh: W. Blackwood and Sons, 1927).

17. Both quotations in this paragraph are from Martin, "Mongol Army," 49-50.

18. Referring to the Jurchen tribes that were not part of the Chin Empire.

19. Ratchnevsky, *Genghis Khan,* 105.

20. Constant fluctuations in the pattern of alliances among the smaller and larger powers of Central Asia make it almost impossible to use those alliances as a reliable indicator of national utilities in the manner typically formulated in rational choice theory. See, e. g., Bruce Bueno de Mesquita, *The War Trap* (New Haven: Yale University Press, 1981), 111-12.

21. Calculations are based on the following estimates: Black Irtysh (10,000 troops); Kirghiz (10,000); Xi-Xia (125,000); Jurchen (75,000); Oirat (10,000); Uighur (20,000); Karluk (10,000); Naiman/Kerait (20,000); Merkit (10,000); Ubsa Noor (10,000); Tumat (10,000); Naiman under Kuchlug (20,000). Estimates based on Ratchnevsky, *Genghis Khan,* 101-34; Howorth, *History of the Mongols,* 4-7, 62-77; Ye. I. Kychanov, "Mongolo-Tangutskiye voyny i gibel' gosudarstva Si Sya" [Mongol-Tangut wars and the demise of the state of Xi-Xia] in S. L. Tikhvinskiy, ed., *Tataro-Mongoly v Azii i Yevrope* [Tatar-Mongols in Asia and Europe] (Moscow: Nauka, 1970), 46-54; Benson, *The Mongol Campaigns,* 58-81.

22. ad-Din, *Sbornik letopisey,* vol. I/2, 163; Martin, "Chingiz Khan's First Invasion," 194.

23. Ratchnevsky, *Genghis Khan,* 116.

24. From the perspective of substantive rationality, geography affects the strategic proclivities of a land power in three major ways: power declines monotonically with distance; the rate of power decline is in reverse proportion to a nation's power at home; the rate of decline declines with advances in technology. Bueno de Mesquita, *The War Trap,* 103-4.

25. Martin, "Mongol Army," 51.

26. Martin, "Chingiz Khan's First Invasion," 196.

27. Benson, *The Mongol Campaigns,* 137; Edward B. Espenshade, Jr., *Rand McNally Goode's World Atlas,* 18th ed. (Chicago: Rand McNally, 1986), 158-59.

28. The method of probability estimates in expected utility theory—one of the primary exponents of the rational choice tradition—was applied. See Bueno de Mesquita, *War Trap,* 101-26; for the formulas used, see ibid., 107-9. Assuming one cavalryman was worth five infantrymen, the Mongol army proper is counted as 110,000 strong (all cavalry); the armies of the intermediate powers that could join the Mongol forces at 30,000 (bringing the total Mongol army size to 140,000—consistent with the high-end estimates); resisting or neutral intermediate powers at 162,000 (assuming that half of their armed forces were cavalry); the Chin army at 220,000; and the army of the Khwarazm-shah at 140,000. As documented earlier in this chapter, the populations from which these armies were drawn are counted at around 1 million for the Mongols; 500,000 for the supporting intermediate powers; and 2.7 million for the resisting or neutral intermediate powers. The Chin Empire population exceeded 48 million as recorded in a census, and 10 million was projected for Khwarazm. Sung capabilities were not included in the calculations for reasons described in this chapter. On sources regarding the Mongol, Chin, and Khwarazm armies and population, see this chapter, notes 5 and 11. Sources for the intermediate powers are listed in note 21 to this chapter.

29. Herbert Franke, *Studien und Texte zur Kriegsgeschichte der Suedlishen Sungzeit* (Wiesbaden: Otto Harassowitz, 1987), 16, quoted in Modelski and Thompson, *Coevolution,* 152; C. P. Fitzgerald, *China: A Short Cultural History* (London: Cresset Press, 1942), 430.

30. See an article on Wang Chi by Charles Peterson, in Igor de Rachewiltz et al., *In the Service of the Khan: Eminent Personalities of the Early Mongol-Yuan Period, 1200-1300* (Wiesbaden: Harrassowitz Verlag, 1993), 181-82.

31. Charles A. Peterson, "First Sung Reactions to the Mongol Invasion of the North, 1211-17," in John Winthrop Haeger, ed., *Crisis and Prosperity in Sung China* (Tucson: University of Arizona Press, 1975), 222-23, 228, 233-34.

32. Ratchnevsky, *Genghis Khan,* 105-6.

33. Ibid., 106.

34. Rachewiltz et al., *In the Service of the Khan,* 17; Benson, *Mongol Campaigns,* 72.

35. Benson, *Mongol Campaigns,* 73; Ratchnevsky, *Genghis Khan,* 106-7.

36. According to *Yuan-shi*, Genghis Khan "did not yet dare to put this decision into action" in 1206. Quoted in Ratchnevsky, *Genghis Khan*, 107.

37. ad-Din, *Sbornik letopisey*, vol. I/2, 163-65.

38. *Meng-wu-erh Shih*, Biography of A-la-hu-shih Ti-chi (Alakush-Tagin), quoted in Martin, "Chingiz Khan's First Invasion," 186-92; also see Ratchnevsky, *Genghis Khan*, 109.

39. Quoted in Rachewiltz et al., *In the Service of the Khan*, 98.

40. Wei Yuan, *Yuan Shih Hsin Pein*, quoted in Martin, "Chingiz Khan's First Invasion," 187; *Meng- wu-erh Shih*, Chinese biography of Yeh-lu Liu-Ke, quoted in Martin, "Mongol Army," 60; Ratchnevsky, *Genghis Khan*, 111.

41. *Secret History*, para. 249; ad-Din, *Sbornik letopisey*, vol. I/2, 153.

42. For details of the Uighur submission, see ad-Din, *Sbornik letopisey*, vol. I/2, 152-53; quote is in Ratchnevsky, *Genghis Khan*, 102.

43. Martin, "Chingiz Khan's First Invasion," 203; *T'hung-tsian-gan'-mu*, quoted in *Istoriya pervykh chetyrekh khanov iz doma Chingisova* [A history of the first four Khans of the House of Genghis], trans. Monk Hyacinth (St. Petersburg: Karl Kray Publishers, 1829), 52-53.

44. *Yuan-shi*, 149, 20a, quoted in Ratchnevsky, *Genghis Khan*, Martin, "Mongol Army," 107; ibid., 59, 70-76.

45. *T'hung-tsian-gan'-mu* [General Chinese History], quoted in Hyacinth, *Istoriya pervykh chetyrekh khanov*, 43.

46. The title by which the Mongols referred to the emperors of China.

47. ad-Din, *Sbornik letopisey*, vol. I/2, 263.

48. H. G. Raverty, *Tabakat-i-nasirt*, vol. 2, 954, quoted in Ratchnevsky, *Genghis Khan*, 109.

49. Vladimirtsov, *Gengis-Khan*, 55.

50. Ratchnevsky, *Genghis Khan*, 108; Martin, "Chingiz Khan's First Invasion," 109, estimates Genghis Khan's army at 110,000, of which 20,000 were left behind in the Mongolian heartland to guard against any insurrection by the conquered tribes. Hence, the estimate of about 90,000 for the Mongol army of invasion.

51. ad-Din, *Sbornik letopisey*, vol. I/2, 263.

52. Grekov and Yakubovsky, *Zolotaya orda*, 48; Ratchnevsky, *Genghis Khan*, 122, 124.

53. Barthold, *Turkestan*, 378-79; Nasawi, *Zhizneopisaniye*, 87.

54. Nasawi, *Zhizneopisaniye*, 85.

55. Petrushevskiy, "Pohod mongol'skih voysk," 103.

56. Barthold, *Turkestan*, 379-80.

57. ad-Din, *Sbornik letopisey*, vol. I/2, 188.

58. Ratchnevsky, *Genghis Khan*, 120-23.

59. ad-Din, *Sbornik letopisey*, vol. I/2, 197; also see *Secret History*, para. 254, on the selection of Genghis Khan's successor. A good summary of other primary sources on this issue can be found in Ratchnevsky, *Genghis Khan*, 125-29.

60. D'Ohsson, *Histoire*, vol. 1, 212; Ratchnevsky, *Genghis Khan*, 129.

61. Nasawi, "Sirat as-sultan Jalal ad-din Mankubirti," in *Histoire du sultan Djelal ed-din Mancobirti*, 2 vols., ed. O. Houdas, (Paris, 1891-1895), vol. 2, 61-63.

62. Grekov and Yakubovsky, *Zolotaya orda*, 49.

63. Ibn al-Asir, "Al-Kamil fi-t-tarih," in *Sbornik materialov, otnosyashchihsya k istorii Zolotoy ordy* [Collected works related to the history of the Golden Horde], ed. V. G. Tizengauzen, vol. 1: *Izvlecheniya iz sochineniy arabskikh* [Excerpts from Arabic sources] (St. Petersburg: Izdatel'stvo Akademii Nauk, 1884), 6. See also Barthold, *Turkestan*, 404.

64. Petrushevskiy, "Pohod mongol'skikh voysk," 109; for the role of the Kankalis tribe in the formation of the military aristocracy in the Sultanate of Khwarazm, see Howorth, *History of the Mongols*, vol. 1, 74.

65. Barthold, *Turkestan*, 405.

66. Ibid., 375-76.

67. Nasawi, *Zhizneopisaniye*, 147; Petrushevskiy, "Pohod mongol'skih voysk," 111. Most likely the caliph's mission to Genghis Khan took place in 1217, when Muhammad's army marched on Baghdad.

68. Based on primary sources analyzed in Ratchnevsky, *Genghis Khan*, 118-19.

69. With the Mongol army split in two on the march to Khwarazm, the segment under Genghis Khan numbered approximately 40,000 to 50,000 cavalry, plus two companies of siege engines. See a passage from C. C. Walker, *The Mongol Invasion of Khwarazm*, quoted in Martin, "Mongol Army," 63-64. Barthold estimated the strength of the Mongol army for their invasion of Khwarazm at 150,000 at a minimum and 200,000 at a maximum, and he correctly mentions that the 62,000-strong left wing under Mukhali remained

in China. But Barthold (*Turkestan*, 404) counts the size of the right wing twice by adding it to the estimate of the total strength of Genghis Khan's army proper (set at 129,000 by Rashid). We know from other sources, however, that the number of 129,000 most probably encompassed the center, the left, and the right wings which would indicate an error in Barthold's calculations. Desmond Martin, a specialist in Mongol military history, having analyzed the Chinese and Central Asian sources, concluded that the Mongol army at Samarkand "can hardly have exceeded 80,000 or 90,000 effectives." The impression of larger numbers might have been conveyed by the use of thousands of captives as a human battering ram.

70. Juzjani, *The Tabakat-i Nasiri,* trans. Major Raverty, 1004, quoted in Barthold Turkestan, 404.

71. Ratchnevsky, *Genghis Khan,* 121.

72. *Secret History,* para. 256.

73. Nasawi, *Zhizneopisaniye,* 82-83.

74. Martin, "Mongol Army," 59; Nasawi, *Zhizneopisaniye,* 82-83; Ratchnevsky, *Genghis Khan,* 129-30.

75. Juvaini, *History of the World Conqueror,* vol. 1, 145, quoted in Ratchnevsky, *Genghis Khan,* 129.

76. Martin, "Mongol Army," 58; Martin, "Chingiz Khan's First Invasion," 194, 196; Barthold, *Turkestan,* 403-5.

77. The Chinese general who wrote extensive chronicles collected in *Meng Ta Pei-lu* and considered as a major source on the Mongol military organization. See Martin, "Chingiz Khan's First Invasion," 182n.

78. *Meng Ta Pei-lu,* quoted in Martin, "Mongol Army," 58.

79. Martin, "Mongol Army," 58-59.

80. The Mongol army must have been exhausted and unprepared for major battle after crossing the desert, for afterward Genghis Khan suspended operations and passed the summer of 1211 camping at Ta-shui-luan. See Martin, "Chingiz Khan's First Invasion," 196-97.

81. *Meng-wu-erh Shih,* biography of Po-lu (Boru) of Wu-mu-hu, quoted in Martin, "Mongol Army," 81.

82. See Ratchnevsky, *Genghis Khan,* 112-13, for a comprehensive summary of the primary sources on cannibalism as a means of providing food for the Mongol army. See also N. Ts. Munkuyev, "Novye materialy o polozhenii

mongol'skih aratov v XIII-XIV vv." [New materials regarding the state of the Mongol arats in the thirteenth-fourteenth centuries], in S. L. Tikhvinskiy, ed., *Tataro- Mongoly v Azii i Evrope,* [Tatar-Mongols in Asia and Europe] (Moscow: Nauka, 1970), 386-402. On an outbreak of plague during the siege of Zhongdu in 1214, see Rachewiltz et al., *In the Service of the Khan,* 18.

83. *Ssu Ch'ao Pieh Shih* (Biography of Mukhali), quoted in Martin, "Chingiz Khan's First Invasion," 203.

84. Howorth, *History of the Mongols,* pt. 3, relates that King Haython estimated the strength of the Mongol army at 30,000 men, and Malakia put the Seljuk army at 150,000; William of Rubruck gave lower estimates for both parties: 10,000 for the Mongols and 100,000 for the Seljuks. In Howorth's opinion the numbers of the Seljuk army were exaggerated. Nevertheless, all diverse records point to a large numerical superiority of the Seljuks over the Mongols. Quoted in Martin, "Mongol Army," 81.

85. William McNeill, *The Pursuit of Power* (Chicago: University of Chicago Press, 1983), 40; T. Kinugawa, ed., *Collected Studies on Sung History Dedicated to Professor James T. C. Liu* (Kyoto: Dohosha, 1989), 282, quoted in Modelski and Thompson, *Coevolution,* 152; Haeger, "Introduction," 5.

86. E. O. Reischauer and John Fairbank, *East Asia: The Great Tradition* (Boston: Houghton Mifflin, 1960), 202; and John Richard Lebadie, "Rulers and Soldiers: Perception and Management of the Military in Northern Sung China, 960–ca. 1060" (Ph.D. dissertation, University of Washington, 1981), 206-7, quoted in Modelski and Thompson, *Coevolution,* 235, n. 3.

87. Peterson, "First Sung Reactions," 223, 224n; Pi Yuan, comp., *Hsu tzu-chih t'ung-chien* (Beijing: Ku-chi ch'u-pan-she, 1957), 4297, quoted in Peterson, "First Sung Reactions," 224.

88. Peterson, "First Sung Reactions," 226; Fitzgerald, *China,* 430.

Notes to Chapter 6

1. See William R. Thompson, *On Global War: Historical-Structural Approaches to World Politics* (Columbia: University of South Carolina Press, 1988), 105-8. Nine major studies in international relations that define the wars of 1793-1815 in terms synonymous to global war are R. B. Mowat, *A History of European Diplomacy* (London: Edward Arnold, 1928); Quincy Wright, *A Study of War* (Chicago: University of Chicago Press, 1942/65); Arnold J. Toynbee, *A Study of History,* vol. 9 (London: Oxford University Press, 1954);

L. L. Farrar, Jr., "Cycles of War: Historical Speculations on Future International Violence," *International Interactions* 3 (1977), 161-79; George Modelski, "The Long Cycle of Global Politics and the Nation-State," *Comparative Studies in Society and History* 20 (1978), 214-35; Robert Gilpin, *War and Change in World Politics* (New York: Cambridge University Press, 1981); Immanuel Wallerstein, *The Politics of the World Economy: The States, the Movements, and the Civilizations* (Cambridge: Cambridge University Press, 1984); Manus I. Midlarsky, "Some Uniformities in the Origins of Systemic War" (paper presented at the annual meeting of the American Political Science Association, Washington, D.C., 1984); Jack S. Levy, "Theories of General War," *World Politics* 37 (April 1985), 344-74. A comparative analysis of conceptual elements in the definition of systemic war by Gilpin, Modelski, Wallerstein, Midlarsky and Levy shows high levels of agreement on participation of all major actors (global powers) and concrete or potential structural change in the world system. See Karen A. Rasler and William R. Thompson, *The Great Powers and Global Struggle, 1490-1990* (Lexington: University of Kentucky Press, 1994), 203.

2. Paul Kennedy, *The Rise and Fall of the Great Powers: Economic Change and Military Conflict from 1500 to 2000* (New York: Vintage Books, 1989), 120-21; T. Walter Wallbank and Alastair M. Taylor, *Civilization: Past and Present* (Chicago: Scott, Foresman, 1956), 306; David H. Willson, *A History of England* (New York: Holt, Rinehart and Winston, 1967), 602, 606-10.

3. Kennedy, *Rise and Fall*, 121; Willson, *A History of England*, 607.

4. Kennedy, *Rise and Fall*, 124.

5. George Lefebvre, Raymond Guyot, and Philippe Sagnac, *La révolution française* (Paris: Librairie Felix Alcan, 1930), 156, 179; Grenville to General Williamson, January 7, 1792, C.O. 138/42; Dundas to Governor of Barbados, August 3, 1792, C.O. 28/63, quoted in Rose, Newton, and Benians, *Cambridge History*, 38.

6. Estimates are based on data in George Modelski and William R. Thompson, *Seapower in Global Politics, 1494-1993* (Seattle: University of Washington Press, 1988), 70, 111, 121; Rasler and Thompson, *The Great Powers and Global Struggle*, 194-95, 197; Kennedy, *Rise and Fall*, 99, 122, 149. Contemporary official figures on the size of the French, Austrian, and Prussian armies were also verified with Lefebvre et al., *La révolution française*, 184, 223; Thompson, *On Global War*, 140. The author's calculations of the odds of French challenge succeeding (expected success probability) are based on the formula $P_i = cap_{ik}/(cap_{ik} + cap_{kk})$ where P_i denotes the probability P of success for actor i (France) against coalition k (First Coalition).

7. Estimates are based on Modelski and Thompson, *Seapower,* 70, 121; Thompson, *On Global War,* 140; Rasler and Thompson, *The Great Powers and Global Struggle,* 43. Calculations are based on the same expected probability method, see the formula in note 6 above.

8. Lefebvre et al., *La révolution française,* 179.

9. Rose, Newton, and Benians, *Cambridge History,* 32, 39, with reference to *Dropmore Papers,* vol. II, 319, 332, 339, 341, 344, 351; William E. H. Lecky, *History of England in the Eighteenth Century,* 8 vols. (New York: D. Appleton and Company, 1891), vol. 5, 566.

10. William Windham Grenville, *The Manuscripts of J. B. Fortescue Esq. preserved at Dropmore,* vol. 2, Historical Manuscripts Commission, Fourteenth Report, Appendix, pt. v (London: HMSO, 1894), 352, quoted in T. C. W. Blanning, *The Origins of the French Revolutionary Wars* (London: Longman, 1986), 154.

11. James Harris Earl of Malmesbury, *Diaries and Correspondence of James Harris First Earl of Malmesbury,* vol. 2 (London: Bentley, 1844), 501-2.

12. Lefebvre et al., *La révolution française,* 173.

13. W. T. Laprade, "England and the French Revolution, 1789-1797," *John Hopkins University Studies in Historical and Political Science* 27 (1909), 521-30.

14. Albert Sorel, *L'Europe et la révolution française,* vol. 1: *Les moeurs politiques et les traditions* (Paris: E. Plon, Nourrit, 1926); Burke's remark is from William Cobbett, ed., *The Parliamentary History of England,* vol. 29 (London: T. C. Hansard, 1817), 77.

15. Blanning, *French Revolutionary Wars,* 48.

16. Harold W. Temperley and Lillian M. Penson, eds., *Foundations of British Foreign Policy from Pitt (1792) to Salisbury (1902), or Documents Old and New* (Cambridge: Cambridge University Press, 1938), 7-8.

17. Ibid.

18. Lefebvre et al., *La révolution française,* 159.

19. Steven T. Ross, *Quest for Victory: French Military Strategy, 1792-99* (New York: A. S. Barnes and Company, 1973), 43-44. See also A. W. Ward and G. P. Gooch, *The Cambridge History of British Foreign Policy, 1783-1919,* 2 vols. (New York: Macmillan, 1922); J. Holland Rose, *William Pitt and the Great War* (London: G. Bell and Sons, 1912).

20. Lefebvre et al., *La révolution française*, 153-55.

21. Blanning, *French Revolutionary Wars*, 143-45.

22. Ibid., 145; Sir Robert Murray Keith, *Memoirs and Correspondence (Official and Familiar) of Sir Robert Murray Keith, envoy Extraordinary and Minister Plenipotentiary at the Courts of Dresden, Copenhagen, and Vienna, from 1769-1792*, ed. Mrs. A. Gillespie Smyth, 2 vols. (London: H. Colburn, 1849), vol. 2, 518; William Eden Auckland, *Diary and Correspondence of William, Lord Auckland*, 4 vols. (London: Bentley, 1861), vol. 2, 403, 408, 421, 423.

23. Eugene C. Black, *The Association: British Extraparliamentary Political Organization, 1769-1793* (Cambridge: Harvard University Press, 1963), 252; Austin Mitchell, "The Association Movement of 1792-9," *Historical Journal 4* (1961), 60-63; Lefebvre et al., *La révolution française*, 158-59.

24. Blanning, *French Revolutionary Wars*, 156.

25. Ibid.; see chaps. 5 and 6 on the political and economic factors of Britain's global leadership. The career of Charles Fox is itself a good indication of the influence of the British political institutions on strategic preferences. Thus, despite welcoming the French Revolution and later being sympathetic toward Napoleon, Fox opposed Napoleon's offers of peace on terms that would have weakened Britain's global trade while serving as foreign secretary in what became known as the Ministry of All Talents (1806). See John P. Kenyon, *The Wordsworth Dictionary of British History* (Ware: Wordsworth Reference, 1994), 143.

26. On these persistent factors in British strategy, see George Modelski and Sylvia Modelski, eds., *Documenting Global Leadership* (Seattle: University of Washington Press, 1988), 237-39; also Kennedy, *The Rise and Fall*, 97-99.

27. France, National Convention. Seance du 1er janvier. Discours de Kersaint sur l'imminence d'une guerre avec la Grande-Bretagne [Session of January 1. Speech by Kersaint on the inevitability of war with Great Britain], in *Histoire parlementaire de la Révolution Française, ou Journal des Assemblés Nationales, depuis 1789 jusqu'en 1815*, ed. P.-J.-B. Buchez and P.-C. Roux, (Paris: Paulin, Libraire, 1835), 367-68.

28. Archives parlementaires de 1787 à 1860, Recueil complet des débats législatifs et politique des chambres françaises, 127 vols. (Paris: Librairie administrative de Paul Dupont, 1879-1913), vol. 37, 574; Jones, French Revolution, 157, based on Samuel F. Scott, The Response of the Royal Army to the French Revolution: The Role and Development of the Line Army, 1787-93 (Oxford: Clarendon Press, 1978); Archives parlementaires, vol. 36, 607.

29. Théodore Iung, *L'Armée et la révolution: Dubois-Crancé, mousquetaire, constituant, conventionnel, général de la Guerre* (Paris: G. Charpentier, 1884), 341.

30. Jones, *French Revolution*, 24, 26, 31.

31. Ibid., 156; Ross, *Quest for Victory*, 45, with reference to Min. de la Guerre, Archives historiques, "Armées de la République: Situations générales, 1792-1800," carton B1245.

32. Iung, *Dubois-Crancé*, 327-45.

33. See the sources for French army size in chap. 5.

34. E. H. Jenkins, *A History of the French Navy: From Its Beginnings to the Present Day* (London: MacDonald and Jane's, 1973), 204-6.

35. The evidence was provided by Antiboul, a member of the committee on the marine, in a testimony at the interrogation by the *comissaires* at Marseilles on June 24, 1793, who inquired into the reasons for the French naval failures, quoted in Léon Lévy, "Le Conventionnel Jeanbon Saint-André, 1749-1813" (Ph.D. dissertation, University of Paris, 1901), 311.

36. Lévy, "Le Conventionnel Jeanbon Saint-André," 311-12.

37. Ibid., 313.

38. Jenkins, *History of the French Navy*, 206.

39. Iung, *Dubois-Crancé*, 333; Buchez and Roux, *Histoire parlementaire*, 368.

40. Blanning, *French Revolutionary Wars*, 109.

41. Buchez and Roux, *Histoire parlementaire*, 366, 368-69, 377.

42. Jacques Droz, *Histoire diplomatique de 1648 à 1919*, 3d ed. (Paris: Dalloz, 1972), 189; Andre Fribourg, *Discours de Danton* (Paris: Société de l'Histoire de la Révolution Française, 1910), 203.

43. Blanning, *French Revolutionary Wars*, 136-37; Fribourg, *Discours de Danton*, 211ff.

44. Henry Collins, "The London Corresponding Society," in *Democracy and Labour Movement: Essays in Honour of Dona Torr*, ed. John Saville (London: Lawrence & Wishart, 1954), 110; Jean Albert-Sorel, *Histoire de France et d'Angleterre: La rivalité, l'entente, l'alliance* (Amsterdam: Les Éditions Françaises d'Amsterdam, 1950), 179.

45. Lefebvre et al., *La révolution française*, 152.

46. Blanning, *French Revolutionary Wars*, 155; Iung, *Dubois-Crancé*, 333; Fribourg, *Discours de Danton*, 269.

47. Alfred Cobban, *Aspects of the French Revolution* (New York: W. W. Norton, 1968), 192-95, based on La Luzerne to Montmorin, May 13, 1791, A. A. E., C. P. Angleterre 577, fo. 238; Dispatches of Barthelemy August 26, September 9, September 30, October 14, November 4, November 11, December 2, 1791, A. A. E., C. P. Angleterre, 578, fos. 182, 229-30, 311; 579, fos. 34, 130, 142, 238; Camille Desmoulins, *Fragment de l'histoire secrète de la révolution, sur la faction d'Orléans, le comité Anglo-Prussien et les six premiers mois de la république,* 5-6 (British Museum F 255-56).

48. Sorel, *L'Europe et la révolution française,* vol. 3: *La Guerre aux Rois,* 174-75; Laprade, "England and the French Revolution," 521-32; Blanning, *French Revolutionary Wars,* 153, 157; Buchez and Roux, *Histoire parlementaire,* 371.

49. Buchez and Roux, *Histoire parlementaire,* 368.

50. For the complete list of the archival documents, see Cobban, *Aspects,* 306-13.

51. See also Oscar Browning, ed., *The Despatches of Earl Gower, English Ambassador at Paris from June 1790 to August 1792* (Cambridge: Cambridge University Press, 1885), 2-4.

52. Cobban, *Aspects,* 214.

53. George III to Pitt, May 26, 1787, quoted in ibid., 217.

54. Alfred Cobban, *Ambassadors and Secret Agents: The Diplomacy of the First Earl of Malmesbury at the Hague* (London: Jonathan Cape, 1954), 114, based on Fraser to Harris, January 4, 1785, FO. 37/6. Fraser served as undersecretary to Carmathen, Secretary of State for Foreign Affairs.

55. Cobban, *Aspects,* 200, with reference to parliamentary papers, Civil List accounts, treasury warrants and order books, audit office accounts and discharges, and Foreign Office registers; also see Harvey Mitchell, *The Underground War against Revolutionary France: The Mission of William Wickham, 1794-1800* (Oxford: Clarendon Press, 1965), 256.

56. Mitchell, *Underground War,* 256.

57. Cobban, *Ambassadors and Secret Agents,* 110-16, 200-3.

58. Sorel, *L'Europe et la révolution française,* vol. 3, 165.

59. Blanning, *French Revolutionary Wars,* 152-53.

60. J. T. Murley, "The Origin and Outbreak of the Anglo-French War of 1793" (D. Phil. dissertation, Oxford University, 1959), 148.

61. Quoted in Blanning, *French Revolutionary Wars,* 153.

62. Quoted in Albert-Sorel, *Histoire de France et d'Angleterre,* 175, and Fribourg, *Discours de Danton,* 268-69.

63. For the French declaration of war, see John Hall Stewart, *A Documentary Survey of the French Revolution* (New York: Macmillan, 1951), 398-401. For Britain's declaration of war, see Modelski and Modelski, eds. *Documenting Global Leadership,* 247-56.

64. Modelski and Modelski, *Documenting Global Leadership,* 247-56; see also the discussion of British capabilities earlier in this chapter.

65. Ibid.

66. Stewart, *Documentary Survey of the French Revolution,* 398-401. John Hall Stewart, other editors of this collection of documents, and experts at the U.S. Library of Congress Reference Department found no documents confirming the establishment of Anglo-Prussian secret coalition in January 1793.

67. Modelski and Modelski, *Documenting Global Leadership,* 247-56.

Notes to Chapter 7

1. Robert V. Daniels, *Russia: The Roots of Confrontation* (Cambridge: Harvard University Press, 1985), 348-49.

2. See, for example, Stephen E. Ambrose, *Rise of Globalism: American Foreign Policy Since 1938,* 7th ed. (New York: Penguin Books, 1993), 303 and chap. 15; for the Soviet rhetoric, see Sergei S. Sergeev, *Total'nyy shpionazh* [Total espionage] (Moscow: Voenizdat, 1984), 3-4.

3. For a comprehensive and vivid account of U.S.-Soviet arms control negotiations, which informed many conventional interpretations, see Strobe Talbott, *Deadly Gambits: The Reagan Administration and the Stalemate in Nuclear Arms* Control (New York: Vintage Books, 1985).

4. Raymond L. Garthoff, *Deterrence and the Revolution in Soviet Military Doctrine* (Washington, D.C.: Brookings Institution, 1990).

5. Sherman Kent, "The Law and Custom of the National Intelligence Estimate," DCI Miscellaneous Studies, MS-12, February 1976, 4-10. This in-house CIA paper, marked "secret," was declassified only in February 1994 as part of the CIA's Historical Review Program.

6. Ibid., 43.

7. See John Barron, *KGB Today: The Hidden Hand* (New York: Berkeley Books, 1985), 379; and Amy W. Knight, "The KGB and Soviet Foreign Policy," in *Contemporary Issues in Soviet Foreign Policy,* eds. Frederick J. Fleron, Jr., Erik Hoffmann, and Robert Laird (New York: Aldine de Gruyter, 1995), 466.

8. USSR, Komitet gosudarstvennoy bezopasnosti [KGB], Attachment to No. 2126/PR, in Christopher Andrew and Oleg Gordievsky, eds., *Comrade Kryuchkov's Instructions: Top Secret Files on KGB Foreign Operations, 1975-1985* (Stanford: Stanford University Press, 1993), 17.

9. For example, when an NIE was scheduled on important subject, TRs served as special guides for collection at home and abroad by all major players in the U.S. intelligence community. As Sherman Kent put it, "the desirability of certain collection chores" would then be specified to the CIA's Deputy Directors of Planning/Operations, the Foreign Broadcast Information Services, and the Domestic Collection Division. To representatives from the Bureau of Intelligence and Research (INR) at the State Department, TRs signaled that "the right embassies" must be alerted. Representatives from the military would "go to the field and lay some new requisitions on their attaches. See Kent, "Law and Custom of the National Intelligence Estimate," 45.

In the Soviet case, the KGB was better positioned to reflect Politburo priorities than the other major agency involved in collection abroad, Glavnoye razvedyvatel'noye upravleniye (GRU) of the General Staff. The KGB was larger, better funded, and able to pull rank on its "military neighbors." None of the GRU heads was ever even a candidate (nonvoting) member of the Politburo, whereas KGB chairmen, including Andropov, Chebrikov, and Kryuchkov, were full Politburo members. The GRU organizational chart included the KGB group at the highest level of command, an arrangement not paralleled in the KGB's organizational structure. See Christopher Andrew and Oleg Gordievsky, eds., "More 'Instructions from the Center': Top Secret Files on KGB Global Operations, 1975-1985," *Intelligence and National Security* 7 (January 1992), 14; and Desmond Ball, *Soviet Signals Intelligence (SIGINT)* (Canberra: Strategic and Defense Studies Center, Research School of Pacific Studies, The Australian National University, 1989), 9.

10. U.S. Congress, House Committee on Foreign Affairs, *The Role of Intelligence in the Foreign Policy Process* (Washington, D.C.: U.S. Government Printing Office, 1980), 25.

11. Thirteen NIEs in the 11-3/8 and 11-4 series represent most of the declassified 23 estimates used in this study. The 11-3/8 series of NIEs addressed the

potential utilization and development of defensive and offensive elements of the Soviet capability to wage intercontinental war, while the 11-4 series was intended to assess trends in military policy, given the impact of Soviet politics and ideology. The 11-4 series, as may well be expected in a bean-counting intelligence paradigm, was more limited in scope and appeared less regularly than the annual NIE 11-3/8 series.

In practice, however, each series examined both military and economic capabilities, as well as the political intentions of the Soviet leadership relative to the use of force. Scope notes, or brief statements describing the purpose of each individual NIE in the 11-3/8 series, routinely contained the following wording (or something close to it): "It [NIE] assesses Soviet policies and doctrine applicable to strategic nuclear forces for intercontinental attack, peripheral attack, and strategic defenses." See NIE 11-3/8-80, *Soviet Capabilities for Strategic Nuclear Conflict through 1990* (December 16, 1980), i.

12. Leonov, *Likholet'e* (Moscow: Mezhdunarodnye otnosheniya, 1994), 130.

13. Washington Platt, *Strategic Intelligence Production: Basic Principles* (New York: Praeger, 1957), 207-11 (Platt was a brigadier general, U.S. Army); Lawrence Freedman, *U.S. Intelligence and the Soviet Strategic Threat* (Boulder, Colo.: Westview Press, 1977), 41. A complete set of phrases, matched with ranges of certainty, was as follows:

"ALMOST CERTAIN": Chances: about 9:1 or more in favor. Range of possibility: 0.85-0.99 in favor; 0.01-0.15 against (1=100%). Synonyms: A flat statement about a situation which evidently cannot be verified is equivalent to saying, "It is almost certain that." Any flat statement regarding the *future* is in this class: "————indicated that," "We believe that," "It is evident that (or apparent that)," "There is little doubt that (or will undoubtedly)."

"CHANCES ARE GOOD": Chances: about 3:1 in favor. Range of possibility: 0.60-0.84 in favor; 0.16-0.40 against. Synonyms: "It is probable that" (or any other use of "probably"), "It is fairly certain that," "It is likely that appears to," "should be," "is expected (or anticipated)," "It is logical to assume," "It is reasonable to conclude."

"CHANCES ARE ABOUT EVEN": Chances: about 1:1 or 50-50. Range of possibility: 0.40-0.59 in favor; 0.41-0.60 against.

"CHANCES ARE GOOD THAT—NOT": Chances: about 1:3 in favor or 3:1 against. Range of possibility: 0.15-0.39 in favor; 0.61-0.85 against. Synonyms: Same as for "Chances are Good," plus the inclusion of NOT or another negative.

"ALMOST CERTAIN THAT—NOT": Chances: about 1:9 in favor or 9:1 against. Range of possibility: 0.01-0.14 in favor; 0.86-0.99 against. Synonyms: Same as for "Almost Certain," plus the inclusion of NOT or another negative.

INCONCLUSIVE: Only when the writer is unwilling to indicate even approximately the probability of a statement being true will he use the following phrases without further qualification: "It is possible that," "may" (might is not expected to be used unless followed by a condition), "It could have."

14. NIE 11-3/8-80, 3; U.S. Central Intelligence Agency, NIE 11-4-78, *Soviet Goals and Expectations in the Global Power Arena*, M/H (July 7, 1981), 3; U.S. Central Intelligence Agency, *Soviet Policy in the Middle East and South Asia under Andropov* (February 2, 1983), 3.

15. Donald P. Steury, *Estimates on Soviet Military Power, 1954-1984: A Selection* (Washington, D.C.: Center for the Study of Intelligence, Central Intelligence Agency, 1994), x; ed. Philip D. Morehead, *The American Roget's College Thesaurus* (New York: Signet, 1978), 91.

16. In contrast, the palm-reading approach would require focusing mainly on indicators of political aggressiveness, whether linked to military capabilities or not.

17. The text of each NIE's "key judgements" was searched for words indicating that there was a change underway in the state of Soviet strategic capabilities relative to the United States. If this change implied gains in the Soviet position, the relevant threat factor was assigned a score of "1" (and "-1" when NIEs mentioned changes favorable to the United States). If such statements of relative change were absent, a score of "0" was given. Positive assessments of the state of the Soviet economy in the NIEs (by comparison with the prior assessments) were coded as "1," negative assessments as "-1," and the absence of change as "0." Repeated positive or negative assessments were coded as "0" when no indication was given whether the situation changed, unless the statement related to a dynamic factor such as growth rates. Thus, if the Soviet Union was said to have "problems in the energy sector," the score of "-1" would result. If repeated next year without specifications indicating whether the same problem worsened or was being resolved, a score of "0" was assigned. The same approach was applied to statements regarding changes in political and ideological aspects of Soviet power (indicator categories 4 and 5). Statements suggesting that a change in any given political or ideological factor would result in a more aggressive Soviet posture were scored as "1," and mentions of factors expected to lead to less aggressive or more peaceful Soviet

policies as "-1." The score of "0" reflected the absence of statements regarding changes in the impact of ideology or domestic politics on the level of the war threat. Trend in estimated Soviet threat levels were constructed by aggregating these scores. Scores for any given year are a sum of scores for all previous years, representing changes in Soviet threat potential over the 1975-1984 period.

18. Quoted respectively from U.S. Central Intelligence Agency, NIE 11-4-78, *Soviet Goals and Expectations in the Global Power Arena* (May 9, 1978), vi; U.S. Central Intelligence Agency, NIE 11-3/8-76, *Soviet Forces for Intercontinental Conflict through the Mid-1980s* (December 21, 1976), 7.

19. NIE 11-3/8-80, A-1.

20. William T. Lee, *CIA Estimates of Soviet Military Expenditures: Errors and Waste* (Washington, D.C.: American Enterprise Institute, 1995).

21. Rodion Malinovskiy, *Bditel'no stoyat' na strazhe mira* [Vigilantly standing guard over the peace] (Moscow: Voenizdat, 1962), 12, 13, 21; Foreign Broadcast Information Service, USSR, July 6, 1965 (see Brezhnev's comments); David S. Sullivan, "Evaluating U.S. Intelligence Estimates," in *Intelligence Requirements for the 1980s: Analysis and Estimates,* ed. Roy Godson (New Brunswick, NJ: National Strategy Information Center, 1980), 49-73; Dr. Robert Gates, presentation at "The New Structures of European Security" of the Pacific Northwest Colloquium on International Security, March 10, 1995, from author's notes.

22. On the linkage between NIEs and NCS-68, see John Prados, *The Soviet Estimate: U.S. Intelligence Analysis and Soviet Strategic Forces* (Princeton: Princeton University Press, 1986), 21- 22; on the adoption of PD-59 and its similarity with NSC-68, see Walter LaFeber, *America, Russia, and the Cold War, 1945-1990* (New York: McGraw-Hill, 1991), 300.

23. This concept was officially rejected at the Twentieth Congress of the Soviet Communist Party in 1956; see ed. A. M. Prohorov, *Sovetskiy entsiklopedicheskiy slovar* [Soviet encyclopedic dictionary], 4th ed. (Moscow: "Sovetskaia entsiklopediia," 1990), 239.

24. Quoted in LaFeber, *America, Russia, and the Cold War,* 299.

25. For Andropov's views on these issues stated to KGB colleagues and Politburo members, see Nikolai S. Leonov, *Likholet'ye,* 191-216.

26. This evidence also challenges revisionist historians who claim that Reagan deliberately spent the Soviet Union into the grave, given that he operated within the "limits of the known world" and institutional information flows represented by the NIEs.

27. U.S. Central Intelligence Agency, NIE 11-3/8-75, *Soviet Forces for Intercontinental Conflict through the Mid-1980s* (October 9, 1975), 6; other estimates that addressed this question pursued the same argument.

28. U.S. Central Intelligence Agency, SNIE 11/80/90-82, *Soviet Policies and Activities in Latin America and the Caribbean* (June 25, 1982), 9, 13-14, 17-18.

29. Cf. Kommunisticheskaya partiya Sovetskogo Soyuza [Communist Party of the Soviet Union], *Materialy XXV s'ezda KPSS* [Materials of the Twenty-fifth Congress of the CPSU] (Moscow: Politizdat, 1976), 11-16; and idem, *Materialy XXVI s'ezda KPSS* [Materials of the Twenty-sixth Congress of the CPSU] (Moscow: Politizdat, 1981), pp. 11-15. At a course in Marxist-Leninist political economy at Kiev State University, attended by the author in the 1982-1983 academic year, professor Nikolai Grebnev, who also served as a consultant to the Council of Ministers and the Central Committee of the Communist Party of Ukraine, emphasized the significance of this change. On the Twenty-seventh Congress, see idem, *Materialy XXVII s'ezda KPSS* [Materials of the Twenty-seventh Congress of the CPSU] (Moscow: Politizdat, 1986). For Andropov's shift of emphasis to "mutually advantageous cooperation," "complete non-interference with sovereignty," greater reliance on "correct domestic policies" of the LDCs, and proportioning Soviet aid to economic capabilities, see Yuri Andropov, *Rech na Plenume Tsentral'nogo Komiteta Kommunisticheskoy Partii Sovetskogo Soyuza* [Speech at the Plenary Meeting of the Central Committee of the Communist Party of the Soviet Union], June 15, 1983, in Yuri Andropov, *Izbrannyye stat'i i rechi* [Selected articles and speeches] (Moscow: Politizdat, 1983), 297.

30. U.S. Central Intelligence Agency, NIO M 76-021J, *Soviet Strategic Objectives: An Alternate View* (December 1, 1976), 1.

31. See USSR, Komitet gosudarstvennoi bezopasnosti [KGB], No. 551/PR, Attachment 891/PR/52, "Plan of Requirements on Chinese Subjects for 1977" (March 14, 1977), in *Instructions,* ed. Andrew and Gordievsky, 196; and idem, No. 1058/PR/61, "The Organization of Intelligence Work against the European Economic Community (EEC) from the Standpoint of 'Legal' Residencies" (April 15, 1977), ibid., 156.

32. See, respectively, idem, No. 373/PR/52, "Permanent Operational Assignment to Uncover NATO Preparations for a Nuclear Missile Attack on the USSR" (February 17, 1983), in *Instructions,* ed. Andrew and Gordievsky, 69; idem, No. 2126/PR, Attachment (November 21, 1983), ibid., 16; idem, No. 156/54, "Chief Conclusions and Views Adopted at the Meeting of

Heads of Service" (February 1, 1984), ibid., 6, 8; No. 367/MP (July 10, 1984), ibid., 89; idem, No. 2106/PR, "Measures Designed to Step Up Work on Problems of Military Strategy" (December 17, 1984) in Andrew and Gordievsky, "More Instructions," 15; idem, No. 337/PR (February 13, 1985), in Andrew and Gordievsky, *Instructions,* 107.

33. Andrew and Gordievsky, *Instructions,* 67.

34. Vadim Bakatin, *Izbavleniye ot KGB* [Getting rid of the KGB] (Moscow: Novosti, 1992), 44.

35. The share of these factors would be even higher if the content analysis included two other regular parts of the instructions outlining "active measures," such as misinformation and staged events, and agent recruitment. This was done to eliminate a potential bias in favor of the tested hypothesis.

36. USSR, Komitet gosudarstvennoi bezopasnosti [KGB], Attachment to No 337/PR (February 13, 1985), in Andrew and Gordievsky, *Instructions,* 110.

37. Ibid., 107; see this point corroborated in the memoirs of Andropov's foreign policy adviser, Andrei Aleksandrov-Agentov, *Ot Kollontay do Gorbacheva* [From Kollontai to Gorbachev] (Moscow: Mezhdunarodnye otnoshenia, 1994), 281-82.

38. USSR, Komitet gosudarstvennoi bezopasnosti [KGB], No. 156/54, "Chief Conclusions and Views Adopted at the Meeting of Heads of Service" (February 1, 1984), in Andrew and Gordievsky, *Instructions,* 4-14.

39. See No. 2126/PR, Attachment (November 21, 1983), in Andrew and Gordievsky, *Instructions,* 17; Andrew and Gordievsky, *Instructions,* 1-3.

40. No. 156/54, Andrew and Gordievsky, *Instructions,* 6.

41. Ibid. The pledge not to use nuclear weapons first was made by Brezhnev in 1982.

42. Ibid.

43. Ibid., 7-8.

44. Ibid., 12.

45. The abbreviation consists of the last three words, taken from a KGB acronym, in Russian, *vnezapnoye raketno-yadernoye napadeniye* [surprise nuclear missile attack].

46. In fact, this is a shorter version that has gained usage in the West, omitting the Russian for *vnezapnoye* (surprise) nuclear attack.

47. Bakatin, *Izbavleniye*, 89-90.

48. USSR, Komitet gosudarstvennoi bezopasnosti [KGB], No. 373/PR/52, in Andrew and Gordievsky, *Instructions*, 75.

49. Christopher Andrew and Oleg Gordievsky, *KGB: The Inside Story of Its Foreign Operations from Lenin to Gorbachev* (New York: Harper Perennial, 1991), 583; Andrew and Gordievsky, "More Instructions," 1.

50. Andrew and Gordievsky, *KGB*, 584; KGB, No. 373/PR/52, in Andrew and Gordievsky, *Instructions*, 70.

51. KGB, No. 373/PR/52, Attachment 1, in Andrew and Gordievsky, *Instructions*, 71-72.

52. Aleksandr Feklisov, *Za okeanom i na ostrove: Zapiski razvedchika* [Over the ocean and on the island: Notes of an intelligence officer] (Moscow: DEM, 1994), 222.

53. KGB, No. 373/PR/52, Attachment 1, in Andrew and Gordievsky, *Instructions*, 73.

54. KGB, No. 373/PR/52, Attachment 2, in Andrew and Gordievsky, *Instructions*, 76-77; Talbott, *Deadly Gambits*, 35. It should be noted that credible technical data was obtained by the Soviet General Staff that Pershing II could acquire range to reach Moscow. Yet, technical improvements on the United States part in previous decades failed to trigger a scare similar to Operation RYAN's. This time, however, information on Pershing's capability potential was received at the time of the Kremlin's rising fear of the United States' allegedly aggressive intentions. Threat assessments thus implicitly emphasized the political will to upgrade Pershing rather than the existing capabilities.

55. KGB, No. 373/PR/52, Attachment 2, in Andrew and Gordievsky, *Instructions*, 76-77.

56. Ibid., 85; Andrew and Gordievsky, *KGB*, 600.

57. KGB, No. 373/PR/52, Attachment 2, in Andrew and Gordievsky, *Instructions*, 77-81; Andrew and Gordievsky, *Instructions*, 85; Andrew and Gordievsky, *KGB*, 599-600; Aleksandrov-Agentov, *Ot Kollontay do Gorbacheva*, 281.

58. Andrew and Gordievsky, "More Instructions," 1.

59. Andrew and Gordievsky, *KGB*, 603.

Notes to Chapter 8

1. United States. President's Commission on Strategic Forces. *Report of the President's Commission on Strategic Forces,* submitted to the president by chairman Brent Scowcroft, April 6, 1983, 3. Participating in the commission were many top military and intelligence officials, including several past and future CIA directors. Commission members were Nicholas Brady, William Clements, John M. Deutch, Alexander M. Haig, Jr., Richard Helms, John M. Lyons, William J. Perry, Thomas C. Reed, Levering Smith, and R. James Woolsey. Senior counselors to the commission were Harold Brown, Lloyd N. Cutler, Henry M. Kissinger, Melvin R. Laird, John McCone, Donald Rumsfeld, and James R. Schlesinger.

2. *Report of the President's Commission on Strategic Forces,* 8.

3. Raymond L. Garthoff, *The Great Transition: American-Soviet Relations and the End of the Cold War* (Washington, D.C.: Brookings Institution, 1994), 101.

4. See line marked Total Threat in Figure 7.1, chap. 7.

5. Robert M. Gates, *From the Shadows: The Ultimate Insider's Story of Five Presidents and How They Won the Cold War* (New York: Simon and Schuster, 1996), 319.

6. Central Intelligence Agency, Office of Soviet Analysis, *USSR: Economic Trends and Policy Developments,* Joint Economic Committee Briefing Paper (September 14, 1983), 8-11, 18, quoted in Garthoff, *The Great Transition,* 41. See also Raymond L. Garthoff, "The Spending Gap," *Bulletin of the Atomic Scientists,* 40 (May 1984), 5-6.

7. Gates, *From the Shadows,* 319.

8. Lawrence Kaagan, "Public Opinion Trends and the Defence Front: Trends and Lessons," in *Defense and Consensus: The Domestic Aspects of Western Security,* ed. Christopher Bertram (New York: St. Martin's Press, 1983), 15, 22.

9. John Lewis Gaddis, *The United States and the End of the Cold War: Implications, Reconsiderations, Provocations* (New York: Oxford University Press, 1992), 125-26; Garthoff, *The Great Transition,* 505.

10. Quoted in Gaddis, *The United States and the End of the Cold War,* 126.

11. U.S. Central Intelligence Agency, *Domestic Stresses on the Soviet System,* NIE 11-18-85 (November 1985), 8.

12. NIE 11-18-85, 8-9, 13. Soviet consumer demands for quality and variety of food were correctly viewed as unsatisfied, although the CIA spared the high-level consumers of its estimates from graphic descriptions of a typical Soviet workers' diet, such as greasy salted smelt eaten with watery boiled potatoes, pickles, and slabs of pork fat.

13. Ibid., 10. On the share of Muslims in the Soviet population and its spectacular growth, both numerically and proportionately, see Hélèn Carrére d'Encausse, *Decline of an Empire* (New York: Harper Colophon Books, 1981 [1978]), 65-70.

14. In the coordinated intelligence community view, laid out in the NIE, anti-Russian sentiments were considered "most virulent" among Balts, Western Ukrainians, Georgians, and the peoples of Central Asia (Uzkeks, Kazakhs, Tajiks, the Turkmen, and the Kirgiz). The estimate, however, recorded a dissenting view of the Bureau of Intelligence and Research at the State Department, suggesting that anti-Russian aspirations in Central Asia were dampened by greater assimilation and lack of any recent experience of political independence, unlike in Western Ukraine and the Baltics. While noting that the separatist movements in these areas remained "politically insignificant" and that anti-Russian national consciousness was often directed against other non-Russian minorities, the estimate nevertheless concluded: "Ethnic self-consciousness and resentment of Russian dominance is steadily rising inside the USSR, along with the growth of the non-Russian population." The CIA also registered the galvanizing impact of Poland's mass popular unrest led by Solidarity on the Western Ukraine and the Baltics as well as the impact of the war in Afghanistan on the peoples of Central Asia. NIE 11-18-85, 11, n. 2.

15. The estimate correctly pointed out that "those who gave moral support to the visible dissenters of the recent past are still there" and that small numbers of dissenters had gone underground and became radicalized, even to the point of considering "violent actions against the system." NIE 11-18-85, 12. A famous Russian rock singer, Boris Grebenshchikov, whose career took off in the 1980s while he was banned from making records by the Soviet government, suggested in one his songs that the sweeping changes in the Soviet Union were brought about by a "generation of janitors and street sweepers," occupations taken up by many of that small group of political and human rights dissenters mentioned in the CIA reports who remained at large in the early 1980s. For a comprehensive account of dissent in the USSR during this period, see Lyudmila Alexeyeva, *Soviet Dissent: Contemporary*

Movements for National, Religious, and Human Rights (Middletown, Conn.: Wesleyan University Press, 1987).

16. Though no such actions rivaled the 1962 food riots in the southern Russian city of Novocherkassk, growing potential for unrest was noted. The CIA drew the attention of U.S. decision makers to a strike in 1980 by tens of thousands of workers in the center of Russia's automobile industry, Togliatti. In another act of dramatic defiance, party members in the city of Perm in the Urals turned in their party cards in protest over food shortages. NIE 11-18-85, 12.

17. Ibid., 13.

18. Ibid., 16-17, 10.

19. Ibid., 8.

20. Quoted by David Kennedy, *Sunshine and Shadow: The CIA and the Soviet Economy,* Case Study C16-91-1096.0 for the Intelligence and Policy Project, John F. Kennedy School of Government (Cambridge: Harvard University, 1991), 18.

21. Quoted in Henry S. Rowen and Charles Wolf, Jr., *The Impoverished Superpower: Perestroika and the Soviet Military Burden* (San Francisco: Institute of Contemporary Studies, 1990), 15. These views were also expressed frequently in the mainstream American media, e.g., in a *New York Times* editorial October 22, 1995: "The CIA considered the Soviet Union an economic power when it was actually an economic wreck." In the *Wall Street Journal,* Adam Wooldridge argued that the CIA "continued to endorse the myth that the [Soviet] communists had transformed an agricultural backwater into a mighty industrial power capable even of higher levels of economic development." For a book-length review of these arguments, see Nicholas Eberstadt, *The Tyranny of Numbers: Measurement and Misrule* (Washington, D.C.: American Enterprise Institute Press, 1995).

22. NIE 11-18-85, 1.

23. Ibid., 9. For example, the estimate pointed out that the Soviet military and workers in defense industries were affected by deteriorating disease control, alcoholism, corruption, and educational deficiencies. Some long-term problems were also foreseen: "As military technologies become more complex and diffuse, Soviet military power is becoming more constrained by low technology levels in the society at large, a source of worry to Soviet military authorities."

24. U.S. Congress, Joint Economic Committee, *Allocation of Resources in the Soviet Union and China, 1985,* Hearings Before the Subcommittee on Economic Resources, Competitiveness, and Security Economics of the Joint Economic Committee, Part 11, 99th Cong., 2d sess., March 19, 1986, 6-7; U.S. Central Intelligence Agency, Directorate of Intelligence, Office of Soviet Analysis, *Gorbachev's Modernization Program: Implications for Defense,* SOV 86-10015X, March 1986, 9-10; Memorandum to the Deputy Director for Intelligence [Richard J. Kerr] from Douglas J. MacEachin, Director, Office of Soviet Analysis, NIE 11-3/8: Force Projections, April 22, 1986, Records of the Directorate of Intelligence, Job 90-60135, Box 2, Folder 20.

25. U.S. Central Intelligence Agency, Directorate of Intelligence, Office of Soviet Analysis, *Gorbachev's Challenge: The Looming Problems,* SOV 87-10009, 4; U.S. Central Intelligence Agency, Directorate of Intelligence, Office of Soviet Analysis, *Gorbachev: Steering the USSR into the 1990s,* SOV 87-10036X, July 1987, ix; U.S. Congress, Joint Economic Committee, *Allocation of Resources,* 72.

26. U.S. Central Intelligence Agency, Directorate of Intelligence, Office of Soviet Analysis, *Soviet National Security Policy: Responses to the Changing Military and Economic Environment,* SOV 88- 10040CX, June 1988, vii-viii.

27. U.S. Central Intelligence Agency, Douglas J. MacEachin, Director of Soviet Analysis, Memorandum to Richard Kerr, Deputy Director for Intelligence, "Leadership Situation in the USSR, September 27, 1988, attachment, "Prospects for a Leadership Crisis," n.d., 1, 3, 4; U.S. Central Intelligence Agency, Director of Intelligence, Office of Soviet Analysis, *Gorbachev's September Housecleaning: An Early Evaluation,* SOV 88-10079X, December 1988, iv, 1-2, 10; U.S. Central Intelligence Agency, Directorate of Intelligence, Office of Soviet Analysis, *The Soviet Economy in a Global Perspective,* SOV 89-10017, March 1989, i-ii.

28. Ronald Reagan, *National Security Strategy of the United States* (Washington, D.C.: Pergamon-Brassey's, 1988), xi, 5, 12, 13.

29. For example, in 1990, according to declassified Soviet documents, the International Department of the Central Committee disbursed close to $11 million dollars to communist parties ("leftist workers' organizations") of the United States, France, Portugal, Greece, Israel, Chile, India, Lebanon, Venezuela, Argentina, El Salvador, Brazil, Colombia, and Uruguay (of which $2 million went to the U.S. Communist Party). Evgenii Lisov, "'Zelenye' dlya krasnikh" [Greenbacks for the "reds"], *Ogonyok,* 9 (February 1992), 6.

30. "Deputy at CIA warns of Soviets," *Washington Times,* February 2, 1988, A3, quoted in Garthoff, *The Great Transition,* 340.

31. Garthoff, *The Great Transition,* 340-41.

32. "Rech' M. S. Gorbacheva v Organizatsii Ob'edinennyh Natsii," *Pravda,* December 8, 1988; Ronald Reagan, "Presidential Address to the Nation on Soviet-United States Relations," December 10, 1988, *Presidential Documents,* vol. 24 (December 19, 1988), 1613-14.

33. Garthoff, *The Great Transition,* 365-66; Mikhail Gorbachev, *Zhizn' i reformy* [Life and Reforms], 2 vols. (Moscow: Novosti, 1995), vol. 2, 131-32. Gorbachev writes that he treasured the 1988 UN speech because it embodied "a complete switchover to new thinking." Gorbachev saw the speech as "Fulton in reverse," referring to Winston Churchill's 1946 Iron Curtain speech in Fulton, Missouri. The former Soviet leader asks retrospectively in his memoir, "What did I consider as the most important in that speech?" After listing some of the arms reductions proposals, Gorbachev concludes, "This, however, was not the main thing. I tried to demonstrate to the world community that we all were entering a principally new period of history, when the old, traditional principles of interstate relations—based on the correlation of forces *[sootnosheniye sil]* and competition—must give way to new principles—based on cocreativity and co-development" (132).

34. Hanson, *Time and Revolution,* 237, n. 1; Michael R. Beschloss and Strobe Talbott, *At the Highest Levels: The Inside Story of the End of the Cold War* (Boston: Little, Brown, 1993), 33-34.

35. Christopher Simpson, *National Security Directives of the Reagan and Bush Administrations: The Declassified History of U.S. Political and Military Policy, 1981-1991* (Boulder, Colo.: Westview Press, 1995), 896.

36. Simpson, *National Security Directives, 1990-1991,* 897-98.

37. George Bush, *National Security Strategy of the United States: 1990-1991* (Washington, D.C.: Brassey's, 1990), 31, 34. On the central role of military capabilities, the paper further stated: "Even as tensions ease and military forces are reduced on both sides, maintaining the global strategic balance is inescapably an American concern; there is no substitute for our efforts," 31.

38. Reagan, *National Security Strategy,* 13; Bush, *National Security Strategy,* 32.

39. U.S. Congress, Joint Economic Committee, *Allocation of Resources in the Soviet Union and China,* pt. 15, April 20, May 16, June 28, 1990, 1.

40. The committee reviewed a 72-page joint paper of the Central Intelligence
Agency and Defense Intelligence Agency (DIA), entitled "The Soviet
Economy Stumbles Badly in 1989," and listened to the testimony of high-
level intelligence officials in open and closed sessions. Representing the CIA
were John Helgerson, Deputy Director for Intelligence, George Kolt,
Director of the Office of Soviet Analysis, and John McLaughlin, Director of
European Analysis. The DIA's position was articulated by Dennis Nagy,
Acting Deputy Director for Foreign Intelligence, as well as their support
staff. For the complete list of names, see *Allocation of Resources in the Soviet
Union,* p. 15, 144.

41. Ibid., 154-58. Of the three questions dealing with Soviet intentions, only one
focused on the political dimension of the Soviet threat (i.e., military policy
debate); the other two questions on Soviet intentions (to withdraw from
Eastern Europe and to continue economic reform involving military
spending reductions) directly linked intentions with costs. This further
suggests that political intentions in their own right were downplayed in the
general scheme of Soviet threat assessment.

42. Ibid., 17.

43. Ibid., 165.

44. Garthoff, *The Great Transition,* 507, n. 10. It is also likely, judging from that
note, that intelligence estimates assuming 95 percent manning levels for
Soviet military units in Europe were challenged, suggesting instead 85
percent manning levels.

45. *Allocation of Resources in the Soviet Union,* pt. 15, 166, 167.

46. Ibid., 2, 6, 11, 145, 171-72.

47. Ibid., 171.

48. U.S. Central Intelligence Agency and Defense Intelligence Agency, "The Soviet
Economy Stumbles Badly in 1989" (joint paper presented to the Technology and
National Security Subcommittees of the Joint Economic Committee, Congress
of the United States, April 20, 1990), ibid., 30, 36, 43, 85-93.

49. Gates, *From the Shadows,* 511, 527.

50. Allocation of Resources in the Soviet Union, pt. 15, 153.

51. Gates, *From the Shadows,* 528.

52. Christopher Andrew and Oleg Gordievsky, *KGB: The Inside Story of Its
Foreign Operations from Lenin to Gorbachev* (New York: Harper Perennial,
1991), 604-5.

53. Gorbachev, *Zhizn'i reformy*, vol. 1, 260-61; Andrew and Gordievsky, *KGB*, 605.

54. Andrew and Gordievsky, *KGB*, 605-24.

55. Quotes from the BBC/PBS documentary series, *Messengers from Moscow*, pt. 4 (1995).

56. "A world united in its diversity" was one of Gorbachev's buzz phrases used in almost every speech on Soviet "new thinking." For an extended original explanation of new thinking as both a concept and a guide to Soviet foreign policy, see Mikhail Gorbachev, *Perestroika: New Thinking for Our Country and the World* (New York: Harper & Row, 1987), pt. 2.

57. Gorbachev, *Zhizn' i reformy*, vol. 2, 8.

58. For this insightful textual analysis and English translation of quotes from the Congress report, see Garthoff, *The Great Transition*, 255-59. The original Russian-language quotes are from L. I. Brezhnev, *XXVI s"yezd Kommunisticheskoy partii Sovetskogo Soyuza, 28 fevralya - 3 marta 1981 goda: stenograficheskiy otchet* [The Twenty-sixth Congress of the Communist Party of the Soviet Union, February 28–March 3, 1981: Stenographic Report] (Moscow: Politizdat, 1981), vol. 1, 33; and M. S. Gorbachev, *Politicheskiy doklad tsentral'nogo komiteta KPSS XXVII s"yezdu Kommunisticheskoy partii Sovetskogo Soyuza* [Political report of the CPSU Central Committee to the Twenty-seventh Congress of the Communist Party of the Soviet Union] (Moscow: Politizdat, 1986), 7-29.

59. Gorbachev, *Zhizn' i reformy*, vol. 2, 16.

60. Anatoliy Chernyayev, *Shest' let s Gorbachevym: Po dnevnikovym zapisyam* [Six years with Gorbachev: According to the diary records] (Moscow: Kultura, 1993), 114.

61. Chernyayev, *Shest' let s Gorbachevym*, 115; Gorbachev, *Zhizn' i reformy*, vol. 2, 15; Chernyayev, *Shest' let s Gorbachevym*, 115.

62. Nikolai Leonov, *Likholet'ye* [The stormy years] (Moscow: Mezhdunarodnye otnosheniya, 1994), 198.

63. This section of the Twenty-sixth Congress report consisted of progressively subordinate subsections covering Moscow's relations with the world socialist system (second circle), the newly liberated countries and the world communist movement (third circle), and the capitalist states (fourth circle). See Brezhnev, *XXVI s"yezd Kommunisticheskoy partii*, 33.

64. Quoted in Raymond L. Garthoff, "The KGB Reports to Gorbachev," *Intelligence and National Security* 11 (April 1996), 226. For the bibliographical data on the original KGB documents, see ibid., 242-43.

65. Quoted ibid., 226-27.

66. Quoted ibid., 227-28.

67. Quoted ibid., 228, 230-31. Also, the report on 1988 posted "reducing international tensions" as the main objective of KGB active measures, a distinctly new element as compared with the 1985 and 1986 reports.

68. Leonov, *Likholet'ye*, 298.

69. Andrew and Gordievsky, *KGB*, 620.

70. BBC, *Survey of World Broadcasts*, SU/0708 B/3 (March 9, 1990); *Pravda*, April 22, 1990.

71. Vadim Bakatin, *Izbavleniye ot KGB* [Getting rid of the KGB] (Moscow: Novosti, 1992), 239.

72. Leonov, *Likholet'ye*, 319.

73. Ibid., 321.

74. Chernyayev, *Shest' let s Gorbachevym*, 113, based on the list of Soviet delegation.

75. Leonov, *Likholet'ye*, 323.

76. Ibid., 324. The concept of minimal reasonable sufficiency did imply major conceptual changes in the Soviet military doctrine—stressing the prevention of war, a defensive posture even in the event of war, and arms reductions. See Gorbachev's speech to the Eighteenth Congress of the Soviet Trade Unions, in *Pravda*, February 26, 1987; "On the Military Doctrine of the Member States of the Warsaw Pact," *Pravda*, May 30, 1987. Gorbachev sincerely believed that couching defense sufficiency in terms of general principles— such as cutting all strategic nuclear forces by half—was vital to the disarmament process *precisely* because such an approach "would spare us from making all those calculations, mutual mistrust, and accusations in hostile intentions." See the transcript of Gorbachev's conversation with the American delegation led by George Shultz, Moscow, April 14, 1987, in Gorbachev, *Zhizn' i reformy*, vol. 2, 44.

77. Leonov, *Likholet'ye*, 328.

78. Ibid., 326-27. According to Georgii Kornienko, then First Deputy Foreign Minister of the Soviet Union, the Defense Ministry initially agreed to include SS-23s in the Intermediate Nuclear Forces Treaty (despite these missiles having a range 100 kilometers under the 500 kilometer treaty threshold) in exchange for lowering the threshold itself to 400 kilometers—which would have barred the United States from deploying the modernized version of

Lance-2 missiles with a 450-470 kilometer range. In April 1987, Gorbachev and Shevardnadze told George Shultz in Moscow that they would have no problem classifying SS-23 as a shorter range missile (500-1,000-kilometer range), and that they would let the experts work out the details. Representatives of the General Staff were not invited to the experts meeting held at the Foreign Ministry the evening after the talks and were not shown minutes of the meeting. As the talks continued, Gorbachev confirmed Soviet agreement to include SS-23s in the INF package without lowering the threshold from 500 to 400 kilometers. Marshal Sergei Akhromeyev was not invited to this part of the talks but joined the negotiations later to discuss the Strategic Arms Reductions Treaty. Gorbachev intended to show his domestic critics that SS-23s could, in fact, attain the 500-kilometer range and ordered the chief designer of SS-23s, S. Nepobedimiy, to stage a confirmation test shooting. The tests were cancelled after the chief designer and Marshal Akhromeyev said that when in flight beyond 400 kilometers, the SS-23's control system would automatically switch off with potentially disastrous consequences. See Georgi Kornienko, *Kholodnaya voyna: Svidetel'stvo yeë uchastnika* [The Cold War: Testimony of a participant] (Moscow: Mezhdunarodnyë otnosheniya, 1995), 252-55.

79. Leonov, *Likholet'ye*, 327. This also explains the frustrations of the military who agreed to Gorbachev's initiatives as "the soldiers of the party," against their best professional judgements. Thus, Marshal Sergei Akhromeyev, the chief Soviet negotiator at Reykjavik, considered resigning as Chief of the General Staff of the Soviet Armed Forces but stayed to maintain the appearance of Soviet political unity, after Gorbachev agreed to equal force levels without any compensation for the U.S. forward-based systems and NATO allied offensive arms. See Sergei M. Akhromeyev and Georgii M. Kornienko, *Glazami marshala i diplomata* [Through the eyes of a marshal and a diplomat] (Moscow: Mezhdunarodnyë otnosheniya, 1992). Akhromeyev also "asked God's forgiveness" for signing the document, drafted at the foreign ministry, by which naval forces were excluded from the talks on the Conventional Forces in Europe Treaty (signed in 1990). See Leonov, *Likholet'ye*, 327.

80. Leonov, *Likholet'ye*, 325-26.

81. Quoted in Christopher Andrew and Oleg Gordievsky, eds., *Comrade Kryuchkov's Instructions: Top Secret Files on KGB Foreign Operations, 1975-1985* (Stanford: Stanford University Press, 1993), 213-15.

82. Andrew and Gordievsky, *Comrade Kryuchkov's Instructions*, 216-17.

83. Gorbachev, *Zhizn' i reformy*, vol. 2, 36.

84. Leonov, *Likholet'ye*, 333, 360; Bakatin, *Izbavleniye ot KGB*, 176, 92.

85. Leonid Shebarshin, *Ruka Moskvy: Zapiski nachal'nika sovetskoy razvedki* [The hand of Moscow: Notes of the chief of Soviet foreign intelligence] (Moscow: Tsentr-100, 1992), 274.

86. Shebarshin, *Ruka Moskvy*, 219.

87. Leonid Shebarshin, *Iz zhizni nachal'nika razvedki* [Sketches from the life of a foreign intelligence chief] (Moscow: Mezhdunarodnye otnosheniya, 1992), 24.

88. Shebarshin, *Ruka Moskvy*, 222-23.

89. Leonov, *Likholet'ye*, 360-84.

Notes to the Conclusion

1. H. G. Wells, *The Invisible Man* (New York: Bantam Books, 1987), 115.

2. Ibid., 26.

3. George Modelski and William R. Thompson, *Leading Sectors and World Powers: The Coevolution of Global Politics and Economics* (Columbia: University of South Carolina Press, 1996), 216.

4. "Meeting with Soviet Leader in Geneva: Themes and Perceptions," *National Security Decision Directive*, no. 194, Washington, D.C., October 25, 1985, 2; "Soviet Initiatives in International Economic Affairs," *National Security Study Directive*, no. 2-86, Washington, D.C., September, 16, 1986, 1-2.

5. Allan E. Goodman, "Intelligence in the Post-Cold War Era," in *In From the Cold*, Report of the Twentieth Century Fund Task Force on the Future of U.S. Intelligence (New York: Twentieth Century Fund Press, 1996), 35-36.

6. Goodman, "Intelligence in the Post-Cold War Era," 47.

7. Aaron Karp, "The New Politics of Missile Proliferation," *Arms Control Today* 26 (October, 1996), 10-14.

8. John F. Sopko, "The Changing Proliferation Threat," *Foreign Policy* 105 (Winter 1996-97), 3-14.

9. Ibid., 16.

10. Goodman, "Intelligence in the Post-Cold War Era," 107-8. On France bribing Brazil to get the radar contract, see ibid., 114 (with reference to *New Republic,* March 27, 1995, 10)—after the CIA told the State Department about this case, the State Department complained to Brazil and, in the end, Raytheon got the contract (ibid.). Regarding post–Cold War security threats, cf. testimony of then-Director of Central Intelligence, James Woolsey, in U.S. Congress, Senate, *Current and Projected National Security Threats to the United States and Its Interests Abroad,* Hearing before the Select Committee on Intelligence, 103d Cong., 2nd sess., January 25, 1994, 5-11.

11. Dan Glickman, U.S. Congress, House, Hearing before the Permanent Select Committee on Intelligence, 103d Cong., 1st sess., March 19, 1993, 2.

12. David Briscoe, "Experts Disagree on Number of Wars," *Fort Pierce Tribune,* December 30, 1996, A3; Allan E. Goodman, "Shifting Paradigms and Shifting Gears: A Perspective on Why There Is No Post-Cold War Intelligence Agenda," *Intelligence and National Security* 10 (October 1995), 6.

13. Walter Pincus, "CIA Wonders Why Young Spies Are Quitting: Fighting Drugs Rather than Cold War, Some Say Thrill Is Gone," *Seattle Times,* November 26, 1996, A3.

14. Robert David Steele, "Private Enterprise Intelligence: Its Potential Contribution to National Security," *Intelligence and National Security* 10 (October 1995), 213-14.

15. Jeffrey T. Richardson and Desmond Ball, *The Ties That Bind: Intelligence Cooperation between the UKUSA Countries—the United Kingdom, the United States of America, Canada, Australia and New Zealand* (Boston: Allen and Unwin, 1985), 1.

16. Ibid., 6, 301. Consistent with the Cold War paradigm, the United States accounted for about 90 percent of the total budgets and personnel of all the UKUSA agencies (Britain was responsible for another 8 percent) and set intelligence collection and assessment priorities. The cooperative collection and analysis effort on a global scale was put in place and has been partially replicated in intelligence cooperation going beyond UKUSA (involving NATO member states and the British Commonwealth).

17. Paula L. Scalingi, "Intelligence Community Cooperation: The Arms Control Model," *International Journal of Intelligence and Counterintelligence* 5 (1992), 401-10. Scalingi served in various analytical positions at the CIA, on the U.S. Delegation to the Strategic Arms Reductions Talks, and was a

staff member of the U.S. House of Representatives Permanent Select Committee on Intelligence and the Arms Control Intelligence Staff (ACIS). Among the new problems demanding intensified intelligence efforts with the demise of the Cold War were "international aspects of the environment, natural resource scarcities (such as water), global health problems, international research and development efforts." See, "Intelligence Capabilities, 1992-2005," *National Security Directive*, no. 67, November 15, 1991, 2.

18. SIPRI, *Yearbook: World Armaments and Disarmament* (New York: Oxford University Press, 1989), 475-79.

19. See Russia's government resolution, "O naznachenii rossiiskogo organa po zashchite informatsii, kotoroi obmenivaiutsia Rossiiskaia Federatsiia i Organizatsiia Severoatlanticheskogo dogovora" [On designating a Russian government body to be responsible for the protection of information exchanged by the Russian Federation and the North Atlantic Treaty Organization], in Russia, Ministry of Foreign Affairs, *Diplomaticheskii Vestnik*, No. 4, April 1997, 4; Hugh Smith, "Intelligence and U.N. Peacekeeping," *Survival* 36 (1994), 174-93; Craig Covault, "Cooperative Recon Gains Momentum," *Aviation Week and Space Technology*, October 9, 1995, 28-29.

20. Smith, "Intelligence and U.N. Peacekeeping," 175; Sir David Ramsbotham, "Analysis and Assessments for Peacekeeping Operations," *Intelligence and National Security* 10 (October 1995), 170-71.

21. On China's "sweatshop socialism"—a system that centralizes control of the local Communist Party, industrial enterprises (including joint ventures with the West), and trade unions in the hands of one person—resulting in scanty wages, physical and psychological harassment of the workforce, draconian work rules, and suppression of organized labor, see Anita Chan and Robert A. Senser, "China's Troubled Workers," *Foreign Affairs* 76 (March–April 1997), 104-17.

22. Stacy Mosher, "Patriotism is Enough," *Far Eastern Economic Review*, April 16, 1992, 16.

23. Dent Ocaya-Lakidi, "U.N. and the U.S. Military Roles in Regional Organizations in Africa and the Middle East," in *Peace Support Operations and the U.S. Military*, ed. Dennis Quinn, (Washington, D.C.: National Defense University Press, 1994), 158; Donna Cassata, "Can U.N. Keep a Secret?" *Congressional Quarterly Weekly Report* 53, March 18, 1995, 826; Jesse Helms, "Saving the U.N.: A Challenge to the Next Secretary General,"

Foreign Affairs 75 (September–October 1996), 2-7; Boutros Boutros-Ghali, *Agenda for Peace* (New York: United Nations, 1992).

24. Walter Dorn, "Early and Late Warning by the U.N. Secretary General" (paper presented at the Synergy in Early Warning conference, Center for International and Strategic Studies, York University, Toronto, Canada, March 17, 1997); Idem, "Early Warning of Armed Conflict by the UN Secretary-General: Article 99 Revisited," (paper prepared for the Canadian foreign ministry, July 22, 1997). Personal interviews, Toronto, March 15-18, August 4, 1997.

25. Tai Ming Cheung, "Arm in Arm: Warming Sino-Russian Military Ties Worry U.S.," *Far Eastern Economic Review,* November 12, 1992, 28; Evan S. Medeiros, "U.S. Considers Sanctions on China for Weapons, Technology Transfers," *Arms Control Today* 26 (February 1996), 21-22; Nigel Holloway et al., "Going Ballistic: American Intelligence Reports That Pakistan Has Deployed Chinese M-11 Missiles Could Hurt Sino-U.S. Relations and Raise Stakes in the Subcontinent," *Far Eastern Economic Review* 159, June 27, 1996, 14-15; Open Media Research Institute, *Daily Digest,* pt. 1, March 1, 1996.

26. Frank J. Gaffney, Jr., "The IAEA's Dirty Little Secret," *International Economy* 8 (September–October 1994), 52-55.

27. Mikhail A. Alexseev, "Russia's 'Cold Peace' Consensus: Transcending the Presidential Election," *Fletcher Forum of World Affairs* 21 (Winter–Spring 1997), 37-38. See the position paper featuring 133 authors representing Russia's intelligence community, *Belaya kniga Rossiyskikh spetssluzhb* [White Book of the Russian special services] (Moscow: Obozrevatel', 1995).

28. Craig Covault, "Russia Launches Three Spy Satellites," *Aviation Week and Space Technology,* September 27, 1993, 24.

29. Cf. Andrei Kozyrev, "Russia: A Chance for Survival," *Foreign Affairs* 71 (1992), 1-17; and SVR's views (under Primakov) expressed in Sluzhba vneshney razvedki Rossiyskoy Federatsii [Foreign Intelligence Service of the Russian Federation], *Rossiya-SNG: Nuzhdayetsia li v korrektirovke pozitsiya*

Index